Regulatory Aspects of Artificial Intelligence on Blockchain

Pardis Moslemzadeh Tehrani
University of Malaya, Malaysia

A volume in the Advances in Computational
Intelligence and Robotics (ACIR) Book Series

Published in the United States of America by
IGI Global
Engineering Science Reference (an imprint of IGI Global)
701 E. Chocolate Avenue
Hershey PA, USA 17033
Tel: 717-533-8845
Fax: 717-533-8661
E-mail: cust@igi-global.com
Web site: http://www.igi-global.com

Library of Congress Cataloging-in-Publication Data

Names: Tehrani, Pardis Moslemzadeh, editor.
Title: Regulatory aspects of artificial intelligence on blockchain / Pardis
  Moslemzadeh Tehrani, editor.
Description: Hershey, PA : Engineering Science Reference, (an imprint of
  IGI Global), [2022] | Includes bibliographical references and index. |
  Summary: "This book provides relevant legal and security frameworks and
  the latest empirical research findings in the area of blockchain and AI
  striving to identify and overcome the legal consequences of the
  application of Artificial Intelligence into the blockchain system"--
  Provided by publisher.
Identifiers: LCCN 2021027705 (print) | LCCN 2021027706 (ebook) | ISBN
  9781799879275 (hardcover) | ISBN 9781799879282 (paperback) | ISBN
  9781799879299 (ebook)
Subjects: LCSH: Blockchains (Databases)--Law and legislation. | Artificial
  intelligence--Law and legislation. | Blockchains (Databases).
Classification: LCC K564.C6 R4496 2022 (print) | LCC K564.C6 (ebook) |
  DDC 343.09/99--dc23
LC record available at https://lccn.loc.gov/2021027705
LC ebook record available at https://lccn.loc.gov/2021027706

This book is published in the IGI Global book series Advances in Computational Intelligence and Robotics (ACIR) (ISSN: 2327-0411; eISSN: 2327-042X)

British Cataloguing in Publication Data
A Cataloguing in Publication record for this book is available from the British Library.

For electronic access to this publication, please contact: eresources@igi-global.com.

Advances in Computational Intelligence and Robotics (ACIR) Book Series

Ivan Giannoccaro

University of Salento, Italy

ISSN:2327-0411
EISSN:2327-042X

MISSION

While intelligence is traditionally a term applied to humans and human cognition, technology has progressed in such a way to allow for the development of intelligent systems able to simulate many human traits. With this new era of simulated and artificial intelligence, much research is needed in order to continue to advance the field and also to evaluate the ethical and societal concerns of the existence of artificial life and machine learning.

The **Advances in Computational Intelligence and Robotics (ACIR) Book Series** encourages scholarly discourse on all topics pertaining to evolutionary computing, artificial life, computational intelligence, machine learning, and robotics. ACIR presents the latest research being conducted on diverse topics in intelligence technologies with the goal of advancing knowledge and applications in this rapidly evolving field.

COVERAGE

- Intelligent Control
- Automated Reasoning
- Natural Language Processing
- Artificial Life
- Heuristics
- Evolutionary Computing
- Fuzzy Systems
- Artificial Intelligence
- Computational Intelligence
- Cyborgs

IGI Global is currently accepting manuscripts for publication within this series. To submit a proposal for a volume in this series, please contact our Acquisition Editors at Acquisitions@igi-global.com or visit: http://www.igi-global.com/publish/.

Titles in this Series

For a list of additional titles in this series, please visit: www.igi-global.com/book-series/advances-computational-intelligence-robotics/73674

Genetic Algorithms and Applications for Stock Trading Optimization
Vivek Kapoor (Devi Ahilya University, Indore, India) and Shubhamoy Dey (Indian Institute of Management, Indore, India)
Engineering Science Reference • © 2021 • 262pp • H/C (ISBN: 9781799841050) • US $225.00

Handbook of Research on Innovations and Applications of AI, IoT, and Cognitive Technologies
Jingyuan Zhao (University of Toronto, Canada) and V. Vinoth Kumar (MVJ College of Engineering, India)
Engineering Science Reference • © 2021 • 570pp • H/C (ISBN: 9781799868705) • US $325.00

Decision Support Systems and Industrial IoT in Smart Grid, Factories, and Cities
Ismail Butun (Chalmers University of Technology, Sweden & Konya Food and Agriculture University, Turkey & Royal University of Technology, Sweden)
Engineering Science Reference • © 2021 • 285pp • H/C (ISBN: 9781799874683) • US $245.00

Deep Natural Language Processing and AI Applications for Industry 5.0
Poonam Tanwar (Manav Rachna International Institute of Research and Studies, India) Arti Saxena (Manav Rachna International Institute of Research and Studies, India) and C. Priya (Vels Institute of Science, Technology, and Advanced Studies, India)
Engineering Science Reference • © 2021 • 240pp • H/C (ISBN: 9781799877288) • US $245.00

AI Tools and Electronic Virtual Assistants for Improved Business Performance
Christian Graham (University of Maine, USA)
Business Science Reference • © 2021 • 300pp • H/C (ISBN: 9781799838418) • US $245.00

Transforming the Internet of Things for Next-Generation Smart Systems
Bhavya Alankar (Jamia Hamdard, India) Harleen Kaur (Hamdard University, India) and Ritu Chauhan (Amity University, India)
Engineering Science Reference • © 2021 • 173pp • H/C (ISBN: 9781799875413) • US $245.00

Handbook of Research on Machine Learning Techniques for Pattern Recognition and Information Security
Mohit Dua (National Institute of Technology, Kurukshetra, India) and Ankit Kumar Jain (National Institute of Technology, Kurukshetra, India)
Engineering Science Reference • © 2021 • 355pp • H/C (ISBN: 9781799832997) • US $295.00

701 East Chocolate Avenue, Hershey, PA 17033, USA
Tel: 717-533-8845 x100 • Fax: 717-533-8661
E-Mail: cust@igi-global.com • www.igi-global.com

Table of Contents

Section 1
Legal and Regulatory Framework of the Blockchain

Section 2
Technical Challenges of the Blockchain in Addressing Regulatory Framework

Detailed Table of Contents

Section 1
Legal and Regulatory Framework of the Blockchain

The blockchain is a registry shared among different participants intending to eliminate the need for a central authority to maintain information. The first proposal of this technology was to eliminate financial authorities in transactions of value. However, the application of the same technique for the transaction of information could facilitate trades and offer traceability and diamond tracking around the world. The consensus is at the core of the network because it orchestrates nodes to accept new information, but it operates over a data structure in an open network, consequently leading to many complex behaviours that introduce different vulnerabilities. This work aims to highlight the vulnerability within the blockchain network based on the different participant behaviours that dominate the shared registry. Moreover, different malicious behaviour can appear on the networking layer by taking advantage of the network topology.

The application of AI technology in different sectors can intrude on the data subjects' privacy rights. While the data protection laws attempt to regulate the use and processing of personal data, these laws obstruct the growth and development of AI technology. Current regulations are unable to cope with the AI revolution due to the pacing problem and Collingridge dilemma. In view of the regulatory gaps and the complexity of technology, there is a strong justification to regulate AI technology. It is increasingly important to safeguard privacy without encumbering AI technology with regulatory requirements that will hinder its progress. With the convergence of AI and blockchain technology, privacy challenges are exacerbated. In this chapter, several types of regulations will be analysed to decipher a suitable regulatory framework for AI. This is to ensure effective regulation of AI and to allow AI to flourish with the use and application of blockchain features.

Chapter 3

This study seeks to understand and explain the technological and regulatory challenges of blockchain technology particularly in execution mechanism of smart contracts as compared to regular contracts and to explore legal implication attached the blockchain technology. While evaluating the early days of regulatory framework of blockchain, the current study provides a focused review of relevant studies to identify the legal challenges arising from the application of AI in smart contracts and to find solutions to overcome these challenges. The study has emphasized certain areas related to the blockchain such as AI application and execution of smart contracts and finds that that there is currently a lack of legal certainty as to how various requirements of a valid contract would be satisfied. Hence, it highlights the need of regulation without disrupting the key yet essential features of blockchain. Keywords: Blockchain, Smart contract, AI, Framework, Legislation, Cryptocurrency

Chapter 4

Blockchain technology can be leveraged to record information securely, ranging from public sector data to private records. It has the potential of being ubiquitous due to its far-reaching use cases and revolutionary features. The deployment of blockchain technology can radically transform corporate and government operations and services. The blockchain legislative landscape is rapidly evolving, and an in-depth analysis is provided to offer a legal and contextual perspective of the regulatory trends across the globe. Part I explores the widespread use of blockchain technology for various industries and business applications. It also outlines two types of legislation that can be enacted, namely enabling and prohibitive legislation, to advance the policy objectives of a country. Part II examines the regulatory responses of various countries relating to blockchain use cases and applications.

Chapter 5

This chapter compares the current legal and regulatory landscape of cryptocurrency regulations of selected countries. Countries have adopted distinct and disparate regulatory approaches in regulating cryptocurrency. Countries such as Gibraltar, Malta, Switzerland, Singapore, and certain states in the United States have enacted proactive, enabling, and industry-specific laws to regulate cryptocurrency. The Philippines and Denmark are relatively forward-looking in their endeavour to regulate cryptocurrency by allowing its utilization and/or trade but with a restrictive and cautious approach. Certain countries have imposed rigorous restrictions or banned the usage or trade of cryptocurrency. With the rapid evolution and emergence of cryptocurrency markets, policymakers are adopting different trajectories to develop a suitable regulatory framework to regulate cryptocurrency. Countries around the world should harness the capabilities of cryptocurrency by devising favourable regulations rather than inhibit the application of cryptocurrency.

Chapter 6

Andasmara Rizky Pranata, University of Malaya, Malaysia
Pardis Moslemzadeh Tehrani, University of Malaya, Malaysia

This chapter discuss the legality of smart contract in a decentralized autonomous organization (DAO). The regulation framework of blockchain is developing rapidly with many countries such as Malta and Estonia utilizing and allowing the use of blockchain. While many researchers have discussed the legality of smart contract, its relation to DAO as one of blockchain's applications is rarely discussed. There are three issues discussed in this chapter: the definition of DAO, the definition of smart contract, and the legality of smart contract in DAO. Each country has their own legal threshold of a contract's legality, but there are generally five elements in a legal contract, namely offer and acceptance, consideration, intention, certainty, and completeness. It is possible for the smart contract to fulfil the five legal elements of a contract. As there are different regulations in different countries, there may have been different elements to the law. In conclusion, the legality of smart contracts, like blockchain itself, depends on who uses it, where it is used, and how it is used.

Chapter 7

Poshan Yu, Soochow University, China
Ruixin Gong, Independent Researcher, China
Michael Sampat, Independent Researcher, Canada

Compared with the traditional industrial economy, the Chinese digital economy uses brand-new production factors and production organization methods to bring changes to human society and promote the transformation of the economy. This chapter aims to explore the practical problems of adopting blockchain technology in China's digital economy and study how different cities (managed by various local governments) enhance their unique financial technology ecosystem's economic performance and promote RegTech policy in order to improve the digital economy under the central government's institutional setting. This chapter in turn analyzes the recent cases of blockchain in China's financial industry, compares the application and development of the latest financial technology related policies in major cities, and demonstrates how these regulations can promote the development of blockchain technology in the transformation of China's digital economy.

Section 2
Technical Challenges of the Blockchain in Addressing Regulatory Framework

Chapter 8

Soheil Saraji, University of Wyoming, USA
Christelle Khalaf, University of Wyoming, USA

The current energy transition from a fossil-fuel-based economy to a zero-carbon has significantly accelerated in recent years, as the largest emitters have committed to achieving carbon-neutral goals in the next 20-30 years. The energy industry transition is characterized by modernization through digital technologies, increased renewable energy generation, and environmental sustainability. Blockchain technology can play a significant role in providing secure digital distributed platforms facilitating digitization, decarbonization, and decentralization of the energy systems. Several promising blockchain applications in the energy sector are under research and development, including peer-to-peer energy trading; carbon monitoring, management, and trading; and IoT-enabled electric grid management. However, several challenges are slowing down the commercialization of these applications, including outdated legislation and regulations, slow pace of adaptation from the traditional energy industry, and risks associated with the new, untested technology.

Chapter 9

    Namrata Dhanda, Amity University, Lucknow, India

As the technologies are evolving day by day, they are able to rejuvenate any sector either individually or by incorporating other technologies. There are many prominent sectors in the market such as healthcare, education, entertainment, business, information technology, retail, etc. Every sector has its own set of profits and consequences, but apart from all, the banking or finance sector is the only sector that provides dynamicity to all other sectors and helps them to generate maximum revenue from their principal investment. In this chapter, the authors are focusing on the traditional and modern ways of banking, currencies such as cryptocurrency like Bitcoin, Ethereum, Litecoin, and how the modern currency will change the transaction procedure in the global banking system, creating an amalgamation of such currency with a current transaction system with the role of technology such as Blockchain in the betterment of the global banking system making the system fully decentralized, distributed, transparent, fast, immutable, and efficient.

Chapter 10

    Dhiviya Ram, University of Malaya, Malaysia

One of the most unique forms of contracting is apparent in cloud computing. Cloud computing, unlike other conventional methods, has adopted a different approach in the formation of binding contract that will be used for the governance of the cloud. This method is namely the clickwrap agreement. Click wrap agreement follows a take it or leave it basis in which the end users are provided with limited to no option in terms of having a say on the contract that binds them during the use of cloud services. The terms found in the contract are often cloud service provider friendly and will be less favourable to the end user. In this article, the authors examine the terms that are often found in the cloud computing agreement as well as study the benefit that is entailed in adopting this contracting method. This chapter has undertaken a qualitative study that comprises interviews of cloud service providers in Malaysia. Hence, this study is a novel approach that also provides insight in terms of the cloud service provider perspective regarding the click wrap agreement.

Chapter 11

Aatif Jamshed, ABES Engineering College, Ghaziabad, India
Asmita Dixit, ABES Engineering College, Ghaziabad, India

Bitcoin has gained a tremendous amount of attention lately because of the innate nature of entering cryptographic technologies and money-related units in the fields of banking, cybersecurity, and software engineering. This chapter investigates the effect of Bayesian neural structures or networks (BNNs) with the aid of manipulating the Bitcoin process's timetable. The authors also choose the maximum extensive highlights from Blockchain records that are carefully applied to Bitcoin's marketplace hobby and use it to create templates to enhance the influential display of the new Bitcoin evaluation process. They endorse actual inspection to check and expect the Bitcoin technique, which compares the Bayesian neural network and other clean and non-direct comparison models. The exact tests show that BNN works well for undertaking the Bitcoin price schedule and explain the intense unpredictability of Bitcoin's actual rate.

Foreword

No other discipline or technology will have more impact on shaping our future than computer science and technology. It is thus of utmost importance to design, develop and evaluate upcoming technologies in a more general context, including a societal and ethical perspective as well as economic considerations and legal frameworks. While many scientific publications focus on the technical achievements, literature discussing this broader context is still parse. This book fills this gap in the field of blockchain technologies, which are an emerging platform for establishing fair and transparent data sharing where unauthorized data modifications can be audited and traced. Initially used for financial transactions, blockchain applications currently extend to a wide variety of use cases in other industries as well as in the government and public sector.

This book consists of a valuable collection of contributions on blockchain technology with a focus on addressing privacy and security in cloud computing from an interdisciplinary perspective. It covers the necessary basics for understanding the general operational principles of blockchain technology. The individual chapters are self-contained articles written by experts in their individual fields. Topics covered by the book range from a discussion of security vulnerabilities and appropriate counter measures, to studies on regulatory and legal frameworks, smart contracts, applications in energy industries, or blockchains as enabling technology for digital economies.

As a collection, this book provides an excellent source of reference for everybody interested in understanding the basics of blockchain technology along with economic, societal and legal implications and considerations. It serves as a good starting point for scholars who want to get familiar with the state of the art in the field but also for stakeholders in the industrial, business, government or public sector who want to better understand the potentials of this upcoming technology.

Gabriele Kotsis
Department of Telecooperation, Johannes Kepler Universität Linz, Austria

Gabriele Kotsis *received her Master 's degree (1991, honoured with the Award of the Austrian Computer Society), her PhD (1995, honoured with the very prestigious Heinz Zemanek Preis PhD award) and the venia docendi in computer science (2000) from the University of Vienna. After visiting professor positions at the Business Schools in Vienna and Copenhagen, she accepted a position as full professor in computer science at Johannes Kepler University Linz where she has been since 2002. She is head of the Department of Telecooperation with a research focus in mobile computing, multimedia and hypermedia systems as well as cooperative and collaborative systems. In 2014, Kotsis has been recognized as ACM Distinguished Scientist for her scientific contributions. She was appointed in 2007 and reelected in 2011 as Vice Rector for Research at Johannes Kepler University Linz. At a national level, she is a member of the Austrian Computer Society and was one of the cofounding* *chairs of the Society's working group for professors in computer science. From 2003 to 2007 she was president of the Austrian Computer Society. At an international level, she was a founding member of the ACM Europe Council and currently elected member at large in the ACM Council which is the leading worldwide organisation in computer science. From July 2020 to June 2022, she is President of ACM.*

Preface

Blockchain technology is a new general-purpose technology that poses significant challenges to the existing state of law, economy, and society (Dimitropoulos, 2020). Blockchain similar to other technological innovations are changing existing social patterns and putting pressure on the legal status quo. One feature of the blockchain which makes it more distinctive than other disruptive innovations is that it is a global and transnational technology by nature and design. Blockchain was initially developed as Bitcoin blockchain to a by-pass commercial financial institution and central banks, while later recognised as general-purpose technology that can be used to achieve multiple goals and welcomed by various private and public commercial actors and bodies.

It is a trustless technology exchanging for value over a computer network that can be verified, monitored, and enforced without demanding a trusted third party or central institution. Due to the authenticity and verification technology, more efficient title transfers and ownership verification can be done by this technology as it is programmable, it can enable conditional "smart" contracts. The decentralized feature of the blockchain enables it to perform functions with minimal trust without using centralized institutions. Finally, the borderless and frictionless feature provides a cheaper, faster infrastructure for exchanging units of value. In other words, this technology has broad implications in transacting and the potential for innovation is hard to overstate (Kiviat, 2015).

Blockchain was developed to circumvent national borders by facilitating the transmission of data and the economic value of the participants in the blockchain network. The various blockchain used cases indicated the influence of blockchain on society, economy and law. Blockchain provides the facilitation of cryptocurrencies and other crypto-assets as the first and most important application of blockchain which led to a regulatory backlash by governments in different parts of the world to protect national interests and re-embed money into national jurisdictions. However, potential applications of blockchain technology are not limited to money transfers and payments, it also facilitates the exchange of value. It can solve an important problem of electronic value transfers. It doesn't only move the value, but also it integrates several components of the trading-clearing settlement value chain in an elegant, efficient, and mathematical way. Thus, it should be of interest to any industry engaged as an alternative currency (Dimitropoulos, 2020).

Another broad area of innovation is decentralized smart contracts in which the blockchain enables it. It leverages a secure public ledger as an enforcement mechanism. Parties in blockchain might use smart contracts to design contractual relationships that are automatically executed without the additional costs of monitoring or enforcement. In real-world transactions, intermediaries establish trust and reduce risk between counterparties. While, in decentralized smart contracts, parties may transact at arm's length, with total strangers, without the worry of fraud, and the cost of third-party enforcement. It provides new markets to develop by disintermediating contract markets in which parties do not have concern for counterparty risk. Therefore, smart contract opens up a market for future trading in a simpler approach due to two conditions. First, futures agreements involve objectively verifiable conditions about the state of the world, and second, they are highly standardized to ensure that contracts can be easily traded and priced (Kiviat, 2015).

Based on the legal actor perceptions of the threat posed by crypto-assets and their underlying technology, the country regulatory responses have taken multiple forms. The adoption of blockchain by governments come with challenges. It shifts the power from governmental legal regulations to code-based rules and protocols administered by decentralized blockchain-based networks, while posed a severe challenge to the monopoly of the state over "the promulgation, formation, keeping and verification of institutions and the public record" (Gürcan, 2019).

It is pertinent for policymakers to view blockchain as an adaptable technology. This powerful technology demands comprehensive regulation to mitigate the relevant risks. However, this is the duty of policymakers to exercise caution and precision in tailoring the scope of regulation. The function of blockchain technology is beyond the transmitting value in the traditional money-transfer system. Considering the experiment of countries in regulating blockchain technology and the issues raised in this regard, it would be helpful for other states when considering their model. This book will further emphasise that alternative applications of blockchain technology will necessitate additional guidelines and regulations outside of banking and financial regulatory frameworks. Understanding the concepts and discussion in different aspects of blockchain outlined in this book would be a strong starting point as blockchain technology can support different kinds of dreams.

THE CHALLENGES

Several legal concerns existed based on blockchain technology. Many benefits are inherent to blockchain technology which have been discussed in the above section. However, these benefits are the same features that have raised challenges for regulatory groups that seek to prevent abusive uses of the new technology. Companies and organizations have already taken advantage of this technology. The development of blockchain influences all areas of human interactions; while, It is becoming relevant in various sectors such as energy production, energy production, health system, supply chain system, education, financing, banking, public service management, logistics, and transport. The widespread impact of such development is reflected in the legislative challenges and efforts from regulating the blockchain-related processes to standardizing the applicable terminology and method for resolving disputes arising from the application of Blockchain technology (Cvetkovic, 2020).

Blockchain concept brings a paradigm shift in contractual relations by eliminating the prerequisite notion of trust in another party which is replaced by reliance on technology. It is troublesome to assess if this "trustless" system can also have an impact on the fundamental principle of contract law. It is worth mentioning that an essential element in interpreting a contract is the trust notion. Blockchain technology which enables the automation of contracts reaffirms the 'pacta sunt servanda' principle. However, the necessity of the interpretation cannot be fully excluded. The importance of the smart contract has been recognized by national and international legal systems. They are already used in a variety of settings independently from blockchain technology. A smart contract -from a legal perspective- is a blockchain-based computer program that authenticates, monitors, and implements contractual obligations which have been converted into a program code (De Caria, 2018).

As smart contracts become the reality of the new technological world, an adequate legal response is required. Due to the brink between law and technology, the requisite response is highly specific. The intersection of law and technology open a plethora of new issues and challenges which demand the revision of the old ones. A key issue in the smart contract is whether legal flexibility embodied in legal standards can be transported into a program code. In other words, the standards must be converted into codes which require reducing the codes to the boundaries of the programming language which is complex and demanding (Cvetkovic, 2020).

However, the smart contract has its limitation in the current format. Despite the potential, it is limited to machine-readable terms. The computer could only understand the desire of the programmer as AI is not involved. It seems that in the real-world scenario smart contract works better with terms involving numbers and contracts which do not need much translation of natural language into codes with two-party contracts to combine the advantages of both ex-ante and ex-poste contracts. It has also been suggested to combine smart contracts with traditional contracts and let those terms which could be executed via computer be smart contracts while the rest remained as traditional contracts as well as contract law. To put it simply, the main source of interpretation should remain in traditional contracts and the smart contract could act as a supplement. In case of any disputes arise, parties can always refer to the traditional contract for clarification. Transferring from a traditional contract to a smart contract without supplementary measures is an unrealistic choice and it is dangerous. Therefore, three issues need to be investigated further: first, the applicability of translating all contractual terms into codes and execute through mathematics and algorithm; second, the basis of the smart contract which is a binary zero-sum logic that does not appear in real-life contract cases and finally, the decentralized concept of the smart contract which aims to solve all contractual issues ex-ante. The coexistence of traditional contracts and smart contracts to supplement each other for the time being is the best option (Hsiao, 2017).

SEARCHING FOR A SOLUTION

Blockchain's characteristics such as decentralization, immutability, and anonymity attract many users seeking a secure and anonymous transaction platform, while simultaneously attracts users who have illegal intentions. However, such characteristic does not outweigh the benefits of the blockchain technology. The of blockchain technology can be addressed by appropriate regulation. Smart contracts will remove friction by seamlessly including agreement and enforcement into one protocol, thereby eliminating the possibility of a breach. Blockchain application's main goal in the context of smart contracts is to make the contractual relationship more efficient and economically viable, with fewer opportunities for contractual breach and subsequent disputes. Notably, the process will sharpen its basic structure, clarify the most critical issues, and provide an array of possible solutions, the most important of which is a liability (Cvetkovic, 2020). Legislative responses must consider an application of contract law to this new form of the agreement must be considered by the legislative responses. Legislative responses also require adjusting the rules or create a new regulatory scheme that governs contracts of this type (Fulmer, 2019).

The world has already witnessed the importance and impacts of policies and regulations in the blockchain industry, yet other policies and regulations' impact may be hard to estimate. As digital technology, no one can claim jurisdiction over blockchain technology. Due to the increasing usage of blockchain in various transactions and services, countries and governments began to set rules for blockchain technologies. However, these regulations are not set with a full understanding of either the technology or how existing rules applied to those technologies which led to inadequate or substandard regulation. In federal countries, it led to the regulatory uncertainty that encouraged some blockchain businesses to locate offshore. Thus, it is pertinent to set clear and thoughtful rules aiming both to protect the public and open the situation for innovation. Different countries pursue different objectives through the articulation of policies and regulations. Given that each country has various objectives to seek to achieve, it is impractical to enumerate and evaluate all objectives that countries pursue in the blockchain space. Following a careful assessment of the impacts of the number of policies and regulations, it is fair to conclude that some of the objectives of existing policies and regulations were fulfilled while others were not (Jiaying, 2019).

To sum up, regulators in different jurisdictions have adopted different approaches and pursued varying regulatory initiatives. The majority of countries have not adopted a concise regulatory framework to regulate the blockchain ecosystem. Even though some countries have regulated blockchain in some form, legislation remains in the early stages.

This book targeted a wide range of audiences and readers since it covers blockchain both from legal and technical perspective. The book is intended to add to the growing literature in the fields of the regulatory framework of the blockchain. It also would be relevant to academicians, practitioners, researchers, postgraduates' level of study and experts. It will also be of interest to policymakers and technical experts working in the field of blockchain. This 12-chapters book seeks to advance critical scholarship on several issues relating to the regulatory framework of the blockchain ranging from technical and social aspects to legal ones.

The contributors of this book have framed the technical, legal and policy issues in their unique ways, but together, the collection offers complementary perspectives on many critical issues facing blockchain technology. Therefore, this book aims to move that process along, by presenting scholarship that examines both how the law does, and should, apply to blockchain technology. In doing so, it is not possible to escape from the economic and technical aspects of blockchain. As it has been illustrated, to have an inclusive rule in Blockchain technology, the economic and technical aspects cannot be ignored. Included in this book are chapters discussing an array of blockchain-related public policy and legal issues beginning with an overview of the specific features of blockchain technology, then describing the regulatory framework of Artificial intelligence, blockchain technology and public policy and governance issues, practical use cases, and lastly exploring broader technical and economic issues.

ORGANIZATION OF THE BOOK

The book is organized into 11 chapters. A brief description of each of the chapters follows:

Chapter 1 by Mohamed Ikbal Nacer and Simant Prakoonwit is titled "Vulnerability of Blockchain Network From Consensus Perspective". This chapter offers an introduction and overview on blockchain technology from a security vulnerability perspective based on the different participant behaviours that dominate the shared registry. It addresses the consensus mechanism at the core of its functioning by providing the vulnerability within each step and analyses how each element of the platform can lead to exterior manipulation. Along with this welcome overview framework, the author examines different malicious behaviour which can appear on the networking layer by taking advantage of the network topology. The author also finds that the implementation of standards before the generation of a solution that manages the creation of networks between different peers is of high need, which will dictate that governmental consensus law is a very important step for wide adoption on a horizontal level.

Chapter 2 by Karisma Karisma is titled "A Pragmatic Regulatory Framework for Artificial Intelligence: Regulating Artificial Intelligence". This chapter's intriguing discussions around the application of AI technology in different sectors which can intrude on the data subjects' privacy rights. Despite the attempt of data protection law to regulate the use and processing of personal data, these laws obstruct the growth and development of AI technology. Current regulations are unable to cope with AI revolution due to the pacing problem and Collingridge dilemma. The author analyses several types of regulations to decipher a suitable regulatory framework for AI, by taking into consideration the potential deployment of Blockchain technology in the realm of AI. This is to ensure the effective regulation of AI and to allow AI to flourish with the utilization and application of Blockchain features.

Chapter 3 by Mohammad Abdullah Fazi, titled "A Contextual Study of Regulatory Framework for Blockchain", examines regulatory and legal challenges to blockchain and identifies areas where legal and regulatory intervention is required through. This discussion is important and timely, as it evalutes the proposed legal framework for blockchain-AI convergence to determine whether those regulations fit with nature and objectives of blockchain technology. It discusses the features of a smart contract, while emphasizing the need for regulation and governance of blockchain transections to mitigate the risk and increase the security features for the parties involved.

Chapter 4 by Karisma Karisma is titled "Legal and Regulatory Landscape of Blockchain Technology in Countries: Legislations Addressing Blockchain Technology". This chapter furthers the discussion around the use of blockchain technology for various industries and business applications and examines the regulatory responses of various countries relating to blockchain applications. It also gives an overview about various use cases and applications which have emerged from the deployment of blockchain technology and their potential in revolutionizing and transforming corporate and government operations and services. The author highlights four types of regulatory approaches that can be adopted by various countries, namely (a) wait and see; (b) enacting new legislation; (c) issuing guidance; and (d)regulatory sandboxing.

Chapter 5 by Karisma Karisma is titled "Comparative Review of the Regulatory Framework of Cryptocurrency in Selected Jurisdictions: Insights on Cryptocurrency Regulations". This chpater discusses about the Cryptocurrency as the first major blockchain innovation and the most notable blockchain application. This chapter focuses on cryptocurrency policies, legislations, and regulations in selected jurisdictions. The pertinent areas explored are matters relating to legality and limits in the utilisation of cryptocurrency. The regulatory approaches adopted by countries are divided into three categories, encompasses countries that have enacted proactive and enabling laws; jurisdictions that are relatively proactive in their endeavour to regulate cryptocurrency, allowing the utilisation and/or trade of cryptocurrency but with a restrictive and cautious approach; and the third category which examines countries that have completely restricted or banned the usage and trade of cryptocurrency.

Chapter 6 by Andasmara Rizky Pranata and Pardis Moslemzadeh Tehrani, titled "The Legality of Smart Contract in Decentralized Autonomous Organization", focuses upon the legality of smart contract used in DAO and DAO definition. It also discusses the legal framework of smart contract and whether it fulfils the criteria of a legal contract. It discusses deeply discuss deeply on the technical aspect and the issues in the uses of smart contract, and the importance of smart contract to DAO. Finally, the discussion proceeds to the legal framework of smart contract.

Chapter 7 by Poshan Yu, Ruixin Gong, and Michael Sampat is titled "Blockchain Technology in China's Digital Economy: Balancing Regulation and Innovation". This chapter explores the practical problems of adopting blockchain technology -including regulatory framework- in China's digital economy, and study how different cities (managed by various local governments) enhance their unique financial technology ecosystem's economic performance, and promote RegTech policy, in order to improve the digital economy under the central government's institutional setting. It also analyses the recent cases of blockchain in China's financial industry, compares the application and development of the latest financial technology related policies in major cities, and demonstrates how these regulations can promote the development of blockchain technology in the transformation of China's digital economy.

Chapter 8 by Soheil Saraji and Christelle Khalaf is titled "Blockchain Applications in the Energy Industry". This chapter identifies the impact of emerging blockchain commercialization on different industries, especially the energy industry. To facilitate this discussion, the authors provide a brief overview of the global energy transition and its disruptive impacts on the traditional fossil fuel industry. The chapter examines current implementations, use-cases, and potential futuristic blockchain applications in the energy industry.

Chapter 9 by Namrata Dhanda is titled "Cryptocurrency and Blockchain: The Future of a Global Banking System". This chapter expands on academic literature and navigates the discussion on the traditional and modern ways of banking, currencies such as cryptocurrency like Bitcoin, Ethereum, Litecoin and how the modern currency will change the transaction procedure in the global banking system. An amalgamation of such type of currency with a current transaction system, the role of technology such as Blockchain in the betterment of the global banking system by making the system fully decentralized, distributed, transparent, fast, immutable and efficient. It also discusses about the prominent challenges of the blockchain's adoption in baking system, particularly on the regulatory framework.

Chapter 10 by Dhiviya A/P Ramanathan is titled "Clickwrap Agreement: An Analysis of the Terms of the Cloud Agreement and Studying the Benefits of Adopting Such Methods". The author examines smart contracts as a clickwrap agreement with a different approach in the formation of a binding contract that will be used for the governance of the cloud. The author focuses on the terms that are often found in the clickwrap agreement as well as studies the benefit that is entailed in adopting this contracting method. This study also uses a novel approach that provides insight in terms of the cloud service providers perspective regarding the clickwrap agreement.

Chapter 11 by Atif Jamshid and Asmita Dixit is titled "Bitcoin Prediction Using Multi-Layer Perceptron Regressor, PCA, and Support Vector Regression (SVR)". Bitcoin has gained a tremendous amount of attention late because of the innate nature of entering cryptographic technologies and money-related units in the fields of banking, cybersecurity, and software engineering. This chapter investigates the effect of Bayesian neural structures or networks (BNNs) with the aid of manipulating the Bitcoin process's time table. The author chooses the maximum extensive highlights from Block-chain records that are carefully applied to Bitcoin's marketplace hobby and use it to create templates to enhance the influential display of the new Bitcoin evaluation process.

REFERENCES

Cvetkovic, P. (2020). *Liability in the context of blockchain-smart contract nexus: Introductory considerations*. Academic Press.

De Caria, R. (2018). *The legal meaning of smart contracts*. Academic Press.

Dimitropoulos, G. (2020). *The law of blockchain*. Academic Press.

Fulmer, N. (2019). *Exploring the legal issues of blockchain applications*. Academic Press.

Gürcan, B. (2019). *Various Dimensions and Aspects of the Legal Problems of the Blockchain Technology*. Academic Press.

Hsiao, J. (2017). *Smart contract on the blockchain-paradigm shift for contract law*. Academic Press.

Jiaying, J. (2019). *Regulating Blockchain? A Retrospective Assessment of China's Blockchain Policies and Regulations*. Academic Press.

Kiviat, T. (2015). *Beyond bitcoin: Issues in regulating blockchain transactions*. Academic Press.

Acknowledgment

The editor would like to acknowledge the help of all the people involved in this project and, more specifically, to the authors and reviewers that took part in the review process. Without their support, this book would not have become a reality.

First, the editor would like to thank each one of the authors for their contributions. Our sincere gratitude goes to the chapter's authors who contributed their time and expertise to this book.

Second, the editor wishes to acknowledge the valuable contributions of the reviewers from various parts of the world including Australia, Austria, China, Oman the United Kingdom, the United States of America and Malaysia regarding the improvement of quality, coherence, and content presentation of chapters. The timely engagement and superiority of evaluative review offered collegial support towards the author's vision as well as the consequential distinction of the completed book.

Finally, the editor wants to thank her parents and brothers for their continued support during all of my academic and professional adventures; their constant love, support, and patience helps me to achieve my goals.

Pardis Moslemzadeh Tehrani
University of Malaya, Malaysia

Introduction

BLOCKCHAIN FEATURES

The new generation of emerging technologies has made states increasingly dependent on digital technology (ConsenSys, 2018). A blockchain is a series of consecutive blocks each containing data on various transactions that includes a 'hash value' header for the previous block that, in turn, has a hash-value header of its previous block, and so on. Together, these blocks form a chain that are linked through their hashes. The hash is a function that converts a block and all its contents to a unique fixed-length output which represents the fingerprint of the block. Blockchains determine the hash once a block is created. Any attempt to tamper with data in a particular block in the chain will be detectable, as the hash of its data will no longer match the value included in the next block, thereby breaking the chain (Salman et al., 2019). Thus, a blockchain is an appropriate technology for parties to interact in the absence of a trusted third party. The desired security is achieved as the interactions are recorded in the blockchain database and the data cannot be altered without the consensus of the whole network. Blockchain can be compared with Google doc where work can be carried out simultaneously on one document and in which information is distributed rather than copied. The system is controlled by all those on the blockchain network thus enabling them to approve new entries. To make it even simpler, a blockchain user can broadcast transactions to the blockchain network when interacting with another user. The validity of the transaction will be verified by the nodes (user or computer) in the network and a new block of valid transactions will then be constructed. When the validity of the blockchain is confirmed, it will be attached to the blockchain database and cannot then be deleted or altered. In fact, both transactions and the blocks are signed which make them irreversible and undeniable in the future (Salman et al., 2019). Currently, blockchains are among one of the best creations of the new technology as they maintain an accurate and secure record of an entity's technology assets. This also enables their configurations to become a critical part of the organisation's risk management and mitigation strategies.

Intelligent contracts, also known as smart contracts, are gaining in importance due to the advent of blockchain technology and the benefits of cryptocurrencies. In the blockchain context, smart contracts are considered to be scripts which are stored on particular blockchains. (Konstantinos Christidis, 2016) Smart contracts, as used with blockchain technology, are computer programs which directly control the transfer of assets or digital currency between agreeing parties under prescribed conditions. Blockchains facilitate the existence of distributed peer-to-peer networks in which members who lack mutual trust can interact with each other without reliable intermediaries in a verifiable way. That is, smart contracts include a piece of software code, implemented on blockchain platforms, which guarantees the autonomous and self-enforcing character of its terms. It is initiated by conditions established in advance and subsequently applied to blockchain assets. (Alexander Savelyev, 2017) In other words, they are programs which execute code according to parameters previously agreed upon by two or more counterparties. Such contracts can either be fully coded in stand-alone software, associated with a traditional contract, or be partially governed by rules which have been agreed to by the parties. Smart contracts make it possible to digitally enable, confirm and impose the negotiation and execution of a contract. The contract is recorded in a distributed manner simultaneously on multiple nodes in a blockchain network. (Oscar W, 2018) The most well-known example of smart contract use is seen in Ethereum, a public blockchain-based distributed computing platform which features smart contract characteristics. However, smart contract protocols are currently far from perfect, and suffer from both imperfect governance and limited computing capacity. Their application has been limited due to the complex nature of the underlying programming. However, with wider acceptance and increased use of artificial intelligence, smart contracts may be able to code and verify on a blockchain with more complex trading relationships between the parties.

Artificial intelligence (AI) is changing the way we live, and a number of industries are embracing AI. Embracing blockchain technology implies a willingness to embrace AI where appropriate, however, and failing to do so is in effect moving backwards rather than forwards. The lack of integration of AI with blockchain technologies is the true reason smart contracts have not gained widespread acceptance and usage to date. AI-enabled smart contracts are a much-needed feature that is missing in all major blockchains. Smart contracts are 'smart' due to underlying technology which helps contracting parties agree on terms instantiated in computer code which specifies machine readable instructions for computers to execute under certain conditions. If the conditions are fulfilled, the transmission takes place automatically. However, using AI-enabled smart contracts creates legal challenges which must be understood and met.

It is worth mentioning that the increasing usage of Ethereum over time represents a dramatic increase in value over recent years. (Christidis and Devetsikiotis, 2016) However, recent research notes that Ethereum's smart contract ecosystem has a considerable lack of diversity. Most contracts re-use substantial portions of code, and the number of code developers is low relative to the number of overall contracts. (Macdonald, 2017) This may reflect the relative youth of the smart contract field. (Dave Levin Lucianna Kiffer, Alan Mislove, 2018) That is, the relative newness of the field as a whole may cause lack of diversity. The substantial reuse of code poses a potential threat to reliability and security. It is possible that Ethereum is the most suitable platform at present. Other platforms are yet to achieve the same level of development as Ethereum. The emergence of new contracts enabled by artificial intelligence and new modes of interaction will increase the diversity of the field, while at the same time eliminating the legal problems of current contracts. It is worth mentioning that, although these emerging technologies will bring huge number of advantages, the relevant legal issues raised by these features can't be ignored.

CATEGORIES OF BLOCKCHAINS: PUBLIC AND PERMISSIONED BLOCKCHAINS

Blockchain networks can be broadly categorised as public and permissioned blockchains. Public blockchains have an open network which allows anyone with the technological capability to access the network and the data. For instance, anyone can view the blockchain, propose adding new blocks to it, and validate transactions by following established protocols. Permissioned blockchains are an invitation-only blockchain. Its network can only be accessed by parties that have obtained permission to participate in its platform. Permissioned blockchains can be adopted by a consortium of companies or a single entity relying upon a governance structure to control access, apply and enforce rules, and respond to incidents. However, owing to the degree of trust among participants in permissioned blockchains, less complicated mechanisms are normally used. Traditional security features can be incorporated in permissioned blockchains such as access controls managed through a cloud platform as well as those that are customized to the particular blockchain (English, 2017). Permissioned blockchains can protect critical infrastructures as they provide a more secure environment by preventing unauthorized nodes/users from accessing data. In this system, data collected at each node/user in the private blockchain is measured by a corresponding sensor in the power system thus making it distinct from any earlier measurement and removing the need to examine earlier blocks prior to the voting process. Permissioned blockchain also has unique features aimed at mitigating cybersecurity risks and in detecting, preventing, and combating cyber-attacks. The capability of being used in a wide variety of industries and practice areas has transformed the Permissioned blockchains platform into a fundamental and essential technology. (Liang et al., 2018). Both public and permission blockchain have certain and distinct attributes, encryptions and consensus mechanisms (English, 2017).

ARTIFICIAL INTELLIGENCE AND SMART CONTRACT

Smart contracts, as used with blockchain technology, are computer programs which directly control the transfer of assets or digital currency between agreeing parties under prescribed conditions. Blockchains facilitate the existence of distributed peer-to-peer networks in which members who lack mutual trust can interact with each other without reliable intermediaries in a verifiable way. The concept of smart contracts creates many challenges and concerns when trying to apply conventional concepts of contract law to transactions. The main problem exists in the fact that smart contracts are created and evolve in a technological world "parallel" to the legal field without reference to legal considerations, in a manner similar to the Internet in its infancy. They do not create bonds in the legal sense of the term.

Fundamentally, smart contracts are programs which execute code according to parameters previously agreed upon by two or more counterparties. Such contracts can either be fully coded in stand-alone software, associated with a traditional contract, or be partially governed by rules which have been agreed to by the parties. One of the key attributes of smart contracts is their ability to execute transactions automatically and relentlessly without the need for human intervention. However, this automation, and the fact that smart contracts cannot easily be amended or terminated unless the parties incorporate such capabilities during the creation of the smart contract, present some of the greatest challenges facing widespread adoption of smart contracts. Their application has been limited due to the complex nature of the underlying programming.

For instance, in a traditional context of the contract's world, a party can easily excuse a breach simply by not enforcing the available penalties. In a case of late payment, the vendor may give the option to the customer to pay it later, to preserve the long-term commercial relationship as he/she believes that it is more important than any available termination right or late fee. While, if this transaction had been occurred in smart contract, the option not to enforce the agreement on an ad hoc basis likely would not exist. Consequently, late payment will result in the automatic extraction of a late fee from the customer's account or the suspension of a customer's access to a software program or an internet-connected device if that is what the smart contract was programmed to do. Therefore, the automated execution provided by smart contracts might not align with the manner in which many businesses operate in the real world.

On a similar note, in a conventional contract relationship, a party may be willing to accept, on an ad hoc basis, partial performance to be deemed full performance, either because of an interest in preserving a long-term relationship or a party determines that partial performance is preferable to no performance at all. In this juncture, the desired purpose in smart contract code might not reflect the realities of how contracting parties interact. However, with wider acceptance and increased use of artificial intelligence, smart contracts may be able to code and verify on a blockchain with more complex trading relationships between the parties. (Levi, 2018)

Initially, it may not have appeared so complex to write contracts for digital transactions. However, when these systems began to interact with the physical world, the need for greater intelligence emerged. AI systems capable of translating information from a wide variety of sources into precise terms on which smart contracts can act will be required. Many countries currently maintain legal codes of considerable complexity. Attempts to produce formal digital versions of legal codes are ongoing (Codex, 2014). Eventually, these systems will be used to solve legal problems and perhaps even function as arbitrators or judges. Sophisticated AI systems comprising knowledge of legal systems will be used to simplify and develop legislation.

Artificial intelligence techniques useful for automated negotiations and intelligent contract control include search, expert systems, neural networks and the Minmax algorithm. If the parties give their consent, AI could use these algorithms to negotiate on behalf of the parties as an electronic agent. The application of AI in smart contracts is difficult, however. A large number of issues, such as the interpretation of terms and factors related to contractual language, have emerged. The same words can have multiple meanings, and it is the function of the AI software to appropriately interpret the language. For example, the term "execute" is often used in the context of agreements but means "to apply" and not "to kill". Developers could entrust many tasks to AI which involve interpreting terms. Artificial intelligences must be capable of executing algorithms in accordance with dynamically adjusted, user-defined parameters for certain terms such as price and quality range. They must be able to employ learning techniques and mine data to obtain optimal prices. Gap filler terms are also commonly used in commercial agreements. For example, in some states in the United States, some elements of commercial codes are uniform while others employ space filler terms which may be adjusted to reflect agreements related to time arrangements, delivery method or notice of termination.

Artificial intelligence routines in smart contracts must include dynamic elements able to adapt to the parties' specific needs. AI researchers, particularly in the field of Natural Language Processing (NLP), have made significant advances in automated contract drafting and analysis. Therefore, self-executing code and parameterization based on analysis of typical manually created contracts could be used to generate intelligent contracts via AI. The use of artificial intelligence in smart contracts, that is to say the use of machines in transactions, may lead to more adaptive decisions in the course of executing contracts and observing obligations. Intelligent contracts activated by AI will solve legal problems that have not been anticipated in normal smart contract. It is arguable that smart contract platform providers should be required to disclose how AI-based smart contracts will be executed. Therefore, legal issues raised by AI-based intelligent contracts should be anticipated, so that programmers can prepare relevant code that can be executed on the blockchain.

One of the outstanding legal issues regarding the use of AIs to conclude smart contracts is whether a party has truly given effective consent given that AIs may adapt dynamically and perhaps engage in unexpected behavior. Yet, this issue has not yet been ruled on in court. The extent of provider liability is another undecided issue in this context. Traditional contracts are enforced in distinct phases. If a contract is breached, the injured party must recognize and document the damage and establish the other party's liability. The injured party must then in some cases initiate legal proceedings to establish the breach and enforce payment of damages. Thus, the enforcement phase of traditional contracts requires the involvement of centralized institutions (courts) to intermediate conflicts, forcing the applicant to access multiple types of resources.

The traditional enforcement of contracts thus consumes significant resources and can be rather complex. It is this perceived inefficiency which largely motivates the enthusiasm generated by smart contracts. (Levy, 2017) Intelligent AI contracts remove to some extent these legal hurdles. The AI of the future could conceivably rely on datasets residing on blockchains and on distributed calculations based on blockchain innovations. In addition, AI-mediated blockchains could potentially monetize user data, create autonomous organizations and create a market for AI models. These features of AI-enabled smart contracts on the blockchain present both challenges and opportunities to the legal profession. It is not inconceivable that, with proper regulation and implementation, advances could revolutionize law and business.

However, it should be pointed out that concern about bad code is the same as the concern about bad law. Conditions in this field will not be stable for much longer. Although there are different approaches to addressing the problems inherent in traditional contracts, integrating artificial intelligence into the blockchain and integrating it into smart contracts is an attractive solution. However, without improving the capabilities of smart contracts, there are significant problems with putting in place real-world applications. There is no doubt that enabling AI on smart contracts in the blockchain would involve legal challenges. Regulation and enforcement will be essential in overcoming these problems.

LEGAL FRAMEWORK GOVERNING BLOCKCHAINS

The inherent nature and features of blockchains pose challenges to existing legal frameworks. As described in the first section of this paper, blockchain technology allows transactions and data to be recorded and shared across a distributed network of members without a trusted intermediary, host, and central party. The temptation to use blockchains by organizations and other entities is high and this has brought forth a new set of risks and issues. A world based on centralized governance and control requires new kinds of technologies such as blockchain. This in turn has created new challenges and associated challenges from the legal and regulatory aspects and in enforcement of rules and regulations (Salmon, 2019b). The process of reconciling new technologies with established legal principles and regulatory models is often messy and protracted. The advent of new technology and the growing use of digital technology have given rise to a tendency to replace current laws with technical ones that have the potential to be enforced ex-ante (identify problems beforehand and shape behaviour and responses through regulatory intervention) through codes such as smart contract in blockchain. In other words, it is necessary to adapt regulation so that it would not become obsolete and imposed prospectively to regulate future conduct. However, transforming legal rules to technical ones is a difficult process. Traditionally, legal rules are inherently ambiguous allowing software developers to incorporate their own interpretations into code via formal algorithms and mathematical models such as legal rules that incorporated into codes in smart contract.

The impact of digital technology on legal systems is something that cannot be ignored. It creates a reciprocal effect where code replaces some of the traditional functions of the law, and the law progressively starting to assume the characteristics of code. The emergence of blockchain technology reinforces

Figure 1.

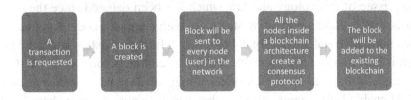

the tendency to rely on codes to regulate the actions of individuals. It presents a novel type of regulation (smart contracts) which transforms the traditional conceptions of law into something that can be better assimilated into code. Thus, it will tempt lawyers and legislators to draft legal contracts and laws that are closer to how technical rules are drafted. Smart contracts are self-executing software codes that run on a blockchain. The code in the smart contract defines the terms of an agreement on an "if" and "else" basis and then automatically enforces those terms if the specific criteria programmed into the code are met. A smart contract is executed by the verification of the users on a blockchain system, removing the requirements of having a trusted third-party intermediary.

The decentralized characteristics of blockchains can bring benefits while posing legal and regulatory challenges since there is no central party that is responsible and can be held accountable (Salmon, 2019a). Even before the advent of blockchains, regulators faced similar issues in determining accountability on the Internet. In Google Spain v AEPD, the Court of Justice of the European Union (CJEU) ruled that a search engine could be held accountable for the protection of personal data in respect of third-party websites accessible through its service (Google Spain SL, Google Inc. v Agencia Espanola de Proteccion de Datos (AEPD), 2014). In a public chain system, no party can easily be held accountable as in the case of a search engine. However, in a private blockchain system, there is clear ownership and responsibility. As such, those running the system might be accountable for data added as in a search engine since the system owner could be seen as enabling the distribution of data through the blockchain.

Blockchains show promise in facilitating secure data exchanges through embedded systems that are increasingly interconnected. Blockchain is a promising solution for many distributed applications where trust and transparency are critical factors.

The simplicity of smart contracts may not be fully appreciated at present, but their limitations may constitute a threat to future applications of blockchain. Blockchain-based smart contracts enforce obligations without relying on a central authority. In reality, contracts fulfill many functions that are not explicitly of a legal nature. Smart contracts on blockchain represents a judicious solution to certain legal problems posed by conventional contracts. However, they require some modifications to make them suitable for multi-channel transactions.(Macdonald, Liu-Thorrold, & Julien, 2017) Smart contract technology neglects the fact that people use contracts as social resources to manage their relationships. (Levy & Society, 2017) As AI becomes more and more powerful and ubiquitous, tremendous efforts are being made to enable smart contract AI.(Solum, 2014) Therefore, AI-empowered intelligent contracts offer a unique opportunity to remedy the deficiencies of simple smart contracts, while simultaneously introducing legal challenges which need to be addressed and identified. Without improving the capabilities of smart contracts, it is difficult to implement decentralized, real-world applications of the blockchain.

The autonomous nature of AI creates problems of predictability and control that could render ineffective *ex-post* regulation, especially if an AI system poses a very significant risk. Traditional regulatory methods, such as research and development supervision, product licensing and tort, seem rather ill-suited to managing the risks associated with autonomous and intelligent machines.(Scherer & Tech., 2015) One long-standing issue of technology and law which has been debated since the advent of the computer program is how to capture a normative statement with computer code. Another is the question of how to make such normative statements legally binding. A further question triggered by the emergence of the blockchain is how to turn legal contracts into smart contracts and vice versa.(Governatori et al., 2018) Yet another question raised by the latest technology advancements is how to overcome the legal issues raised by AI-enabled smart contracts in such a way as to obtain a more beneficial result for both developers and customers. These questions will be addressed in this book.

Pardis Moslemzadeh
Tehrani, University of Malaya, Malaysia

REFERENCES

Christidis, K., & Devetsikiotis, M. (2016). Blockchains and Smart Contracts for the Internet of Things. *IEEE Access: Practical Innovations, Open Solutions, 4*, 2292–2303. doi:10.1109/ACCESS.2016.2566339

ConsenSys. (2018). *Why Military Blockchain is Critical in the Age of Cyber Warfare.* Retrieved from https://media.consensys.net/why-military-blockchain-is-critical-in-the-age-of-cyber-warfare-93bea0be7619

English, Kim, & Nonaka. (2017). *Advancing Blockchain Cybersecurity: Technical and Policy Considerations for the Financial Services Industry.* Academic Press.

Google Spain, S. L. (2014). Google Inc. v Agencia Espanola de Proteccion de Datos (AEPD), Mario Costeja Gonzalez. *CASE (Philadelphia, Pa.), C-131*(12).

Governatori, G., Idelberger, F., Milosevic, Z., Riveret, R., Sartor, G., & Xu, X. (2018). *On legal contracts, imperative and declarative smart contracts, and blockchain systems.* Academic Press.

John Salmon, G. M. (2019a). *Blockchain and Associated Legal Issues for Emerging Markets. International Finance corporation.* World Bank Group. doi:10.1596/31202

John Salmon, G. M. (2019b). *Fresh Ideas about Business in Emerging Market.* Retrieved from www.ifc.org/thoughtleadership

Levi & Lipton. (2018). *An Introduction to Smart Contracts and Their Potential and Inherent Limitations.* Harvard Law School Forum on Corporate Governance. Retrieved from https://corpgov.law.harvard.edu/

Levin, Kiffer, & Mislove. (2018). Analyzing Ethereum's Contract Topology. IMC '18.

Levy, K. (2017). *Book-smart, not street-smart: blockchain-based smart contracts and the social workings of law.* Academic Press.

Levy, K. E. C. (2017). Book-Smart, Not Street-Smart: Blockchain-Based Smart Contracts and the Social Workings of Law. *Engaging Science, Technology, and Society, 3*, 1–15. doi:10.17351/ests2017.107

Macdonald, M., Liu-Thorrold, L., & Julien, R. (2017). The Blockchain: A Comparison of Platforms and Their Uses Beyond Bitcoin. *Work. Pap*, 1–18.

Macdonald, M., Liu-Thorrold, L., & Julien, R. (2017). *The blockchain: A comparison of platforms and their uses beyond bitcoin*. Academic Press.

Oscar, W. (2018). *Ai on Blockchain—What's the Catch?* https://hackernoon.com/how-cortex-brings-ai-on-the-blockchain-86d08922bb2a

Savelyev, A. (2017). Contract Law 2.0:'Smart'contracts as the Beginning of the End of Classic Contract Law. *Information & Communications Technology Law, 26*(2), 116–134. doi:10.1080/13600834.2017.1301036

Scherer, M. (2015). *Regulating artificial intelligence systems: Risks, challenges, competencies, and strategies*. Academic Press.

Solum, L. (2014). *Artificial meaning*. Academic Press.

Section 1
Legal and Regulatory Framework of the Blockchain

Chapter 1
The Vulnerability of the Blockchain Network From the Consensus Perspective

Mohamed Ikbal Nacer
Bournemouth University, UK

Simant Prakoonwit
Bournemouth University, UK

ABSTRACT

The blockchain is a registry shared among different participants intending to eliminate the need for a central authority to maintain information. The first proposal of this technology was to eliminate financial authorities in transactions of value. However, the application of the same technique for the transaction of information could facilitate trades and offer traceability and diamond tracking around the world. The consensus is at the core of the network because it orchestrates nodes to accept new information, but it operates over a data structure in an open network, consequently leading to many complex behaviours that introduce different vulnerabilities. This work aims to highlight the vulnerability within the blockchain network based on the different participant behaviours that dominate the shared registry. Moreover, different malicious behaviour can appear on the networking layer by taking advantage of the network topology.

INTRODUCTION

The bitcoin white paper (Nakamoto, 2019) pushed the boundaries of knowledge by regarding an old problem from a different angle by implementing competency among different maintainers to gain a reward for block validation. This technique has led to the rise of cryptocurrency and has been followed by the introduction of many proposals, such as Blackcoin and Zerocash (Vasin P., 2014), (Sasson et al., 2014). The implementation of business logic through the adoption of a smart contact following the Nick Zabo approach has been conveyed in the Ethereum white paper (Wood, 2014). Chen in (Chen, 2018) proposed the use of traceability mechanisms to validate business information, but the consensus was

DOI: 10.4018/978-1-7998-7927-5.ch001

based on the follower and leader mechanism. These different stages have declared the beginning of a new era within blockchain technology through the implementation of different mechanisms to handle various kinds of information. Nevertheless, the platform as a whole suffers from heavy state transition, monopoly, or vulnerability to attacks.

The goal of the blockchain was to eliminate the bank as a trusted third party as part of a financial verification of the transaction. However, the techniques can be adopted in many industries. It has been found through numerous observations that it can be applied to provide identity verification, secure diamond grading, and track shipments around the world. (Dillenberger et al., 2019). Since the blockchain network's first proposal, there was a huge hype that tended to show the virtue of its adoption. The rapid development of this technology has highlighted the different ways in which it can make everyday life easier. Thus, many works on the heart of blockchain technology, which is consensus, attempt to promote the importance of the approach to ensure confidentiality, transparency, accountability, traceability, and management of identities. Singh et al. in (Singh. et al., 2018) point out that blockchain technology is a game-changer in the IoT industry before discussing the security issues within the technology that arise from decision distribution, which provides transparency to different battery holders. Moreover, the paper introduced an architecture that separated the user and the miner to keep a record of the validity of the ledger. Fakhri et al. in (Fakhri. & Mutijarsa., 2018) implemented a blockchain and non-blockchain system to provide a test comparison of their performance, in which they were dedicated to the storage of data generated by IoT device. The comparison showed the conceptual contribution in terms of security provided by the blockchain implementation.

Buccafurri et al. in (Buccafurri. et al., 2017)studied the suitability of the blockchain within the context of the IoT. They claimed that the advantages of the network, such as record-keeping, coordination among stakeholders, transparency, and irrevocability of transactions, are characteristics that are also desirable within the IoT sector. Mendki in (Mendki, 2019) proposed an architecture to enable the use of the blockchain within a fog system to secure communication between a user and the fog end server, taking into consideration the limitations on horizontal scalability. The work by Singh et al in (Singh. et al., 2018) studied the possible impacts on the internet from the integration of the blockchain as a backbone communicative mechanism. They found that cyberattacks, such as the denial of service, arise from the centralization of the different services offered by the network. El Kafhali et al. (El Kafhali et al., 2019) introduced a raw data stream within the fog and cloud base by proposing the use of different blockchain networks for each part of the platform.

The work of Nada et al. in (Alasbali et al., 2020) raised concerns over the lack of standards of interoperability within the growing market of blockchain implementation. They proposed a model to handle heterogeneous data. The growth of the different sources to gather data within one running technique led to the discussion of the blockchain as a web by Naim et al. in (Naim et al., 2020). The solution aimed to propose an extension of the semantic blockchain platform by adding a layer of service to handle the different sources of data. Chou et al. (Chou et al., 2020) discussed the problem of data bloating within the blockchain due to immutability within the ledger. The solution was an integration of IPFS to manage the data through the injection of a clustering algorithm that aims to spot the cold and hot data to speed up the validation of the new data. Ismail et al. in (Ismail, et al., 2020) implemented and evaluated a platform that decentralizes access to the health care sector with the use of blockchain technology.

This work aims to provide a study on blockchain technology from a security vulnerability perspective. It addresses the consensus mechanism at the core of its functioning by providing the vulnerability within each step and analyses how each element of the platform can lead to exterior manipulation. The next section introduces blockchain technology, consensus, and different security problems. The third section discusses the different problems within blockchain technology in terms of a consensus approach.

BACKGROUND

The blockchain is a technology that aims to function over an open network without the domination of a central authority. The advantage of such an intention is to offer traceability and transparency among users of the system. Most of the prototype markets incline toward cryptocurrencies, in which the proof of work (PoW) dominates the underlying incentive for its functioning. Different solutions have adopted different mechanisms to optimise the drawback of the latter approach. Many pieces of research have studied the impact of different sources of information on how interoperability will delay the functioning of the system; consequently, there have been various attempts to address the traceability of information over the data structure, such as (Chen, 2018).

The process of consensus is divided into two steps; one is internal, and the other is external. The internal step is based on binding to the incentive rules by doing work, and random coin tossing (Nakamoto, 2019) (Bentov I. et al., 2014); however, the external step is based on the propagation of the information in the network. The two behaviours have a big impact on the delay in finalizing a list of transactions in the network (Decker & & Wattenhofer, 2013). It is essential to state that the different leader-based solutions that are available, such as PoW (Nakamoto, 2019), proof of stake (Bentov I. et al., 2014), proof of useful resources (Turesson, 2019), and the byzantine fault tolerance, are designed to make it practically impossible for the attacker to invest time and resources in acting maliciously. However, theoretically, a different type of attack has been detected.

The work in (Eyal & Sirer, 2014) identified that the PoW is prone to 51% malicious nodes. Networking attacks such as the eclipse lead to forking more than double-spending; however, the network is based on almost ten thousand nodes that are interested in ledger validity. The work on (Malkhi et al., 2019) by Malkhi et al. identified a special kind of attack where different nodes intend to keep the platform alive but attack safety, and this kind of behaviour is comparable to the selfish mining by mining cartels (Eyal & Sirer, 2014). The proof of the stake depends on the assumption that the stakeholder will always be interested in the ledger's validity. However, different kinds of attack, such as the long-range attack (Roy et al., 2018), stake bleeding (Gaži et al., 2018) beside the capability to monopolize the system, and the rise of stake cartels, can lead the system to malicious behaviour. Proof of useful resources lacked some conceptual criteria that let them stand with an open context where randomness is a key for convergence and criteria for trust. The work (Malkhi et al., 2019) claimed the use of byzantine fault tolerance within a permissionless network by trying to make a flexible quorum that observes and penalizes different participants. Nevertheless, the high level of oriented message complexity introduced by the BFT approach makes it more suitable for a private version.

The research by Liu et al. in (Liu et al., A survey on applications of game theory in blockchain, 2019) aimed to investigate the vulnerability within the blockchain from bitcoin ideology. The block withholding, hopping, and all selfish behaviour exhibited by the miners have been analysed according to a game theory approach, which is the mathematical modeling of actors' rational behaviours. The work in (Buccafurri et al., 2017) studied the PoS and highlighted the rise of stake cartels. Moreover, it discussed the monopoly issues within this kind of approach. The hyper ledger fabric that follows the BFT has been dedicated to the transaction of information, but it is incapable of dealing with an unlimited number of nodes due to high message complexity. The IOTA approach introduces a monopoly due to the zero-reward given to a maintainer; consequently, the monopolist can manipulate the data besides the expensive search algorithms.

The work of Zheng et al. in (Zheng, 2018) had surveyed blockchain technology in which different consensus studies were investigated and explained in addition to defining the technology as separate components. The work of Mohamed et al. in (J & N, 2019) discussed the different horizontal applications of this solution such as its application to the financial sector, stock trading, cryptocurrency, and healthcare. He also broadly studied challenges such as security, scalability, privacy, and integration issues across many industries, trading in stocks, cryptocurrency, and healthcare. He also broadly studied challenges such as security, scalability, privacy, and integration issues across many industries. Software engineering studies have been carried out in (Porru et al., 2017) to highlight the conceptual drawback of the system in the architectural construction of it alongside the safety and reliability of the platform. This work focuses on security vulnerability from a consensual perspective, it addresses the different techniques implemented and proposed from literature. In addition, the study devoted part of it to the vulnerability of networking resulting from a consensual choice.

CONSENSUAL VULNERABILITY

The perspective of maintaining information between different nodes interested in its validity through the sharing of the distributed ledger has received much attention in recent years. Consequently, this work investigates all the vulnerabilities stated in the literature in a comparative approach to highlight the drawbacks within the blockchain network by focusing on the consensus as the central problem within this approach. The study will show the impact of the data structure and networking due to consensus choices. The work in (Liu et al., A survey on applications of game theory in blockchain.) discussed the different game theory analyses dedicated to the PoW and concluded that the PoW is vulnerable to 50% attack and many other types of behaviours that depends depend on the selection of the forks. Moreover, the consensus can be subjected to latency due to the selfish behaviour of miners or pools. PoS suffers from various disadvantages such as monopoly, long-range attack, uncle's block, and pool cartels (Eyal & Sirer, 2014). The IOTA approach suffers from centralization and resource consumption that can grow massively (Jiang & Lian, 2019). Moreover, BFT suffers from a high message complexity towards the leader that makes it unsuitable for permissionless blockchain.

Proof of Work

The PoW was first proposed in the hash cash to discourage spammers from sending emails. However, it was later adopted within the bitcoin platform to discourage malicious nodes from participating in the validation process. The solution leads to probabilistic finality, where the miners' resources play the role of decision-making. PoW consists of solving a mathematical puzzle in exchange for rewards. Nakamoto et al. (Nakamoto, 2019) proposed the first implementation of a peer-to-peer network to eliminate double-spending in the financial transaction named bitcoin. The solution has started a huge hype around blockchain technology. it proposed to use different distributed peers to exchange a block containing a set of user transactions to be validated before propagating. The approach introduced a race between different validators called miners because of the reward generated by the network for each validated block.

Each transaction is authenticated through the use of a digital signature. Therefore, the introduction of the solution of a probabilistic gain is based on the resource invested by each miner.

Figure 1. Function of mining

$$P_i = \frac{w_i}{\sum_0^n w_j} \quad \ldots \ldots \ldots \ldots \ldots \ldots \ldots (1)$$

Where P represents the probability of winning in the race, which is described as the resources dedicated by a specific miner over the resource dedicated by the entire network. J represents each data point up to n, and W represents hardware resources.

Although PoW and its first implementation, bitcoin has gained worldwide attention, the solution operates on a network that follows certain standards that cannot simply change to accommodate cryptocurrency needs. Nevertheless, the technique as well as prone to many concerns such as being subject to monopoly (Nacer et al., 2020), the 51% attack can be used to undermine the network for the competitor (Kroll, The economics of bitcoin mining, or bitcoin in the presence of adversaries, 2013), or the need for continually increased resource consumption which can increase massively with rapid community growth.

Stale Block

The data structure takes a tree form, in which it will always choose the longest path following the longest chain rule. However, the idea of which path to take based on the predictability technique of the games theory has been explored (Jiang Y. &., 2019). Forking appears when miners come with a different solution to the block, at the same time leading to a different scope of miners. It leads to either soft or hard forking, in which the latter can be exhibited by cropping the network to mine different versions of the ledger or the stable block, which are the blocks that have been left behind, or the ones that did not make it in the chosen longest chain. The miners will recalculate the stale blocks and send them back to be added to the strongest path. However, it has been concluded that increasing difficulty in the PoW is the main factor in decreasing the appearance of the stale block. The work in (Gervais et al., 2016) has provided details that the generation time of ten minutes in the bitcoin platform leads to the stale average block of 534.8KB. The work in (Stifter et al., 2019) highlighted that raising the problem of stale block appearance is dependent on the difficulty of the puzzle. *Figure 1* stands for major forking that happened on the bitcoin platform.

Figure 1 shows some forks within the bitcoin blockchain, regular forks were initiated in the first step with the low number of miners. It can observe the unintentional large fork created in 2013 which was later abandoned. The Bitcoin Knots hard fork is based on a floured version of the bitcoin system, which has the same name, it was launched in 2013. Libbitcoin was followed in 2014. Bitcoin ABC, as well as Bitcoin Cash in 2017 and Bitcoin SV, was released in 2018. Each solution besides adopting the maintenance of a hard fork has the intention to ensure securities consideration and scalability on top of the already existing platform.

Figure 2. Major bitcoin forks

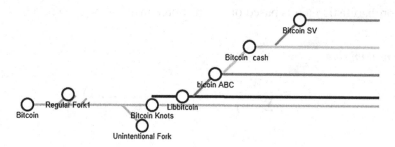

Mining Cartels

Mining cartels are the result of the competency among different nodes to maintain the ledger validity. Many nodes implemented protocols such as Stratum (Stifter N. S., 2019) to secure the advantageous probability of winning the race. However, the mining cartels' competency leads to different behaviour to take advantage of each other. Selfish mining is malicious behaviour from one cartel against another to secure the reward. Most of the cartels are managed by a pool manager, in which the search is divided among the participants in the pool. Block withholding is a malicious technique based on the participation of an attacker within the victim pool; the work will be divided among the registered nodes (Bag et al., Bitcoin block withholding attack: Analysis and mitigation., 2016). Rosenfeld in (Rosenfeld, 2011) was the first to propose the problem and has studied it since the bitcoin paper. Eyal discussed block withholding (BWH) and raised concerns about the double-spending that can take place by taking advantage of this vulnerability. Bag et al. in (Bag et al., Bitcoin block withholding attack: Analysis and mitigation., 2016) studied the different strategies that the user can use to maximize the revenue. Moreover, they offered suggestions on how to counter BWH. The work by Rosenfeld (Rosenfeld, 2011) was the first work that addresses a general concept of BWH, which is lying in wait (Bag et al., Bitcoin block withholding attack: Analysis and mitigation., 2016). The paper stands for the different options that the miner could have after he solves the mined block, such as continuing mining with more resources to secure more rewards than his peers or being an infiltrating miner that is loyal to another cartel. Although the mining cartel is a very good option due to the huge level of difficulty, it introduces many problems within the blockchain network, such as the capability of monopoly, which is the real hurdle to eliminating the trusted party. Pool hopping is a special case of block withholding, in which the attacker has been sent specially to capture information regarding the progress in solving the NP-completed problem of the PoW. The information found will be shared with the source.

Consensus Attacks

The consensual attack is a special kind of attack that addresses the different techniques used to double-spend or pass a malicious transaction. The first one is the 51% attack, in which the miner or a group of miners own the resources that can comprise more than half of the system, thereby generating more blocks than what rest. The system will be under the sole control of the monopolist. However, a specific cartel used to hold more than 50% of a system before it ceased to exist due to the need for trust that comes from a high distribution, which can lead people to lose belief in the bitcoin ideology. Liao and

Katz (Liao, 2017) studied the possibility of providing a bribery transaction in exchange for shifting from one chain to another for major miners. The study has a strong assumption that such an action can take place; however, the high distribution that can appear by eliminating any appearance of a major miner will eliminate such behaviour. The Goldfinger proposed by Kroll et al. in (Kroll, The economics of bitcoin mining, or bitcoin in the presence of adversaries, 2013) is an attack proposal that aims to clarify the fact that the domination of the platform by an exterior force to destroy the system can be done by monopolizing more than delaying many transactions and different malicious behaviour.

Proof of Stake

The PoS is an incentive mechanism that will be adopted by the Euthrieum Foundation instead of the PoW. The approach is based on fostering a large community through the use of PoW before immigration to the new approach. The power of the approach lies in the lack of any resource investment. Moreover, many other solutions based on the PoS have been proposed in the literature, such as (Bentov et al., Proof of activity: Extending bitcoin's proof of work via proof of stake [extended abstract], 2014), and implemented to serve as a cryptocurrency, such as (Vasin P., 2014). The community raises many questions regarding the trust that will be transferred to stakeholders to manage funds. Many kinds of proof of stake can be found in the literature, which can be categorized into three forms: the chain-based PoS, the community-based proof of stake, and the BFT proof of stake. Although proof of stake depends on different stakeholders, the latter approach can make the functioning very different in terms of finality, propagation, and security.

The chain-based PoS can be described as a generation mechanism that depends on many factors. PeerCoin (Kriskó, 2013) is a stake-oriented consensus for cryptocurrency. The solution tried to address the small size of the community by offering a reward to small stakeholders based on the age of the hold coins. On the other hand, nxt (Popov, A probabilistic analysis of the nxt forging algorithm., 2016) has raised concerns over lowering the cost of participants, which raises the risk of the negligible interest that one miner may have in the network, leading to many kinds of malicious activities. Another type of proof of stake, which is the best-known, implements an algorithm called Follow the Satoshi Algorithm (FTSA). The solution implements a random search over the ledger for the selection of specific coins that will be checked for ownership by stakeholders. The community-based approach selects a community based on different metrics and criteria before creating a validation community that takes a sequential turn on the validation of the information. However, the validation mechanism among the different validators follows the BFT approach. Auroboros (Kiayias, 2017) is a protocol that implements a dynamic community, in which each block validation is called an epoch. The epoch will be divided into an N slot at a specific time; the slot stands for one leader time to generate a block. The community has the potential to change its members in each new epoch. Snow White is another approach that falls under the community-based blockchain, in which it tries to address the disconnection among the different validators by making the stakeholder take the entire blockchain as input and generates a list of peers randomly to stand for the new committee. Finally, the BFT is directed among the different members. Tendermint (Kwon, 2014) was the first solution that proposed the use of BFT within the validation step, in which it developed many rounds of exchanged messages. The messages stated different stages of consensus, which are Propose, Prevote, Pre-commit. The solution finalizes a transaction by the recipient of two-thirds of the community pre-commit message to the leader.

Cartels can rise in the system and many behaviours that can be a potential thread within PoW can also appear in this incentive. The criteria that can be shared among the two techniques is the fact there are means that can be detailed as stakes or resources to converge into one ledger. Consequently, the aim of the convergence between many nodes with an underlying reward that can be entitled to different validators based on the version of the ledger leads to a probabilistic finality that can be delayed or enforced by the use of many techniques, such as cartel building. The 'nothing at stake' (Houy, 2014) is a mechanism that invests in the costless efforts to generate a block. It is, however, comparable to the PoW, in which miners have many versions of the ledger. This case can be very expensive in PoS due to the need for convergence, but the probabilistic finality introduces competency. However, some miners try to distribute their functioning over the different versions to eliminate any financial loss that may come from choosing one chain over another. Moreover, the costless effort can give flexibility to different stakeholders to accept bribery, known as posterior corruption (Liao, 2017), in which the user can double-spend the same coins but only after some time, or send the same coins with a significant transaction fee to an important stakeholder to stimulate a race to the longest chain. A long-range attack (Homoliak, 2019) is the capability of the minter to recreate the entire history of the blockchain, claiming all the rewards in the network. Stake bleeding is another technique that invests in collecting transaction that forgot to be validated and needs to be resubmitted or selected from the malicious chain before claims all the fees when the side chain is the main one. This approach is prone to result in a monopoly, which occurs when there is an investment in the probabilistic finality beside the domination on the means to come to consensus can lead the validator to be the sole monopolist and manipulate the network growth (Nacer et al., 2020).

PoS has received much attention in recent years due to the inefficiency that comes with PoW. The solution cannot secure the user's privacy due to the domination of the network by stakeholders that can run many analytic techniques to track users. Moreover, the solution does not support full randomness because it is a partial execution of the community that owns the platform. However, the network has been adopted in many solutions within the internet of things. The adoption of the solution for an open system that can eliminate the trusted party cannot be the case due to the lack of security measures; the solution is based on voting that may lead to oriented attacks in which stakeholders will be targeted. Conversely, the adoption of PoS can be one of the best in private blockchains run by a group of companies, in which important documents or values are exchanged.

IOTA Approach

The Tangle IOTA is a solution proposed by Popov in (Popov, The tangle., 2016), in which the high submission rate from a huge number of users that will be solving a small PoW puzzle will be far greater than any other force that aims to alter the system's belief. The solution dedicated to the internet of things (IoT), in which it has been adopted, has been analysed in several studies. The Tangle is a directed acyclic graph (DAG) that stands for an ensemble of transactions linked together through the use of the PoW, in which each transaction is called a site. The leaves of the graph are called tips. The tips are invalidated transactions, and through the use of a random selection algorithm, two tips will be selected for validation in exchange for the injection of a new transaction. The initiator of each transaction runs one of the three selection algorithms proposed by Popov such as a uniform random walk, an unweighted random walk, or a weighted random walk (Popov, The tangle., 2016). The cumulative weight rule is the solution to calculate before predicting the finality of a transaction. The solution does not reward other maintainers, making it prone to monopoly by stakeholders. Consequently, it is not suitable for the public blockchain.

The IOTA approach has been built specifically to serve within the IoT sector as a zero-fee transaction; however, the approach used hash cash (Back, 2002) proof of work within each user device. Consequently, it has eliminated the resource dedicated by the server, but at the cost of consistency in the user's performance. Many works in the literature have adopted the IOTA ideology to build a solution within the IoT sectors, such as (Florea, 2018). However, the search within the DAG is random, and the algorithm starts from the initiation of the graph. Consequently, when the graph grows, the search for tips can be an extensive process. The work in (Shabandri, 2019) has raised concerns about the computation power that will be invested in the validation of a transaction when the graph grows massively. However, the system does not provide a reward for a maintainer. Consequently, it is managed only by stakeholders. The splitting attack is a specific state the system can encounter, in which the graph can be cropped into two parts whereby the attacker can double-spend by attaching the same transaction into the two paths.

The solution has many drawbacks relating firstly to the lack of a consensual means of eliminating double-spending in an open environment. There are many behaviors that the attacker can invest in that were discussed in Tangle's whitepaper, such as double-spend attacks, parasite chain, and network splitting. Jiang et al. in (Jiang Y. W., 2018) proposed the use of ReRam, a non-volatile memory that can respond with the high performance expected in terms of computation when the DAG massively grows. Bu et al. in (Bu, 2019), discussed the selection algorithm developed by IOTA, in which many transactions are left behind and require resubmission. Numerous works have studied the vulnerability of 34% of attacks, in which it is claimed to be the secure part-owned by IOTA stakeholders. However, the system does not have any rewards for those responsible for maintenance to attract participants outside the community who can increase the integrity of the system. Therefore, centralization and replay attacks have been discussed by De Roode et al. (Roode & G., 2018)

The solution has been widely discussed in use cases in the IoT industries. However, although the publicity which made the approach has received a lot of attention in recent years, it does not have a valid mechanism to deal with the open system, it does not provide the purpose of block modification, which is the elimination of the relying party. However, from a technical point of view, the solution does not solve the zero-fee, but it transfers the computation by forcing the user to run a lightweight PoW. So, the IOTA entanglement approach is not a promising solution in the blockchain industry, and it does not even provide the basics of block modification.

Byzantine Fault Tolerance

Byzantine fault tolerance (BFT) has been proposed to serve as a consensual approach within the distributed blockchain nodes. The problem was first proposed and then solved by Lamport (Lamport, 1982), in which the solution aimed to make the different processes come to a consensus on the order of the event. The BFT system must fulfill the following requirement (Xiao et al., 2019.):

Termination: All processes, which are not faulty, within the system generate an output.

Agreement: All processes, which are not faulty, within the system eventually converge on the same output y.

Validity: If all processes begin with the same input x then y=x.

Integrity: the consensus value y and the decision made by each process must be generated from a non-faulty process.

Paxos is a solution that has been proposed to reach the consensus on 2f+1, where f is the number of a faulty node without any consideration of a byzantine behaviour. Oki and Liskov proposed that the use of view stamped replication is based on attaching the leader replicate to each view that will manage votes before deciding on the event based on the received N of the message, in which N>2f+1. Kastro and Liskov proposed the practical BFT (Castro, 1999), which is based on a high exchange of messages between the different nodes. The messages exchanged by the different replicas and leaders are pre-preparation, preparation, validation, and response. The leader initiates the validation message when he receives 2f + 1, in which f is the supposed Byzantine peers that make up a third of the platform. The complexity of the algorithm is $O\left(N^2\right)$.

The discussion of adopting BFT in blockchain technology has been discussed in (Stifter N. J., 2019). Malkhi et al. (Mendki, 2019) proposed flexible BFT where the different nodes. The flexibility is linked to the different quorums that will be managed by the active nodes to eliminate any malicious behavior from other nodes. The solution obviously leads to a monopoly, which makes it practically unsuitable for a public blockchain. The approach attempted to solve a certain problem called Alive-but-Corrupt. Due to the monopoly introduced due to the introduction to access the quorum, the rise of a node that intends to save the liveliness of the system but to attack the security is very important. The work of Amir et al. (Salzman et al., 2010) explained the danger of the leader-oriented approach by targeting the leader to delay messages, delay manipulation after the denial of service attack. Moreover, the monopoly can lead a malicious node to orchestrate the performance of the system. Amir et al. proposed a performance-based accuracy criterion for use with the BFT model. In the Zyzzyva protocol, replicas respond directly to the customer, and the customer has the power to help them adjust their order number if there is any inconsistency. Therefore, Ronget et al. (Rong et al., 2019). claimed that the optimization stemming from Zyzzyva was more suitable as a basis for blockchain technology than PBFT.

Safety within the BFT depends on many behaviors that can take place due to structured decision-making. Malkhi (Malkhi D. N., 2019) introduced the living-but-corrupt problem, in which the malicious one can be part of behavior that can threaten the security of users' funds. He proposed the use of a dynamic quorum that constantly observes and penalizes Byzantine participants. The leader can be attacked by outside forces who have details of inside elements. For example, a community participant can provide an outside force with an IP address of the leader; the attacker can use many networking techniques such as flooding the network with data, a man-in-the-middle attack (Ekparinya, 2018), or RBG hijacking isolation. While adopting a solution within a consortium blockchain to serve as a consensus mechanism within a high trust network between companies or within a different party within an organization, the solution suffers from high complexity of messages which cannot be passed in a high submission system. The solution has also been proposed for use in the IoT sector in many works, but the system suffers from the centralization of decision making leading to its adoption as a cryptocurrency, the target of malicious behavior.

Figure 2 shows the message exchange implemented by the Byzantine fault tolerance practice, in which five steps have been proposed to reach a consensus. First of all, it starts with a request from the client to the leader. Second, the leader will inform the other replicas to pre-prepare in advance the consensus, in which all the servers will exchange the message to be on time. Third, prepare is a type of message that builds on the last upcoming exchange to validate the consensus. Fourth, the commit message will write the consensus value before confirming it by another message exchange cycle. Fifth, each server will respond directly to the client. It can be observed that in the permissionless system, the complexity of the message exchange is almost unmanageable.

Figure 3. Practical Byzantine fault tolerance

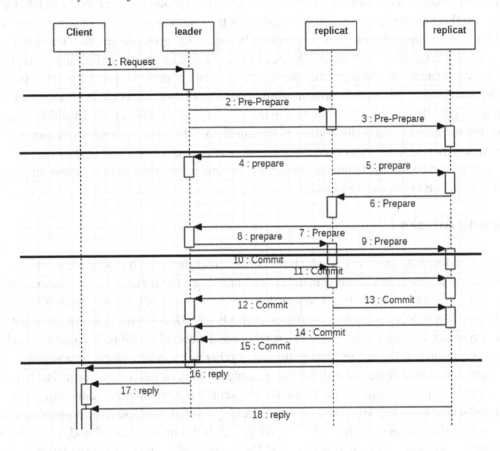

The Chain Approach

TheChain (Nacer et al., 2020) is a solution that aims to invest in the fact that solidarity is not an act of charity, but is many forces that come together for a mutual objective. The proposal dropped the consensus to look at the old problem from a different angle, where intersected regions of interest have been implemented. The data structure has taken a different form from the normal data structure shared in previous work; it has taken advantage of the Petri network regarding its suitability, in which the place was exchanged as a list of wallets and the transition as a list of transactions. The ledger is open for any injection of a new place and transition. It takes advantage of the procedure that leads to the use of graph reachability as a checking mechanism to validate a block. The solution links all similar transactions with the use of memory references, leading to faster injection and generating an accurate local and global sequential number. The token within places can be exchanged with any type of information with more complex symbolic criteria. The governance algorithm is the last element within the platform that has the goal of building boundaries in many regions before securing the intersection among them.

The solution raised the concern of monopoly within different approaches due to their investment through mean to converge into one version of the ledger. TheChain introduced the concept of node independence, in which the intersection of operating territories among the different validators forces them to watch over each other. The solution discussed how the elimination of the convergence on the chain could eliminate much vulnerability that comes with the probabilistic finality. The global and local sequential numbers are a precise integer that stands for the transaction locally, in which many transactions with the same identity will generate an exact balance. However, the solution keeps the usage of coins based on the UTXO model due to the need for privacy and the capability of parallel treatment that will be stimulated from such a technique. Moreover, the chain runs over the graph, but problems of splitting and forking that usually appear within the means-based convergences are not expected to take part in its growth, due to each validator's independence and a double layer of validation that firstly addresses the balance and secondly addresses the injection with a precise sequential number. Finally, different cartels' behaviour that has been discussed previously cannot be a part of the system. TheChain invested in such behaviour due to partial networking centralization and tried to address this underlying networking vulnerability in a different way.

Networking Attacks

Blockchain is a distributed network in which peers communicate through independently-built channels to come to a consensus. Consequently, many attacks that target the network have been explored in the literature, such as (Saad et al., 2019). The search for peers within blockchain technology is a very important step in which the bitcoin implementation depends on a DNS server that provides a list of peers that will be a source of truth for the user. On the other hand, networks such IOTA use the search for the IP address of the closest one before sharing the list of other peers. Many blockchain solutions can differ from centralization to complete distribution, passing by a decentralized platform. The hyper ledger fabric is an IBM implementation of the blockchain system in a permissionless environment; it runs on a centralized server owned by IBM with different access provided to users. The decentralized platform can be found in the proposal, such as flexible BFT, due to the importance of nodes and distribution being completed in proposals such as bitcoin and TheChain. The open system provided to different users makes different cyber-attacks easy, with various means that can take advantage of the user or the distribution of decisions.

The DNS attack occurs by taking advantage of the vulnerability that the user needs to connect to peers. Consequently, one option is the use of the DNS server as a bootstrapping mechanism. The user will enquire about the table of peers from the DNS server before opening a connection with those peers. The network architecture will be centralized around the server for the extraction of true peers. The users will be vulnerable to many attacks, such as the man in the middle attack, cache poisoning, and stale records. The attackers will inject a malicious list of peers into the server to crop the network, and the user will be the subject of many manipulations that can take place. The latter approach introduces the territorial distribution of miners among the network. The bitcoin mining process is distributed in China, USA, and Germany. This concentration leads to a type of attack that targets the network structure, such as RBG hijacks, about which a study has shown that the hijacking of less than 100 gateway can eliminate 50% of the network hashing power (Saad et al., 2019)., which is more than the majority that can secure the system's normal functioning. Another type of attack is called the eclipse attack. The idea to isolate nodes in the network after being their only source of the truth; the attacker can provide those nodes through his own view of the network (Saad et al., 2019). This type of attack is likely to happen within unstructured networks such as bitcoin-related cryptocurrencies that aim to serve the same purpose of providing privacy in terms of transaction validations. The distributed denial of service attacks DDOS can be performed within the blockchain network through the domination of the network and by eliminating any additional blocks that are added, flooding the network with data, or taking down the DNS server. These techniques can lead to delays, resulting in the probabilistic finality to double-spend or undermining the network of a competitor.

The work in Kadcast (Rohrer & & Tschorsch, 2019) highlights that the network that takes unstructured topology can perform poorly in transaction propagations and can build upon a Kadamilia a structured one that can perform up to 30% better than the old version. The adoption of blockchain technology within different sectors should consider the different perspectives of the attack that can be executed within a public network and the security of user funds. Moreover, the transaction of information in the blockchain model can raise many privacy concerns. Thus, the blockchain technology runs under a topology that may suffer from the structured approach and the unstructured one at the same time, which need to be addressed before the discussion of the open adoption of the technique. However, the running of the technique in a private environment can secure to the consortium a huge

DISCUSSION

This section provides a comparison table that summarizes the blockchain technology in terms of six platform components, which are the monopoly, liveliness attacks, safety attacks, complexity, type of finality, propagation protocol. Figure 3 shows a comparison of TheChain with other consensus-based approaches. Consensual approaches aim to converge on one version of the general ledger at a time. These approaches are vulnerable to monopoly and manipulation due to dependence on resources, stakes, or votes. Therefore, PoS and PoW are subject to fault data injection, network failure, and double-spend by the monopolist due to the reliability of the longest chain rule. IOTA has a central feature, which makes it vulnerable to more than the third attack alongside the data structure choice, which is vulnerable to double spending and the injection of fault data by the monopolist via the splitting attack. The transaction finality depends on the longest chain convergence in PoW, PoS, or the cumulative weighting rules in the IOTA approach. However, in TheChain is based on broadcasting transactions initially to all the stars before converging on the most relevant regions.

Figure 3 demonstrates that TheChain has shifted from a probabilistic finality to a deterministic one by eliminating the act of dictating data from the exterior super force, which led to a chain of intersected regional parties that share common interests regionally. It is inspired by the world financial sector, in which many villages intersect interest with the next, incorporated into several distinct that share it with others before passing the same ideology on national then international level. The use of work incentive has made the use of the Proof of work very expensive process in term of complexity; however, Proof of stake suffer from a complexity of the voting that can be very complex depending on the exterior factor of the number of participants. The idea of regions within TheChain has eliminated the over duplication of data leading the gossip algorithm to be unsuitable within that context and limited the complexity of gossiping from $O(\log n)$ to a complexity of $O((\log(n/region)+region*B)$ where n stand for the number of participants, B for the considered stars (leaders of broadcasting). As it has been explained before the system will be cropped into many regions consequently if we assume that all regions with the same size long(n/region) are a complexity to propagate with one region, before broadcast to other regions leaders.

Moreover, enabling regions had to lead to high scalability because each region is responsible for maintaining their part besides watching their next. Due to the elimination of exterior dictation of data, the fault tolerance is 100% regionally(this concept can be proved only with a security assessment) (For example, central regions, if it comes to cooperate with all its intersected regions, it can alter information. However, TheChain aims are to encompass the whole world under one system, which leads to high complexity that is impossible to be altered. Nevertheless, if a nation decided to alter some data due to a mistake, it is possible by making all regions come to the same decision. The introduction of the concept of growing business within the system decided to claim reward with a complexity of 1.

FUTURE RESEARCH DIRECTIONS

Blockchain technology is an immerging solution that has got much attention in recent years. This work has provided a background survey for the consensual mechanism and its vulnerability. The future trend of research that can be built upon this paper:

A survey study on privacy within blockchain technology.

A specific networking vulnerability within each platform and how the information propagation can delay it.

A novel solution that addresses the network layer.

An implementation of governmental laws regarding connectivity to peers.

Injecting this approach as a global solution must address these issues, it is well known that websites suffer from cyber attacks to extract their data. However, the servers are still prone to such attacks, but the registration of the company will allow legal action to deter attackers. Blockchain technology suffers from the disadvantage of anonymity, which makes the solution with unfulfilled legal requirements. So, the network vulnerability study applied to the delay in reaching consensus and finalizing a transaction is very important. In addition, the study of privacy is very important to ensure that the technology itself lives up to the promises claimed. Thus, a solution must address connectivity through government laws is very necessary to ensure user privacy as well as security because in a peer-to-peer system it will be very important whom the application is connected to. In addition, the network architecture should be discussed to ensure that many non-delayed structures are well understood and undermine any infiltration behavior.

CONCLUSION

Blockchain technology has got much attention in recent years to the potential of the technology to eliminate the security is an issue within the blockchain technology due to the novelty of the solution that aims to

Table 1. Comparision of approaches

Table 1: Comparison Table

	monopoly	liveliness	safety	complexity	type of finality	propagation protocol.
BFT	Depends on the rules of voting are set on initiation	More than a third of the community	More than a third of the community	PBFT is ?? ??^{2}	Two types probabilistic and Deterministic	Gossip
PoW	Prone	50% hash power (Saad et al. 2019	50% hash power (Saad et al. 2019	O(1) but with a constant time of (Dos Santos 2017) 4, 26× 10^{18} (solving the puzzle)	Probabilistic (Gervais et al. 2016)	Gossiping
PoS	prone	50% stake value(Xiao et al. 2020)	50% stake value(Xiao et al. 2020)	Usage of voting to converge (O(c2 + cn)) where n is the number of replicas and c the committee number. Jalalzai et al. (2019)	Probabilistic (Gervais et al. 2016)	Gossiping
Tangle IOTA	Prone	1/3 of network hashing power (Sayeed·& Marco-Gisbert 2019),	Splitting attack (Liao & Katz 2017)	Usage of voting to converge (O(c2 + cn)) where n is the number of replicas and c the committee number. Jalalzai et al. (2019)	Probabilistic (Bu et al. 2019)	Gossiping
TheChain approach	Not prone	Taking all nodes down	Investing the intersection of regions to build confusion	O(1)	Deterministic	Broadcast among committee

address a conceptual problem by making it impractical to break the link among many nodes interested in its validity. The work can be summarized as follows:

The introduction of blockchain technology.

The discussion of security problems within blockchain technology.

The discussion of the different consensual mechanisms within blockchain technology.

The classification of the consensual approach gives good readability to the reader.

This work began by introducing the need to study the vulnerability of the blockchain network due to the huge hype surrounding the technology, which will lead to rapid adoption with the lack of legal understanding of the limitation of the technology. Therefore, identify the consensus on the core of the technology before introducing radically different approaches. Each approach has been criticized and discussed based on the various vulnerabilities identified previously. Finally, the different solutions were compared to summarize their drawbacks in a simple table.

The study can be summarized in facts that Byzantine fault tolerance is a voting mechanism that depends on a 1/3 rule of malicious activity. The PoW suffers from derivational problems such as forking, transaction finality, or monopoly. Additionally, the PoS suffers from the inability to operate in an open environment without monopolization. However, TheChain's ideology is based on making the network with a huge level of intersection by maintainers who take the financial benefits of clients, which make it in need of huge scale to function properly.

Research that can be built on, or with this work, to produce the right context for lawmakers to decide on circumstance happened above a solution. The consideration of privacy on the different implementation of blockchain technology besides its benefits and risks for users must be accompanied by a certificate of user acceptance for a certain service. In addition, networking capabilities must be studied in the precise term to define the limits of social digital existence, which represent the user's right to be forgotten and to the non-public exposure. Thus, the implementation of standards before the generation of a solution that manages the creation of networks between different peers is of high need, which will dictate that governmental consensus law is a very important step for wide adoption on a horizontal level.

ACKNOWLEDGMENT

This research was supported by Bournemouth University under the grant: a novel artificial intelligence method for decision chain within the blockchain technology.

REFERENCES

Alasbali, N., Azzuhri, S., & Salleh, R. (2020). A Blockchain-Based Smart Network for IoT-Driven Smart Cities.*Proceedings of the 2020 2nd International Electronics Communication Conference.*

Back, A. (2002). *Hashcash-a denial of service counter-measure*. Academic Press.

Bag, S., Ruj, S., & Sakurai, K. (2016). Bitcoin block withholding attack: Analysis and mitigation. *IEEE Transactions on Information Forensics and Security*, 1967–1978.

Bentov, I., Lee, C., & Mizrahi, A. (2014). Proof of activity: Extending bitcoin's proof of work via proof of stake [extended abstract]. *Performance Evaluation Review*, 34–37.

Bu, G. G.-B. (2019). G-iota: Fair and confidence aware tangle. In *IEEE Conference on Computer Communica- tions Workshops (INFOCOM WKSHPS)* (pp. pp. 644–649.). IEEE.

Buccafurri, F., Lax, G., Nicolazzo, S., & Nocera, A. (2017). Overcoming limits of blockchain for IoT applications. *Proceedings of the 12th International Conference on Availability, Reliability and Security*, 1-6.

Castro, M. (1999). Practical Byzantine fault tolerance. OSDI, 99, 173-186.

Chen, R. Y. (2018). A traceability chain algorithm for artificial neural networks using T–S fuzzy cognitive maps in blockchain. *Future Generation Computer Systems*, 198–210.

Chou, I., Su, H., Hsueh, Y., & Hsueh, C. (2020). BC-Store: A Scalable Design for Blockchain Storage. *Proceedings of the 2020 2nd International Electronics Communication Conference*, 33-38.

Decker, C., & Wattenhofer, R. (2013). Information propagation in the bitcoin network. In IEEE P2P 2013 Proceedings (pp. 1-10). IEEE.

Deirmentzoglou, E. P. (2019). A survey on long-range attacks for proof of stake protocols. *IEEE Access: Practical Innovations, Open Solutions*, 28712–28725.

Dillenberger, D., Novotny, P., Zhang, Q., Jayachandran, P., Gupta, H., Hans, S., & Vaculin, R. (2019). Blockchain analytics and artificial intelligence. *IBM Journal of Research and Development*, 63(2/3), 5–1.

Ekparinya, P. G. (2018). Impact of man-in-the-middle attacks on ethereum. In *2018 IEEE 37th Symposium on Reliable Distributed Systems (SRDS)* (pp. 11-20). IEEE.

El Kafhali, S., Chahir, C., Hanini, M., & Salah, K. (2019). Architecture to manage Internet of Things data using blockchain and fog computing. *Proceedings of the 4th International Conference on Big Data and Internet of Things*, 1-8.

Eyal, I., & Sirer, E. G. (2014). Majority is not enough: Bitcoin mining is vulnerable. In *International conference on financial cryptography and data security* (pp. 436-454). Springer.

Fakhri, D., & Mutijarsa, K. (2018). Secure IoT communication using blockchain technology. In *2018 International Symposium on Electronics and Smart Devices (ISESD)* (pp. 1-6). IEEE.

Florea, B. C. (2018). Blockchain and Internet of Things data provider for smart applications. In *2018 7th Mediterranean Conference on Embedded Computing (MECO)* (pp. 1-4). IEEE.

Gaži, P., Kiayias, A., & Russell, A. (2018). Stake-bleeding attacks on proof-of-stake blockchains. In *2018 Crypto Valley Conference on Blockchain Technology (CVCBT)* (pp. 85-92). IEEE.

Homoliak, I. V. (2019). A security reference architecture for blockchains. In *2019 IEEE International Conference on Blockchain (Blockchain)* (pp. 390-397). IEEE.

Houy, N. (2014). *It will cost you nothing to'kill'a proof-of-stake crypto-currency*. Available at SSRN 2393940.

Ismail, L., Materwala, H., & Khan, M. (2020). Performance Evaluation of a Patient-Centric Blockchain-based Healthcare Records Management Framework. *Proceedings of the 2020 2nd International Electronics Communication Conference*, 39-50.

J, A.-J., & N, M. (2019). Blockchain in industries: A survey. *IEEE Access*, 7, 36500-36515.

Jiang, Y. &. (2019). High performance and scalable byzantine fault tolerance. In *IEEE 3rd Information Technology, Networking, Electronic and Automation Control Conference (ITNEC)* (pp. 1195–1202). IEEE.

Jiang, Y., & Lian, Z. (2019). High performance and scalable byzantine fault tolerance. In *IEEE 3rd Information Technology, Networking, Electronic and Automation Control Conference (ITNEC)* (pp. 1195–1202). IEEE.

Jiang, Y. W. (2018). A cross-chain solution to integration of iot tangle for data access management. In *2018 IEEE Interna- tional Conference on Internet of Things (iThings) and IEEE Green Computing and Communications.* IEEE.

Kiayias, A. R. (2017). Ouroboros: A provably secure proof-of-stake blockchain protocol. *In Annual International Cryptology Conference* (pp. 357-388). Springer.

Kriskó, A. (2013). Crypto currencies–currencies governed by belief Bitcoin, Piggycoin, Monero, Peercoin, Ethereum and the rest. Conference book Konferenciakötet.

Kroll, J. A. (2013). The economics of bitcoin mining, or bitcoin in the presence of adversaries. *Proceedings of WEIS*, 11.

Kwon, J. (2014). *Tendermint: Consensus without mining.* Draft v. 0.6, fall, 1(11).

Lamport, L. S. (1982). *The byzantine generals problem acm transactions on progamming languages and syetems.* Academic Press.

Liao, K. (2017). Incentivizing blockchain forks via whale transactions. In *International Conference on Financial Cryptography and Data Security* (pp. 264–279.). Springer.

Liu, Z., Luong, N. C., Wang, W., Niyato, D., Wang, P., Liang, Y.-C., & Kim, D. I. (2019). *A survey on applications of game theory in blockchain.* arXiv preprint arXiv:1902.10865.

Malkhi, D. N. (2019). Flexible byzantine fault tolerance. *Proceedings of the 2019 ACM SIGSAC Conference on Computer and Communica- tions Security*, 1041–1053.

Mendki, P. (2019). Blockchain enabled IoT edge computing. *Proceedings of the 2019 International Conference on Blockchain Technology*, 66-69.

Nacer, M., Prakoonwit, S., & Alarab, I. (2020). TheChain: A Fast, Secure and Parallel Treatment of Transactions. In *Proceedings of the 2020 2nd International Electronics Communication Conference* (pp. 81-89). ACM.

Naim, B., Hronsky, M., & Klas, W. (2020). From Blockchain to Web: Paving the Last Mile for Releasing Chained Data from the Blocks. *Proceedings of the 2020 2nd International Electronics Communication Conference*, 24-32.

Nakamoto, S. (2019). *Bitcoin: A peer-to-peer electronic cash system.* Manubot.

Paxos made simple. (2001). *ACM Sigact News, 32*(4), 18–25.

Popov, S. (2016). A probabilistic analysis of the nxt forging algorithm. *Ledger*, 69-83.

Popov, S. (2016). *The tangle.* Academic Press.

Porru, S., Pinna, A., Marchesi, M., & Tonelli, R. (2017). Blockchain-oriented software engineering: challenges and new directions. In *IEEE/ACM 39th International Conference on Software Engineering Companion* (pp. 169-171). IEEE.

Rohrer, E., & Tschorsch, F. (2019). Kadcast: A structured approach to broadcast in blockchain networks. In *Proceedings of the 1st ACM Conference on Advances in Financial Technologies*, (pp. 199-213). ACM.

Rong, Y., Zhang, J., & Bian, J. (2019). Erbft: efficient and robust byzan- tine fault tolerance. In *2019 IEEE 21st International Conference on High Per- formance Computing and Communications*. IEEE.

Roode, D., & G., U. I. (2018). How to break iota heart by replay- ing. In *2018 IEEE Globecom Work- shops (GC Wkshps)* (pp. 1–7.). IEEE.

Rosenfeld, M. (2011). *Analysis of bitcoin pooled mining reward systems.* arXiv, preprint arXiv:1112.4980.

Roy, N., Shen, S., Hassanieh, H., & Choudhury, R. R. (2018). Inaudible voice commands: The long-range attack and defense. In *15th USENIX Symposium on Networked Systems Design and Implementation (NSDI 18)*, (pp. pp. 547-560). USENIX.

Saad, M., Spaulding, J., Njilla, L., Kamhoua, C., Shetty, S., & Nyang, D. (2019). *Exploring the attack surface of blockchain: A systematic overview.* preprint arXiv:1904.03487.

Saad, M. S. (2019). *Exploring the attack surface of blockchain: A systematic overview.* preprint arXiv:1904.03487.

Salzman, N. H., Hung, K., Haribhai, D., Chu, H., & Karlsson-Sjöberg, J., & A., E. (2010). Enteric defensins are essential regulators of intestinal microbial ecology. *Nature Immunology*.

Sasson, A., C., C., G., M., G., I., M., E., T., & Virza. (2014). Zerocash: Decentralized anonymous payments from bitcoin. In *IEEE Symposium on Security and Privacy*, (pp. 459-474). IEEE.

Shabandri, B. (2019). Enhancing IoT Security and Privacy Using Distributed Ledgers with IOTA and the Tangle. In *2019 6th International Conference on Signal Processing and Integrated Networks (SPIN)* (pp. 1069-1075). IEEE.

Singh, M., Singh, A., & Kim, S. (2018). Blockchain: A game changer for securing iot data. In *2018 IEEE 4th World Forum on Internet of Things (WF-IoT)* (pp. 51–55.). IEEE.

Stifter, N. J. (2019). Revisiting Practical Byzantine Fault Tolerance Through Blockchain Technologies. In Security and Quality in Cyber-Physical Systems Engineering (pp. 471-495). Springer.

Stifter, N. S. (2019). Echoes of the past: Recovering blockchain metrics from merged mining. *International Conference on Financial Cryptography and Data Security*, 527-549.

Turesson, H. R. (2019). *Privacy-preserving blockchain mining: Sybil-resistance by proof-of-useful-work.* arXiv preprint:1907.08744.

Vasin, P. (2014). *Blackcoin's proof-of-stake protocol v2.* https://blackcoin. co/blackcoin-pos-protocol-v2-whitepaper

Wood, G. (2014). *Ethereum: A secure decentralised generalised transaction ledger.* Ethereum project yellow paper.

Xiao, Y., Zhang, N. J. L., & Lou, A. Y. (2019.). Distributed consensusprotocols and algorithms. Block-chain for Distributed Systems Security, 25.

Zheng, Z. X. (2018). Blockchain challenges and opportunities: A survey. *International Journal of Web and Grid Services*, 352–375.

Chapter 2
A Pragmatic Regulatory Framework for Artificial Intelligence

Karisma Karisma

University Malaya, Malaysia

ABSTRACT

The application of AI technology in different sectors can intrude on the data subjects' privacy rights. While the data protection laws attempt to regulate the use and processing of personal data, these laws obstruct the growth and development of AI technology. Current regulations are unable to cope with the AI revolution due to the pacing problem and Collingridge dilemma. In view of the regulatory gaps and the complexity of technology, there is a strong justification to regulate AI technology. It is increasingly important to safeguard privacy without encumbering AI technology with regulatory requirements that will hinder its progress. With the convergence of AI and blockchain technology, privacy challenges are exacerbated. In this chapter, several types of regulations will be analysed to decipher a suitable regulatory framework for AI. This is to ensure effective regulation of AI and to allow AI to flourish with the use and application of blockchain features.

INTRODUCTION

The emergence of AI has had a profound impact on our lives. As AI evolves, it heightens the ability to use personal data in ways that intrude the right to privacy of individuals. Therefore, a comprehensive regulation on AI can protect the right to privacy and promote societal values.(Dignum, 2019; Wischmeyer & Rademacher, 2019) Regulation is an instrument that facilitates the development of economic sectors and it is a prerequisite for the proper functioning of markets that can enable competition and improve consumer welfare.(MacCarthy, 2020) It can provide specific high-tech service sectors with legal certainty and stability.(European Commission, 2020)

AI regulations can be used to achieve goals that are vital for the betterment of the society and to encourage AI technological innovations to flourish because the interaction between innovation and

DOI: 10.4018/978-1-7998-7927-5.ch002

regulation is mutually inclusive.(Wischmeyer & Rademacher, 2019) Having considered the definition of regulation and reasons to regulate AI technology, it is important to evaluate the challenges faced by legal systems in regulating AI.

Various challenges have arose from the use of AI in different sectors. AI systems use large volumes of data to gather meaningful insights and patterns about data subjects. The usage of large datasets can result in the loss of individual control over the data subjects' personal data and consequently, diminish human dignity, agency and choice. Besides that, opacity in the processing of personal data by AI systems may infringe privacy of data subjects because they are not provided adequate information or explanation of the manner in which their personal data is collected, used or processed. This can lead to data exploitation where users of AI-based systems may not be aware that their information is being repurposed for uses not disclosed at the time the data was collected. AI systems may link disparate information that might result in re-identification or deanonymisation and can intrude the data subjects' right to privacy. Besides that, AI systems can predict and infer sensitive information from the data provided, which significantly heightens privacy intrusion. The application of AI challenges data protection laws that currently exist, including the principle of data minimisation, purpose limitation, transparency, right to erasure, and storage limitation. The convergence of AI with blockchain technology is no doubt beneficial to enhance the function and applicability of AI. Nevertheless, with the deployment of blockchain in the realm of AI, privacy issues are exacerbated. Though the amalgamation of these two technologies is still at its infancy, a regulatory framework for AI should be deployed to address challenges in the realm of privacy especially with the applicability of blockchain features in AI.

The burden imposed by the present data protection regulations may hamper the growth and development of AI in various sectors. Thus, due to the lack of AI regulations, this chapter evaluates various regulatory frameworks that can be adopted to safeguard privacy and promote AI development. This author proposes a suitable regulatory model as AI is "too promising to be governed in a hands-off fashion, waiting for problems to develop and then trying to fix them after the fact".(MacCarthy, 2020) Due to the dynamic nature of AI, regulators, stakeholders and the government have to actively engage in dialogues on the regulation of AI technology to ensure that right to privacy becomes an integral part of the future AI development.

BACKGROUND

Roger Brownsword and Morag Goodwin defines regulation as "encompassing any instrument (legal or non-legal in its character, governmental or non-governmental in its source, direct or indirect in its operation and so on) that is designed to channel group behaviour".(Brownsword & Goodwin, 2012) The application of AI is subject to existing laws, namely consumer rights laws, human rights laws, and data protection laws. However, these laws may be unsuitable to address various concerns and issues that arise, because they are devised around a "socio-technical context" of the distant past.(Clarke, 2019)

In comparison to the fast development of AI technology, the legal frameworks relied on by the society to regulate these emerging technologies have not progressed as rapidly. There are growing concerns as to the mounting gap between the rate of technological advancement and its regulation through legal mechanisms. The existing legal frameworks take a "static" rather than a "dynamic" approach.(Marchant et al., 2011) They are "mired in stagnation, ossification and bureaucratic inertia".(Marchant et al., 2011) Scholars have proposed two options to address the growing gap between the two. Firstly, to slow down the pace of technological progress and secondly, to device better regulatory framework to adapt with the growing AI technology.(Marchant et al., 2011) The first option is implausible because AI technology has significant economic advantages. Therefore, regulators must keep up with the efforts to regulate AI technology in a dynamic and flexible manner to be on par with technological advances.(Marchant et al., 2011)

Collingridge stated that for particular technologies, the social consequences cannot be foreseen at the early stages of development before it is widely utilised. However, when the technology has been societally embedded, implementation of the regulation will be expensive and challenging. This dilemma is faced by regulators in regulating AI technology.(Coeckelbergh et al., 2018)

Regulators are confronted with the "uncertainty paradox" because they are compelled to make decisions without dependable risk information or hindsight regarding technological advances.(Moses, 2013; van Asselt et al., 2010) Besides that, AI technologies gain "momentum" with their growth and are consequentially more resistant to "regulatory prodding".(Moses, 2013) Therefore, regulators have to act fast, at the early stages of technological development to minimize privacy and other social risks.

CONVERGENCE OF AI WITH BLOCKCHAIN TECHNOLOGY

The convergence of AI with blockchain technology can further transform AI, as AI stands to benefit from a decentralized platform. Firstly, the decision-making process of AI can be recorded on the blockchain ledger in a transparent manner as blockchain technology provides for a tamper-proof mechanism, to ensure that data which is recorded on the network is not tampered with.(Salah et al., 2019) Consequentially, it ensures data integrity throughout the data lifecycle. AI can operate in an autonomous manner with high efficiency as the validation of datasets occur at a much faster pace, therefore allowing for greater data management and deployment, and adding greater value from the data extracted from AI based devices. (Salah et al., 2019) Various AI applications can function autonomously in certain complex operations, namely during automatic computation, optimization, execution of planning strategies, knowledge discovery, reasoning and learning.(Salah et al., 2019)

Besides that, with the convergence of AI and blockchain technology it can potentially lead to collective and decentralised decision making without the presence of a centralized authority. For example, swarm robotics approach in robotic applications, where robots can vote on a certain outcome. The voting results is verified by other robots in a decentralized and transparent manner. This can consequentially enhance the decision-making task in that robotic swarm, as the process is repeated to reach a conclusion. (Salah et al., 2019; Singh et al., 2020)

However, blockchain technology is said to be facing "privacy poisoning" and the discussion would be narrowed to three areas, namely informational privacy, decisional privacy and transactional privacy. Informational privacy can be described as the right of an individual to determine who has access to their personal data and to what degree, whilst decisional privacy can be described as the right against "unwanted access such as unwanted interference" in an individual's determinations.(Lanzing, 2019) The immutability of public blockchain data structure is in conflict with the right to be forgotten. The personal data fed into the network cannot be deleted, replaced or removed, which is at odds with an individual's informational privacy. Various concerns can arise from such "eternal records".(Gupta, 2020) Individuals may not want the recorded information to be present eternally as it may include sensitive data. Besides that, as elucidated by scholars, there might be an issue of "ownership" over the information recorded on the blockchain network.(Gupta, 2020) Without clarity on the "ownership rules", it might result in the access and sale of the information without the consent of parties to the transaction.(Gupta, 2020)

On the aspect of decisional privacy, blockchain-based smart contracts are self-executing, self-enforcing and decentralized contracts, which may result in individuals having no autonomy to control, halt, or alter the manner of execution of contracts. This could limit the adoption of blockchain-based smart contracts.

Transactional privacy concerns the protection of one's transactional data, namely the value of transactions and the records generated from them. The lack of transactional privacy arises from the decentralized blockchain ledger which is publicly shared with a record of transactions containing pertinent information involving data analysis, transferred values, timestamp and signature of sender.(Baghery, 2019) Even if the details concerning the parties to the transaction are anonymised, other transactional data can still be assessed. The information which is accessible can be correlated and extrapolated, and this can lead to the revelation of identity.(de Haro-Olmo et al., 2020) This is similarly a challenge to sensitive information which is stored on the blockchain network. Even though the sensitive data is encrypted, it can be compromised due to the activity of hackers, resulting in unauthorized usage and access of information. (Gupta, 2020)

TYPES OF REGULATION

Various regulatory frameworks will be assessed to decipher a suitable regulatory structure to regulate AI that will protect individuals from privacy intrusion and promote innovation and growth in various sectors, whilst ensuring that there is no trade off on one against the other.

1. Principle-Based Regulation

Principle-based regulation can be connoted as turning away from the dependence on "detailed" and "prescriptive rules" and relying on broadly stated principles to set the standard.(Black et al., 2007) This type of regulation facilitates and allows for greater openness and flexibility, and prevents AI technology from being burdened in the "regulatory thicket" that arises from a rule-focused approach.(Fenwick et al., 2016) By the adoption of a principle-based approach, it "facilitates action and allows future revisions" as and when there is an innovative development in the realm of AI technology, such as the deployment of blockchain features.(Fenwick et al., 2016) It is durable and effective as it is able to adapt to both innovation and market conditions.(Black, 2008) It does not impose detailed processes but rather, outcomes to be realized. Therefore, the principle-based regulation encourages "substantive compliance" by organizations.(Black, 2007)

2. Precautionary Regulation

The precautionary regulation permits the enactment of regulations in the absence of a comprehensive evidence of the risk. The uncertainty of the risks rationalises the enactment of this type of regulation. The regulation prohibits the potentially risky activity until the activity demonstrates acceptable risk or no risk at all.(Lofstedt, 2003)

AI technology is developing fast and there are "legitimate concerns" on how AI will affect an individual's quality of life.(Weaver, 2014) Nevertheless, scholar Adam Thierer asserts that the precautionary-based regulation should be avoided in the realm of technological advances.(Thierer, 2014)[1] This regulatory approach is similar to "permissioning" innovation which can be a rigid and inflexible approach.(Thierer, 2014) The problem with its usage is that it holds AI systems to extremely high standards, which would result in a technological stillness. (Samp & Phillips, 2020) Besides that, precautionary regulation is based on "hypothetical problems" that may never arise in the near or distant future.(Thierer, 2014)

3. Adaptive Regulation

The definition of adaptive regulation is "regulation that can be modified or changed in response to (and to be suitable for) new situations".(Bennear & Wiener, 2019) Various scholars have asserted that the regulatory process for AI should be more adaptive. Rigidity in regulations might be counter intuitive to the evolving nature of AI technology. It is important that the regulatory framework utilised to regulate AI is one that is flexible and has the ability to adapt in accordance with the risk and benefits of AI technology, devised from time to time.(Pagallo et al., 2019) An adaptive regulation improves net benefits, reduces countervailing risks such as the possible intrusion to privacy and allows technological innovation. It ensures that a more "adaptive approach to innovation" is complemented by a more "adaptive approach to regulation".(Bennear & Wiener, 2019)

4. Outcome-Based Regulation

Outcome-based regulation can be defined as a regulation specifying the outcome that should be achieved rather than prescribing the process or action to be abided with to achieve compliance. Outcome-based regulation allows the developers, deployers or organizations that use the AI system to decide on measures they wish to adopt to meet the regulatory requirements.(Moolman, 2017) This introduces flexibility in the regulatory framework without hampering technological innovation.(Moolman, 2017) The regulated parties can utilise cost saving and technological channels that achieve the regulatory outcome.

5. Ex-Ante and Ex-Post Regulations

Ex-ante and ex-post regulations, respectively mean "before the fact" and "after the fact". The "fact" refers to the adoption and implementation of AI systems.(Danaher, 2015) Matthew Scherer stated that, the challenges of AI arise both during the research and development stage and when AI is utilised in various industries and becomes more embroiled into our day to day lives. Due to problems of "discreetness" [2], "diffuseness",[3] "discreteness" [4] and "opacity",[5] it may be challenging and impractical to regulate AI technology via an ex-ante regulatory framework.(Scherer, 2016) As for ex-post regulations, the issues of "foreseeability and control" causes this form of regulation to be ineffectual.(Scherer, 2016) AI systems are unforeseeable as they have the ability to produce solutions that humans may not have considered, or having considered may have rejected such solutions.(Scherer, 2016) It would be iniquitous and unfair for the designers to be liable for the unforeseeable harm of AI systems. Another risk created by the AI system is the problem of control. Loss of control transpires when the AI system cannot be controlled by individuals legally responsible for its operation and oversight.(Scherer, 2016) The challenge in controlling the actions of the AI system may render the ex-post regulatory framework futile.

6. Risk-Based Regulation

An option that was proposed by the German Data Ethics Commission (GDEC) was the risk-based approach for AI regulation. The notion underlying the risk-based approach is "the greater the potential for harm, the more stringent the requirements and the more far-reaching the intervention by means of regulatory instruments".(Opinion of the Data Ethics Commission, 2019) The potential for harm must be assessed by considering the "sociotechnical system as a whole" such as the datasets used for algorithmic application. The GDEC proposes a five-level risk-based system. AI applications that fall under Level 1, lowest level with "negligible potential for harm" do not require any special oversight measures and specifications on the transparency and explainability of AI systems.(Opinion of the Data Ethics Commission, 2019) The AI applications that fall under Level 4, associated with a "serious potential for harm" would be subject to "enhanced oversight and transparency".(Scherer, 2016)

The risk-based regulatory framework is more adaptable to the risks posed by AI applications, and it is effective in achieving regulatory outcomes. It requires regulators to tailor their enforcement responses in a transparent manner on the grounds of severity and risks. (Department of Finance, 2016)

7. Self-Regulation and Co-Regulation

According to Haufler, self-regulation occurs when organizations which need to be regulated, "design and enforce the rules themselves".(Haufler, 2013) The rules that regulate their behaviour are implemented voluntarily, either going past the present regulatory requirements or forming new standards in areas where there is a dearth of government rules or standards. Even though the rules are adopted voluntarily, it may be complemented with various "formal and informal" enforcement methods.(Haufler, 2013)

Self-regulatory partnerships[6] may denote a positive step forward of institutionalizing and operationalizing ethical and social dialogues.(Partnership on AI, 2016) Nevertheless, the self-regulatory framework tends to focus on industry vision and goals rather than those of other stakeholders.(Cath et al., 2018) The self-regulatory framework have to be closely supervised and while self-regulation is laudable, it cannot be substituted for national laws.(Eyers, 2019)

Co-regulation can be defined as "initiatives in which government and industry share responsibility for drafting and enforcing regulatory standards".(Hirsch, 2010) It is neither purely government regulation nor industry self-regulation but rather a hybrid of them both. It has been asserted by scholars that co-regulation offers flexibility and adaptability of self-regulation whilst incorporating the supervision and rigor of government rules.

The following are the advantages of a co-regulatory framework. Firstly, the unique knowledge possessed by companies deploying technological solutions can be utilised to enact more realistic, cost-effective, flexible and adaptable regulations.(Hirsch, 2010) AI presents significant regulatory challenges, more so with the application of blockchain features. The uneven allocation of specialised and expert knowledge between companies using or developing AI technology and regulators, result in complications when devising a proper regulatory framework.(Spiro, 2020) A co-regulatory model fills in these regulatory gaps by incorporating "industry self-regulation and stakeholder involvement with government oversight". (Spiro, 2020)

AI can be properly regulated when there is a strong involvement of market actors, such as companies in various sectors who are also involved in the "design and implementation" of regulation.(OECD, 2008) These companies will have a strong "sense of ownership" over the regulations and will observe the regulations more readily.(Hirsch, 2010) Co-regulation denotes "joint responsibilities" between companies and the State.(Marsden, 2004) These ensures commitment to the objectives of the regulation and accountability towards the regulations enacted.(OECD, 2008)

The regulations enacted will not be one sided but would focus on public goals over and above their own self-interest.(Hirsch, 2010) This cooperation will improve government-industry relations and a good solution can be devised towards combatting the threat of privacy in the realm of AI.

AI GUIDELINES AND FRAMEWORK THAT ADDRESS SAFEGUARDS TO PRIVACY

An ethical framework can ensure integrity amongst data users, developers and deployers of AI. It can manage various risks related with AI, enabling a speedier and a more consistent and effective adoption of AI.(Saif & Ammanath, 2020) Throughout the years, there have been a wealth of soft-law instruments which have thoroughly articulated a proliferation of "principles" to provide guidance in relation to AI technology. These documents have been issued by different actors, namely the civil society, multi-stakeholders, private sectors, governments and inter-governmental organizations. In this section, reference is made to the following soft-law instruments: (a) AI Principles of Telefonica; (b) Ethics Guidelines for Trustworthy AI; (c) Beijing AI Principles; and (d) Singapore's Model Artificial Intelligence Governance Framework. It is important to illustrate the soft-law instruments in this section because soft laws can significantly complement hard-laws.

1. AI Principles of Telefonica

Some individual companies have implemented their own company-specific soft laws by issuing principles or guidelines for AI. In 2018, Telefonica, a multinational telecommunications provider based in Spain published the "Principles of AI".(Fjeld et al., 2020) One of the principles incorporated by Telefonica is the principle of privacy and security by design.(Telefonica, 2018) When designing AI systems, the element of privacy forms an integral part in the system's lifecycle. The framework also encompasses principles of fairness, transparency and explainability, and human centricity.(Benjamins et al., 2019) Other companies such as Google[7], Microsoft[8] and International Business Machines Corporation (IBM)[9] have similarly adopted their own AI principles.(Fjeld et al., 2020; Google, 2018; Microsoft, 2018; Rossi et al., 2019)

2. European Commission's High-Level Expert Group on AI

The AI Ethics Guidelines produced by the High-Level Expert Group on Artificial Intelligence is a framework to promote Trustworthy AI. The respect of human dignity and freedom of the individual and citizens rights enunciated therein closely relate to information and decisional privacy. As elucidated in the Ethics Guidelines, the human dignity of individuals should not be "diminished, compromised or repressed" by AI technology.(High-Level Expert Group on Artificial Intelligence, 2019) Therefore, AI systems should be developed in a way that respects and protects human dignity and sense of identity. (High-Level Expert Group on Artificial Intelligence, 2019) "Privacy should be grafted as a first-order branch to the trunk of human dignity".(Floridi, 2016) The freedom of the individual as exemplified in the ethical guidelines entails the right to privacy and the freedom from the intrusion of the said right.

The Guidelines also elucidate four ethical principles which must be respected to ensure that the development, deployment and usage of AI systems are conducted in a trustworthy manner. The four ethical principles are respect for human autonomy, prevention of harm, fairness and explicability.(High-Level Expert Group on Artificial Intelligence, 2019) Besides that, the ethics guidelines provides guidance by way of seven requirements. One of the seven requirements is privacy and data governance. AI system must safeguard the right to privacy and data protection.(High-Level Expert Group on Artificial Intelligence, 2019) It includes personal data or information given by the data subject and the information generated by the AI system over the progression of the interaction between the user and the AI system. (High-Level Expert Group on Artificial Intelligence, 2019)

3. Beijing AI Principles

Beijing AI Principles were issued in May 2019.(Beijing AI, 2019)[10] The 15 principles stipulated therein call for "the construction of a human community with a shared future, and the realization of beneficial AI for humankind and nature". (Beijing AI, 2019) The principles are divided into three categories, namely research and development, use and governance. The area of research and development includes the principles to do good, be responsible, serve humanity and to be consistent with human values such as "privacy, dignity, freedom and autonomy.(Beijing AI, 2019) To align with the principle of being ethical, the AI system should be made as fair, transparent, explainable and predictable as possible. Open platforms of AI should be encouraged to avoid data exploitation and to "promote equal development opportunities for different regions and industries".(Beijing AI, 2019) The document states that AI should be utilised wisely to "maximize its benefits and minimize the risks".(Beijing AI, 2019) The principle of informed consent ensures that stakeholders provide their informed consent regarding potential effect of the system on their rights and interests.(Beijing AI, 2019)

Other multi-stakeholder groups have adopted principles of AI, namely the Partnership on AI[11], the Future of Life Institute[12], the Institute of Electric and Electronic Engineers[13] and Montreal Declaration.[14](Fjeld et al., 2020; Montreal Declaration, 2017)

4. Governance Framework of Singapore

In 2019, Singapore published a Model Artificial Intelligence Governance Framework (Model Framework) which had been developed by consulting "academics, industry leaders and technologists from different backgrounds and jurisdictions".(Personal Data Protection Commission Singapore, 2019) The Model Framework aims to structure discussions around the challenges faced by the utilisation of AI technology and possible solutions to utilise AI in a responsible manner.(Personal Data Protection Commission Singapore, 2019)[15]

It stipulates "good data accountability practices" namely understanding where the data originates from, by looking at how it was "collected, curated and moved" and maintaining its accuracy; ensuring data quality (Personal Data Protection Commission Singapore, 2019)[16]; and reducing inherent bias. (Jonker & Petkovic, 2008) Given that this is an accountability-based framework, implementing this framework will assist in demonstrating whether an organisation had implemented "accountability-based practices in data management and data protection".(Personal Data Protection Commission Singapore,

2019) Other countries have published similar soft-law frameworks, namely United Kingdown, Dubai and Mexico.(Fjeld et al., 2020)

In summary, the guidelines discussed above converge on the ethical principle of privacy. Privacy is portrayed as a value to uphold (IEEE Global Initiative on Ethics of Autonomous Intelligent Systems, 2017; Partnership on AI, 2016) and a right to be safeguarded.(Future of Life Institute, 2017; Telefonica, 2018) Privacy is often presented in connection with data protection.(Future of Life Institute, 2017; Google, 2018; Montreal Declaration, 2017; Telefonica, 2018) Certain guidelines relate privacy to freedom(Future of Life Institute, 2017) or trust.(NITI Aayog, 2018) The recommended modes to safeguard privacy encompass technical solutions(Microsoft, 2018) such as differential privacy(NITI Aayog, 2018) and privacy by design(Google, 2018; Telefonica, 2018) or regulatory approaches, namely the creation of laws specific to AI.(ARTICLE 19, 2018; Intel, 2017)

There are two limitations to soft-law instruments which include guidelines, best practices and private standards. Firstly, the soft-law provisions are unenforceable and there is no obligation nor guarantee that the developers, deployers and users of AI will comply with soft-law instruments.(Marchant, 2019) Secondly, there are confusing proliferations of various soft-law AI instruments, and it is cumbersome for an actor to access the overlaps, gaps or contradictions of these instruments.(Marchant, 2019) Edward Santow, the Human Rights Commissioner said that "An ethics framework can help to make good choices but is different to the law which sets baselines for proper conduct."(Eyers, 2019)

CONCLUSION

In contrast with the growth and development of AI technology, the legal framework relied on to regulate these emerging technologies have not evolved as rapidly. Regulators are confronted with various uncertainties because they are constrained to make decisions without dependable risk information or hindsight on the technological advances, more so with the convergence of AI with blockchain technology. Various types of regulatory frameworks have been elucidated and assessed in the previous sections. The adoption of principle-based regulation facilitates flexibility and openness, in tandem with the growth and innovation of AI technology. On the other hand, precautionary regulations can be seen to limit technological advances by protecting different sets of values, namely the impact of AI on an individual's quality of life. Adaptive regulation removes rigidity and adapts to different inventions, thus removing the impact of regulation on technological advances. Outcome-based regulations can allow industry players to adopt various measures to be aligned with regulatory outcomes. Whilst ex-post regulations may be rendered ineffective, it might be unfeasible to adopt the ex-ante regulatory framework due to various challenges such as opacity. Risk-based regulations have to be adaptable to the risks present from the application of AI and deployment of blockchain technology. Co-regulation denotes joint responsibility between industry players and regulators, whilst self-regulation is directed towards the voluntary implementation of rules and standards by industry players. Soft-law instruments on AI are "imperfect governance tools" because of the inability to enforce the provisions in the instruments, and the lack of accountability.(Marchant, 2019) A suitable regulatory framework that is flexible, adaptable and inclusive will be recommended by the author in the next section.

PROPOSED REGULATORY FRAMEWORK FOR AI TECHNOLOGY

Based on the discussion in previous sections, application of AI and the deployment of various blockchain features within it can intrude the right of information and decisional privacy, and the application of rigid and inflexible data protection laws can result in conflict with AI development.

1. Principle-Based Regulation to Safeguard the Right to Privacy

The author proposes a principle-based regulatory framework for regulating AI technology as it provides flexibility, promotes innovation and growth and enhances competitiveness between market players. The framework should be "technology-neutral" and "industry-neutral" and can be applied to other industries. The principle-based regulatory framework can work hand-in-hand with the outcome focused approach by framing the principles as outcome-based standards.(Black et al., 2007) The shifting focus from inputs or prescriptive regulation to an outcome-focused approach can create "operational efficiencies" for regulators and encourage innovation for the developers of AI. This model of regulatory framework allows companies and corporations to decide on ways to comply with the regulation which focuses on high-level principles and outcomes, thus affording greater freedom. The specifics and procedures to be adopted are left to the companies, as long as the outcome as stipulated in the regulation is achieved. (Edelman et al., 2018) Five main principles that safeguards individuals' right to information and decisional privacy will be articulated below.

a. Transparency and Explainability

The first principle is the transparency and explainability principle. In the present context, AI systems are alleged to have the "black box" or opacity problem, in that the input and operations are unknown and not evident to the data user or other stakeholders. However, not all AI systems are "inscrutable black boxes".(Wischmeyer & Rademacher, 2019) Opening the black box is essential to identify and address privacy infringements.

The level of transparency of AI models should depend on the impact of the technology on individuals. The greater the impact, the more imperative it is for AI to be transparent.(Deloitte, 2019) Secondly, the importance of the sector in which AI system is utilised and the significance of AI systems in that sector are important factors in the transparency architecture of AI.(Ginart et al., 2019) Thirdly, how closely the AI technology is assimilated into the decision-making process of individuals is vital for a meaningful transparency strategy. Transparency of AI systems can be heightened if AI systems significantly contribute to the decision-making process. The element of transparency provides stakeholders, data subjects, and regulatory agencies adequate knowledge required to initiate an action in Court against the company responsible.(Wischmeyer & Rademacher, 2019) It also provides enough information to provide a sense of agency to individuals' likely to be directly affected by such decisions.(Wischmeyer & Rademacher, 2019)

The explainability principle would require AI systems which have been developed, to provide evidence or justification for each output. The AI systems must be able to give an explanation. Explanations provided to the user of the AI-based products or services may differ from explanations provided to regulators and compliance auditors. Various AI-based products and services, such as sentiment analysis or personalised recommendations would need to utilise explainable AI algorithms to ensure greater understanding and reduce privacy concerns by generating trust and acceptance.(Phillips et al., 2020)

Besides articulating a suitable principle to ensure transparency and explainability of AI, a practical solution is to adopt blockchain technology. Developing a trustworthy AI would require the deployment of emerging blockchain technology which augments a transparent AI system and develops resilience against biasness.(Nassar et al., 2020) Nevertheless, the adoption of blockchain technology within the AI system presents its own challenges which should be tackled.

b. Use and Deletion Principle

The principle of data use is particularly important in the area of AI. The minimisation of data usage and the limitation of its purpose should be adopted in a practical fashion and should not be applied rigidly. Customers should be allowed to consent to various processing purposes, provided the consent given is an informed consent. It should not be limited to "specified" purposes, but include and obtain consent for wider purposes, such as "certain application classes, providers, regions or other specifically designated types of data use".(European Banking Federation, 2019) The data minimisation principle should be understood in a flexible manner by allowing deployers and developers of AI systems to process large quantities of personal data, provided it is carried out in an "ethical and accurate way".(Weber et al., 2020)

The implementation of the data deletion principle has a serious impact to AI and big data. Therefore, the principle of data deletion or erasure must be worded with caution taking into consideration the complexity, technicality, and impracticability, to encourage efficient deletion of data.(Villaronga et al., 2018) The regulation should include exceptions to the principle in circumstances where erasure is impractical, and is likely to affect the service received by other users. In such circumstances that fall within the exceptions, data subjects should have a right to anonymity to anonymize their data so that it is not "personally identifiable".(Wallace & Castro, 2018) Regulators should provide guidance or standards on the compliance with the principle of data deletion in line with the development of AI technology in particular sectors.(Villaronga et al., 2018)

The focus of the principle of data deletion should be placed on deletion efficiency of AI models. More interdisciplinary research is necessary to understand the deletion efficiency of AI systems and the identification of potential methods that support such efficiency.(Ginart et al., 2019)

Nevertheless, as mentioned above, due to the immutability feature of blockchain technology, the right to be forgotten is technically impossible to achieve. The regulatory framework should be able to provide guidance on the manner to fulfil the standards on data deletion, such as by way of destruction of the private key that is required to decrypt the data, causing the encrypted data to be inaccessible or by adopting the avenue of "redactable blockchain".(European Parliamentary Research Service, 2019)

c. Reasonable Inferences Principle

As mentioned above, AI systems draw "non-intuitive" and "unverifiable" inferences and predictions from data subjects' data about their behaviours, sentiments and preferences. Inferences are the least protected in data protection laws, though they pose the greatest threat to privacy. Therefore, in the realm of AI and big data, the principle of reasonable inferences should be introduced. This principle would provide data subjects with safeguards against inferences drawn through AI analytics.(Wachter & Mittelstadt, 2019) In line with the risk-based approach the "reasonable inferences" principle should be primarily applicable to "high-risk inferences" which have a privacy-invasive nature.(Wachter & Mittelstadt, 2019) The existence of this principle will require data controllers to determine whether an inference is reasonable.

d. Human Control or Oversight Principle

When developing AI-systems, the principle of human control and oversight is vital to safeguard privacy. Companies must be able to make informed decisions regarding AI systems. Besides that, they should also be able to "reasonably self-assess or challenge the system" and make informed choices regarding the usage, processing and analysis of individuals' personal data. Above all, this principle is to be observed by companies and organizations to ensure that they are not subjected to the sole decision of automated processing. Human oversight is important during the "design cycle" of the system and to "oversee the overall activity" of the AI system.(High-Level Expert Group on Artificial Intelligence, 2019) Exercising human oversight over the AI system can ensure that safety and security features are in place.

e. Accountability Principle

AI system should be accompanied by a chain of accountability. Accountability can be defined as the "ability to determine whether a decision was made in accordance with procedural and substantive standards and to hold someone responsible if those standards are not met".(Doshi-Velez et al., 2017) Every individual involved in the AI-system at any step of the way should be held accountable for the impact of the AI-system.(Rossi et al., 2019) The designers, deployers and decision-makers play an important role in the design, development, processes and outcomes of AI systems and therefore it is important to prevent those accountable individuals from "hiding" behind the AI systems.(Doshi-Velez et al., 2017; Rossi et al., 2019)

2. Co-Regulation

Co-regulation generally involves a "statutory tip of regulatory principles and authorisation for the regulator, a co-regulator layer that sets out regulatory design, and a base of industry-shaped rules and codes to provide the detailed implementation".(European Parliament, 2019)

In practice, this involves companies in various sectors agreeing to participate in a multi-stakeholder process to devise codes of conduct that are enforceable. These codes of conduct are created against the backdrop of national laws that elucidate the process, the substantive requirement to be satisfied and the legal consequences of such codes of practice.(Rubinstein, 2016) Besides that, precisely-detailed prerequisites can be created depending on its necessity.(Wrigley, 2018) The flexibility and clear guidance afforded by the co-regulatory framework is vital to the regulatory toolbox. The adherence to the code of conduct could make an organisation more transparent and accountable, as well as safeguard the rights to privacy of data subjects.

The code of practice for the implementation by industry players can include the element of privacy by design. The concept of privacy by design has 7 foundational principles which can be adopted.(Waldman, 2019)[17] Privacy by design ensures that privacy protection mechanisms are built in into AI systems from the start to ensure good privacy management.(Vitale et al., 2017) This is an important framework that protects privacy at all stages of AI systems, throughout the design and lifecycle of products and services. Privacy by design can incorporate elements usually encompassed in privacy laws such as notice, consent, anonymity and pseudonymity, access, and recourse.(Yanisky-Ravid & Hallisey, 2018) Essentially, privacy by design can combat privacy-implicating issues present in AI systems.

REFERENCES

Article 19. (2018). *Privacy and Freedom of Expression In the Age of Artificial Intelligence.* https://www.article19.org/wp-content/uploads/2018/04/Privacy-and-Freedom-of-Expression-In-the-Age-of-Artificial-Intelligence-1.pdf

Baghery, K. (2019). On the efficiency of privacy-preserving smart contract systems. *International Conference on Cryptology in Africa.* Beijing AI. https://www.baai.ac.cn/news/beijing-ai-principles-en.html

Benjamins, R., Barbado, A., & Sierra, D. (2019). Responsible AI by Design in Practice. *Proceedings of the Human-Centered AI: Trustworthiness of AI Models & Data (HAI) track at AAAI Fall Symposium.*

Bennear, L. S., & Wiener, J. B. (2019). *Adaptive Regulation: Instrument Choice for Policy Learning over Time.* https://www.hks.harvard.edu/sites/default/files/centers/mrcbg/files/Wiener_2.14.19.transcript.pdf

Black, J. (2007). *Principles based regulation: risks, challenges and opportunities.* http://eprints.lse.ac.uk/62814/

Black, J. (2008). Forms and paradoxes of principles-based regulation. *Capital Markets Law Journal, 3*(4), 425–457. doi:10.1093/cmlj/kmn026

Black, J., Hopper, M., & Band, C. (2007). Making a success of principles-based regulation. *Law Financial Markets Review, 1*(3), 191–206. doi:10.1080/17521440.2007.11427879

Brownsword, R., & Goodwin, M. (2012). *Law and the Technologies of the Twenty-First Century: Text and Materials.* Cambridge University Press. doi:10.1017/CBO9781139047609

Cath, C., Wachter, S., Mittelstadt, B., Taddeo, M., & Floridi, L. (2018). Artificial intelligence and the 'good society': The US, EU, and UK approach. *Science and Engineering Ethics, 24*(2), 505–528. doi:10.100711948-017-9901-7 PMID:28353045

Clarke, R. (2019). Regulatory alternatives for AI. *Computer Law & Security Review, 35*(4), 398–409. doi:10.1016/j.clsr.2019.04.008

Coeckelbergh, M., Loh, J., Funk, M., Seibt, J., & Nørskov, M. (2018). *Envisioning Robots in Society – Power, Politics, and Public Space: Proceedings of Robophilosophy.* IOS Press. https://books.google.com.my/books?id=jLh9DwAAQBAJ

Danaher, J. (2015). *Is effective regulation of AI possible? Eight potential regulatory problems.* https://philosophicaldisquisitions.blogspot.com/2015/07/is-effective-regulation-of-ai-possible.html

de Haro-Olmo, F. J., Varela-Vaca, Á. J., & Álvarez-Bermejo, J. A. (2020). Blockchain from the Perspective of Privacy and Anonymisation: A Systematic Literature Review. *Sensors (Basel), 20*(24), 7171. doi:10.339020247171 PMID:33327652

Deloitte. (2019). *Transparency and Responsibility in Artificial Intelligence.* Retrieved May 29, 2021 from https://www2.deloitte.com/content/dam/Deloitte/nl/Documents/innovatie/deloitte-nl-innovation-bringing-transparency-and-ethics-into-ai.pdf

Department of Finance. (2016). *Guidance for regulators to implement outcomes and risk-based regulation.* http://productivity.nsw.gov.au/sites/default/files/2018-05/Guidance_for_regulators_to_implement_outcomes_and_risk-based_regulation-October_2016.pdf

Dignum, V. (2019). *Responsible Artificial Intelligence: How to Develop and Use AI in a Responsible Way.* Springer International Publishing. https://books.google.com.my/books?id=EEO8DwAAQBAJ

Doshi-Velez, F., Kortz, M., Budish, R., Bavitz, C., Gershman, S., O'Brien, D., . . . Wood, A. (2017). *Accountability of AI under the law: The role of explanation.* arXiv:1711.01134 [cs.AI].

Edelman, K., Hurley, B., Devan, P., Khan, A., & Bhat, R. (2018). *The future of regulation: The principles for regulating emerging technologies.* https://www2.deloitte.com/content/dam/insights/us/articles/4538_Future-of-regulation/DI_Future-of-regulation.pdf

European Banking Federation. (2019). *EBF position paper on AI in the banking industry.* https://www.ebf.eu/wp-content/uploads/2020/03/EBF-AI-paper-_final-.pdf

European Commission. (2020). *White Paper on Artificial Intelligence - A European approach to excellence and trust.* https://ec.europa.eu/info/sites/info/files/commission-white-paper-artificial-intelligence-feb2020_en.pdf

European Parliament. (2019). *Regulating disinformation with artificial intelligence: Effects of disinformation initiatives on freedom of expression and media pluralism.* https://www.europarl.europa.eu/RegData/etudes/STUD/2019/624279/EPRS_STU(2019)624279(ANN1)_EN.pdf

European Parliamentary Research Service. (2019). *Blockchain and the General Data Protection Regulation: Can distributed ledgers be squared with European data protection law?* https://www.europarl.europa.eu/RegData/etudes/STUD/2019/634445/EPRS_STU(2019)634445_EN.pdf

Eyers, J. (2019). *We need laws about AI, not self-regulation.* Retrieved May 29, 2021 from https://www.afr.com/technology/we-need-laws-about-ai-not-self-regulation-20191216-p53k8r

Fenwick, M., Kaal, W. A., & Vermeulen, E. P. (2016). Regulation tomorrow: What happens when technology is faster than the law. *American University Business Law Review, 6,* 561–594. doi:10.2139srn.2834531

Fjeld, J., Achten, N., Hilligoss, H., Nagy, A., & Srikumar, M. (2020). *Principled artificial intelligence: Mapping consensus in ethical and rights-based approaches to principles for AI.* Berkman Klein Center Research Publication.

Floridi, L. (2016). On human dignity as a foundation for the right to privacy. *Philosophy & Technology, 29*(4), 307–312. doi:10.100713347-016-0220-8

Future of Life Institute. (2017). *Asilomar AI Principles.* Retrieved May 29, 2021 from https://futureofife.org/ai-principles/

Ginart, A., Guan, M., Valiant, G., & Zou, J. Y. (2019). Making AI forget you: Data deletion in machine learning. *Advances in Neural Information Processing Systems*.

Google. (2018). Artificial Intelligence at Google: Our Principles. *Google AI*. https://ai.google/principles

Gupta, N. (2020). Security and privacy issues of blockchain technology. In *Advanced Applications of Blockchain Technology* (pp. 207–226). Springer. doi:10.1007/978-981-13-8775-3_10

Haufler, V. (2013). *A Public Role for the Private Sector: Industry Self-Regulation in a Global Economy*. Brookings Institution Press. https://books.google.com.my/books?id=TxKNYxTRA-cC

High-Level Expert Group on Artificial Intelligence. (2019). *Ethics Guidelines for Trustworthy AI*. https://digital-strategy.ec.europa.eu/en/library/ethics-guidelines-trustworthy-ai

Hirsch, D. D. (2010). The law and policy of online privacy: Regulation, self-regulation, or co-regulation. *Seattle UL Rev.*, *34*, 439.

IEEE Global Initiative on Ethics of Autonomous Intelligent Systems. (2017). *Ethically Aligned Design: A Vision for Prioritizing Human Well-being with Autonomous and Intelligent Systems, Version 2*. IEEE.

Intel. (2017). *Artificial Intelligence: The Public Policy Opportunity*. Retrieved May 29, 2021 from https://blogs.intel.com/policy/files/2017/10/Intel-Artificial-Intelligence-Public-Policy-White-Paper-2017.pdf

Jonker, W., & Petkovic, M. (2008). *Secure Data Management: 5th VLDB Workshop, SDM 2008, Auckland, New Zealand, August 24, 2008, Proceedings*. Springer. https://books.google.com.my/books?id=8Bd_6cxbkDgC

Lanzing, M. (2019). "Strongly recommended" revisiting decisional privacy to judge hypernudging in self-tracking technologies. *Philosophy & Technology*, *32*(3), 549–568. doi:10.100713347-018-0316-4

Lofstedt, R. (2003). The precautionary principle: Risk, regulation and politics. *Process Safety and Environmental Protection*, *81*(1), 36–43. doi:10.1205/095758203762851976

MacCarthy, M. (2020). *AI needs more regulation, not less*. https://www.brookings.edu/research/ai-needs-more-regulation-not-less/

Marchant, G. (2019). "Soft Law" Governance of Artificial Intelligence. *UCLA: The Program on Understanding Law, Science, and Evidence (PULSE)*. https://escholarship.org/uc/item/0jq252ks

Marchant, G. E., Allenby, B. R., & Herkert, J. R. (2011). *The growing gap between emerging technologies and legal-ethical oversight: The pacing problem* (Vol. 7). Springer Science & Business Media. doi:10.1007/978-94-007-1356-7

Marsden, C. T. (2004). Co-Regulation in European Media and Internet Sectors. *Communications and the Law*, *9*(5), 187–195.

Microsoft. (2018). *Microsoft AI Principles*. https://www.microsoft.com/en-us/ai/responsible-ai?activetab=pivot1%3aprimaryr6

Montreal Declaration. (2017). *Montreal Declaration for a Responsible Development of Artificial Intelligence*. https://recherche.umontreal.ca/english/strategic-initiatives/montreal-declaration-for-a-responsible-ai/

Moolman, J. (2017). *Are you ready for outcomes-based regulation?* https://www.linkedin.com/pulse/you-ready-outcomes-based-regulation-juanita-moolman

Moses, L. B. (2013). How to think about law, regulation and technology: Problems with 'technology' as a regulatory target. *Law, Innovation and Technology, 5*(1), 1–20. doi:10.5235/17579961.5.1.1

Nassar, M., Salah, K., & Rehman, M. H. (2020). Blockchain for explainable and trustworthy artificial intelligence. *Wiley Interdisciplinary Reviews. Data Mining and Knowledge Discovery, 10*(1), 1340. doi:10.1002/widm.1340

NITI Aayog. (2018). *Discussion Paper National Strategy for Artificial Intelligence*. https://niti.gov.in/writereaddata/files/document_publication/NationalStrategy-for-AI-Discussion-Paper.pdf

OECD. (2008). *APEC-OECD Co-operative Initiative on Regulatory Reform Proceedings of the Fourth APEC-OECD Workshop on Regulatory Reform*. OECD Publishing. https://books.google.com.my/books?id=gbBFF4_XXBUC

Opinion of the Data Ethics Commission. (2019). *Data Ethics Commission of the Federal Government*. https://www.bmjv.de/SharedDocs/Downloads/DE/Themen/Fokusthemen/Gutachten

Pagallo, U., Aurucci, P., Casanovas, P., Chatila, R., Chazerand, P., Dignum, V., . . . Valcke, P. (2019). *AI4People - On Good AI Governance: 14 Priority Actions, a S.M.A.R.T. Model of Governance, and a Regulatory Toolbox*. https://www.eismd.eu/wp-content/uploads/2019/11/AI4Peoples-Report-on-Good-AI-Governance_compressed.pdf

Partnership on AI. (2016). *Tenets*. https://www.partnershiponai.org/tenets/

Personal Data Protection Commission Singapore. (2019). *Model Artificial Intelligence Governance Framework*. https://ai.bsa.org/wp-content/uploads/2019/09/Model-AI-Framework-First-Edition.pdf

Phillips, J. P., Hahn, C. A., Fontana, P. C., Broniatowski, D. A., & Przybocki, M. A. (2020). *Four Principles of Explainable Artificial Intelligence* [Unpublished Paper]. https://www.nist.gov/system/files/documents/2020/08/17/NIST%20Explainable%20AI%20Draft%20NISTIR8312%20%281%29.pdf

Rossi, F., Sekaran, A., Spohrer, J., & Caruthers, R. (2019). Everyday Ethics for Artificial Intelligence. *IBM Design Program Office*. https://www.ibm.com/watson/assets/duo/pdf/everydayethics.pdf

Rubinstein, I. (2016). The Future of Self-Regulation is Co-Regulation. In *The Cambridge Handbook of Consumer Privacy*. Cambridge University Press.

Saif, I., & Ammanath, B. (2020). Trustworthy AI' is a framework to help manage unique risk. *MIT Technology Review*. https://www.technologyreview.com/2020/03/25/950291/trustworthy-ai-is-a-framework-to-help-manage-unique-risk/

Salah, K., Rehman, M. H. U., Nizamuddin, N., & Al-Fuqaha, A. (2019). Blockchain for AI: Review and open research challenges. *IEEE Access: Practical Innovations, Open Solutions, 7*, 10127–10149. doi:10.1109/ACCESS.2018.2890507

Samp, T., & Phillips, S. R. (2020). *White House issues guidelines for regulatory and non-regulatory approaches to artificial intelligence.* https://www.dlapiper.com/en/us/insights/publications/2020/01/white-house-issues-guidelines-for-regulatory-and-nonregulatory-approaches-to-artificial-intelligence/

Scherer, M. U. (2016). Regulating artificial intelligence systems: Risks, challenges, competencies, and strategies. *Harvard Journal of Law & Technology, 29*, 353–400.

Singh, P. K., Singh, R., Nandi, S. K., Ghafoor, K. Z., Rawat, D. B., & Nandi, S. (2020). An efficient blockchain-based approach for cooperative decision making in swarm robotics. *Internet Technology Letters, 3*(1), 140. doi:10.1002/itl2.140

Spiro, M. (2020). The FTC and AI Governance: A Regulatory Proposal. *Seattle Journal of Technology. Environmental Innovation Law, 10*(1), 2.

Telefonica. (2018). *Telefonica: Our Artificial Intelligence Principles.* Retrieved May 29, 2021 from https://www.telefonica.com/documents/

Thierer, A. (2014). *Problems with Precautionary Principle-Minded Tech Regulation & A Federal Robotics Commission.* https://medium.com/tech-liberation/problems-with-precautionary-principle-minded-tech-regulation-a-federal-robotics-commission-c71f6f20d8bd

van Asselt, M., Vos, E., & Fox, T. (2010). *Regulating technologies and the Uncertainty paradox.* Wolf Legal Publishers.

Villaronga, E. F., Kieseberg, P., & Li, T. (2018). Humans forget, machines remember: Artificial intelligence and the right to be forgotten. *Computer Law & Security Review, 34*(2), 304–313. doi:10.1016/j.clsr.2017.08.007

Vitale, J., Tonkin, M., Ojha, S., Williams, M.-A., Wang, X., & Judge, W. (2017). Privacy by design in machine learning data collection: A user experience experimentation. *The AAAI 2017 Spring Symposium on Designing the User Experience of Machine Learning Systems Technical Report.*

Wachter, S., & Mittelstadt, B. (2019). A right to reasonable inferences: Re-thinking data protection law in the age of big data and AI. *Colum. Bus. L. Rev.*, 494.

Waldman, A. E. (2019). Privacy's Law of Design. *U.C Irvine Law Review, 9.* https://scholarship.law.uci.edu/ucilr/vol9/iss5/8

Wallace, N., & Castro, D. (2018). *The impact of the EU's new data protection regulation on AI.* Centre for Data Innovation.

Weaver, J. F. (2014). *We Need to Pass Legislation on Artificial Intelligence Early and Often.* https://slate.com/technology/2014/09/we-need-to-pass-artificial-intelligence-laws-early-and-often.html

Weber, Lenne, & Poirier. (2020). AI, Machine Learning & Big Data: France. Academic Press.

Wischmeyer, T., & Rademacher, T. (2019). *Regulating Artificial Intelligence*. Springer International Publishing. https://books.google.com.my/books?id=FQ3BDwAAQBAJ

Wrigley, S. (2018). Taming Artificial Intelligence: "Bots," the GDPR and Regulatory Approaches. In Robotics, AI and the Future of Law (pp. 183-208). Springer.

Yanisky-Ravid, S., & Hallisey, S. (2018). 'Equality and Privacy by Design': Ensuring Artificial Intelligence (AI) Is Properly Trained & Fed: A New Model of AI Data Transparency & Certification As Safe Harbor Procedures. *Fordham Urb. L.J., 46*(2).

ENDNOTES

[1] The "top-down" technology-specific regulatory framework should be avoided, instead a "bottom-up" solution should be utilised.

[2] Discreetness portrays the fact that the development of AI technology can be carried out with "limited visible infrastructure" such as being assembled online.

[3] Diffuseness refers to the fact that individuals that are working on a particular component may be located at a great distance away from each other, in a different organisation, jurisdiction or geographical location.

[4] Discreteness means that distinct components of the AI system may be designed and constructed at a different place and time.

[5] Opacity refers to the situation where the "inner workings" of AI maybe kept hidden and may not be subject to reverse engineering, as the manner in which AI systems operate are more opaque than other technologies.

[6] 'Partnership of AI' is a "multi-stakeholder" organization, comprising of organizations and companies building and utilising AI technology, civil society organizations, academic institutions, researchers and other groups. Its mission is to "shape best practices, research, and public dialogue about AI's benefits for people and society". It has more than 100 partners in 13 countries.

[7] Artificial Intelligence at Google: Our Principle was published in 2018. It incorporates 7 objectives, one of which is the incorporation of privacy design principles.

[8] Microsoft AI Principles was published in 2018. It incorporates principles of fairness, reliability and safety, privacy and security, inclusiveness, transparency, and accountability.

[9] IBM Everyday Ethics for AI was published in 2019. It focuses on 4 areas namely, accountability, value alignment, explainability, fairness and user data rights.

[10] The coalition includes the "Beijing Academy of Artificial Intelligence (BAAI), Peking University, Tsinghua University, Institute of Automation and Institute of Computing Technology in Chinese Academy of Sciences, and an AI industrial league involving firms like Baidu, Alibaba and Tencent".

[11] "Partnership on AI" published a document known as "Tenets" in 2016.

[12] The "Future of Life Institute" published the "Asilomar AI Principles" in 2017.

[13] The "Institute of Electric and Electronic Engineers" published the "Ethically Aligned Design" in 2019.

[14] The "Montreal Declaration for a Responsible Development of Artificial Intelligence" was issued in 2017.

15   The Model Framework aims to "collect a set of principles, organise them around key unifying themes, and compile them into an easily understandable and applicable structure".

16   The "accuracy of the dataset", "completeness" of the dataset, "veracity" of the dataset, how recently the dataset was compiled or updated, "relevance" of the dataset and the context for data collection, "integrity" of the dataset that has been joined from multiple datasets, "usability" of the dataset, "human interventions if any human has filtered, applied labels, or edited the data".

17   (a) proactive not reactive; (b)privacy as default setting; (c) privacy embedded in design; (d) fully functional protection of privacy; (e) transparency and visibility; (f) end to end security during the products' entire lifespan; (g) respecting user's privacy.

Chapter 3
A Contextual Study of Regulatory Framework for Blockchain

Muhammad Abdullah Fazi
Multimedia University, Malaysia

ABSTRACT

This study seeks to understand and explain the technological and regulatory challenges of blockchain technology particularly in execution mechanism of smart contracts as compared to regular contracts and to explore legal implication attached the blockchain technology. While evaluating the early days of regulatory framework of blockchain, the current study provides a focused review of relevant studies to identify the legal challenges arising from the application of AI in smart contracts and to find solutions to overcome these challenges. The study has emphasized certain areas related to the blockchain such as AI application and execution of smart contracts and finds that that there is currently a lack of legal certainty as to how various requirements of a valid contract would be satisfied. Hence, it highlights the need of regulation without disrupting the key yet essential features of blockchain. Keywords: Blockchain, Smart contract, AI, Framework, Legislation, Cryptocurrency

INTRODUCTION

Since its beginning, an interest in regulatory framework of blockchain technology has been found among the experts and stakeholders. In order to inquire the regulation of blockchain technology within the areas of law, this chapter provides a literature review of blockchain based applications in a wider spectrum as it pertains to law. The objective is to explore the existing state of rules and regulations of blockchain and their implications. Therefore, this study is structured as follows: It starts with the examination of regulatory and legal challenges to blockchain and identifies areas where legal and regulatory intervention is required through a focused review of the most significant studies on the subject. For this, first, it provides a cursory overview on technological aspects of the issue and identifies the features of 'decentralised' nature and functionality of blockchain while highlighting the considerable regulatory

DOI: 10.4018/978-1-7998-7927-5.ch003

implications attached to it. Second, it discusses blockchain-AI convergence and the existing and proposed legal framework along with the challenges to determine whether those regulations fit with nature and objectives of blockchain technology. Lastly, while discussing the features of a smart contract, this study, report the results emphasizing the need for regulation and governance of blockchain transections to mitigate the risk and increase the security features for the parties involved. For this, the regulatory framework should be drafted to support blockchain's innovative potential rather limiting it. With this, the proposed regulations should target to disrupt the criminal and fraudulent transactions without killing the innovation of blockchain. In conclusion, while focusing on the intersection between the technology and the law, study has identified several vulnerabilities particularly related to legal execution of smart contracts such as lacking formal legal requirements of a contract, lack of jurisdiction and scalability etc. Hence, the proposed paradigms for the new technology, its untraceable nature of applications and agreements are not of easy to converge with the conventional legal or regulatory parameters that arises biggest concern pertaining to reliability of blockchain technology and hinders its large-scale acceptability as a trusted medium of trade.

BACKGROUND

Blockchain: A Primer

The blockchain technology prompted much attention in 2009, first decentralized digital currency emerged in the form of Bitcoin (Nakamoto, 2008). A new technology was introduced to utilize a database to keep record of all transactions in a distributed ledger. This new technology has become known as blockchain. With blockchain, people can buy and sell commoditize without a third-party or centralized intermediary. This peer-to-peer payment system allow participants to transfer cryptocurrency anywhere in the world without involving any bank or central financial institute. Blockchain based distributed system challenges the supervisory role of the central banks and the regulatory structure of different jurisdictions. For instance, Bitcoin, a blockchain based payment product doesn't require a person's identity to be disclosed while performing a transection (Lee and L'heureux, 2019). Now, because of its smartness and usefulness, industries have seen its potential in many other fields beyond the purpose of its creation. Due to its great potential, over 4.5 billion USD funds have been invested and over 2500 blockchain related patents were flied until 2017 (Jesse, McWaters, et. al., 2016).

Here, according to Finck, it is pertinent to differentiate between cryptocurrency and blockchain. As stated earlier, blockchain technology emerged as an enabling technology that provides peer-to-peer digital payment. Due to its initial application, cryptocurrency and blockchain are often considered as the same although they are not. Apart from Bitcoin, since its beginning innovators have enabled many other blockchain based applications (Finck, 2018). The vary common feature of all of these applications is their reliance on central feature of blockchain technology, that provides distributive yet accurate record of data. The blockchain technology decentralizes the information and data storing that makes it unique. This decentralization feature alone opens a wide range of technological and financial opportunities which makes it a far-reaching innovation. Before this, an intermediary was inevitable, hence, it was not possible to coordinate any internet activity. However, blockchain technology enabled transections and payments to be made between any two or more anonymous parties without involving any third party or central authority (Finck, 2018). Thus, it by passes the monitoring and approval requirements prior to any transection or trade. For this, data and information stored on a blockchain based application can be effectively maintained through public and private keys and electronic signatures.

Fink further describes the operational mechanism of blockchain as the application has the tendency to code trust into blockchain application as it codes a singular automated trusted state without trusted actors. This automated code enables "trust the outputs of a system without trusting any actor within it (Fink, 2018)." This mechanism enables the parties to trust the system. Hence, this automated "trusted code" provides a wide range of opportunities to the corporations, persons and machines to trade directly without monitoring of any central authority. While ensuring the anonymity and privacy of the parties intact, for entities, trust in the blockchain system or code is enough to enable them to trade. The automated code with ensures the trust in a transection opens a ray of possibilities for billions of smart, efficient and anonymous transections worldwide.

At its core, blockchain is just a recordkeeping or record-tracking product that reliably stores data on a network in a secure way. Like a virtual databas, the blockchain is also described as "spreadsheet in the sky" (Vaughn and Outzen, 2017). The simplicity of its function made the application of this technology extended beyond digital currencies (Fulmer and Nathan, 2019). Decentralized nature of blockchain makes this technology secure and fair as compared to a centralized data center or authority where data is placed in a single location. However, the decentralized nature also invites some legal and technical challenges which will be discussed under coming sections of this article.

In terms of data management and effective and secure transactions, Artificial Intelligence (AI) based applications increases machine learning capabilities which is essential yet a requirement for blockchain. While enhancing the efficiency, the convergence of AI and blockchain can create even new products. In continuation to this, the next section of the study focuses on potential of combining both of these technologies together and discusses regulatory implications attached to it.

AI in Blockchain: Application, Implications and Legal Issues

Over the past decade blockchain and artificial intelligence (AI) have demonstrated their efficiency in many technological and monetary applications. Blockchain technology has proven its capability to perform automated payments and give access a shared ledger, logs and transections in a decentralized mechanism. With this, the Blockchain application while operating through AI has ability to apply smart contract and provides solutions for the participants without any intermediator or third-party governance (N.A. Team, 2018). While operating with the Blockchain, AI offers decision making facilities for the machine to govern the contract as a human. AI is developed to work with big volumes of data, and blockchain technology has now been considered as a platform to store a huge volume of data (K. Salah, Rehman, et. al., 2019).

Consequently, to operate with blockchain, the revolutionary concept of decentralisation of AI has been emerged. Decentralisation of AI is actually a combination of blockchain where a decentralized software or application of AI enables to govern the decision making on a digitally signed, trusted and secure shared data that has been stored on the blockchain, in a distributed and decentralized manner, without intermediaries or third parties (K. Salah, Rehman, et. al., 2019).

Applications of AI in Blockchain Technology

From the utility aspects of convergence of AI into blockchain technology, Ahmed Banafa has provided comprehendible yet insightful overview. According to Banafa, both technologies are inevitable from the future needs of the financial and technological needs of the market. Therefore, AI can be seen as catalyst for effective functionality of blockchain. For instance, from the aspects of data protection, AI is highly dependent on data provided to it. Through the large amount of data provided to AI, it enables it to improve itself and perform an accurate function. On the other hand, blockchain also needs data to allow its encrypted storage on distributive ledger. Combining AI and blockchain enable the application to back up the system for highly valuable and sensitive data of parties. Storing data on AI enabled blockchain provide a more secure enjoinment for any trade which only allow access to the specific parties in an automated manner (Ahmed, 2019). Similarly, AI also improves decision making of a blockchain based computer program. Through the AI enabled blockchain application it is possible to access and process a large amount of data that can be used for improved performance of the computer program. AI application-based decision making also makes the audit process easier as it analyses a large amount of provided data effectively (Ahmed, 2019). Thus, with an appropriate AI-based blockchain program steps from data entry to conclusion of transection can be made transparent particularly form a legal point of view.

However, the technologies are still in the process of evolution and therefore, facing multidimensional challenges in different applications particularly when it applies on monetary transections or into a smart contract. For example, in case of a centralized AI where data is managed in a centralized fashion (Lee and L'heureux, 2019), it may subject to tempering or hacking with the authenticity of data generated by the sources is also not guaranteed to be accurate (Qi and Xiao, 2018). Here, the N.A. Team, pointed out another crucial area of concern regarding the centralized nature of AI where corporations like Google and Amazon provides cloud services using AI computing. However, as a single company they can stop providing these services at any time (N.A. Team, 2018). With this, the corporations are also in constant pressure of countries to access data as per their geographical restrictions that leads to breach of privacy. In relation to this, monopolization of AI power by few big corporations is also a concern to acquire data and computing resources (N. Dinh & T. Thai, 2018). In terms of secure data sharing, obtaining data for module training and research is difficult unless one of the big corporations i.e., Facebook or Google is involved in the study. Eventually, it stops the competition between corporation and researchers which is required to boost AI (N. Dinh & T. Thai, 2018). These issues with several other changes may affect the AI decision making and can lead to dangerous outcomes.

The literature produced and contributions to unfold the subject, lacks comprehensive reviews on the role that blockchain plays in the context of law particularly when AI comes into operation. Existing literature on the subject reveals that researchers studied blockchain and law in isolation, due to which there are very few studies on the subject available to provide a viable solution regarding legal issues related to the technology when it comes to business.

Technical and Legal Issues Related to AI Based Blockchain

There are some legal issues that identify gap in the existing literature which need to be discuss under this research as follow.

Data Tempering

The data stored in centralized AI application may lead to the possibility of data tampering and breach, as data can be subject to hacking and manipulation as it is managed and stored in centralized manner (K Salah, Rehman, et. al., 2019).

Here, the researchers have rightly identified the core issue of the blockchain and AI technologies when both comes into operation together. In case of tampered data entries or wrong command due to some hacking or malicious activity the whole transaction become invalid and in worst cases a huge amount of money theft also can occur. Although the corporations relying on centralized data application have security agreements and protocols, still these centralized corporations face internal data leaks. Resultingly, complete data security guarantee against any breach is not possible (N.A. Team, 2018). It suggests that despite of their usability and great efficiency both technologies are prone to attack which make them quite vulnerable for any kind of business application. Though the blockchain systems provide a good security mechanism which is not easy to breach still 8,833 out of 19,366 existing Ethereum contracts are reported vulnerable (X. Li, P. Jiang, T. Chen, et. al., 2017). Hence, to counter the issues pointed out in centralized AI application, the N.A. Team suggested two viable solutions i.e. shared computing platforms using AI and a programming decentralized AI application.

An Expensive Medium

Conventional blockchain is a very expensive medium for storing large amounts of data. For example, storing large files or documents on Bitcoin blockchain is very expensive as the size limit per block is limited to one megabyte. To solve this problem, a decentralized storage medium is used for storing such data and hashes of the data are linked with the blockchain blocks or used within the blockchain smart contract code (K Salah, Rehman, et. al., 2019).

Again, the researchers have suggested to remove a technological obstacle by providing a cheaper data storage (decentralization) mechanism. However, the decentralized data storage may arise legal issues related to breach of data and privacy. Here, the researchers did not provide a computing solution to avoid data breach in case of hacking activity.

Cyber-Attacks and Hacking

Similarly, another study has shown the tendency of cyber-attacks and hacking against these technologies as:

at present, the defined standards regarding smart contract security is still lacking which means the hidden vulnerabilities found in new or existing smart contracts could potentially lead to undesired results, e.g., monetary losses. In 2017 alone, the hack of Ethereum's Parity wallet caused a total loss of $180 million; while in 2016, a bug (The DAO, 2016) found in Ethereum's DAO (i.e., decentralized autonomous organization) enabled a hacker to siphon $50 million from its smart contract (Marwala, Tshilidzi, et. al., 2018). The hacker managed to exploit several errors and mistakes made in the computing of the smart contracts that enabled multiple transactions (The DAO, 2016).

Other than data tempering and hacking issues attached to the AI and blockchain applications, there are several other issues have emerged as a constant threat to the use of these technologies.

For instance, with a huge volume of personal data embedded in blockchain mechanism, the data encryption becomes a significant challenge for ensuring and guaranteeing participant's/user's privacy participating in smart transections. This aspect is somehow related to security issue as well. The experts have said that until now "no one has managed to develop a public-key algorithm that is free from weaknesses". However, there are relatively secure options like operating through a private key is available but for large number of transactions available to many participants at the same time is not possible through using private key. Despite of its better security, private key has its own limitations such as the private blockchain platforms limits the access of large amount of data that is necessary for AI functions to make correct decisions.

Smart Contracts: A Viable Solution

In 2013, Vitalik Buterin has developed Ethereum as an improvement and extension of bitcoin while expanding its capabilities. The Ethereum was developed with the capabilities of self-execution of its code that called "smart contract". Ether (ETH) is now trading around 2150 USD and having shared the market with 278 billion USD that makes it second biggest blockchain after Bitcoin (Adam, 2018). With a built-in code and distributed machine, the Ethereum applications can perform innumerous functions without having a centralized authority or third-party.

The term "smart contract" was first used by Nick Szabo a computer scientist in 1994 (Brent Miller, Brent, 2016). In his article Szabo describes a smart contract as:

Smart contracts combine protocols with user interfaces to formalize and secure relationships over computer networks. Objectives and principles for the design of these systems are derived from legal principles, economic theory, and theories of reliable and secure protocols. (Szabo, 1997)

He further explains the contract as:

The basic idea behind smart contracts is that many kinds of contractual clauses (such as collateral, bonding, delineation of property rights, etc.) can be embedded in the hardware and software we deal with, in such a way as to make breach of contract expensive (if desired, sometimes prohibitively so) for the breacher.

Here, first time Szabo presented the idea very precisely and simply to generate a computer code language or command with a legal sense of virtual contractual agreement having capabilities of self-execution with security features embodied in the application.

While unfolding the mechanism of a smart contract that how it works in real life, Sazbo gave the example of vending machine as:

A canonical real-life example, which we might consider to be the primitive ancestor of smart contracts, is the humble vending machine. Within a limited amount of potential loss (the amount in the till should be less than the cost of breaching the mechanism), the machine takes in coins, and via a simple mechanism, which makes a freshman computer science problem in design with finite automata, dispense change and product according to the displayed price. The vending machine is a contract with bearer: anybody with coins can participate in an exchange with the vendor. The lockbox and other security mechanisms protect the stored coins and contents from attackers, sufficiently to allow profitable deployment of vending machines in a wide variety of areas.

In this example, Sazbo also recognized the essential feature of security which is actually the most important concern so far. However, in legal sense there are a lot of more complexities have to be mitigated before recognition of smart contract in everyday life as a binding agreement.

From legal point of view Fulmer and Nathan have pointed out three main features of smart contract i.e. automation, decentralization and anonymity (Fulmer and Nathan, 2019). Besides of providing the novel applications and new ventures for ease of business, decentralization, automation and anonymity features of blockchain are also instigating more legal challenges in terms of imposing liabilities and duties in a contract. Since, Nevada Act provides significant guidelines for using blockchain technology. However, without solving the issues related to legal challenges its quite difficult to ensure the trust of participants fully in blockchain technology.

Legislation Governing Smart Contracts

In terms of real-world regulations and legislation behind the smart contract, Nevada has taken a lead by adopting a first ever pro-blockchain legislation called Nevada Senate Bill 398 (Nevada Act, 2019). This Act establishes provisions and definitions related to smart contact and blockchain technology. In promotion and adoption of new technology, the Act prohibits the local government to impose tax or restrictions on blockchain technology.

In providing definitions, section 4 of the Act defines blockchain as:

"Blockchain" means an electronic record created by the use of a decentralized method by multiple parties to verify and store a digital record of transactions which is secured by the use of a cryptographic hash of previous transaction information (Nevada Act, 2019)."

While defining "smart contract," section 9 of the Act provides as:

Smart contract" means a contract stored as an electronic record pursuant to chapter 719 of NRS which is verified by the use of a blockchain.

These definitions allow smart contracts to be produced as evidence in litigation. Moreover, it also acknowledges the electronic record where a written deed is required to enforce and an agreement.

In pursuance of this, the Act states as:

(1) A smart contract, record or signature may not be denied legal effect or enforceability solely because a blockchain was used to create, store or verify the smart contract, record or signature.

AND

(2) In a proceeding, evidence of a smart contract, record or signature must not be excluded solely because a blockchain was used to create, store or verify the smart contract, record or signature.

(3) If a law requires a record to be in writing, submission of a blockchain which electronically contains the record satisfies the law.

(4) If a law requires a signature, submission of a blockchain which electronically contains the signature or verifies the intent of a person to provide the signature satisfies the law (Nevada Act, 2019).

Beside establishing evidentiary value of smart contract, the -Act also puts restrictions on kind of notices issued by blockchain participants i.e., notice of default, notice of cancellation, notice of foreclosure etc (Fulmer and Nathan 2019).

By providing essential definitions of blockchain and smart contract, this landmark legislation established a great yet significant example for other States and courtiers to initiate similar steps in recognition of blockchain technology at world level.

However, due to the blockchain's immutable characteristic of construction, it is challenging yet difficult for any legislation or regulation to completely mitigate the legal risks involved in blockchain transaction at this stage. For instance, blockchain can only verify whether the particular transaction can occur without verifying the input information. This problem can lead to serious consequences from legal and security point of view. Therefore, a participant can steal the right of ownership from other participants by exploiting the code feature which ensures only the rightful seller can sell the property, but it doesn't ensure that the rightful buyer get the title. In context of smart contract for sale, the question arises that who will be held responsible if the contract doesn't execute automatically? Considering the fact that data in blockchain might be immutable or very difficult to change.

With this, regarding the decentralised nature of blockchain, there are also jurisdictional issues attached. As the blockchain based on networks of many computers which could be placed in different parts of the world a jurisdictional issue can be faced as where the agreement was made or which law to be applied in enforcement of the contract terms in case of conflict etc (Fulmer and Nathan 2019). Similarly, there is no central authority to make complains in case of malfunction or to sue. However, the jurisdictional issue can be addressed by making an international arbitration body or through making a universal code on which all the participants are agreed upon. Similarly, the anonymity feature of blockchain on hand provides a significant ease of use for many participants but on the other hand this feature alone make things difficult for law enforcements agencies to identify the criminal activity or financial crimes and fraudulent activities under blockchain because of anonymous participants.

Legal Issues Relating to Smart Contract

In context of the above-mentioned discussion, the idea of smart contract which also enables legal liabilities, duties and rights to the parties involved is quite compelling. However, there are still many questions that has to addressed from a legal point of view to mitigate the risk.

Lacking Formal Legal Requirements of Regular Contract

No matter the Nevada state legislation acknowledges the smart contract there are still many jurisdictions where formal requirements of legal contract has to be met before creation any liability. For instance, in Sweden, notaries are not required by the Swedish law. Likewise, it may require that the contract should be in a language that both the parties can fully understand. In this particular scenario, can the "code" be regarded such a commonly understandable language? If yes, does the code need "translations" of terms in other languages? and thereby also require rules for what constitutes a legally binding translation of a smart contract to say German, French, or Italian? (Thematic report, 2019).

Signature Requirement

As seen above in the Nevada Act, that recognizes an electronic signature, similarly in EU, signature on a smart contract must need to valid under to be legally valid under eIDAS and must be verified by a TSP (Thematic report. (2019). However, the verification requirement of signature might risk the anonymity feature of the smart contract which is an essential rather most significant part of the blockchain technology.

Question of Jurisdiction

Transnationality is another vital feature of blockchain technology where any individual can initiate the transection and participate in a trade by aiding blocks to the ongoing ledger. However, this feature alone raises the issue of legal jurisdiction that under which country or law that smart contract can be governed. Each country has their own contract laws that creates different types of liabilities and duties. Therefore, in the absence of "universal jurisdiction" it is difficult to govern a smart contract in a uniform and equitable manner.

Regulatory Challenges to Smart Contracts

Regarding the regulatory framework for the smart contract in blockchain application. The biggest challenge involves the regulation and how the duties and rights of the parties to a smart contract can be effectively incorporated and regulated. Regarding regulatory framework, till now blockchain systems standards yet to be formed. With this at global and domestic levels a uniform regulation is needed to synchronize the business among many parties belongs to different countries and regions. Similarly, governance issues also need to be discussed according in line with the regulatory framework.

Being a new technology, there are hardly any existing laws governing the operation of smart contracts. In the absence of legislation this part is also very crucial to apply and monitor the smart contracts on large scale.

Scalability of Smart Contracts

Scalability is one of the biggest challenges in blockchain transection. For example, bitcoin blockchain can only perform four transactions per second. Similarly, the Ethereum performs a little higher number of 12 transactions per second. In comparison to Facebook where millions of transactions occur in every second, these very low number of transactions is not sufficient to make them a reliable platform in future.

Issue of Vulnerability

Smart Contract vulnerability is a very crucial area to ensure and build the trust on blockchain systems. Therefore, it is necessary to explore and design a bug free a smart contract to secure the transection and data against cyber-attacks. In this regard it is important to secure and write the code of the contract as it may be vulnerable to attack.

Lacking Dispute Resolution Mechanism

Regarding the dispute resolution mechanism, it is also not clear that how the conventional contract law will apply on the disputes of smart contracts. As mentioned by Green, "Currently, when the meaning of a contract is disputed by the parties to it, a court will consider what that agreement would mean to a reasonable human observer. Where that agreement is written in computer code, however, and intended for communication to an artificial intelligence, the significance of a reasonable human observer's interpretation is a matter of contention" (Smart contracts, 2017). Current legal practices will have to be updated in order to manage smart contracts appropriately. Another challenge is that the success of smart contracts is highly dependent on the code programmed into them and the individuals writing the programs. Smart contracts execute exactly as instructed, so a lot of care and effort must be put into understanding what the code entails, both for contract developers and the parties entering into agreement. There have already been instances where the code in smart contracts were exploited (Law, 2017).

These questions, with several other challenges are rarely addressed in the existing literature which provides a gap to study and explore the areas and implications of mergence between AI and blockchain.

CONCLUSION

Admitting that blockchain is a future of all internet trades and the great potential of technological revolution that it has. It is equally important to keep in view that the technology is still in its premature stage. That is why, it demands considerable time and technological advancement to further develop its full realization that is an essential to promulgate appropriate and sustainable legislation. From the focused review of existing literature, it is also evident that there is gap between technological aspects of blockchain and legal efforts to mitigate the risks of a smart contract. This requires, further understanding of evolving technology and also harmonize efforts to embrace the blockchain as a legal trade. Despite of its huge potential and far-reaching ray of possibilities, still form a regulatory point of view, study find that the blockchain is far away from real world infusion due to the liability and risk issues attached. For instance, in execution of a smart contract, study finds that automated code or smart contract is lacking the basic feature and requirements of contract law as established in many countries. Therefore, issues related to jurisdiction, anonymity of parties and formal requirement of a valid contract are still lacking. Further critical issues, such as no dispute resolution mechanism, vulnerability of smart contracts (in case of cyber-attacks/hacking), scalability of transactions concluded through the blockchain, lack of uniformity and issues related to data security are the main challenges against the widescale acceptability of the blockchain technology. Therefore, in order to achieve a wide scale adoption of blockchain, this study recommends joint efforts of key players and states to propose a universal jurisdiction upon its maturity. Thus, study concludes that if the smart contract continues and the blockchain technology improves and evolves further, in order to gain the reliability and across the globe acceptability, these novel legal questions have to be answered to mitigate the legal and security challenges attached to it.

REFERENCES

Banafa, A. (2019). *Blockchain and AI: A Perfect Match?* https://www.bbvaopenmind.com/en/technology/artificial-intelligence/blockchain-and-ai-a-perfect-match/

Dinh & Thai. (2018). AI and Blockchain a disruptive integration. *Computer, 51*, 48-53. http://www.people.vcu.edu/~tndinh/papers/IEEEComp18_Blockchain+AI.pdf

Financial Conduct Authority. (2019). *Guidance on Cryptoassets*. Accessed at https://www.fca.org.uk/publication/consultation/cp19-03.pd

Finck, M. (2018). Blockchains: Regulating the Unknown. *German Law Journal, 19*(4), 665–692. doi:10.1017/S2071832200022847

Fulmer, N. (2019). Exploring the Legal Issues of Blockchain Applications. *Akron Law Review, 52*(1), 5. https://ideaexchange.uakron.edu/akronlawreview/vol52/iss1/5

Hayes, A. (2018). Is Ethereum More Important than Bitcoin? *Investopedia*. https://www.investopedia.com/articles/investing/032216/ethereum-more-important-bitcoin.asp

Jesse McWaters, R. (2016). The Future of Financial Infrastructure: An Ambitious Look at How Blockchain Can Reshape Financial Services. *World Economic Forum*. http://www3.weforum.org/docs/WEF_The_future_of_financial_infrastructure.pdf

Law, A. (2017). *Smart Contracts and their applications in supply chain management*. MIT Thesis. Accessed at https://dspace.mit.edu/handle/1721.1/114082

Lee, J., & L'heureux, F. (2019). A regulatory framework for cryptocurrency. *European Business Law Review*. https://ore.exeter.ac.uk/repository/handle/10871/120627

Li, Jiang, Chen, Luo, & Wen. (2017). A survey on the security of blockchain systems. *Future Gener. Comput. Syst., 107*, 841-853. . doi:10.1016/j.future.2017.08.020

Marwala, T., & Xing, B. (2018). *Blockchain and Artificial Intelligence*. https://arxiv.org/abs/1802.04451

Miller, B. (2016). *Smart contract and the role of lawyers (Part 1)- About smart contracts*. http://biglawkm.com/2016/10/20/smart-contracts-and-the-role-of-lawyers-part-1-about-smart-contracts/

Nevada Senate Bill 398 at https://www.leg.state.nv.us/Session/79th2017/BDR/BDR79_59-0158.pdf

Qi, Y., & Xiao, J. (2018). Fintech: Ai powers financial services to improve people's lives. *Communications of the ACM, 61*(11), 65–69. doi:10.1145/3239550

Salah, K., Rehman, M. H. U., Nizamuddin, N., & Al-Fuqaha, A. (2019). Blockchain for AI: Review and Open Research Challenges. *IEEE Access: Practical Innovations, Open Solutions, 7*, 10127–10149. doi:10.1109/ACCESS.2018.2890507

Smart Contracts. (2017). *Oxford faculty of law*. https://www.law.ox.ac.uk/business-law-blog/blog/2017/03/smart-contracts?cv=1

Szabo, N. (1997). Formalizing and Securing Relationships on Public Networks. *First Monday*, 2(9). Advance online publication. doi:10.5210/fm.v2i9.548

Team, N. A. (2018). *Nebula AI (NBAI) decentralized ai blockchain whitepaper*. https://nebulaai.org/_include/whitepaper/NBAI_whitepaper_EN.pdf

The DAO: Theft is property. (2016). *The Economist, 419*(8995), 66.

Thematic Report. (2019). Legal and regulatory framework of blockchains and smart contracts. *EU Blockchain*. Accessed at https://www.eublockchainforum.eu/sites/default/files/reports/report_legal_v1.0.pdf

Vaughn & Outzen. (2017). *Understanding how blockchain could impact legal industry*. https://www.law360.com/articles/879810/understanding-how-blockchain-could-impact-legal-industry

Chapter 4
Legal and Regulatory Landscape of Blockchain Technology in Various Countries

Karisma Karisma
University Malaya, Malaysia

Pardis Moslemzadeh Tehrani
iD https://orcid.org/0000-0001-9698-8698
University Malaya, Malaysia

ABSTRACT

Blockchain technology can be leveraged to record information securely, ranging from public sector data to private records. It has the potential of being ubiquitous due to its far-reaching use cases and revolutionary features. The deployment of blockchain technology can radically transform corporate and government operations and services. The blockchain legislative landscape is rapidly evolving, and an in-depth analysis is provided to offer a legal and contextual perspective of the regulatory trends across the globe. Part I explores the widespread use of blockchain technology for various industries and business applications. It also outlines two types of legislation that can be enacted, namely enabling and prohibitive legislation, to advance the policy objectives of a country. Part II examines the regulatory responses of various countries relating to blockchain use cases and applications.

INTRODUCTION

The utilization of blockchain technology has expanded beyond the realm of digital currencies, permeating into other domains. This occurrence has triggered a regulatory response from various jurisdictions. Blockchain technology is envisaged to be ubiquitous and has the potential to disrupt business practices. It is pertinent to consider regulatory solutions as blockchain technology is further developed and leveraged for far-reaching applications. This chapter expands on academic literature and navigates the regulatory landscapes beyond digital currencies, namely other blockchain use cases and industry applications.

DOI: 10.4018/978-1-7998-7927-5.ch004

As the regulatory apparatus is evolving significantly, it is apt to embark on a discussion relating to the regulatory initiatives that have been adopted by various countries, to facilitate the implementation and deployment of blockchain technology. Several states in the United States (US) and other countries have either proposed or enacted laws and regulations that address blockchain technology. Part I explores the widespread use of blockchain technology for various industries and business applications. It also outlines two types of legislation that can be enacted, namely enabling and prohibitive legislation, to advance the policy objectives of a country in the area of blockchain. Part II examines the regulatory responses of several countries relating to blockchain use cases and applications. This chapter highlights four types of regulatory approaches that can be adopted by various countries, namely (a) wait and see; (b) enacting new legislation; (c) issuing guidance; and (d)regulatory sandboxing. A descriptive method is adopted in Part I and II of this chapter. This chapter also serves as a blueprint for future work in conducting a comparative analytical study on the regulatory initiatives of each country.

BACKGROUND

Blockchain technology is a tamper-proof digital ledger that records data, transactions, and digital assets in a distributed manner without the need for central authorities or intermediaries to process and validate the data. (Suda et al., 2017) Therefore, unlike a centralized system, the decentralized structure of blockchain is not susceptible to a single point of failure nor responsible for the entire task as the workload is distributed to the "computing nodes".(Raj et al., 2020) Every node maintains the same encrypted copy and can "record, store and update" the ledger. (Furlonger & Uzureau, 2019; Quasim, 2020) The decentralized structure ensures transparency, anonymity and efficiency of the blockchain ecosystem. (Bashir, 2018) Besides that, consensus mechanisms are utilized in blockchain to deal with "faults" in a distributed system, to ensure that all the participating nodes provide an agreement towards a single source of truth. (Bashir, 2018) The participating nodes on the blockchain network maintain and rely on the same distributed ledger, which functions as a "golden record" and is immutable. (Suda et al., 2017) The immutability of blockchain suggest that transaction data located on blockchain networks are tamper-evident in that they cannot be eliminated or altered easily. (Politou et al., 2019) The term "immutable" means "perpetual after some time or unfit to be changed". (Kumar et al., 2020) In the realm of blockchain, this term is interpreted as "practically immutable, for all intent and purposes", and immutability can be achieved with the assistance of a "cryptography hash value". (Kumar et al., 2020; Raj et al., 2020) Blockchain technology was first proposed by Satoshi Nakamoto in 2008 where a paper on bitcoin was published. (Nakamoto, 2008) The paper suggested an electronic payment system that allows payment to be made from one willing party to another, directly without reliance or interference from third-party intermediaries. (Hughes, 2017; Suda et al., 2017)

The more prominent and notable applications of blockchain technology are cryptocurrencies. These applications rely on the extensive capability of blockchain systems to "record, transfer and store data" in a secure manner. (Hughes, 2017) Currently, blockchain technology is utilized in various domains such as the energy trading sector, health care sector, supply chain management, and financial services. Countries have begun to explore the use and implementation of blockchain technology and whether the technology should be regulated, including the manner to regulate it. Scholar Benedetto Neitz outlined two reasons for regulating blockchain technology. (Neitz, 2020) Firstly, it protects members of the public from harm. Cryptocurrency has led to a surge of scams in the past years. Scammers continue to find different methods to deceive individuals into fraudulent investments. As threats to the public increase, regulators can no longer adopt a hands-off approach. Besides that, regulators use blockchain-enabling laws to attract blockchain-related companies to their jurisdiction. Countries like Switzerland and Malta have implemented regulatory structures to "win interjurisdictional competition" and provide a conducive environment for technological innovation to gain the reputation of a blockchain-friendly country.(Neitz, 2020) Nevertheless, there is resulting friction between protecting the public and furthering innovation. It is pertinent to look to other jurisdictions for guidance before drawing up legislation as a multitude of approaches has been applied by regulators in different jurisdictions to achieve policy objectives. On the one hand, delayed legislative enactments might lead towards a more measured approach in regulating blockchain, though it may risk losing interjurisdictional competition. On the other hand, passing legislation hastily may cause harm in the long term if policies underlying the legislation are not deliberated upon before the enactment of legislation. (Neitz, 2020)

STATE-OF-THE-ART OF BLOCKCHAIN TECHNOLOGY

Blockchain has developed as a leading technology underlying the application of cryptocurrencies (or digital currencies). As previously stated, the use of blockchain as a technology layer was first envisioned for financial applications. In recent years, blockchain-based applications and use cases are increasing. Blockchain technology is emerging as a disruptive technology that can radically transform other domains which go beyond financial applications. Blockchain technology can be leveraged by various industries to record information in an immutable ledger, ranging from public data to private records. (Al-Megren et al., 2018)

Blockchain technology has numerous real-world use cases.

- **Education**: Higher-educational institutions can use blockchain technology to store educational information such as academic degrees, thus eliminating "degree fraud".(Chen et al., 2018)
- **Banking and Finance**: The use of blockchain facilitates speedier transactions while maintaining high levels of security, privacy and transparency.(Osmani et al., 2020) Instead of storing data on a centralized database that is susceptible to attacks, data can be stored on a decentralized platform. (Osmani et al., 2020)
- **Real Estate**: Fraudulent activities concerning real estate transactions can be prevented with the use of blockchain technology which serves as a decentralized platform to store and manage real estate information in a tamper-proof manner. (Joy & Sebastian, 2020; Pankratov et al., 2020) In furtherance to the above, blockchain technology can replace intermediaries in real-estate transactions, resulting in time and cost savings.(Joy & Sebastian, 2020; Pankratov et al., 2020) There is also a vast increase in transparency and security in real-estate management.(Joy & Sebastian, 2020)
- **Supply Chain Management**: Blockchain technology can be used in the management of the supply chain and has the potential to resolve the challenges ordinarily faced by centralized systems. (Lacity, 2020)
- **Transportation**: A complete record of the transportation process is stored on a blockchain ledger, allowing senders to monitor their shipment.(Humayun et al., 2020)

- **Energy**: There is great potential for the use of blockchain technology in the energy sector. Utility companies adopting traditional business models are inefficient due to the amount of energy wastage from converting and transmitting energy resources to consumers. Blockchain-based energy trading can facilitate prosumers to trade energy effectively by the creation of peer-to-peer energy market platforms.(Y. Zhou et al., 2020)
- **Healthcare**: Health records of patients can be managed securely while preserving data privacy. Besides that, patients have the private key to their data stored on a blockchain network and have control over the access and use of healthcare data. Blockchain technology also facilitates the cross-border sharing of data. Hence, data can be shared seamlessly by patients with healthcare professionals in other jurisdictions.(Attaran, 2020)
- **Governance**: Blockchain technology is capable of facilitating government operations and services. It enables "smart administration" by reducing administrative costs and revolutionizes citizens engagement and involvement by allowing a "technology-enabled community-based model of governance".(Shen & Pena-Mora, 2018)

The following section expands on the discussion of real-world blockchain use cases.

1. Blockchain for Companies

Blockchain is capable of resolving issues associated with the companies' inability to keep accurate and timely records.(Singh et al., 2019) This is because, blockchain technology is ideal for record-keeping and can create and retain corporate records efficiently in a verifiable manner, particularly due to its features of transparency, security and immutability.(Kaal & Evans, 2019) The simplicity offered by blockchain-based record-keeping can substantially decrease the time and cost of data verification as blockchain ledgers consisting of ownership information are updated in real-time. On the aspect of security, the centralization of corporate registries generates considerable challenges, such as hacking of corporate databases which can consequentially destroy or modify records. With the adoption of blockchain technology, corporations can rely on the decentralised and distributed nature of technology, where there can be no "single point of failure".(de Jong et al., 2017) Besides that, blockchain is capable of preventing fraud and increasing trust because every transaction on the blockchain is "encoded" by way of cryptography and validated by other individuals using consensus mechanisms. After validation, the blockchain ledger is updated with the transaction and treated as authentic. The endeavour to subsequently alter, modify or get rid of information on a blockchain ledger by malicious individuals can be detected by other nodes and prevented.(de Jong et al., 2017; Kiviat, 2015)

Blockchain technology can revolutionize stock trading as it facilitates corporations to retain records regarding stock transactions accurately, in real-time. By taking advantage of the features of blockchain, corporations can employ a more effective method of keeping records of each transfer such as the number of shares and participants of the transfer.(Tu, 2020) Before the legislative recognition of blockchain technology in Delaware, by the amendments made to the Delaware General Corporation Law (DGCL), DGCL functioned on a simplified model. Under this model, the "corporate secretary maintains a document called the stock ledger" and the stock ledger contains "legally relevant transactions in the corporation's shares", including the date of share acquisition by any individual and the number of shares bought.("In re Appraisal of Dell Inc," 2015) It also contains information on the date of share transfer and the number of shares traded.("In re Appraisal of Dell Inc," 2015) Nevertheless, if a transfer has occurred but the corporation is not notified of such transfer, the corporation relies on the existing records in the stock ledger until the stockholder takes measures to notify the corporation.("In re Appraisal of Dell Inc," 2015) Delaware amended their legislation to allow corporations to use blockchain technology to effectively maintain stock ledgers. Corporations that use blockchain technology for stock ledgers can also adopt blockchain-based smart contracts. This is an effective administrative mechanism for corporations with "complex capital structures", such as different classes of stocks that have different rights, concerning voting and payment. (Laster & Rosner, 2017) Blockchain technology can be used to send information securely to stockholders, thus increasing the efficiency of communication.

2. Blockchain for the Public Sector and Government Services

Blockchain has the potential of improving government operations and services and furthering state policies effectively. It can reduce operational costs whilst augmenting transparency between public sector agencies and citizens. Based on academic literature, the prominent use cases of blockchain technology in the public sector include (a) managing digital identities of citizens in an effective manner to facilitate the application of government services; (b) enabling the registration of asset ownership by storing signature and timestamp linked to the document on a blockchain network, which can be validated by peers using consensus mechanisms; (c) employing blockchain-based voting systems to provide transparency of the entire process and to maintain immutability of voting records; and (d) storing health records of its citizens securely on a blockchain network. (Alketbi et al., 2018) As stated by the then United Kingdom (UK) Government Chief Scientific Adviser, Sir Mark Walport, "Distributed ledger technology has the potential to transform the delivery of public and private services. It has the potential to redefine the relationship between government and the citizen in terms of data sharing, transparency and trust and make a leading contribution to the government's digital transformation plan." (Government Office for Science, 2016) Besides the UK, Global Blockchain Council, a public-private initiative was set up by the Dubai Government to allow collaboration of local and international entities and government agencies to promote the development of blockchain technology. (Alketbi et al., 2018) In furtherance that, Hawaii's proposed legislation to establish a working group to explore best practices concerning blockchain technology "recognizes the vast potential for this technology to drastically change and improve public sector operations and private industry capabilities". ("H.B. 1418, 29th Leg., Reg. Sess. (Haw.)," 2017)

3. Blockchain in Finance

A pertinent use case of blockchain technology is blockchain-based tokenization. "Tokenization converts the value stored in tangible or intangible object into a token".(Ernst & Young, 2020) Tokenization can convert almost any asset, regardless of whether it is a real or virtual asset. Blockchain technology facilitates the ownership, storage, and transfer of these tokens in a frictionless, secure and efficient manner without the need of a third party, thus providing various benefits to a variety of sectors.(Ernst & Young, 2020; Kharitonova, 2021; Uzsoki, 2019) There are four different types of tokens, namely "currency tokens", "security tokens", "utility tokens" and "asset-backed tokens". Even though most of these tokens are generated via Initial Coin Offerings ("ICO"), these tokens can be allotted without ICOs such as currency tokens and asset-backed tokens.(Garcia-Teruel & Simón-Moreno, 2021) Diverse token designs enable different applications.

1. Currency tokens are used to make payments or exchanges.
2. Utility tokens allow the holders to have access to and benefit from an application or service.(Garcia-Teruel & Simón-Moreno, 2021; Gurrea-Martínez & Remolina, 2020)
3. Asset-backed tokens are digital tokens that represent the "ownership of a real-world physical asset". (Brukhanskyi & Spilnyk, 2019)
4. Security tokens constitute the digital representation of shares or securities in companies.(Garcia-Teruel & Simón-Moreno, 2021)

There is a multitude of advantages that tokenization offers to investors and issuers. Tokenization can improve the liquidity of assets.(J. Zhou et al., 2020) For example, real estates are illiquid assets due to their high value, thus reducing the demand for such assets, and resulting in non-diversifiable risks.(Baum, 2021) Asset tokenization facilitates fractional ownership of assets. This can generate greater demand for tokens from the wider group of traders, increases the risk-reward characteristics and liquidity of assets. (Baum, 2021) Blockchain can also store ownership records that arise from the trade of fractionalised real estate assets securely. Besides that, tokens are transacted by the use of smart contracts which facilitate speedier and automated transactions.(J. Zhou et al., 2020) It allows for increased transparency and traceability, as the rights and responsibilities of the token holder are attached directly to the token. (J. Zhou et al., 2020)

In comparison to other emerging technologies encompassing the Fourth Industry Revolution, blockchain has portrayed the "most promise for radical disruption".(Verberne, 2018) In furtherance of the discussion above on real-world use cases, jurisdictions have enacted enabling laws to allow seamless adoption of blockchain technology. The Information Technology & Innovation Foundation, in an article titled "A Policymakers' Guide to Blockchain", has elucidated 10 principles to facilitate policymakers in regulating blockchain applications and use cases in various industries.(Castro & McQuinn, 2019) Policies and regulations enacted should enable research and development of blockchain technology and facilitate its use in private and public sectors.(Castro & McQuinn, 2019) The adoption of technology-neutral regulation and flexible regulatory framework can create a "level playing field between the traditional and emerging technology or business model" and allow emerging technological innovations to thrive.(Castro & McQuinn, 2019) In the next section, the author would provide a descriptive overview of blockchain-related legislation in various jurisdictions.

PURPOSE OF ENACTING BLOCKCHAIN-RELATED LEGISLATION

To integrate blockchain-based solutions in various sectors, it is pertinent to bridge the gap by gradual policy shifts. Legal barriers, such as the "incompatibility" of the current legislative framework with blockchain-based applications pose major issues in the evolution and development of blockchain technology.(Allessie et al., 2019) As legislation is generally enacted to advance and achieve policy objectives, the primary policy objective to "increase technological and ecosystem maturity" of blockchain technology can be successfully achieved by rehashing and redefining the "governance" framework.(Allessie et al., 2019) The lack of a proper regulatory structure and governance framework may hamper the utilization of blockchain-use cases as there is no effective regulatory oversight or recognition of blockchain.

Two types of legislation can be passed to address the advent of blockchain technology, namely (a) "enabling legislation" and (b) "prohibitive legislation".(Mills, 2017) Policymakers and regulators can promote blockchain innovation by enacting flexible and enabling legislation. This facilitates a widespread utilization of blockchain-based use cases as it provides certainty to investors and business entities that the adoption of blockchain is "legally authorized" and "legitimate".(Mills, 2017) Besides that, the comprehensive framework of enabling laws steers the conduct of business entities in meeting the requirements of law when adopting blockchain technology. For instance, the companies incorporated in Delaware can now maintain stock ledgers by using distributed ledger technologies. Nevertheless, even though records of the corporation can be kept by way of "1 or more electronic networks or databases (including 1 or more distributed electronic networks or databases)", these records must be capable of being "converted into clearly legible paper form within a reasonable time".("S.B. 69, 149th Gen. Assemb., Reg. Sess, (Del)," 2017) The enactment of "enabling legislation" for blockchain technology may also provide incentives to corporations that adopt blockchain-based solutions. For example, Vermont passed S.B 269 of 2017 relating to Blockchain Business Development that allows a limited liability company to be set up for the purposes of operating a business that utilizes blockchain technology for a significant part of its business activities. ("S.B. 269, Leg., Reg. Sess. (Vt.)," 2017) To safeguard the interest of owners from being personally liable for debts or liabilities, they may elect to form a blockchain-based limited liability company (BBLLC). Besides that, policymakers and regulators can enact legislation to "signal their commitment" to draw investors and blockchain start-ups to their country, thus accelerating the growth of blockchain-based use cases.(Neitz, 2020) As discussed in the section below, several states in the United States and countries like Switzerland, Luxembourg, and Malta have enacted enabling legislation concerning blockchain technology. Other countries are incrementally passing legislation that business entities and corporations can leverage to successfully implement blockchain technology. Besides that, the legal recognition of blockchain technology by policymakers and regulators may confer a "first mover" benefit, which can spur economic growth by attracting investors and harnessing the possibilities of blockchain technology in that country.(Condos et al., 2016) The country can gain a competitive advantage over other countries by legally recognizing blockchain technology. For instance, by the introduction of blockchain laws in Vermont, Jill Rickard, the "Director of Policy at Vermont's Department of Financial Regulation" stated that "We're the first mover in this area[…]" and the adoption of blockchain has "the potential to be huge for the state if we allow these business entities to incorporate here, whereas they're not really possible in other states".(Landen, 2018) Therefore, besides attracting blockchain start-ups and increasing tax revenue, countries can earn the title of a technology-friendly nation.(Neitz, 2020) In the next section, the authors will advance their discussion to provide a factual and descriptive overview of enabling laws that have been passed by regulators in various jurisdictions.

The widespread adoption of blockchain-related legislation has triggered a debate on the necessity of adopting enabling laws. It has to be determined whether the country needs to provide prior authorization before corporations are allowed to leverage blockchain technology.(Tinianow & Klayman, 2017) Besides that, with the deficit of blockchain-related legislation in various sectors and jurisdictions, it has to be ascertained whether the application of blockchain in those areas should be deemed invalid.(Tinianow & Klayman, 2017) In the US, it would be impractical and unfeasible for state governments to enact blockchain-related legislation for every sector.(Tinianow & Klayman, 2017) If this is not thoroughly considered, it might lead to "a hodgepodge of legislation covering different functions, with different standards, and different levels of specificity".(Tinianow & Klayman, 2017) Business entities may be embroiled with uncertainty and face "compliance challenges", more so if businesses operate in more than one jurisdiction.(Tinianow & Klayman, 2017) Scholars suggest the enactment of enabling legislation only when the existing legislation creates "ambiguity regarding the permissibility" of employing blockchain technology.(Tinianow & Klayman, 2017) If the existing laws do not hinder the application of blockchain technology, going through the entire legislative process to enact industry-specific legislation may be superfluous.(Tinianow & Klayman, 2017)

Legislation is also enacted to protect the public from harm by prohibiting several activities related to blockchain-based use cases and applications. As blockchain technology is rapidly evolving, various issues ensue from its adoption. Scholars have divided these issues into various aspects, namely jurisdictional conundrum, security and privacy issues, and "governance impacts".(Salmon & Myers, 2019) Jurisdictional issues can arise by the use of blockchain technology, as multiple "nodes of a decentralized ledger" are not at a particular place and may "span multiple locations". (Salmon & Myers, 2019) There is no consistent approach for determining which country has legal jurisdiction, making it a complex issue to be resolved. Besides that, scholars have asserted that blockchain technology is in conflict with privacy and data protection laws.(Salmon & Myers, 2019) Article 17 of the General Data Protection Regulation (GDPR) exemplifies the "right to be forgotten".("General Data Protection Regulation (GDPR)," 2016) Pursuant to Article 17, a data subject has the "right to obtain from the controller the erasure of personal data […] without undue delay".("General Data Protection Regulation (GDPR)," 2016) However, the data on the blockchain ledger is notoriously difficult to be altered or modified, and therefore it is "practically immutable".(Dunjic, 2018) Secondly, Article 25 of GDPR, requires privacy by design and by default.("General Data Protection Regulation (GDPR)," 2016) It requires the organization to adopt "appropriate technical and organisational measures […] designed to implement data-protection principles". ("General Data Protection Regulation (GDPR)," 2016) It also requires the integration of "necessary safeguards into the processing in order to meet the requirements of this Regulation and protect the rights of data subjects".("General Data Protection Regulation (GDPR)," 2016) The "pseudo-anonymous data" recorded on a blockchain ledger is incongruous with Article 25. Besides that, the data controller and data processor defined under Article 4 GDPR have distinct roles and responsibilities under the GDPR. ("General Data Protection Regulation (GDPR)," 2016) Under Article 24 GDPR, the data controller is required to "implement appropriate technical and organisational measures" to ensure that the processing of personal data is in compliance with the GDPR.("General Data Protection Regulation (GDPR)," 2016) Nevertheless, there appears to be a stark contradiction with blockchain technology because in the blockchain landscape, there is no reliance on third-party intermediaries due to its trustless nature, and absence of control by a centralized authority.(Thukral, 2021) In a peer-to-peer public blockchain network, it is difficult to determine if the blockchain participants are controllers or processors.(Bayle et al., 2018; Salmon & Myers, 2019) This is because all participants have access to the blockchain ledger and are able to contribute to the blockchain network by adding transactions.(Bayle et al., 2018) Conversely, the different levels of participation of peers in a blockchain network might be able to establish the extent to which they are controllers.(Salmon & Myers, 2019) The inconsistency of the provisions set out in GDPR and the application of blockchain technology may be due to the composition and operability of the blockchain system, which was not "anticipated" when enacting GDPR.(Bayle et al., 2018) Blockchain technology poses the risk of cyber-attacks. The blockchain wallet stores the private key and maintains "public-key transaction-history" which is not hack-proof.(Thukral, 2021) Besides that, blockchain systems that utilize the proof of work consensus mechanism are susceptible to 51% attacks where the malicious miner(s) control "more than 50%" of the hash rate. (Mingxiao et al., 2017). Other challenges arise, such as determining who should be accountable in a peer-to-peer blockchain network and questions of liability.(Salmon & Myers, 2019) It is evident that policymakers and regulators play an important role in enacting enabling and prohibitive legislation in line with policy objectives. As a result of rapid development of blockchain technology, regulatory initiatives should be heightened to promote innovation, while protecting members of the public.

BLOCKCHAIN-RELATED LEGISLATION IN VARIOUS COUNTRIES

Various countries have legal and regulatory structures in place pertaining to blockchain-based applications. Blockchain legislative landscape is rapidly evolving, and an in-depth analysis is provided to offer a legal and contextual perspective of the regulatory trends across the globe on real-world blockchain use cases. The legislation enacted by the following countries can be regarded as blockchain enabling legislation. The enactment of such legislation is able to signify the "confidence" of the country in the deployment and adoption of blockchain technology.(Tinianow & Klayman, 2017)

1. United States

On 23 June 2021, the Consumer Safety Technology Act was passed in the House of Representatives. ("H.R. 3723, 117th Congress," 2021) Title II and III of the Consumer Safety Technology Act concern Blockchain Technology Innovation and Digital Token Taxonomy, where Title II is cited as Blockchain Innovation Act, while Title III is cited as the Digital Taxonomy Act. The Blockchain Innovation Act necessitates the Department of Commerce in consultation with the Federal Trade Commission (FTC) to undertake a study on the use cases of blockchain technology and its benefits in preventing fraud. The Digital Taxonomy Act requires a study to be conducted on unfair or deceptive acts or practices in the digital token sector. ("H.R. 3723, 117th Congress," 2021) As the law can only be passed if both the Senate and the House of Representatives debate and vote on the same legislation, it remains to be seen if the Bill will be passed by the Senate.(Drake, 2021) Legislators have until now not passed any significant federal laws concerning the application of blockchain technology. Instead, various states in the US have introduced their legislation on blockchain technology which aim to provide greater certainty to blockchain transactions. These legislations generally relate to three areas, namely corporate law, contract law, and state services. The legislative approach adopted by state legislatures endeavour to provide direction and framework for blockchain technology to facilitate its development without the imposition of unwarranted restrictions. (Suda et al., 2017)

a. Arizona

In 2017, Arizona passed a bill on the amendment of existing legislation to provide recognition to blockchain technology. Arizona House Bill 2417, which was introduced in February 2017 and passed as law in March 2017, amended Title 44, Chapter 26 of Arizona Revised Statutes (ARS) on Electronic Transactions. (Caytas, 2017; "H.R. 2417, 53d Leg., 1st Reg. Sess. (Ariz.)," 2017) It acknowledges the validity of signatures, records and contracts "secured through blockchain technology". By the addition of Article 5, the statute now reads that "a signature that is secured through blockchain technology is considered to be in an electronic form and to be an electronic signature" and "a record or contract that is secured through blockchain technology is considered to be in an electronic form and to be an electronic record". ("H.R. 2417, 53d Leg., 1st Reg. Sess. (Ariz.)," 2017) Besides that, a contract is not to be denied legal effect, validity, or enforceability merely because the contract contains a smart contractual term.

Chapter 26, Article 5 of ARS also defines "blockchain technology"[1] and "smart contract"[2]. ("H.R. 2417, 53d Leg., 1st Reg. Sess. (Ariz.)," 2017) Nevertheless, the definition of data on the blockchain ledger as "immutable and auditable and provides an uncensored truth" appears to pose a conundrum. ("H.R. 2417, 53d Leg., 1st Reg. Sess. (Ariz.)," 2017)

With Ethereum hard fork, blockchain transactions can be reversed through consensus reached from the Ethereum community. (Walch, 2016) Therefore, the inclusion of the phrase "immutable" leads to confusion in the interpretation of the statute, as it does not reflect the practical reality of blockchain. Besides that, data entered on a blockchain ledger may be inaccurate or false. "If a false piece of data is put on a blockchain ledger, it remains false[…]" (Walch, 2017) Ascertaining the truth of blockchain data is contingent on the steps taken externally as the truth of data on the blockchain ledger depends on the quality and verity of data entered on the blockchain ledger. (Finck, 2018a; Walch, 2016; Walch, 2017) For regulators to make sound decisions on blockchain technology, they should comprehend the technology's features and risks, and be aware of the technological terminology used when regulating blockchain technology. (Walch, 2017) The State Senator of Arizona voiced its concerns on the naivety of blockchain technology, security and privacy protections, which needs to be addressed. (Suda et al., 2017)

b. Delaware

On 2 May 2016, Governor Jack Markell launched the Delaware Blockchain Initiative to commemorate the era of blockchain technology. Delaware State Bar Association's Corporation Law Council proposed the amendment of DGCL that would enable corporations registered in Delaware to utilise blockchain technology for the purposes of maintaining stockholders' registries and recording the issuance and/or transfer of shares. (Caytas, 2017) The amendments are reflected under Section 219(a), 219(c), 224, and 232 of Title 8 of DGCL. ("S.B. 69, 149th Gen. Assemb., Reg. Sess, (Del)," 2017) Section 219 provides for the preparation of a list of stockholders permitted to vote at the meeting of stockholders. Before the amendment, the previous Section 219(a) stated that "The officer who has charge of the stock ledger of a corporation shall prepare and make, at least 10 days before every meeting of stockholders, a complete list of the stockholders entitled to vote at the meeting […]".The amendment makes a pertinent change to Section 219(a) where the wording "officer who has charge of the stock ledger" is deleted, and the amended provision provides that "The corporation shall prepare, at least 10 days before every meeting of stockholders, a complete list of the stockholders entitled to vote at the meeting". ("S.B. 69, 149th Gen. Assemb., Reg. Sess, (Del)," 2017) The simplified model requiring an individual to maintain records, consisting of the stock ledger is departed from, and a more liberal approach is instead espoused to facilitate the adoption of distributed ledger technology. (Laster & Rosner, 2017) Section 219(c) defines stock ledger as records administered by or on behalf of the corporation detailing the name, address and number of shares of the "corporation's stockholders of record" and "all issuances and transfers of stock of the corporation" recorded in accordance with Section 224 of Title 8. ("S.B. 69, 149th Gen. Assemb., Reg. Sess, (Del)," 2017) The amendment to Section 219(c) clarifies that the administration of stock ledger can be delegated to third parties and need not be administered internally, within the corporation. (Laster & Rosner, 2017)

Before the amendment of Section 224, it was set out in the legislation that "Any records maintained by a corporation in the regular course of its business […] may be kept on, or by means of, or be in the form of, any information storage device or method". After the amendment, the Act provides that "Any records administered by or on behalf of the corporation in the regular course of its business, […] may be kept on, or by means of […] 1 or more electronic networks or databases (including 1 or more distributed electronic networks or databases)". ("S.B. 69, 149th Gen. Assemb., Reg. Sess, (Del)," 2017) Firstly, the provision no longer exemplifies that the records must be maintained by corporations. Secondly, corporations are permitted to utilise distributed ledger technology to maintain records. Based on the blockchain use cases, the adoption of blockchain technology can accurately reflect shareholder ownership of authorized shares and the number of outstanding shares.(Strassman, n.d.) Therefore, the progressive amendments made by Delaware in the area of corporate law should be applauded.(Strassman, n.d.; Tinianow & Long, 2017)

Besides that, Section 232 of DGCL allows notice to be given in the form of electronic transmission. The definition of Section 232 (c) on electronic transmission is amended to include "[…] the use of, or participation in, one or more electronic networks or databases (including one or more distributed electronic networks or databases) […]". This amendment is necessary to accommodate the utilisation of blockchain technology. ("S.B. 69, 149th Gen. Assemb., Reg. Sess, (Del)," 2017)

With the enactment of the abovementioned legislation, Delaware legally recognizes blockchain technology and provides legal clarity in the area of corporate law. Business entities can streamline operations and business processes by leveraging the benefits of blockchain technology. Nevertheless, several issues emanate from the legislative provisions introduced by Delaware. These provisions imply that the entire stockholder record should be "maintained on the chain" by corporations.(*A Big Lesson from the Delaware Blockchain Amendments*, 2018) As the number of blockchain nodes increase, the system becomes ineffective due to limited storage capacity and scalability. (*A Big Lesson from the Delaware Blockchain Amendments*, 2018)

c. Illinois

The Blockchain Technology Act (BTA) came into effect on 1 January 2020. In line with other State Acts, this Act addresses the validity and enforceability of smart contracts, records or signatures which are created, stored, or verified by blockchain technology. Under Section 10(b), the "evidence of a smart contract, record, or signature must not be excluded solely because a blockchain was used to create, store, or verify the smart contract, record, or signature".("205 ILCS 730 Blockchain Technology Act.," 2020) Besides that, pursuant to Section 10(c), if a law necessitates a "record to be in writing, submission of a blockchain which electronically contains the records satisfies the law".("205 ILCS 730 Blockchain Technology Act.," 2020) In furtherance to that, Section 10(d) provides that if a law necessitates a signature, "submission of a blockchain which electronically contains the signature […]satisfies the law". ("205 ILCS 730 Blockchain Technology Act.," 2020) BTA is a holistic legislation that facilitates blockchain implementation in Illinois. BTA provides the desired legal certainty to business entities and members of the public concerning blockchain and smart contracts, and elucidates the "evidentiary standards". (Milewski, 2020)

Section 15(a) to (e) places several "limitations to the use of blockchain".("205 ILCS 730 Blockchain Technology Act.," 2020) For instance Section 15(a) which provides that if the parties have reached a consensus to conduct transactions via blockchain, and a law necessitates that "a contract or other record relating to the transaction be in writing", the record associated with the transaction can be denied legal validity or enforceability if the blockchain entailing an electronic record of the transaction "is not in a form that is capable of being retained and accurately reproduced" for persons entitled to retain the record of transaction. ("205 ILCS 730 Blockchain Technology Act.," 2020) Besides that, pursuant to Section

15(b) (subject to Section 15(f)), if the law other than this Act necessitates the record to be displayed, communicated or transmitted in a particular manner, the use of blockchain to "post, display, send, communicate, transmit, or store" such record does not meet the requirement of the other law. ("205 ILCS 730 Blockchain Technology Act.," 2020)

The role of local government is stipulated in the Act, where Section 20(b) allows the local government to utilise blockchain or smart contract for the purposes of performance of its powers or duties, in line with the Act. Pursuant to Section 20(a), the local government is not to impose any tax or licensing requirements concerning the utilisation of blockchain or smart contract by an individual or organization. ("205 ILCS 730 Blockchain Technology Act.," 2020) Therefore, unlike other State Acts, the Blockchain Technology Act also deals with the role of the local government in relation to blockchain and smart contract.

Besides that, Public Act 101-0259, cited as Blockchain Business Development Act came into effect on 6 January 2020. Section 10 provides that the Department of Financial and Professional Regulation shall review the possible use cases of blockchain technology to banking provisions and the required legislative changes, and submit a report on it.("IL Public Act 101-0504," 2019) As set out in Section 15, the Department of Commerce and Economic Opportunity shall integrate in its economic development and business support programs topics on blockchain technology. ("IL Public Act 101-0504," 2019)

d. Nevada

Based on the discussion below, Nevada is viewed as a blockchain technology-friendly state. In 2017, Senate Bill 398 was passed into legislation. This Act pertains to electronic transactions and recognises blockchain technology as a form of "electronic record" for the purposes of "Uniform Electronic Transactions Act". ("NV Rev Stat § 719," 2013; "S.B. 398, 79th Leg. Sess. (Nev.)," 2017) Section 1 of SB 398 amends Chapter 719 of Nevada Revised Statutes ("NRS") by defining blockchain as an "electronic record of transaction" which is "uniformly ordered", "processed using a decentralized method[…]", "redundantly maintained […] to guarantee the consistency or nonrepudiation of the recorded transactions" and "validated by the use of cryptography".("S.B. 398, 79th Leg. Sess. (Nev.)," 2017) Section 3 amends NRS 719.090 by including blockchain within the definition of "electronic record".("S.B. 398, 79th Leg. Sess. (Nev.)," 2017) Section 4 and Section 6 of this Act amends Chapter 244 and Chapter 268 of NRS respectively and provides that a local government is prohibited from imposing tax, certification or licensing requirements, and any other requirements in relation to the use of blockchain. ("S.B. 398, 79th Leg. Sess. (Nev.)," 2017) Nevada appears to be the first state in the US to prohibit the imposition of tax on the use of blockchain technology, which confers a "safe harbor" for corporations and business entities to leverage blockchain technology.(Kieckhefer, n.d.) However, licensing fees can still be imposed.(Kieckhefer, n.d.) Legislation enacted by Nevada recognises blockchain technology and includes it under the sphere of "electronic record".(Kieckhefer, n.d.) It facilitates the use of blockchain technology as individuals and business entities have the "comfort of knowing that transactions conducted over a blockchain would be recognized in Nevada's laws".(Kieckhefer, n.d.)

Nevada also passed Senate Bills 161, 162, 163, and 164 into laws in 2019. SB 161 is associated with financial businesses and creates a regulatory sandbox known as the Regulatory Experimentation Program for Product Innovation. It delineates the conditions for the operation of the Regulatory Experimentation Program and confers a temporary exemption for 2 years from regulatory requirements. By the passing of this bill, it creates a conducive and safe environment for companies to test their products without having to undergo the licensing approval process. ("S.B. 161, 80th Leg. Sess. (Nev.)," 2019)

SB 162 revises provisions concerning electronic transactions by amending Chapter 719 of NRS. Section 7 of SB 162 amends the definition of "blockchain" to include "public blockchain". A public blockchain is defined under Section 2 of SB 162.("S.B. 162, 80st Leg. Sess. (Nev.)," 2019) Besides that, referring to the provisions before the amendment (NRS 719.350), government agencies were able to decide whether and to what extent they would "accept, process, use and rely upon an electronic record". With the coming into effect of amendments, Section 5 of SB 162 prohibits government agencies from "refusing to accept, process, use or rely upon a certified copy of a record from another governmental agency", except in the event where that agency will be required to acquire and upgrade their equipment or software to accept such copy. ("S.B. 162, 80st Leg. Sess. (Nev.)," 2019) The additions of these provisions facilitate the adoption of blockchain technology in Nevada.

Section 6 SB 163 which came into effect on 1 October 2019 revises the definition of "electronic transmission" under NRS 75.050, by specifically providing for "any form or process of communication occurring through the use of or participation in a blockchain".("S.B. 163, 80th Leg. Sess. (Nev.)," 2019) Therefore, it allows businesses to distribute notices or other communications on their internal affairs using blockchain. Section 29 of SB 163 defines "blockchain" to also include "public blockchain", and public blockchain is defined under Section 25.("S.B. 163, 80th Leg. Sess. (Nev.)," 2019) Section 8 of SB 163 allows a corporation to keep records "maintained by the corporation in the regular course of business", on or by means of a blockchain, provided such records can be converted into clear and legible paper format within a reasonable time. ("S.B. 163, 80th Leg. Sess. (Nev.)," 2019)

According to Article 10 of the Constitution of Nevada and NRS 361.228, "shares of stock and certain other forms of intangible personal property are exempt from property taxation". ("Nev. Code. Title 32. Chp 361, NRS 361.228 ", 2010; "Nev. Const. Art. 10, §1,") SB 164 clarifies that for the purposes of NRS 361.228, virtual currencies are intangible personal property". SB 164 further defines virtual currencies as a digital representation of value that is (a) created on a public blockchain; (b) "not attached to any tangible asset or fiat currency"; (c) accepted as a mode of payment; and (d) may only be "transferred, stored or traded electronically". ("S.B. 164, 80th Leg. Sess. (Nev.)," 2019)

e. Vermont

Vermont enacted HB.868 of 2016 relating to economic development provisions. By the enactment of this Act, § 1913 is added to Title 12 V.S.A, which sets out that a digital record registered in a blockchain shall be "self-authenticating" under the Vermont Rule of Evidence 902. ("H.B. 868, Gen. Assemb., Reg. Sess. (Vt)," 2016) It is worth mentioning that Vermont's "blockchain enabling" law which came into effect in 2016 does not alter the Electronic Transactions Act unlike the other states but amends Title 12: Court Procedure by adding the blockchain provision as an evidentiary rule. ("H.B. 868, Gen. Assemb., Reg. Sess. (Vt)," 2016)

Besides that, Vermont's legislators incorporated the following presumption which reads "A fact or record verified through a valid application of blockchain technology is authentic". ("H.B. 868, Gen. Assemb., Reg. Sess. (Vt)," 2016) At first glance, it may seem like a provision that provides a "guarantee" on the authenticity of the fact or record. Nevertheless, the statute simply presents a direction to the court on the manner to view data that is verified through the application of blockchain. (Kelly, 2019)

Vermont passed the S.B 269 of 2017 relating to Blockchain Business Development, which came into effect on 1 July 2018. ("S.B. 269, Leg., Reg. Sess. (Vt.)," 2017) It allows setting up a limited liability company for the purposes of operating a business that utilises blockchain technology for a "material portion" of its business activities. ("S.B. 269, Leg., Reg. Sess. (Vt.)," 2017) Therefore, as means to protect owners from being personally liable for debts or liabilities, they may elect to form a BBLLC by specifying in the "articles of organization" of such election and by complying with other additional requirements in the Act such as to (a) stipulate whether the blockchain "enabled by the BBLLC" will be fully or partly decentralized and fully or partly public or private; (b) specify the extent of "participants' access to information and read and write permissions"; (c) espouse protocols in relation to security breaches that might impact the "integrity" of blockchain technology; (d) exemplify the "rights and obligations of each group of participants". ("S.B. 269, Leg., Reg. Sess. (Vt.)," 2017) The BBLLC may provide for its own governance in its entirety or part and may adopt any reasonable algorithms to validate records, in addition to the "requirements, processes and procedures for conducting operations, or making organizational decisions". ("S.B. 269, Leg., Reg. Sess. (Vt.)," 2017) By enacting favourable laws relating to blockchain, it provides a conducive environment for businesses to adopt blockchain technology and to encourage economic development. The Act also creates a Personal Information Protection Company ("PIPC") which is essentially a business that provides "personal information protection services" to individual consumers. Such services encompass "receiving, holding and managing the disclosure or use" of personal information of an individual consumer, pursuant to a written agreement and in the best interest of the consumer. The PIPC has a fiduciary responsibility to the consumer in providing the services. ("S.B. 269, Leg., Reg. Sess. (Vt.)," 2017)

f. California

In 2018, the state legislators of California passed the Assembly Bill 2658 in 2018, which founded the Blockchain Working Group (BWG). (Blockchain Working Group, 2020) BWG was assigned to define "blockchain" and evaluate its use cases, advantages, best practices, and legal consequences. Besides that, BWG was tasked to suggest amendments to other legislations affected by the adoption of blockchain. BWG consisted of 21 members from various disciplines such as law, business, and technology. The consensus was reached by the BWG in that the definition of "blockchain" was pertinent to facilitate clear and precise policy decisions. BWG acknowledged that the definition of blockchain should be "accessible to and understandable by the public, and yet technically specific enough to ensure that the State can reap maximum benefit".(Blockchain Working Group, 2020) The BWG adopted a succinct definition of blockchain after considerable discussion on the subject. Besides that, BWG recognised that almost all of the blockchain use cases can be implemented by a centralized database. The sole reason for the application of blockchain technology is to avoid "dependency on single organizations or individuals" and to keep the ledger "honest and accountable". BWG elucidated the ethical issues concerning the social impact of blockchain technology, namely "fairness, equity, accessibility, trust and transparency, and sustainability".

An ethical framework designed by BWG is primarily addressed to regulators and policymakers. The three principles exemplified in the ethical framework are (a) addressing "key ethical design goals"; (b) considering "ethical uses of blockchain technology"; (c) minimization of "unintended consequences". (Blockchain Working Group, 2020) California's legislature has taken an important step in understanding blockchain technology and evaluating its potential value and risks before developing an extensive regulatory scheme. The Majority Leader of the California State Assembly, Ian Calderon states that

California's legislators can "learn from the mistakes made from other states that have drafted legislation for blockchain and make well informed decisions to come up with legislation that works best for California". (Wolfson, 2019) Nevertheless, California's approach might be counterproductive due to its slow pace in law-making, causing many blockchain organizations to move to other states or countries with more certain and developed legislative frameworks.

This report is off to a good start because due to California's careful deliberation, blockchain legislation grounded on the BWG report is likely to be a more even-handed and successful legislative framework in the fullness of time. (Neitz, 2020) Ian Calderon has stated that "the earliest possible implementation date on blockchain-related policy would be January 1, 2022". (Wolfson, 2019)

g. Wyoming

HB0101 amends the Wyoming Business Corporations Act to authorize corporations to use distributed or other electronic networks or databases to maintain records of the corporation provided that such records can be converted into written form within a reasonable time. ("H.B. 0101, 64th Leg., Budget Sess (Wyo.)," 2018) Besides that, by the enactment of HB0070, the Secretary of State is authorized to develop and implement a blockchain filing system for business entities. Based on the provisions under HB 0185, a business entity may issue stock certificates in the form of certificate tokens. ("H.B. 0185, 65th Leg., Gen. Sess. (Wyo.)," 2019) The certificate tokens represent the shares that are stored in an electronic format that contains certain information such as the "name of the stock recipient and the number and type of shares" which is entered into a blockchain or other secure auditable databases. ("H.B. 0185, 65th Leg., Gen. Sess. (Wyo.)," 2019) By "passing permissive legislation early and often", it signals the unwavering support of state legislators towards the growth of blockchain technology in Wyoming. (Neitz, 2020) Wyoming strives to draw blockchain start-ups/corporations and bring "employment and innovation opportunities" to the state.(Neitz, 2020)

2. Luxembourg

Distributed ledger technology was first introduced into the laws of Luxembourg in 2019, specifically the amendment to the Law of 1 August 2001 on the circulation of securities. ("Law of 1 March 2019," 2019) The new Article 18 provides that electronic recording devices such as distributed electronic registers or databases can be utilised for purposes of maintaining securities accounts or registering securities in securities accounts. ("Law of 1 March 2019," 2019)

Besides that, the Law of 22 January 2021 amending Luxembourg laws of "6 April 2013 on dematerialised securities" (Dematerialised Securities Act 2013) and "5 April 1993 on financial sector" (Banking Act 1993), further encapsulates distributed ledger technologies in Luxembourg. ("Law of 22 January 2021," 2021; Massinon & Nickel, 2021) Luxembourg Act of 6 April 2013 is amended by adding the definition of "issuer account". An issuer account is essentially an account held by a settlement institution or a central account keeper recording the dematerialised securities issued. Issuer account may be held by way of secure electronic registration devices such as distributed ledger technologies. (Kozakiewicz & Fettes, 2021; Prussen, 2021) Therefore, dematerialised securities may now be present in a distributed ledger technology environment.

In addition, the Act of 6 April 2013 (Article 1(10) & (14)) is further supplemented, and Act of 5 April 1993 (Article 28-12) is amended by allowing credit institutions and investment firms in a Member

State of the European Economic Area to partake as Central Account Keepers for purposes of the issuer accounts. This eliminates the need to obtain additional authorization from the Commission de Surveillance du Secteur Financier ("CSSF"). However, certain conditions are imposed on credit institutions and investment firms in providing their services. These entities must be able to establish that they have suitable control and security mechanisms for their computer systems to maintain central accounts which allows for (a) recording in an issuer account of all securities admitted to their operations; (b) "circulation of securities by transfer from one account to another"; (c) "verification that the total amount of each issue admitted to their transactions" and recorded in an issuer account is equivalent to the total sum of securities recorded in the securities accounts of their account holders; (d) "exercise of the rights attached to the securities registered in the securities account". ("Law of 22 January 2021," 2021; Massinon & Nickel, 2021)

3. Liechtenstein

On 3 October 2019, the Parliament of Liechtenstein adopted the "Tokens and Trusted Technology Service Providers Law" ("TVTG", officially known as Token- und VT-Dienstleister-Gesetz). For ease of discussion, the expression Liechtenstein Blockchain Act will be used. ("Token- und VT-Dienstleister-Gesetz," 2019) This Act came into effect on 1 January 2020 and focuses on tokens, expanding beyond its conventional use case of the acceleration of payments through distributed ledgers. This Act is essentially an enabling Act that creates an exhaustive set of laws that facilitate the "commodification" of blockchain-based rights and adopt property law notions in the regulation of tokens and digital assets. Many milestones led to the enactment of the Blockchain Act.

1. 2016: The Liechtenstein Government initiated a working group, which issued a draft on the Blockchain Act. The intention was to offer a conducive environment for the development of the token economy. (Johann, 2018)
2. 2017: The Knowledge Idea of a Token Container Model was developed. (*Liechtenstein is the New Powerhouse for Digital Securities*, 2021)
3. 2018: In August, the Ministry for General Government Affairs and Finance of Liechtenstein published a consultation report on the proposed Blockchain Act. The government of Liechtenstein acknowledged the importance of blockchain technology for the economy and the enactment of laws that can provide legal certainty and facilitate the development of a "token economy". (Dobrauz, 2018)
4. 2018: In November, the findings gathered from the public consultation exercise was implemented.
5. 2019: First reading in Parliament in June
6. 2019: Second reading in Parliament in October
7. 2020: The Act came into force.

The scope of the Liechtenstein Blockchain Act encompasses the regulation of all types of applications of the token economy and is not confined to applications concerning financial markets. (Government of Liechtenstein, 2019, p. 43) Based on the Report by the Government of Liechtenstein ("the Report"), token economy represents "not only purely digital assets but also digitalised rights to physical objects or digitalised rights derived from contracts". (Government of Liechtenstein, 2019, p. 46) The report states the need to draft the law as "abstractly" as possible to facilitate its applicability for future technological inventions. (Government of Liechtenstein, 2019, p. 6) Therefore, the term "transaction systems based on trustworthy technologies" ("TT system") is adopted in Liechtenstein Blockchain Act. By the introduction of legislation on tokens and trustworthy technologies ("TT") service providers, it allows recording of the "real world" in a legally secure way. This law delineates a viable legal structure for all applications of the token economy to provide legal certainty for businesses and organizations. The government of Liechtenstein intends to maintain technological neutrality, and the use of terms like "virtual" or "crypto" which depicts a technological form is not be suitable. (Government of Liechtenstein, 2019, p. 12) Besides that, a narrow classification of tokens as "crypto-currency" and "crypto-asset" disregards many possible applications of the token economy. (Government of Liechtenstein, 2019, p. 38)

Therefore, the Liechtenstein Blockchain Act introduces "tokens" as a new "legal object", considered as a movable asset that can be owned and transferred. (Kulms, 2020); ("Token- und VT-Dienstleister-Gesetz," 2019) The Report further explores the potential application of blockchain systems and clusters the current and potential applications of blockchain systems under the umbrella term of "token economy". (Government of Liechtenstein, 2019, p. 23) The Report illustrates the various use cases encapsulating the token economy. This includes digital payments via tokens, company financing, transaction of securities, asset management, music licensing rights, and supply chains.

The use cases of the token economy are associated with rights, such as movable or immovable property rights, payment claims against the debtor, intellectual property rights and right to lien. The introduction of tokens facilitates the representation of all types of rights on the TT system, in digital form. (Government of Liechtenstein, 2019, p. 54) The token is connoted as a kind of "container" that represents rights.(Allen et al., 2020) However, the creation of tokens does not generate new rights. Only existing rights are subjected to the "transmission and legitimation system of the blockchain". (Government of Liechtenstein, 2019, p. 57)

As for the Token Container Model, the token can represent any kind of right but in certain situations it can be an "empty" container, for instance, cryptocurrencies with no real value security or "collateralization". (Government of Liechtenstein, 2019, p. 54) In most situations, tokens signify the digital representation of real assets on the TT system, such as ownership rights to property. This creates a challenge from the duality of assets, namely "digital and analogue assets" and the need to maintain legal certainty. For the purchaser of the token, it is important for him to be certain that he has acquired the right accompanying the token. On the other hand, for the purchaser of the real asset, it is pertinent for him to be sure that he has acquired the asset and not be imperilled by the risk of being left "empty-handed". (Government of Liechtenstein, 2019, p. 59) Synchronicity is pertinent, both online and offline to create a proper legal framework which would facilitate the transfer of assets. More importantly, on the aspect of legal implications, the token representing a right prompts the application of laws germane to that right. For instance, for security tokens, security laws and financial market laws may be applicable. For tokens representing intellectual property rights, the laws governing intellectual property rights may be relevant. (Duenser, 2020)

The Liechtenstein Blockchain Act defines "tokens as a piece of information on a TT System which: can represent claims or rights of memberships against a person, rights to property or other absolute or relative rights; and is assigned to one or more TT Identifiers". ("Token- und VT-Dienstleister-Gesetz," 2019) Therefore, it can be denoted as a legal object which represents all kinds of rights, but one that has no physicality but only "digital character strings". (Government of Liechtenstein, 2019, p. 55 & 58) By the introduction of a new legal object, ie Token, the legal effects must be specified, particularly concerning the rights to the token and the transfer of the token. This is elucidated in Article 5(2) of the

Liechtenstein Blockchain Act, where the Act introduces two concepts, namely (a) "person possessing the right of disposal" of the token and (b) "holder of a power of disposal without wanting to be the person possessing the right of disposal". (Government of Liechtenstein, 2019, p. 62; "Token- und VT-Dienstleister-Gesetz," 2019)

The right of disposal is closely linked to the TT key as this right can only be exercised by way of a private key. "TT key" is a key that allows for the disposal of Tokens, and TT key holders have the "actual power of disposal of the Token". ("Token- und VT-Dienstleister-Gesetz," 2019) (Government of Liechtenstein, 2019, p. 55) Yet, the TT key holder may "not be the person possessing the right of disposal".(Government of Liechtenstein, 2019) Therefore, if a third party obtains the TT key unaccompanied by any authorisation, the third party obtains "de facto power of disposal over the token" and is able to conduct transactions. Nevertheless, the third party is not one who has the right of disposal and therefore is not entitled to dispose of it. (Government of Liechtenstein, 2019, p. 62)

On a separate note, the person with the power of disposal can be assumed to have the right of disposal of the Token and is considered by the TT system as the "lawful holder" of the right represented in the Token. ("Token- und VT-Dienstleister-Gesetz," 2019) In the eventuality of unauthorised acquisitions, that "assumption can be refuted".(Government of Liechtenstein, 2019) "Rights of disposal" may be delegated wholly or partly to a "deputy" by a person entitled to dispose of the token. The "deputy" would then have the "right of disposal". Such delegation is usually made to a TT Key Depositary defined as "a person who safeguards TT Keys" on behalf of customers.(Government of Liechtenstein, 2019)

This distinction of a "person possessing the right of disposal" and the "holder of a power of disposal" becomes pertinent during the use of machines and smart contracts on the TT system. (Government of Liechtenstein, 2019, p. 63) Machines and smart contracts can be connoted as TT Identifiers. "TT Identifiers" are identifiers that permit the assignment of Tokens. Therefore, machines or smart contracts have a "power of disposal" of the token (Government of Liechtenstein, 2019, p. 63)

The Blockchain Act not only governs the qualifications of Tokens but also their disposal, and this aspect is further exemplified in Articles 6 and 7 of the Act.(Government of Liechtenstein, 2019) ("Token- und VT-Dienstleister-Gesetz," 2019) Disposal transaction can be connoted as the "legal transaction by which a right is transferred, encumbered, amended or revoked". (Government of Liechtenstein, 2019, p. 63) Additionally, besides the transfer of "right of disposal", it includes a restricted right in rem such as the right of usufruct.("Token- und VT-Dienstleister-Gesetz," 2019) Disposal of a Token necessitates that the transferring party possesses the right of disposal, without which disposals are ineffective.("Token- und VT-Dienstleister-Gesetz," 2019)

The Blockchain Act also reproduces bona fide rules where persons that receive "Tokens in good faith, free of charge, for the purpose of acquiring the right of disposal or a restricted in rem right" is not obliged to return the token if he was unaware of the lack of right of disposal, notwithstanding that the transferring party was not entitled to secure such disposal of the Token. (Kulms, 2020) ("Token- und VT-Dienstleister-Gesetz," 2019) (Government of Liechtenstein, 2019, p. 122)

4. Switzerland

The Parliament of Switzerland enacted an Act on the Adaptation of Federal Law to Developments in Distributed Ledger Technology (DLT Act). The following are the important milestones prior to the enactment of the DLT Act. (Gesley, 2021)

1. 2018: In December, the Swiss Federal Council issued a report entitled the Legal Framework for Distributed Ledger Technology and Blockchain in Switzerland.
2. 2019: In November, the Swiss Federal Council issued a draft law concerning blockchain and distributed ledger technology, which went through public consultation.
3. 2020: In September, Parliament enacted the DLT Act
4. 2021: In February, certain parts of the DLT Act came into force. The remaining parts of the Act are scheduled to come into force on 1 August 2021.

With the enactment of the DLT Act, different Federal Laws are adapted. The aim of the DLT Act is not to present specific legislation on blockchain, but to incorporate provisions on crypto-assets into existing laws. (Braun-Dubler et al., 2020) With effect from 1 February 2021, the DLT Act amends the Code of Obligations, Federal Intermediated Securities Act (FISA) and Federal Act on Private International Law. The DLT Act introduces uncertificated securities, known as ledger-based securities, in these Acts.(Raijmakers, 2020) From the exploration of the legal provisions, the law does not invoke the term distributed ledger technologies and remains technology-neutral. (Gesley, 2021) Ledger-based security is defined in Article 973d of the Code of Obligation as a right which "is registered in a securities ledger" and "may be exercised and transferred" only by way of the securities ledger. Four prerequisites must be fulfilled by the securities ledger, namely (a) creditors are given "power of disposal over their rights" via technological processes; (b) its integrity is safeguarded by way of "adequate technical and organizational measures"; (c) the "content of the rights, the functioning of the ledger and the registration agreement is recorded in the ledger"; (d) the information and ledger entries may be accessed by creditors and they may inspect the integrity of the ledger. ("Swiss Federal Code of Obligations," 1911) A person who is legally bound to another, the obligor, is "entitled and obliged to render performance only to the creditor" stipulated in the securities ledger. The transfer of ledger-based securities is dependent on the registration agreement. ("Swiss Federal Code of Obligations," 1911) In furtherance to that, Article 5(h) of FISA introduces ledger-based securities, which consist of the same meaning as that provided under Article 973d of the Code of Obligations. There are far-reaching implications by such amendments to the law, where the issuance and transfer of securities can be carried out in the DLT system without the need for a signature. (Balzli, 2021) The issuance of ledger-based securities does not entail a third-party intermediary or a custodian, such as a licensed bank or a central securities depository to credit these securities to the securities account of the account holder.

With the entry into force of the other provisions of the DLT Act, legislative provisions in other acts will be also amended in line with the DLT Act. This would affect Debt Enforcement and Bankruptcy ("DEBA"), the Financial Services Act ("FinSA"), Financial Institutions Act ("FinIA"), National Bank Act ("NBA"), the Banking Act ("BA"), Anti-Money Laundering Act ("AMLA"), Financial Market Infrastructure Act ("FinMIA"), which is expected to take effect on 1 August 2021. (Güntert & Schnyder 2021)

5. Malta

In 2018, three blockchain enabling laws were enacted in Malta to facilitate innovation in the realm of blockchain and distributed ledger technology. The enactment of the "Malta Digital Innovation Authority Act" (MDIA Act), "Innovative Technology Arrangements and Services Act" (ITAS Act) and "Virtual Financial Assets Act" (VFA Act) provide regulatory certainty to businesses in implementing blockchain technology. The VFA Act will be discussed in the subsequent Chapter.

a. MDIA Act

The Act provides for the establishment of a Digital Innovation Authority to support the "development and implementation of the guiding principles" as set out in the Act, and to advance principles for the development of "visions, skills and other qualities" concerning technological innovation, which includes distributed or decentralized technology.("ACT No. XXXI of 2018," 2018) Parallel to the Preamble of the Act, Article 6 states that the object of the Authority is to explore the development in Malta of "innovative technology arrangements" (ITA) and "innovative technology services" (ITS) and "exercise such supervisory and regulatory functions" in the area of ITA and ITS.("ACT No. XXXI of 2018," 2018) The functions and powers of the Authority are further elucidated under Article 6(3) of the Act, where the Authority is to "regulate, monitor and supervise" the provision of ITA and ITS, and to promote the "interest and legitimate expectations of users" in relation to these arrangements.("ACT No. XXXI of 2018," 2018) ITAs are defined under Article 2 of the Act as "intrinsic elements including software, codes, computer protocols and other architectures which are used in the context of DLT, smart contracts and related applications".("ACT No. XXXI of 2018," 2018) Besides that, Article 3 sets out the guiding principles in that the development of the innovative technology sector shall be carried out, having regard to the significance of not thwarting innovation and making sure that standards are in place to protect consumers and investors, market integrity and public interest.("ACT No. XXXI of 2018," 2018)

b. ITAS Act

With reference to the Preamble, this Act makes provisions for the "regulation of designated" ITAs and ITSs under this Act. Besides that, Article 3(2) of the ITAS Act sets out several "methods of recognition" of ITAs and ITSs.("ACT No. XXXIII of 2018," 2018) This will promote the growth and development of technological innovation. The Authority can also certify different ITAs in relation to its "qualities", "features", "attributes", "behaviours" or "aspects".("ACT No. XXXIII of 2018," 2018) Under Article 7(6), once an ITA is certified, it shall be granted a Certificate which shall set out the "details of how the innovative technology arrangement is identified, including any public key or a brand name".("ACT No. XXXIII of 2018," 2018) The Certificate is also provided with a unique number for identification. The Authority may certify an ITA when the Authority is certain that the general and specific requirements have been complied with.("ACT No. XXXIII of 2018," 2018) The specific requirements include the necessity to have a "registered technical administrator" who can demonstrate the ability of the ITA to comply with the prerequisites for certification, as well as the standards exemplified in the guidelines issued by the Authority.("ACT No. XXXIII of 2018," 2018)

6. Dubai Blockchain Policy

Dubai has developed a Blockchain Policy ('the Policy"), which is a distinct approach from that adopted by legislative bodies of other countries.(Dubai Future Councils) The drafting process of the Policy involved four stages.(Dubai Future Councils) The first stage involved identifying and collating various challenges faced by government entities and private corporations during the deployment of blockchain use cases. The second stage involved conducting numerous workshops to deliberate on requirements and options for Blockchain policies. The third stage encompassed identifying "focus areas" to navigate the development of Blockchain policies. The focus areas are classified into three classes, namely "Network Governance", "Network Operations" and "Foundational Capabilities". Finally, the policy options were evaluated against the "guiding principles" of Dubai. The guiding principles include (a)advancing innovation and evolution of blockchain technology rather than constraining its growth; (b) promoting the efficient implementation of blockchain networks; (c) powering blockchain adoption by promoting collaboration between private sector players and the government to enhance the value of blockchain technology; (d) providing flexible guidelines with the purpose that any particular technology is not restricted in its application; (e) ensuring that the policy is in line with existing laws and regulations; (f) ensuring that security and privacy are prioritised when implementing decisions.(Dubai Future Councils).

A few Articles from the Policy will be discussed to provide an insight into the scope and application of the Policy. Based on Article 3 of the Policy, the policy applies to "Dubai Government Entities" which intend to utilise Blockchain, form a new Blockchain network or join an existing Blockchain Network; (b) "Private Sector Participants" that intend to join "Dubai Government Blockchain Network" or "Government-hosted Blockchain Platform"; (c) "Blockchain Networks and Platforms formed or hosted or joined by a Dubai Government Entity".(Dubai Future Councils) The Policy is divided into three areas, namely "Network Governance" ("NG"), "Network Operations" ("NO") and "Foundational Capabilities" ("FC"). Under the realm of NG, Articles 5 to 8 address intellectual property rights in relation to the blockchain use cases, formation of blockchain networks, on-boarding and off-boarding procedures and development of a transparent operating model, including what the operating model should contain. (Dubai Future Councils) The second area, NO sets out the requirement for publication of standardized data formats and ensuring interoperability between other Blockchain Networks, and covers data privacy and confidentiality, security and policy compliance. The last area is FC and it includes the role of the Smart Dubai City Office, utilization of smart contracts, adoption and compliance with architectures and standards, and utilization of shared services to maintain efficiency.(Dubai Future Councils) Dubai's efforts to introduce blockchain policy is beneficial to support the public and private sector in implementing blockchain technology, whilst addressing the challenges faced during the conception and development of blockchain technology and mitigating these challenges.

CONCLUSION AND RECOMMENDATION

In conclusion, regulators in different jurisdictions have adopted different approaches and pursued varying regulatory initiatives. The majority of countries have not adopted a concise regulatory framework to regulate the blockchain ecosystem. Even though some countries have regulated blockchain in some form, legislation remains in the early stages. Generally, four types of regulatory approaches can be adopted by countries, namely (a) wait and see; (b) enacting new legislation; (c) issuing guidance; and (d)regulatory sandboxing, each of which is analysed in turn. With the advent of blockchain technology and disparate regulatory strategies adopted by various jurisdictions, it has to be determined whether these strategies are "proportionate and limited to what is necessary to protect a specific public interest in a democratic society".(Wright et al., 2008)

Wait and See Approach

Regulators can adopt the wait and see approach to study and evaluate how blockchain systems develop before enacting new legislations. This regulatory strategy should not be regarded as acceding to passivity.(Finck, 2018b) Instead, during this period, regulators are "actively monitoring" the growth of blockchain technology (Parker, 2017) This includes monitoring the inherent risks and implications to the economy and society at large from the application of blockchain technology. The existing legislative framework continues to apply.(Finck, 2018b) For technology systems that have not achieved the desired level of maturity, the wait and see approach can be regarded as an "information-gathering process" before regulators decide on whether or not to legislate.(Finck, 2018b) In gathering information, regulators engage in dialogue with stakeholders, industry players and experts.(Finck, 2018b) Regulations hastily passed may not be feasible in light of technological innovation. In furtherance to that, the enactment of suboptimal regulation may hinder the deployment of blockchain technology.(Akgiray, 2019) Nevertheless, without regulations in place to address the intricacies of blockchain technology, it may result in "regulatory uncertainty" and discourage industry players and investors from investing in such business landscapes because "building a business amid regulatory uncertainty can be like building on quicksand". (Finck, 2018b)

Enacting New Legislation

As exemplified above, numerous countries have enacted new legislation to espouse a dynamic regulatory landscape for blockchain technology.(Finck, 2018b) Countries have enacted blockchain-friendly and enabling laws and regulations due to the advent of blockchain technology. The enactment of laws proves to be beneficial as it can create a level playing field for business entities inclined to adopt blockchain technology. Nevertheless, such regulatory initiatives to effectively regulate real-life blockchain applications may be counterproductive as the law enacted may become outdated due to technological development and necessitate amendments.(Finck, 2018b) It is desirable and ideal for the regulatory scheme to be technologically neutral to ensure that the law can adapt flexibly to rapid technological changes. Besides that, the approach taken by states in the US has been to establish working groups to understand the workings, processes, risks and benefits of the deployment of blockchain technology before the enactment of legislation. The working group members are from diverse backgrounds, such as policymakers, regulators, industry representatives and experts. They are able to produce an all-encompassing report through their collaborative efforts. This all-encompassing report on blockchain technology is a catalyst towards the development of the states' legislative strategy.

Issuing Guidance

Regulators can issue "regulatory guidance" on the application of existing laws. Guidance issued may prove beneficial to industry players and stakeholders as it confers certainty and may offer solutions to legal problems, more so with the evolution and development of blockchain technology.(Finck, 2018b) Besides that, it ensures that industry players are aware of the strategy adopted by regulators through the issuance of guidelines, such as advocating a hands-off approach to blockchain technology regulations. (Finck, 2018b) Industry players can then align their business activities accordingly and prevent "stupefaction when it is formalized".(Finck, 2018a) Nevertheless, guidelines are forms of soft law that do not have a legally binding effect and may be disregarded by courts when presiding over a case.(Finck, 2018a)

Regulatory Sandboxing

Regulators may perceive it to be "premature" to enact a legislative framework due to the constant evolution of blockchain technology.(Finck, 2018b) However, the absence of a legislative framework would effectively mean that investors and industry players face legal uncertainties. It might hinder investors and industry players from investing in the blockchain industry in that country and may leave the country in search of greener pastures and more conducive environments. Therefore, to attract investors, countries can adopt an approach known as regulatory "sandboxing".(Finck, 2018b) A regulatory sandbox is "a set of rules that allows innovators to test their product or business model in an environment that temporarily exempts them from following some or all legal requirements in place".(Finck, 2018b) This approach benefits regulators and business entities within the safe space conditions of a regulatory sandbox. It can facilitate innovation in the particular industry due to low regulatory barriers. Nevertheless, due to the "lack [of] transparency", it can create an unequal level playing field for market players.(Finck, 2018b)

As blockchain-based applications continue to emerge, lawmakers may have to resolve the regulatory conundrum surfacing from the rapid development of blockchain technology. Even though the countries that have enacted legislations (as explained above) are likely to have a competitive lead, there is no fool proof regulatory approach. Therefore, in an attempt to devise an effective regulatory framework, lawmakers could have a policy dialogue by engaging stakeholders in meaningful discussions during the policy development process. Besides that, lawmakers can look to other countries to obtain information on the approach that has been adopted and gather insights on the challenges faced by these countries. Considering that blockchain technology provides promising opportunities in various sectors, it is pertinent to provide a conducive regulatory landscape to allow innovation while ensuring that proper safeguards are in place to minimize risks arising from blockchain technology.

FUTURE RESEARCH DIRECTIONS

This chapter offers a descriptive discussion on legislation adopted by various countries to address blockchain technology. The subsequent chapters, "A Pragmatic Regulatory Framework for Artificial Intelligence: Regulating Artificial Intelligence" and "Comparative Review of the Regulatory Framework of Cryptocurrency in Selected Jurisdictions: Insights on Cryptocurrency Regulations" complements this chapter. The legal implications of blockchain technology have been further addressed in those chapters. This chapter also serves as a blueprint for future work in conducting a comparative analytical study on the regulatory initiatives of each country concerning "enabling" and "prohibitive" legislation.

REFERENCES

A Big Lesson from the Delaware Blockchain Amendments. (2018). https://koreprotocol.medium.com/a-big-lesson-from-the-delaware-blockchain-amendments-9789e34f6c9f

Akgiray, V. (2019). *The Potential for Blockchain Technology in Corporate Governance*. OECD Publishing. https://www.oecd-ilibrary.org/content/paper/ef4eba4c-en

Al-Megren, S., Alsalamah, S., Altoaimy, L., Alsalamah, H., Soltanisehat, L., & Almutairi, E. (2018). Blockchain use cases in digital sectors: A review of the literature. *2018 IEEE International Conference on Internet of Things (iThings) and IEEE Green Computing and Communications (GreenCom) and IEEE Cyber, Physical and Social Computing (CPSCom) and IEEE Smart Data (SmartData).*

Alketbi, A., Nasir, Q., & Talib, M. A. (2018). Blockchain for government services—Use cases, security benefits and challenges. *2018 15th Learning and Technology Conference (L&T).*

Allen, J. G., Rauchs, M., Blandin, A., & Bear, K. (2020). *Legal and Regulatory Considerations for Digital Assets.* https://www.jbs.cam.ac.uk/wp-content/uploads/2020/10/2020-ccaf-legal-regulatory-considerations-report.pdf

Allessie, D., Sobolewski, M., & Vaccari, L. (2019). *Blockchain for digital government.* https://joinup.ec.europa.eu/sites/default/files/document/2019-04/JRC115049%20blockchain%20for%20digital%20government.pdf

Attaran, M. (2020). Blockchain technology in healthcare: Challenges and opportunities. *International Journal of Healthcare Management*, 1-14. doi:10.1080/20479700.2020.1843887

Balzli, T. R. (2021). *New tech act in Switzerland secures legal environment, allows blockchain to flourish.* Retrieved June 30, 2021 from https://www.imd.org/news/updates/new-tech-act-Switzerland-secures-legal-environment-blockchain-flourish/

Bashir, I. (2018). *Mastering Blockchain: Distributed ledger technology, decentralization, and smart contracts explained* (2nd ed.). Packt Publishing. https://books.google.com.my/books?id=3ZlUDwAAQBAJ

Baum, A. (2021). Tokenization—The Future of Real Estate Investment? *Journal of Portfolio Management, 47*(7).

Bayle, A., Koscina, M., Manset, D., & Perez-Kempner, O. (2018). When blockchain meets the right to be forgotten: technology versus law in the healthcare industry. *2018 IEEE/WIC/ACM International Conference on Web Intelligence (WI).*

Blockchain Working Group. (2020). *Blockchain in California: A Roadmap.* https://www.govops.ca.gov/blockchain/

Braun-Dubler, N., Gier, H. P., Bulatnikova, T., Langhart, M., Merki, M., Roth, F., ... der ETH Zürich, H. A. G. (2020). *Blockchain: Capabilities, Economic Viability, and the Socio-Technical Environment.* vdf Hochschulverlag ETH Zurich. https://books.google.com.my/books?id=QLbrDwAAQBAJ

Brukhanskyi, R., & Spilnyk, I. (2019). Cryptographic objects in the accounting system. *2019 9th International Conference on Advanced Computer Information Technologies (ACIT).*

Castro, D., & McQuinn, A. (2019). *A Policymaker's Guide to Blockchain.* https://itif.org/publications/2019/04/30/policymakers-guide-blockchain

Caytas, J. (2017). Blockchain in the US regulatory setting: Evidentiary use in Vermont, Delaware, and elsewhere. *The Columbia Science and Technology Law Review.*

Chen, G., Xu, B., Lu, M., & Chen, N.-S. (2018). Exploring blockchain technology and its potential applications for education. *Smart Learning Environments*, 5(1), 1–10.

Condos, J., Sorrell, W. H., & Donegan, S. L. (2016). *Blockchain Technology: Opportunities and Risks.* https://sos.vermont.gov/media/253f2tpu/vermontstudycommittee_blockchaintechnology_opportunities-andrisks_finalreport_2016.pdf

de Jong, J., Meyer, A., & Owens, J. (2017). Using blockchain for transparent beneficial ownership registers. *Int'l Tax Rev.*, 28, 47.

Drake, E. (2021). *2 new blockchain bills head for US Senate.* Retrieved June 30, 2021 from https://coingeek.com/2-new-blockchain-bills-head-for-us-senate/

Dubai Future Councils. (n.d.a). *Dubai Blockchain Policy.* https://www.smartdubai.ae/docs/default-source/policies-standards/dubai-blockchain-policy.pdf?sfvrsn=ddfaec24_4

Dubai Future Councils. (n.d.b). *Dubai Blockchain Policy Brief.* https://www.smartdubai.ae/docs/default-source/publications/brief---dubai-blockchain-policyd78f44970b3a47269cc95fd6a742df06.pdf?sfvrsn=2ff3e093_2

Duenser, T. G. (2020). *Legalize Blockchain: How States Should Deal with Today's Most Promising Technology to foster prosperity.* https://books.google.com.my/books?id=EcLoDwAAQBAJ

Dunjic, M. (2018). Blockchain Immutability ... Blessing or Curse? *Finextra.* https://www.finextra.com/blogposting/15419/blockchain-immutability--blessing-or-curse

Ernst & Young. (2020). *Tokenization of Assets.* Retrieved June 30, 2021 from https://assets.ey.com/content/dam/ey-sites/ey-com/en_ch/topics/blockchain/ey-tokenization-of-assets-broschure-final.pdf

Finck, M. (2018a). *Blockchain Regulation and Governance in Europe.* Cambridge University Press. https://books.google.com.my/books?id=pMd6DwAAQBAJ

Finck, M. (2018b). Blockchains: Regulating the Unknown. *German Law Journal*, 19(4), 665–692.

Furlonger, D., & Uzureau, C. (2019). *The Real Business of Blockchain: How Leaders Can Create Value in a New Digital Age.* Harvard Business Review Press. https://books.google.com.my/books?id=B5U4wQEACAAJ

Garcia-Teruel, R. M., & Simón-Moreno, H. (2021). The digital tokenization of property rights. A comparative perspective. *Computer Law & Security Review*, 41, 105543.

General Data Protection Regulation (GDPR), (2016).

Gesley, J. (2021). *Switzerland: New Amending Law Adapts Several Acts to Developments in Distributed Ledger Technology.* Retrieved June 30, 2021 from https://www.loc.gov/law/foreign-news/article/switzerland-new-amending-law-adapts-several-acts-to-developments-in-distributed-ledger-technology/

Government of Liechtenstein. (2019). *Report and application of the government to the parliament of the Principality of Liechtenstein concerning the creation of a law on tokens and TT service providers (Tokens and TT Service Providers Act, TVTG) and the amendment of other laws (No. 54/2019).* https://www.naegele.law/files/Downloads/2019-07-12_BuA_TVTG_en_full_report.pdf

Government Office for Science. (2016). *Distributed ledger technology: beyond block chain*. https://www.gov.uk/government/news/distributed-ledger-technology-beyond-block-chain

Güntert, M., & Schnyder, F. (2021). *Ledger-based securities: introduction of DLT shares in Switzerland*. https://pestalozzilaw.com/en/news/legal-insights/ledger-based-securities-introduction-dlt-shares-switzerland/

Gurrea-Martínez, A., & Remolina, N. (2020). Corporate Governance Challenges in Initial Coin Offerings. *Singapore Management University School of Law Research Paper, 19*.

H.B. 0101, 64th Leg., Budget Sess (Wyo.), (2018). https://www.wyoleg.gov/Legislation/2018/HB0101

H.B. 0185, 65th Leg., Gen. Sess. (Wyo.), (2019). https://www.wyoleg.gov/Legislation/2019/HB0185

H.B. 1418, 29th Leg., Reg. Sess. (Haw.), (2017).

H.B. 868, Gen. Assemb., Reg. Sess. (Vt), (2016).

H.R. 2417, 53d Leg., 1st Reg. Sess. (Ariz.), (2017). https://www.azleg.gov/legtext/53leg/1r/bills/hb2417p.pdf

H.R. 3723, 117th Congress, (2021).

Hughes, S. D. (2017). *Cryptocurrency Regulations and Enforcement in the US*. Academic Press.

Humayun, M., Jhanjhi, N., Hamid, B., & Ahmed, G. (2020). Emerging Smart Logistics and Transportation Using IoT and Blockchain. *IEEE Internet of Things Magazine, 3*(2), 58-62. doi:10.1109/IOTM.0001.1900097

IL Public Act 101-0504, (2019).

ILCS 730 Blockchain Technology Act, (2020).

In re Appraisal of Dell Inc, 143 A. 3d 20 (Del: Court of Chancery 2015).

Johann, L. (2018). *Liechtenstein implements Distributed Ledger Technology (DLT)*. Retrieved June 30, 2021 from https://bwb.li/blog/liechtenstein-implements-distributed-ledger-technology-dlt/

Joy, J. G., & Sebastian, K. (2020). Blockchain in Real Estate. *International Journal of Applied Engineering Research, 15*(9), 930–932.

Kaal, W. A., & Evans, S. (2019). Blockchain-based securities offerings. *UC Davis Bus. LJ, 20*, 89.

Kelly, L. (2019). What Is Enabled: How Blockchain Enabling Legislation Fails Commercial Contracts. *Rutgers JL Pub. Pol'y, 16*, 1.

Kharitonova, A. (2021). Capabilities of Blockchain Technology in Tokenization of Economy. *1st International Scientific Conference "Legal Regulation of the Digital Economy and Digital Relations: Problems and Prospects of Development" (LARDER 2020)*.

Kieckhefer, B. (n.d.). *How Nevada Is Preparing For Blockchain Technology*. https://www.mcdonaldcarano.com/news/how-nevada-is-preparing-for-blockchain-technology/

Kiviat, T. I. (2015). Beyond bitcoin: Issues in regulating blockchain tranactions. *Duke Law Journal, 65*, 569.

Kozakiewicz, A., & Fettes, K. (2021). *Impact of new Luxembourg law on the issuance and settlement of securities using blockchain.* Retrieved June 30, 2021 from https://www.ashurst.com/en/news-and-insights/legal-updates/impact-of-new-luxembourg-law-on-the-issuance-and-settlement-of-securities-using-blockchain/

Kulms, R. (2020). Blockchains: Private Law Matters Special Feature. *Sing. J. Legal Stud., 2020*, 63.

Kumar, N., Gayathri, N., Rahman, M. A., & Balamurugan, B. (2020). *Blockchain, Big Data and Machine Learning: Trends and Applications.* CRC Press. https://books.google.com.my/books?id=yzX7DwAAQBAJ

Landen, X. (2018). Vt. Banks on Appeal, Lure Of Blockchain. *Valley News.* https://www.vnews.com/Vermont-bullish-on-blockchain-as-new-law-takes-effect-19810798

Laster, J. T., & Rosner, M. T. (2017). Distributed Stock Ledgers and Delaware Law. *Business Lawyer, 73*, 319.

Law of 1 March 2019, (2019). https://legilux.public.lu/eli/etat/leg/loi/2019/03/01/a111/jo

Law of 22 January 2021, (2021).

Liechtenstein is the New Powerhouse for Digital Securities. (2021). Retrieved June 30, 2021 from https://www.lcx.com/liechtenstein-is-the-new-powerhouse-for-digital-securities/

Massinon, L., & Nickel, C. (2021). *Law of 22 January 2021 amending Luxembourg dematerialised securities law and financial sector law.* https://www.dlapiper.com/en/us/insights/publications/2021/01/law-amending-luxembourg-dematerialised-securities-law-and-financial-sector-law/

Milewski, K. P. (2020). *Illinois Embraces Smart Contracts with New Blockchain Legislation.* https://www.natlawreview.com/article/illinois-embraces-smart-contracts-new-blockchain-legislation

Mills, A. (2017). *An Introduction To Blockchain Technology And Its Legal Implications.* https://www.mmmlaw.com/media/an-introduction-to-blockchain-technology-and-its-legal-implications/

Mingxiao, D., Xiaofeng, M., Zhe, Z., Xiangwei, W., & Qijun, C. (2017). *A review on consensus algorithm of blockchain. 2017 IEEE international conference on systems, man, and cybernetics.* SMC.

Nakamoto, S. (2008). Bitcoin: A peer-to-peer electronic cash system. *Decentralized Business Review*, 21260.

Neitz, M. B. (2020). How to Regulate Blockchain's Real-Life Applications: Lessons from the California Blockchain Working Group. *Jurimetrics: The Journal of Law, Science Technology, 61*(2).

Nev. Code. Title 32. Chp 361, NRS 361.228 (2010).

Nev. Const. Art. 10, §1.

ACT No. XXXI of 2018, (2018).

ACT No. XXXIII of 2018, (2018).

NV Rev Stat § 719, (2013).

Osmani, M., El-Haddadeh, R., Hindi, N., Janssen, M., & Weerakkody, V. (2020). Blockchain for next generation services in banking and finance: Cost, benefit, risk and opportunity analysis. *Journal of Enterprise Information Management.*

Pankratov, E., Grigoryev, V., & Pankratov, O. (2020). The blockchain technology in real estate sector: Experience and prospects. *IOP Conference Series. Materials Science and Engineering.*

Parker, L. (2017). *European Commission 'actively monitoring' Blockchain developments.* https://brave-newcoin.com/insights/european-commission-actively-monitoring-blockchain-developments

Politou, E., Casino, F., Alepis, E., & Patsakis, C. (2019). Blockchain mutability: Challenges and proposed solutions. *IEEE Transactions on Emerging Topics in Computing.* doi:10.1109/TETC.2019.2949510

Prussen, E. H. (2021). *Luxembourg: Luxembourg Law Recognises Issuance of Dematerialised Securities In Blockchains.* Retrieved June 30, 2021 from https://www.mondaq.com/fin-tech/1034224/luxembourg-law-recognises-issuance-of-dematerialised-securities-in-blockchains-

Quasim, M. T. (2020). *Decentralised Internet of Things: A Blockchain Perspective* (Vol. 71). Springer Nature.

Raijmakers, J. (2020). *Entry into force of Swiss DLT bill.* Retrieved June 30, 2021 from https://www.loyensloeff.com/ch/en/news/swiss-dlt-bill-enters-into-force-n21037/

Raj, P., Saini, K., & Surianarayanan, C. (2020). *Blockchain Technology and Applications.* CRC Press.

Salmon, J., & Myers, G. (2019). *Blockchain and Associated Legal Issues for Emerging Markets.* https://openknowledge.worldbank.org/bitstream/handle/10986/31202/133877-EMCompass-Note-63-Blockchain-and-Legal-Issues-in-Emerging-Markets.pdf?sequence=1&isAllowed=y

S.B. 161, 80th Leg. Sess. (Nev.), (2019).

S.B. 162, 80st Leg. Sess. (Nev.), (2019).

S.B. 163, 80th Leg. Sess. (Nev.), (2019).

S.B. 164, 80th Leg. Sess. (Nev.), (2019). https://www.leg.state.nv.us/Session/80th2019/Bills/SB/SB164_EN.pdf

S.B. 269, Leg., Reg. Sess. (Vt.), (2017).

S.B. 398, 79th Leg. Sess. (Nev.), (2017).

S.B. 69, 149th Gen. Assemb., Reg. Sess, (Del), (2017). https://delcode.delaware.gov/title8/c001/sc07/index.html

Shen, C., & Pena-Mora, F. (2018). Blockchain for cities—A systematic literature review. *IEEE Access: Practical Innovations, Open Solutions, 6,* 76787–76819.

Singh, H., Jain, G., Munjal, A., & Rakesh, S. (2019). Blockchain technology in corporate governance: disrupting chain reaction or not? *Corporate Governance: The International Journal of Business in Society.*

Strassman, R. (n.d.). Delaware Explicitly Legalizes Corporate Documentation via Blockchain. *Review of Banking & Financial Law, 37.* https://www.bu.edu/rbfl/files/2018/03/166-176.pdf

Suda, M., Tejblum, B., & Francisco, A. (2017). Chain reactions: Legislative and regulatory initiatives related to blockchain in the United States. *Computer Law Review International, 18*(4), 97–103.

Swiss Federal Code of Obligations, (1911).

Thukral, M. K. (2021). Emergence of blockchain-technology application in peer-to-peer electrical-energy trading: A review. *Clean Energy, 5*(1), 104–123.

Tinianow, A., & Klayman, J. A. (2017). *Enabling or Crippling? The Risks of State-by-State Blockchain Laws.* https://www.coindesk.com/enabling-crippling-risks-state-state-blockchain-laws

Tinianow, A., & Long, C. (2017). *Delaware blockchain initiative: transforming the Foundational Infrastructure of Corporate Finance.* Harv. L. Sch. F. on Corp. Governance Fin. Reg.

Token- und VT-Dienstleister-Gesetz, (2019).

Tu, K. (2020). Blockchain Stock Ledgers. *Industrial Law Journal, 96,* 223.

Uzsoki, D. (2019). *Tokenization of Infrastructure- A blockchain-based solution to financing sustainable infrastructure.* https://www.iisd.org/system/files/publications/tokenization-infrastructure-blockchain-solution.pdf

Verberne, J. (2018). *How can blockchain serve society?* Retrieved June 30, 2021 from https://www.weforum.org/agenda/2018/02/blockchain-ocean-fishing-sustainable-risk-environment/

Walch, A. (2016). The path of the blockchain lexicon (and the law). *Rev. Banking Fin. L., 36,* 713.

Walch, A. (2017). Blockchain's treacherous vocabulary: One more challenge for regulators. *Journal of Internet Law, 21*(2).

Wolfson, R. (2019). *Majority Leader of California State Assembly Pushes for Legal Certainty for Blockchain.* Retrieved June 30, 2021 from https://cointelegraphs.com/news/majority-leader-of-california-state-assembly-pushes-for-legal-certainty-for-blockchain

Wright, D., Gutwirth, S., Friedewald, M., Vildjiounaite, E., & Punie, Y. (2008). *Safeguards in a World of Ambient Intelligence.* Springer Netherlands. doi:10.1007/978-1-4020-6662-7

Zhou, J., Conti, M., Ahmed, C. M., Au, M. H., Batina, L., Li, Z., . . . Majumdar, S. (2020). *Applied Cryptography and Network Security Workshops: ACNS 2020 Satellite Workshops, AIBlock, AIHWS, AIoTS, Cloud S&P, SCI, SecMT, and SiMLA, Rome, Italy, October 19–22, 2020, Proceedings.* Springer International Publishing.

Zhou, Y., Wu, J., Long, C., & Ming, W. (2020). State-of-the-art analysis and perspectives for peer-to-peer energy trading. *Engineering, 6*(7), 739–753. https://doi.org/doi.org/10.1016/j.eng.2020.06.002

ENDNOTES

[1]   "Blockchain technology" means "distributed ledger technology that uses a distributed, decentralized, shared and replicated ledger, which may be public or private, permissioned or permissionless, or driven by tokenized crypto economics or tokenless. The data on the ledger is protected with cryptography, is immutable and auditable and provides an uncensored truth".

[2]   "Smart contract" means "an event-driven program, with state, that runs on a distributed, decentralized, shared and replicated ledger and that can take custody over and instruct transfer of assets on that ledger".

Chapter 5

Comparative Review of the Regulatory Framework of Cryptocurrency in Selected Jurisdictions

Karisma Karisma
University Malaya, Malaysia

ABSTRACT

This chapter compares the current legal and regulatory landscape of cryptocurrency regulations of selected countries. Countries have adopted distinct and disparate regulatory approaches in regulating cryptocurrency. Countries such as Gibraltar, Malta, Switzerland, Singapore, and certain states in the United States have enacted proactive, enabling, and industry-specific laws to regulate cryptocurrency. The Philippines and Denmark are relatively forward-looking in their endeavour to regulate cryptocurrency by allowing its utilization and/or trade but with a restrictive and cautious approach. Certain countries have imposed rigorous restrictions or banned the usage or trade of cryptocurrency. With the rapid evolution and emergence of cryptocurrency markets, policymakers are adopting different trajectories to develop a suitable regulatory framework to regulate cryptocurrency. Countries around the world should harness the capabilities of cryptocurrency by devising favourable regulations rather than inhibit the application of cryptocurrency.

INTRODUCTION

Cryptocurrency is the first major blockchain innovation and the most notable blockchain application. Cryptocurrency is garnering the attention of investors, government, policymakers, academics, and other stakeholders all over the world more than ever before. In recent years, cryptocurrency has been widely used, and with the emergence and evolution of cryptocurrency, the regulatory endeavours of countries have been intensified. This chapter focuses on cryptocurrency policies, legislations, and regulations in selected jurisdictions. The pertinent areas explored are matters relating to legality and limits in the

DOI: 10.4018/978-1-7998-7927-5.ch005

utilisation of cryptocurrency. The regulatory approaches adopted by countries are divided into four categories. The first category encompasses countries that have enacted proactive and enabling laws. The second category explores jurisdictions that are relatively proactive in their endeavour to regulate cryptocurrency, allowing the utilisation and/or trade of cryptocurrency but with a restrictive and cautious approach. The third category examines countries that have completely restricted or banned the usage and trade of cryptocurrency. The fourth category evaluates the regulatory landscape of cryptocurrency in the United States. With the rapid evolution and use of cryptocurrency around the world, regulatory bodies are adopting different trajectories. Some countries aspire to win the inter-jurisdictional race of becoming crypto havens by enacting enabling laws, whilst other countries adopt a cautious and restrictive approach.

BACKGROUND

Cryptocurrency was first introduced by Satoshi Nakamoto in 2008, in a white paper, where Nakamoto proposed "a purely peer-to-peer version of electronic cash [which] would allow online payments to be sent directly from one party to another without going through a financial institution".(Nakamoto, 2008) Cryptocurrencies are decentralized, "peer-to-peer" currency systems that are not controlled by the government or institution, causing them to be resistant to government interference.(Lacity, 2020) Besides that, by the application of cryptocurrencies, there is no reliance on third-party intermediaries, namely banks and financial institutions.(Lacity, 2020) Services concerning transactions through cryptocurrencies are automated and community-driven. The transactions of cryptocurrencies are cryptographically protected and are shared on a blockchain ledger which constitutes a "universal record of truth".(Lacity, 2020)

With the emergence of cryptocurrencies, it has become pertinent to regulate the market with suitable regulatory frameworks. Cryptocurrencies may be used for illicit purposes by malicious individuals or business entities, due to their characteristics of anonymity, immutability, and irreversibility of transactions which makes it a suitable market platform to make possible the cybercrime wave.(Chokor & Alfieri, 2021) Therefore, there is a need to regulate cryptocurrencies to prohibit illegal and illicit activities such as money laundering due to the uncertainties surrounding transactions involving cryptocurrencies. Countries in the first category have enacted robust anti-money laundering laws to protect the interest of consumers. These anti-money laundering laws impose obligations to monitor financial transactions and contain provisions on customer due diligence or know your customer requirements.(Quintais et al., 2019) Cryptocurrency service providers should comply with similar rules applicable to financial institutions because of the nature of cryptocurrency exchanges.(Gürcan, 2019)

The second objective of enacting appropriate laws is to increase government revenues through taxes imposed on individuals or business entities who engage in any cryptocurrency transactions.(Chokor & Alfieri, 2021) Nevertheless, no consensus has been reached by countries on the appropriate legal classification of cryptocurrencies resulting in complexity in the system. (Chokor & Alfieri, 2021) As elucidated below, some countries are facing a massive challenge to delineate national rules with clarity. Besides that, cryptocurrency regulations adopted by different countries are dissimilar, and no unified regulatory approach has been devised thus far. Thirdly, cryptocurrency markets are highly volatile, and by enacting regulations, financial stability can be achieved.(Chokor & Alfieri, 2021)

Scholars have proposed the harmonization and integration of cryptocurrency regulations by the adoption of a unified approach.(Cumming et al., 2019) Facilitating a consistent regulatory approach is pertinent to deter individuals or business entities from transacting in countries that have in place more lenient and friendly regulatory ecosystems of cryptocurrencies resulting in the risk of regulatory arbitrage. Due to the naivety of cryptocurrencies, proper dialogue is required to identify the risks and devise suitable measures to prohibit corruptive practices.

Countries around the world should harness the capabilities of cryptocurrency rather than inhibit its application. An outright ban of cryptocurrency may not be an appropriate solution, as underground cryptocurrency markets may thrive under unmonitored environments, thus increasing the likelihood of illegal and illicit transactions.(Rubio, 2020) Besides that, banning cryptocurrencies and imposing any hard-touch regulatory approach is likely to be ineffective as business entities may shift activities concerning cryptocurrencies to jurisdictions with more favourable regulations. (Nabilou, 2019)

REGULATION OF CRYPTOCURRENCIES

Regulatory bodies have faced challenges to keep pace with the evolution of cryptocurrency. This section critically examines the regulatory framework of cryptocurrency in selected countries, particularly exploring the ambit of protection of investors, ensuring financial steadiness, and market integrity. As mentioned, the jurisdictions may be classified into four categories.

- Firstly, countries that have allowed the cryptocurrency market to function by enacting proactive and enabling laws, such as Gibraltar, Malta, Estonia, Singapore, and Switzerland.
- Secondly, countries that are relatively proactive in regulating cryptocurrency but adopt a restrictive and cautious approach, such as Philippines and Denmark.
- Thirdly, countries that have imposed rigorous restrictions or banned cryptocurrency exchanges, such as Indonesia, Vietnam, Cambodia, Brunei, Russia, Ecuador, Bolivia, and India.
- Fourthly, the incoherent legal conceptualization of cryptocurrency and inconsistent state regulations in the United States.

1. Countries That Have Allowed the Cryptocurrency Market to Function by Enacting Proactive and Enabling Laws

a. Gibraltar

Gibraltar's DLT legislation has made headlines as developing the world's first DLT-specific framework for businesses utilizing Distributed Ledger Technology (DLT) or blockchain. It sets out an arduous application process for businesses, aligned with Gibraltar's vision in setting high standards for regulatory compliance. There are currently 13 licensed business entities operating under Gibraltar's business framework, including eToro, Huobi, Xapo, LMAX, Bitso, and Gnosis.(HM Government of Gibraltar, 2020)

Gibraltar developed a DLT framework which came into effect in 2018. The framework was developed to provide a secure and innovative regulatory structure for DLT firms that use the technology for "transmission or storage of value".(Gibraltar Financial Services Commission, n.d.) There are nine principles under the DLT framework and these principles are listed in the "Financial Services (Distributed Ledger Technology Providers) Regulations 2020" (DLT Regulations 2020). ("Financial Services (Distributed Ledger Technology Providers) Regulations," 2020) Besides that, these principles are substantiated by the DLT framework "Guidance Notes". The "Guidance Notes" provide clarity of pivotal areas and maintain a regulatory structure that is up to date and can evolve with technological innovation. (Gibraltar Financial Services Commission, n.d.)

The principles contained in existing taxation legislation and relevant accounting standards apply to cryptocurrencies, as the treatment of cryptocurrencies is not explicitly stipulated under the legislative framework.(Garcia & Garcia, 2021) There is no "capital gains tax", "value-added tax", inheritance or net worth tax (wealth tax) in Gibraltar. However, the 10% corporate income tax rate is payable on income accrued in or derived from Gibraltar. (Garcia & Garcia, 2021)

In 2018, Gibraltar amended "Proceeds of Crime Act 2015" (POCA) to augment the meaning of "relevant financial business" to include "undertakings that receive [...] proceeds in any form from the sale of tokenized digital assets involving the use of distributed ledger technology or a similar means of recording a digital representation of an asset".(2018) The relevant financial businesses must comply with due diligence requirements and appoint a "Money Laundering Reporting Officer".(Gibraltar Financial Services Commission, n.d.)

A firm utilizing DLT to provide DLT services needs to be authorized by the "Gibraltar Financial Services Commission" as a DLT Provider. Regulation 5 of the DLT Regulations 2020 provides that a DLT Provider is required to comply with regulatory principles.("Financial Services (Distributed Ledger Technology Providers) Regulations," 2020) The Schedule to the DLT Regulations 2020 sets out the Regulatory Principles. Amongst other Regulatory Principles, a "DLT Provider must have systems in place to prevent, detect and disclose financial crime risks such as money laundering and terrorist financing".("Financial Services (Distributed Ledger Technology Providers) Regulations," 2020) AML/CFT obligations are as prescribed under the "European Union Anti-Money Laundering Directives", POCA and "Financial Service Commission's Anti-Money Laundering Guidance Notes". At the very least, DLT providers will be required to comply with POCA and the AML/CFT requirements of any jurisdictions they are carrying out their businesses in.(Gibraltar Financial Services Commission, n.d.)

b. Malta

The enactment of the "Virtual Financial Assets Act" (VFAA) creates a comprehensive legislative framework for cryptocurrencies. The VFAA regulates initial virtual financial asset offerings and virtual financial assets. It also regulates the application by an issuer for an admission to trade virtual financial assets on Distributed Ledger Technology (DLT) exchange, the activities of the VFAA agent, and the provision of VFAA services.(Malta Financial Services Authority, 2018a) There are 4 different kinds of DLT assets pursuant to VFAA, namely "virtual token", "virtual financial asset" (VFA), "electronic money", and "financial instrument".

A virtual token is defined under the VFAA as "a form of digital medium recordation whose utility, value or application is restricted solely to the acquisition of goods or services, either solely within the DLT platform on or in relation to which it was issued or within a limited network of DLT platforms". ("Virtual Financial Assets Act ", 2018 Section 2) On the other hand, VFA is defined under the VFAA as any form of "digital medium recordation that is used as a digital medium of exchange, unit of account, or store of value" which falls outside the scope of electronic money, financial instrument or virtual token. ("Virtual Financial Assets Act ", 2018)

To ascertain the nature of the DLT Asset, a "financial instrument test" can be utilized to determine which of the four classifications does the crypto asset fall within. Having established that the DLT asset constitutes a "virtual token", activities concerning "virtual token" are not within the purview of regulations.(Malta Financial Services Authority, 2018a) If the DLT asset constitutes a financial instrument or electronic money, it can only be traded on "trading venues" within the "Markets in Financial Instruments Directive" (MiFID).(Malta Financial Services Authority, 2018a) It has been set out in the Policy Statement issued by European Securities Markets Authority that an entity that offers services and/or activities concerning financial instruments as defined by the MiFID will need to observe the MiFID requirements. (European Securities and Markets Authority, 2017) Therefore, notwithstanding the "novelty" of the technology forming the basis of that DLT asset, entities are required to comply with the existing regulatory framework. (Buttigieg & Efthymiopoulos, 2019) If the DLT asset is neither a "virtual token" nor "financial instrument" or "electronic money", the DLT asset will be classified as VFA and the VFAA Framework will be applicable to it. Besides that, by examining the proviso under the definition of VFA, a "virtual token […] converted into another DLT asset type shall be treated as the DLT asset type into which it is or may be converted". ("Virtual Financial Assets Act ", 2018) Once it has been determined that the DLT asset amounts to a VFA, the second requirement has to be complied with to prompt the application of VFAA. To fall within VFAA, the entity should offer a service provided within the Second Schedule of the VFAA. ("Virtual Financial Assets Act ", 2018)

Unlike the approach adopted by other jurisdictions, Malta has not banned Initial Coin Offerings (ICOs). Instead, Malta has introduced certain requirements for the regulation of ICOs, which are connoted as "initial VFA offerings". No issuer can make an Initial VFA offering unless a whitepaper is drawn up by the issuer by complying with the conditions under Article 4, and the whitepaper is registered in conformity with Article 3(2). ("Virtual Financial Assets Act ", 2018) According to Article 3(2) the whitepaper must be signed by all the members of the "issuer's board of administration".("Virtual Financial Assets Act ", 2018) The aim of drawing up a whitepaper is to ensure that investors are provided with adequate information on the VFA. (Buttigieg & Efthymiopoulos, 2019) Besides that, under Article 9, numerous principles are also applicable to an issuer such as carrying out the business with honesty and integrity and applying due skill and care. ("Virtual Financial Assets Act ", 2018)

The VFAA regulates entities providing services pertaining to VFA. The VFAA provides for the licensing requirements and sets out the obligations of license holders. These requirements are pertinent to prevent manipulation, such as the "pump and dump" ploys. (Buttigieg & Efthymiopoulos, 2019) As set out under Article 13 (1), no entity can provide a VFA service unless such entity possesses a valid license granted by Malta Financial Services Authority.("Virtual Financial Assets Act ", 2018) Besides compliance with the regulations made under the VFAA, license holders are required to observe "prudential requirements" which include requirements on "administration, compliance, risk management, systems, and security access protocols, financial resources, capital adequacy, [and] professional indemnity insurance […]".("Virtual Financial Assets Act ", 2018) It can be gathered from the VFAA provisions that the issuers and license holders are subjected to a principle-based approach instead of a rule-based approach. (Buttigieg & Efthymiopoulos, 2019)

The VFAA framework also provides for VFA Agents which are defined under Article 2. VFAA sets out the role and obligations of VFA Agents under Article 7 and Article 14("Virtual Financial Assets Act ", 2018). The primary role of the VFA Agent includes advising and guiding his client to ensure adherence with the VFAA provisions and any regulations issued under the Act. The VFA Agent is to ensure that prospective issuers and entities intending to provide VFA services are "fit and proper" for such purpose. ("Virtual Financial Assets Act ", 2018) A VFA Agent is required to cooperate with Malta Financial Services Authority (MFSA) and act as a liaison between MFSA and his client. ("Virtual Financial Assets Act ", 2018) It is crucial for prospective issuers and entities to meet such standards, and for VFA agents to oversee and supervise this area of business. The precepts of investor protection and financial stability will be strengthened. Corresponding to the importance of VFA Agents, the MFSA has issued the Virtual Financial Assets Rulebook, where Chapter 1 is specifically for VFA Agents, providing for the high-level principles and the registration requirements that have to be observed by the VFA Agents. (Malta Financial Services Authority, 2018b)

Crypto assets are vulnerable to the risks of money laundering and financing of terrorism (MLF/FT). With Malta becoming the "blockchain island" or "crypto haven" these risks are exacerbated. Therefore, this section addresses the framework that Malta has put forth regarding anti-money laundering and countering financing of terrorism (AML/CFT). As analysed below, Malta has taken proactive steps to combat ML/FT by devising a comprehensive legal and regulatory framework, and this has led to Malta becoming the "jurisdiction of choice" for investors of VFA. (Buttigieg et al., 2019) As a starting point, Article 2 provides for the term "subject person" which has the same meaning under the "Prevention of Money Laundering and Funding of Terrorism Regulations" (PMLFTR). A VFA agent, license holder, and issuer are subject persons under the VFAA and therefore must comply with the PMLFTR. ("Prevention of Money Laundering and Funding of Terrorism Regulations ", 2018) Under Regulation 5, every subject person is required to implement measures and procedures concerning (a) customer due diligence; (b) record-keeping procedures; (c) risk management, customer risk assessment, compliance management and communication, and (d) employee training and awareness. ("Prevention of Money Laundering and Funding of Terrorism Regulations ", 2018) Another barricade towards ML/FT is the appointment of VFA Agents. VFA Agents connoted as "gatekeeper[s]" are required to engage with the competent authority in a cooperative manner while providing advice and guidance to potential issuers or VFA Service Providers. (Buttigieg et al., 2019; "Virtual Financial Assets Act ", 2018) Besides that, the VFA Rule book sets out the requirement of a "Money Laundering Reporting Officer" to be appointed from the three Designated Persons of the VFA Agent. (Malta Financial Services Authority, 2018b) The Rule book also sets out the requirement of transparency, where pursuant to R1-3.2.8.1.1, VFA agents should espouse apposite and transparent reporting lines to ensure that any risk of non-compliance is prioritized. (Malta Financial Services Authority, 2018b) High-level principles are also incorporated within the legislative framework that should be complied with by the issuers of VFA. (Buttigieg et al., 2019; "Virtual Financial Assets Act ", 2018)

In 2018, the "Commissioner for Revenue" issued "Guidelines on the Income Tax Treatment of transactions or arrangements involving DLT assets".(Commissioner for Revenue, 2018) Pursuant to the Guidelines, the DLT assets are categorized into coins and tokens, namely financial tokens, utility tokens, and hybrid tokens.(Commissioner for Revenue, 2018) For transactions concerning coins, the tax treatment is similar to that of fiat currency. Profits from the sale of coins or mining of cryptocurrency are regarded as ordinary income, and these coins fall outside the bounds of capital gains tax.(Commissioner for Revenue, 2018) The returns obtained by individuals owning financial tokens, such as dividends or interest, are to be treated as income. As for transfers concerning financial and utility tokens, the tax treatment depends on whether the transfer is a "trading transaction or a transfer of a capital asset".(Commissioner for Revenue, 2018) In relation to the former, ordinary tax rules are applicable, where proceeds from the sale of the token are treated as trading profits. If profit is derived from a capital transaction, it has to be determined whether it can fall within Article 5 of the "Maltese Income Tax Act", which is limited to transfer of immovable property, securities, intellectual property, beneficial interest in a trust and partnership.(Commissioner for Revenue, 2018; "Income Tax Act ", 1949)

From the discussion above, Malta has adopted a favourable regulatory regime to attract cryptocurrency businesses. By the passing of the VFAA, regulators in Malta have placed importance on the technological aspects of cryptocurrencies and have adopted solutions to protect users. (Ellul et al., 2020)

c. Estonia

In June 2020, the Parliament of Estonia approved the amendments to the "Money Laundering and Terrorist Financing Prevention Act" ("MLTFPA")("Money Laundering and Terrorist Financing Prevention Act ", 2017) and accordingly transposed the "5th Anti-Money Laundering Directive" (AMLD5) and eliminated deficiencies from the incomplete transposition of the "4th Anti-Money Laundering Directive" (AMLD4) as notified by the European Commission. By such amendment, the definition of money laundering is augmented. Besides that, provisions on "Cooperation and exchange of information" are amended to provide more clarity and to facilitate the sharing of information collected from the due diligence procedures between obliged entities. (Ha, 2021) Martin Helme, the then Minister of Finance stated that "Estonia is not a place for money laundering. The government will do everything possible to make sure that our economic environment continues to be honest and transparent and the current legislation is a very important step forward in this regard[…]".(Republic of Estonia Financial Intelligence Unit, 2020)

Virtual currency is termed under the MLTFPA as "a value represented in the digital form, which is digitally transferable, preservable or tradable and which natural persons or legal persons accept as a payment instrument, but that is not the legal tender of any country or funds[…]".("Money Laundering and Terrorist Financing Prevention Act ", 2017) The MLTFPA applies to the providers of a virtual currency service. Virtual currency service encompasses the virtual currency wallet service and virtual currency exchange service, both of which are defined under the MLTFPA.("Money Laundering and Terrorist Financing Prevention Act ", 2017)

In Estonia, an undertaking providing a virtual currency service is required to obtain authorization, issued by the Financial Intelligence Unit (FIU).(Kasprzyk, 2018) By obtaining a license for the virtual currency exchange service, the undertaking can run a virtual currency exchange platform that allows the exchange of virtual currency against a fiat currency (or vice versa) or a virtual currency against another virtual currency(Kasprzyk, 2018). Besides that, an undertaking having obtained a license for the provision of a virtual currency wallet service can run a platform where "keys are generated for customers or customers' encrypted keys are kept, which can be used for the purpose of keeping, storing and transferring virtual currencies".("Money Laundering and Terrorist Financing Prevention Act ", 2017) The FIU has regulatory powers relating to virtual currencies and performs its duties set out in the MLTPA.

According to the Republic of Estonia Tax and Customs Board, income can be generated by way of price adjustments of virtual currency when buying and selling or exchanging, or mining.(Republic of Estonia Tax and Customs Board, 2021) Virtual currencies are defined as property under § 15(1) Income Tax Act. The income received from virtual currencies by way of "gains from the transfer of property" including exchanges, "income from employment" or "business income" is taxed on a comparable basis as income earned from traditional currency.(Republic of Estonia Tax and Customs Board, 2021) In the case of a gain, it is calculated based on the difference between the "selling price and purchase price of the cryptocurrency". On the other hand, in relation to an exchange, it is the difference between the "price of received property" and "purchase price of virtual currency"(Republic of Estonia Tax and Customs Board, 2021). Therefore, if an individual receives proceeds from the trade, purchase or sale, or exchange of a cryptocurrency for another cryptocurrency or regular currency, the income must be declared. (Republic of Estonia Tax and Customs Board, 2021) From the discussion above, Estonia has adopted a progressive approach towards the regulation of cryptocurrencies.

d. Singapore

In 2017, based on a press release by the "Monetary Authority of Singapore" ("MAS"), MAS made clear that the "offer" or "issue" of digital tokens will be subject to regulation if the digital tokens are capital market products under the "Securities and Futures Act" (Cap 289) ("SFA"). Capital market products comprise "securities, units in a collective investment scheme, derivatives contracts and spot foreign exchange contracts for purposes of leveraged foreign exchange trading". (Monetary Authority of Singapore, 2020) Under paragraph 2.4 of "A Guide to Digital Token Offering" (the Guide), the offers of digital tokens which "constitute securities, securities-based derivatives contracts or units in a CIS" are subject to the SFA ("Offer"). An entity can only make an Offer if the Offer is in compliance with the conditions set out in Part XIII of the SFA and the Offer is made "in or accompanied by a prospectus" prepared in conformity with the SFA and registered with MAS. (Monetary Authority of Singapore, 2020)

Subsequently, in November 2017, MAS published a "consultation paper" on the proposed regulatory framework, the Payment Services Bill and sought feedback from the members of the public. In 2019, the Parliament of Singapore passed the "Payment Services Act 2019" ("PSA") ("Payment Services Act 2019," No. 2 of 2019). Under the PSA, digital payment token service is defined as any service dealing with or facilitating the exchange of digital payment tokens. ("Payment Services Act 2019," No. 2 of 2019) Digital payment tokens are defined under Section 2 of the PSA as "any digital representation of value" that (a) is "expressed as a unit"; (b) is "not denominated in any currency"; (c) "is or is intended to be, a medium of exchange"; (d) can be "transferred, stored or traded electronically"; and (e) "satisfies such other characteristics as the Authority may prescribe". ("Payment Services Act 2019," No. 2 of 2019) An undertaking that offers any kind of payment service will need to obtain a license unless exempted. ("Payment Services Act 2019," No. 2 of 2019) Three types of licenses may be issued, including the "money-changing license", "standard payment institution license" and the "major payment institution license". ("Payment Services Act 2019," No. 2 of 2019) On 4 January 2021, the Payment Services (Amendment) Bill 2021("Payment Services (Amendment) Act 2021," No. 1 of 2021) was passed and the definition of digital payment token service was expanded, amongst other pertinent amendments. By the addition of Section 21A to the PSA, the powers of MAS to impose additional requirements through regulations made under section 103(1) on licensees providing "digital payment token service" are heightened. ("Payment Services (Amendment) Act 2021," No. 1 of 2021)

According to the Guide, "MAS Notice on Prevention of Money Laundering and Countering the Financing of Terrorism (AML/CFT)" applies if an entity is deemed to be an intermediary engaging in regulated activities comprising of digital tokens, specified in paragraphs 2.8 to 2.11 of the Guide. (Monetary Authority of Singapore, 2020) AML/CFT conditions will be imposed on the licensees of digital payment token services as these services "carry significant money laundering and terrorism financing risks or ML/TF risks due to the anonymous and borderless nature of the transactions they enable." (Monetary Authority of Singapore, 2019, 2020)

Singapore has also issued a document on the "Income Tax Treatment of Digital Tokens".(Inland Revenue Authority of Singapore, 2020) The tax treatment of tokens are as follows:

1. **Payment Token**: Even though a payment token amounts to a mode of payment, it is not fiat currency (issued by the government) nor a legal tender. The "Inland Revenue Authority of Singapore" (IRAS) considers a payment token to be an "intangible property" as it signifies a set of rights and obligations.(Inland Revenue Authority of Singapore, 2020) Therefore, transactions entailing the utilization of payment tokens as a mode of payment of goods and services are regarded as "barter trade". Where an undertaking receives payment tokens for the goods and/or services it has provided, the undertaking will be taxed on the value of the goods provided or services rendered. On the other hand, where an undertaking pays for goods and/or services via payment tokens, a deduction is allowed subject to the deduction rules.(Inland Revenue Authority of Singapore, 2020) The value of deduction will be pursuant to the value of goods purchased or services obtained. Nevertheless, there could be a situation where it is necessary to obtain the valuation of payment tokens. This may arise when an individual or business entity contracts with another on the performance of services for an agreed number of payment tokens.(Inland Revenue Authority of Singapore, 2020) The individual or business entity might need to record his income in accordance with the payment tokens received. IRAS does not stipulate any method for the valuation of payment tokens. IRAS states that taxpayers can utilize an "exchange rate that best reflects the value of the tokens received" subject to conditions.(Inland Revenue Authority of Singapore, 2020) IRAS also recognizes that payment tokens may appreciate or depreciate, and situations may arise where gain or loss on disposal of payment tokens is subject to taxation laws.
2. **Utility Token**: The utilization of a utility token in exchange for goods or services may constitute a deductible expense under the deduction rules.(Inland Revenue Authority of Singapore, 2020)
3. **Security Token**: The taxability of the returns from a security token is contingent on the nature of the return, for instance, interest or dividend, to which standard taxation rules are applicable. The tax treatment of the gain or loss on the disposal of a security token will depend on whether the security token is held as a capital or revenue asset.(Inland Revenue Authority of Singapore, 2020)

e. Switzerland

Switzerland is one of the most prominent locations in the realm of DLT. The "Federal Council of Switzerland" issued a report entitled the "Legal framework for distributed ledger technology and blockchain in Switzerland" in 2018.(Federal Council of Switzerland, 2018) The report provided an outline of the current regulatory framework of Switzerland and highlighted that the Swiss framework already provides for sufficient regulations to deal with DLT and blockchain. As Switzerland is receptive to technological developments, the report clarified the need for further improvement to the "innovative-friendly" framework conditions. To that end, the Federal Council elucidated certain principles. Firstly, policymakers should lay out an optimal framework that is favourable to innovation.(Federal Council of Switzerland, 2018) Switzerland should make selective adjustments where required to bridge the gaps in the legal framework so as to facilitate the application of DLT and blockchain technology. (Federal Council of Switzerland, 2018)More importantly, the need to pursue a "principle-based and technology-neutral legislative and regulatory approach" is set out, to portray the openness of the Swiss authorities in relation to new technological developments and innovations.(Federal Council of Switzerland, 2018) The Federal Council highlighted the amendments that should be made in line with the principles underlying the report.

Subsequently in 2019, the Swiss Federal Council issued a draft DLT-law and dispatch of the draft DLT-law, which was approved by the "Swiss Federal National Council" and "Economic Affairs and

Taxation Committee of the Swiss Federal Council of States".(Haeberli et al., 2021) In 2020, the Swiss Parliament adopted the "Federal Act on the Adaptation of Federal Law to Developments in Distributed Ledger Technology" (DLT Act). In February 2021 some parts of the DLT Act came into force.("Federal Act on the Adaptation of Federal Law to Developments in Distributed Ledger Technology," 2020) The remaining provisions are expected to come into force on 1 August 2021.

The DLT Act introduces uncertificated register securities (ledger-based securities) which share similar features as the traditional certificated securities but provides a legal mechanism for their transfer via digital or electronic means. The Act sets out the registration of the ledger-based security in a securities ledger. ("Federal Act on the Adaptation of Federal Law to Developments in Distributed Ledger Technology," 2020) The ledger-based security is a right that may be exercised and transferred to others by way of the securities ledger. There are four technical requirements that a securities ledger (register) must meet which are stipulated under Article 973d(2). ("Federal Act on the Adaptation of Federal Law to Developments in Distributed Ledger Technology," 2020) Firstly, the creditors are given the power of disposal over their rights through technological processes. Secondly, the integrity of the securities ledger is safeguarded by way of technical and organizational measures, preventing any unauthorized changes. Thirdly, the ledger sets out the content of the rights and the registration agreement. The creditors may inspect the information and entries on the register concerning them without third-party intervention. ("Federal Act on the Adaptation of Federal Law to Developments in Distributed Ledger Technology," 2020)

Ledger-based securities are created in accordance with an agreement between the parties and the obligor (the debtor) must ensure that the ledger is administered according to the aforementioned agreement. Under Article 973i, the debtor under ledger-based security is obliged to inform the purchaser of the "content of the ledger-based security", "the mode of operation of the securities ledger" and the "measures taken […] to protect the operation and integrity of the ledger".("Federal Act on the Adaptation of Federal Law to Developments in Distributed Ledger Technology," 2020) The debtor is liable for damage incurred by the purchaser as a result of inaccurate and misleading information provided by the debtor.

The DLT Act introduces amendments to the "Debt Enforcement and Bankruptcy Act" ("DEBA") specifically, Articles 242a and 242b.("Federal Act on the Adaptation of Federal Law to Developments in Distributed Ledger Technology," 2020) These provisions are introduced to set out the treatment of crypto assets in bankruptcy proceedings, in relation to the segregation of crypto assets from custodians in bankruptcy proceedings against them. Similarly, the Banking Act is also amended in the case of bank insolvencies. Besides that, by the enactment of the DLT Act, the following amendments are made to the "Financial Market Infrastructure Act" (FMIA)("Financial Market Infrastructure Act of 19 June 2015," 2015). Article 2 (5a) adds "a trading facility for DLT securities", whilst Article 2(5b) includes "uncertificated securities in accordance with Article 973c of the Code of Obligations (CO) and ledger-based securities in accordance with Article 973d of the CO".("Federal Act on the Adaptation of Federal Law to Developments in Distributed Ledger Technology," 2020) The DLT Trading facility is defined under Article 73a which consist of three characteristics namely an (a) institution for multilateral trading of DLT securities; (b) which has the purpose of simultaneous exchange of bids between several participants, and (c) the conclusion of contracts based on non-discretionary rules.("Federal Act on the Adaptation of Federal Law to Developments in Distributed Ledger Technology," 2020) In furtherance to that, a DLT Trading facility must comply with at least one of the three criteria set out in the Act under Article 73a. Amendments have also been made to the Anti-Money Laundering Act (AMLA)("Anti-Money Laundering Act of 10 October 1997," 1997) of 10 October 1997, where the trading facilities of DLT securities are regarded as financial intermediaries, according to Article 2(2) of AMLA. The duties of due diligence of financial intermediaries are provided for in Chapter 2 Section 1 of AMLA.("Federal Act on the Adaptation of Federal Law to Developments in Distributed Ledger Technology," 2020) Hence, DLT trading facilities are not excluded from complying with the provisions of AMLA to combat money laundering and terrorist financing.

On the area of taxation, capital gains surfacing from private assets of individuals are exempt from income tax. This is similarly applicable to the capital gains arising from cryptocurrencies. On the other hand, cryptocurrencies may not be regarded as part of an individual's private asset, but a business asset from a commercial activity conducted by that individual, which may qualify as self-employment.(Haeberli et al., 2021) In such a situation, the capital gains from cryptocurrencies are subject to taxation laws. (Haeberli et al., 2021) In order to determine whether it falls within a commercial activity, Circular No 36 of 27 July 2012 on professional securities trading is applied by the tax authorities.(Federal Department of Finance, 2012) The assessment criteria are as follows:

1. The volume of transactions and its frequency: The disposal of cryptocurrencies within a short duration of time indicates that the individual is not pursuing nor aiming to pursue a capital investment, but rather is interested in the immediate realization of capital gains. The individual recognizes the possibility of incurring significant losses.(Federal Department of Finance, 2012)
2. The utilization of substantial external financing to finance the transaction (Federal Department of Finance, 2012)
3. The need to raise capital to bear interest and expenses on debts that cannot be covered by periodic income. (Federal Department of Finance, 2012)

In relation to Wealth Tax, cryptocurrencies held by individuals must be converted to Swiss francs to conduct tax assessment. The "Federal Tax Administration" ("FTA") provides the exchange rates for particular cryptocurrencies.(Haeberli et al., 2021) Legal entities are subject to capital tax, corporate income tax, and value-added tax under the taxation laws.(Haeberli et al., 2021)

2. Countries That Are Relatively Proactive in Regulating Cryptocurrency but Adopt a Restrictive and Cautious Approach

a. Philippines

In 2014, the Philippines Central Bank ("BSP") issued a Warning Advisory on Virtual Currencies. (Anti-Money Laundering Council, 2014) It was stated explicitly that virtual currencies like Bitcoin are actively exchanged in the Philippines. Nevertheless, such exchanges are not regulated by BSP nor any other authority. The members of the public were warned of the risks and volatility of virtual currencies and potential financial losses.(Anti-Money Laundering Council, 2014) In 2017, the Central Bank of Philippines issued Circular No.944, Series of 2017 concerning the "Guidelines for Virtual Currency Exchanges". The Guidelines govern the operation of virtual currency exchanges. The provisions contained in the Guidelines are incorporated as Section 4512N of the "Manual of Regulations for Non-Bank Financial Institutions".(Bangko Sentral ng Pilipinas, 2017) Virtual currencies are defined under Subsection 4512N.2 and do not have the status of a legal tender as they are not backed by the Central Bank nor issued or guaranteed by any jurisdiction.(Bangko Sentral ng Pilipinas, 2017) In the Philippines, virtual currencies can be used as a form of payment, namely for remittance payments and payments of utility bills.(*Philippines: Where, How, and What you can buy for bitcoins*, 2018) To mitigate risks related to the usage of virtual currencies, especially when they are utilised to provide financial services, entities offering such services must register with BSP. According to Subsection. 4512N.3, virtual currency exchange entities must obtain a Certificate of Registration (COR) to operate as a "remittance and transfer company".(Bangko Sentral ng Pilipinas, 2017) The procedure governing registration should be complied with by such entities by submitting an "Application for Registration and Notarized Deeds of Undertaking" and paying the registration and annual fees. Besides that, the Guidelines (Subsection 4512N.6) stipulate that the entities must undertake sufficient "risk management and security control" to address risks linked to virtual currencies. (Bangko Sentral ng Pilipinas, 2017) The "virtual currency exchanges" are comparable to remittance and transfer exchanges and therefore, are subject to the Anti-Money Laundering Act 2001.(Bangko Sentral ng Pilipinas, 2017) The Philippines has to a certain extent facilitated the adoption of cryptocurrency in the country by not imposing an outright ban, and recognizing the use of cryptocurrency as a legitimate mode of payment.

b. Denmark

To date, Denmark has not enacted any legislative or regulatory framework that specifically deals with cryptocurrencies. Nevertheless, Denmark has recently increased its safeguards concerning the utilisation of cryptocurrencies by the amendments to the Act on "Measures to Prevent Money Laundering and Financing of Terrorism" (AML Act). This is in line with the implementation of the "5th Anti-Money Laundering Directive". It is illegal to use cryptocurrencies for illicit activities such as money laundering, even though cryptocurrencies are not specifically mentioned in the AML Act. (Hofverberg, 2019)

The applicability of Danish legislation depends on whether cryptocurrencies are classified as a mode of "payment", a "capital asset" or a "financial service".(Hofverberg, 2019) According to the Press Release by the Danish Financial Supervisory Authority (DFSA), the use of cryptocurrencies as a mode of payment remains unregulated in Denmark.(Hofverberg, 2019) DFSA has also stated that cryptocurrencies cannot fall within financial service classifications such as the issuance of "electronic money", "payment for services" and "currency exchanges" and therefore is not subject to financial regulations. (Hofverberg, 2019)

Certain crypto assets may qualify as securities. In such a situation, "Prospectus Regulation", "Market Abuse Regulation", "Capital Markets Act" (CMA), and "Markets in Financial Instrument Directive II" (MiFID II) is generally applicable to the public offering of securities or the admission of securities to trading.(Moalem & Probst Larsen, 2020) For crypto assets that do not constitute securities, they may be subject to laws on consumer protection.(Hofverberg, 2019)

3. Countries That Have Imposed Rigorous Restrictions or Banned Cryptocurrency Exchanges

a. Indonesia

Early 2018, Bank Indonesia issued a statement that virtual currencies are not acknowledged as "valid payment instruments", thus affirming the illegality of cryptocurrencies as payment systems. The press release "warned all parties not to sell, buy, or trade virtual currencies" due to the high financial risk of harm to the public.(Office of Assistant to Deputy Cabinet Secretary for State Documents & Translation,

2018) It was further promulgated that pursuant to Law No. 7 of 2011, the currency of the Republic of Indonesia shall be rupiah and every transaction which is for the purpose of payment or settlement of obligation which is to be settled with money shall be in rupiah.(Office of Assistant to Deputy Cabinet Secretary for State Documents & Translation, 2018) The statement referred to "Bank Indonesia Regulation No. 18/40/PBI/2016 on Implementation of Payment Transaction Processing" and "Bank Indonesia Regulation No. 19/12/PBI/2017 on Implementation of Financial Technology", which states that "Payment System Service Providers" and "Financial Technology Providers" are prohibited from processing payment transactions using virtual currencies.(Governor of Bank Indonesia, 2016)

In June 2018, the "Commodity Futures Trading Regulatory Agency", known as Bappebti, an agency under the Ministry of Trade Indonesia announced that cryptocurrencies are commodities that can be traded in Indonesia's futures exchanges.(Indonesia, 2019) "Minister of Trade Regulation No. 99 of 2018" was issued to permit futures trading of crypto assets. Subsequently, in 2019, the agency's head stated that regulations were in force on cryptocurrency futures trading, to provide legal certainty for investors and consumers. The regulation set 1 trillion rupiah (equivalent to $71.17 million) as the "minimum paid-up capital for a new trader offering future contracts for crypto assets".(Indonesia, 2019) Bappebti issued "Bappebti Regulation No. 5 of 2019" to provide a legal framework on the technical provisions on the operation of physical futures trading of crypto assets.("Peraturan Badan Pengawas Perdagangan Berjangka Komoditi Nomor 5 Tahun 2019 Tentang Ketentuan Teknis Penyelenggaraan Pasar Fisik Aset Kripto (Crypto Asset) Di Bursa Berjangka," 2019) Regulation No. 5 of 2019 read together with "Bappebti Regulation No. 2 of 2019" provides an amended regulatory structure on futures trading. Besides the definition of Crypto Asset under Regulation No.5/2019 as an intangible commodity in the form of a digital asset that utilizes cryptography, definitions are also provided for the following terms, namely "Crypto-Asset Exchanges," "Crypto-Asset Clearing Agencies," "Crypto-Asset Traders, Crypto-Asset Clients," and "Crypto-Asset Storage Providers."("Peraturan Badan Pengawas Perdagangan Berjangka Komoditi Nomor 5 Tahun 2019 Tentang Ketentuan Teknis Penyelenggaraan Pasar Fisik Aset Kripto (Crypto Asset) Di Bursa Berjangka," 2019)

In conclusion, cryptocurrencies can be traded in Indonesia, but are not permitted to be utilised as means of payment.("Peraturan Badan Pengawas Perdagangan Berjangka Komoditi Nomor 5 Tahun 2019 Tentang Ketentuan Teknis Penyelenggaraan Pasar Fisik Aset Kripto (Crypto Asset) Di Bursa Berjangka," 2019) Article 3 of Regulation 5 of 2019 further sets out that Crypto Assets can only be traded on the Crypto-Asset Exchanges if approved by Bappebti. To be approved, minimum requirements have to be satisfied and these requirements are also provided for under Article 3 of the Regulation.("Peraturan Badan Pengawas Perdagangan Berjangka Komoditi Nomor 5 Tahun 2019 Tentang Ketentuan Teknis Penyelenggaraan Pasar Fisik Aset Kripto (Crypto Asset) Di Bursa Berjangka," 2019) In addition to cryptocurrency being prohibited as means of payment, financial services institutions are banned from being involved in activities relating to cryptocurrency. (Buchanan, 2019)

b. Vietnam

In Vietnam, cryptocurrencies are not recognized as legitimate means of instrument nor as legal property. Pursuant to Article 105 of the "Civil Code 2015", property is defined as "objects, money, valuable papers and property rights".("Civil Code," 2015) Article 105 further states that "Property comprises immovable property and movable property. Immovable property and movable property may be existing property and property to be formed in the future".("Civil Code," 2015)

Article 17 of the "Law on the State Bank of Vietnam" states that the State Bank is the only agency entitled to issue banknotes and coins in Vietnam. The banknotes and coins issued are legitimate means of payment".("Law on the State Bank of Vietnam," 2010) "Decree No. 80/2016/ND-CP" amends "Decree No. 101/2012/ND-CP" concerning non-cash payments. Article 1, clause 6 defines non-cash payments as "Non-cash payment instruments in payment transactions (hereinafter referred to as payment instruments), including: Cheques, payment orders, collection orders, bank cards and other payment instruments as prescribed by the State Bank".("No. 80/2016/ND-CP Decree," 2016) Clause 7 states that illegal payment instruments are payment instruments not contained within Clause 6 of Article 1. "Other payment instruments" have yet to be prescribed and defined by the "State Bank of Vietnam".("No. 80/2016/ND-CP Decree," 2016) Therefore, cryptocurrencies are not recognized as legitimate means of payment, nor as legitimate non-cash payment instruments.

In 2017, the "State Bank of Vietnam" further issued "Dispatch No.5747/NHNN-PC" in response to a question on the mining of Bitcoin and Litecoin and other virtual currencies. The Dispatch stated that "As stipulated in Vietnam legislation, cryptocurrencies in general, or Bitcoin and Litecoin in particular, are not currencies and do not act as lawful means of payment".(State Bank of Vietnam, 2017) The Vietnamese government is taking proactive action in relation to virtual assets and cryptocurrencies.

To date, whilst the possession, trade and, investment in cryptocurrencies are not banned in Vietnam, issuing, supplying, and using cryptocurrency is deemed illegal and prohibited.(Prodent, 2021) The Vietnamese government has developed a working plan by way of Decision 1255/ QD-TTg dated August 2017 to (a) review the current legal framework on virtual assets, electronic money, and virtual currency in Vietnam; (b) develop a legal framework on virtual assets, electronic money, virtual currencies.(State Bank of Vietnam, 2017) Besides Decision 1255, Directive No. 10/CT-TTg has been issued to strengthen the "management of activities related to Bitcoin and other similar cryptocurrency".("Directive No. 10 /CT-TTg," 2018)

c. Cambodia

In 2018, the "National Bank of Cambodia", the "Securities and Exchange Commission of Cambodia" and the "General-Commissariat of National Police" issued a Joint Statement on cryptocurrencies.(National Bank of Cambodia, 2018) The "propagation, circulation, buying, selling, trading and settlement" of cryptocurrencies without acquiring a license from the authorities constitutes illegal activities. On this note, individuals or business entities that conduct unlicensed activities will be sanctioned according to applicable laws.(National Bank of Cambodia, 2018) Nevertheless, there is lack of clarity of the "applicable laws" and guidelines from the authorities on the application of license.(Cohen, 2019)

The release of this joint statement denotes the possibility of regulation of cryptocurrencies in Cambodia. The joint statement exemplifies that cryptocurrencies that are not regulated by competent authorities have the tendency to generate risks to the public, including the possibility of being hacked and the potential risks of cybercrime, money laundering, and financing of terrorism.(National Bank of Cambodia, 2018) In late 2020, the National Bank of Cambodia launched its central bank digital currency (CBDC), which adopts a permissioned blockchain system.(Medina, 2020) The digital currency, Bakong can be used by members of the public through a mobile application. Bakong was launched to reduce cash-based transactions and to facilitate payments through a centralized infrastructure.(Medina, 2020) To ensure the security of the financial system, Bakong utilizes a KYC tiered system where users intending to open a "higher-limit account" need to register at a bank branch with their national ID. (Medina, 2020)Users considering opening a lower-limit account can go about it by way of SMS verification. Bakong's digital currencies are backed by reserves held at the central bank.(Medina, 2020)

d. Brunei

In 2017, the Brunei Monetary Authority (Autoriti Monetari Brunei Darussalam, AMBD) issued a press release in relation to cryptocurrencies. In the press release, it was mentioned that "cryptocurrencies are not legal tender in Brunei" and are "not regulated by the AMBD".(Autoriti Monetari Brunei Darussalam, 2017) In furtherance to that, the public was reminded to be "vigilant" and cautious when dealing with publicly issued cryptocurrencies.(Autoriti Monetari Brunei Darussalam, 2017) In 2018, the AMBD issued another press release which stated that, while cryptocurrencies are not considered a legal tender in Brunei, the activities encompassing cryptocurrencies may be subject to regulation if they fall within the domain of any of the activities regulated by AMBD, which includes "extension of loans, remitting funds across the border, [and] foreign exchange services".(Autoriti Monetari Brunei Darussalam, 2018) The AMBD stated that it will constantly monitor the development of cryptocurrencies by balancing innovation and the necessity to protect members of the public.(Autoriti Monetari Brunei Darussalam, 2018) Nevertheless, though not recognized as a legal tender, it should be noted that cryptocurrencies have not been declared illegal, and individuals can still trade cryptocurrencies as a store of value. (Sonksen, 2021)

e. Russia

In mid-2020, the "President of the Russian Federation" signed "Federal Law No. 259-FZ on Digital Financial Assets and Digital Currencies".("Federal Law No. 259-FZ on Digital Financial Assets and Digital Currencies," 2020) By the introduction of this law, it regulates the "issuance, recording, and circulation of digital financial assets". It is prohibited to disseminate any information on the potential settlement by way of digital currencies and to offer or accept digital currencies as payment for goods provided or services rendered.(Brank et al., 2021) Digital currencies do not constitute legal tender in Russia and the Russian Ruble is the only official currency in Russia.

f. Ecuador

The National Assembly of Ecuador whilst allowing payments in "electronic money, approved a bill that bans cryptocurrencies like Bitcoin.(Blakstad & Allen, 2018) Article 98 of the "Código Orgánico Monetario Y Financiero" (Ecuador's Financial Code) states that "Se prohíbe de forma general: La emisión, reproducción, imitación, falsificación o simulación total o parcial de moneda y dinero, así como su circulación por cualquier medio, soporte o forma de representación", which can effectively be translated to "The general prohibition of: The emission, reproduction, imitation, falsification or total or partial simulation of currency and money, as well as its circulation by any means, support or form of representation". ("Código Orgánico Monetario Y Financiero ", 2014) The legislative framework of Ecuador stipulates the sanctions from the violation of the prohibition, including the power to seize the digital currencies.

g. Bolivia

In 2014, the "El Banco Central Bank de Bolivia" banned currencies or money not issued or regulated by the government. This includes bitcoin and other cryptocurrencies.(Sahoo, 2017) The translation of the Central Bank statement elucidates that "It is illegal to use any kind of currency that is not issued and controlled by a government or an authorized entity".(Artemov et al., 2017) The ban was said to be necessary to safeguard the national currency and protect individuals/business entities from "uncontrolled currencies" that can potentially result in losing money or investments.(Rizzo, 2014)

h. India

Press releases issued by the Reserve Bank of India in December 2013, February 2017, and December 2017 portrays India's disinclination towards cryptocurrency. On 24 December 2013, RBI warned "users, holders and traders of Virtual currencies (VCs)" regarding the possible "financial, operational, legal, customer protection and security related risks" associated with VCs.(Reserve Bank of India, 2013) The Press Release elucidates that the creation, trading, or use of VCs may present various risks, such as (a) hacking or malware attacks resulting in losses; (b) no authorized central agency to regulate the payments by VCs; (c) high volatility of VCs exposing users to a greater risk of losses; and (d) unintentional infringement of anti-money laundering and combating the financing of terrorism laws. Subsequently, in February and December 2017, further press releases were issued by RBI, where RBI cautioned users of the potential risk of VCs.(Reserve Bank of India, 2017a, 2017b) RBI also stated that it had not given any license or authorization to any entity or corporation to deal with VCs. (Reserve Bank of India, 2017a, 2017b)

In 2017, the Inter-Ministerial Committee ("IMC") proposed the introduction of two bills but neither of the bills was enacted into law. The first bill, Crypto-token Regulation Bill of 2018 comprised of draft provisions to prohibit entities engaging in activities related to crypto-tokens from "falsely posing these products as not being securities or investment schemes or offering investment schemes", and to provide a regulatory framework directed to VC exchanges and brokers where sale and purchase may be permitted.(Dalmia, 2020)

The second bill, Banning of Cryptocurrency & Regulation of Official Digital Currency Bill, 2019, sought to prohibit "mining, holding, selling, trade, issuance, disposal or use of cryptocurrency in the country".(Ministry of Finance, n.d.) The second bill also proposed to ban the utilization of cryptocurrency as a legal tender. In April 2018, the RBI issued a circular on the Prohibition on Dealing with VCs. (Reserve Bank of India, 2018) Based on the circular, entities regulated by RBI were prohibited from dealing with VCs directly and indirectly. A ban was imposed on such entities to offer services that would facilitate any individual or business entity in dealing with VCs. These services encompassed "maintaining accounts, registering, trading, settling, clearing, giving loans against virtual tokens, accepting them as collateral, opening accounts of exchanges dealing with them and transfer/receipt of money in accounts" in relation to the purchase and/or sale of VCs.(Reserve Bank of India, 2018)

In the Supreme Court (SC) judgment of Internet and Mobile Association of India v. Reserve Bank of India presided by Justices "Rohinton Fali Nariman", "S. Ravindra Bhat" and "V. Ramasubramanian", the SC assessed the case by examining Article 19(1)(g) of the Constitution of India.("Internet and Mobile Association of India v. Reserve Bank of India ", 2020) It was held by the Court that a total ban by way of a directive from RBI of any activity and/or trade of VCs that was not prohibited by law violated Article

19(1)(g) of the Constitution. The circular of RBI was set aside on the grounds of proportionality. The Court stated the need to show some "empirical data about the degree of harm suffered" by the regulated entities. In this case, RBI was unable to demonstrate that any of its regulated entities had suffered any loss or adverse effect due to the provision of banking services to VC exchanges. The Parliament of India has proposed introducing the "Cryptocurrency and Regulation of Official Digital Currency Bill", 2021, which may ban private cryptocurrencies and put forth a legislative framework to facilitate the creation of its official digital currency.(Singh, 2021)

4. Country With an Incoherent Regulatory Framework of Cryptocurrency

a. US

The focus of this section would be on the regulations adopted by state governments of the US rather than the federal government due to the minimal rulemaking by the federal government in this area. On the other hand, several state governments have enacted or proposed laws in relation to blockchain technology and cryptocurrencies. States like Wyoming and Colorado have enacted crypto-friendly laws to be the crypto-hub in the US by attracting entrepreneurs and business entities to their states. (Dewey, 2021)

Within the Federal government, government agencies in the US have not formed a unified approach. The distinct treatment of cryptocurrencies by government agencies has led to uncertainties amongst business entities on the regulatory regime that they will be subject to.(Weinstein et al., 2019) "Securities and Exchange Commission" (SEC) describes cryptocurrencies as securities contingent on the "Securities Exchange Act 1934" (SEA 1934) and "Securities Act 1933" (SA 1933), while the "Commodity Futures Trading Commission" (CFTC) defines it as "commodities". On the other hand, the "Internal Revenue Service" ("IRS") treats virtual currencies as property. (Hughes, 2017)

The SEC has played an active role in cryptocurrency regulation in the past years. In July 2017, SEC in the DAO Report of Investigation stated that "Federal securities law may apply to various activities, including distributed ledger technology, depending on the particular facts and circumstances". (Securities and Exchange Commission, 2017) In December 2017, the Chairman of SEC stipulated that some cryptocurrencies appear to SEC to constitute securities, while others do not. (Clayton, 2017) Therefore, the determination of whether cryptocurrencies amount to securities is case-specific. In the recent case of United States v Zaslavskiy, the defendant obtained money from the investors on the false basis that the cryptocurrencies "Recoin" and "Diamond" were guaranteed by real estate and diamonds.("United States v. Zaslavskiy," 2018) Zaslavskiy was charged under SEA 1934 and SEC Rule 10b-5 due to the employment of manipulative and deceptive practices. The Government was of the position that the investment in cryptocurrencies constituted "investment contracts" within the SEA 1934 and SA 1933. The defendant argued that cryptocurrencies did not constitute securities and it did not meet the elements of Howey test of an investment contract. Besides that, the defendant argued that the 1933 and 1934 Securities legislations were void for vagueness. The application of the three limbs to the Howey("SEC v. WJ Howey Co," 1946) test was deliberated by the Court, as to whether (a) "individuals invested money (and other forms of payment) in order to participate in [the defendant's] schemes"; (b) cryptocurrency "constituted a 'common enterprise'"; and (c) "investors were led to expect profits in [the defendant's cryptocurrencies] to be derived solely from the managerial efforts of [the defendant] and his co-conspirators, not any efforts of the investors themselves." SEC had filed a brief in support of the government stance and discussed the pertinence of treating cryptocurrencies as securities. (Schwinger, 2018) The Court rejected the argument by the defendant that the cryptocurrencies did not constitute securities. This decision establishes that under "proper facts and circumstances" federal laws on securities can apply to cryptocurrencies. Nevertheless, it does not denote that every cryptocurrency should constitute securities. (Schwinger, 2018)

Cryptocurrencies may also fall within the jurisdiction of CFTC. CFTC was established in 1974 and operates under the Commodity Exchange Act 1936 (CEA). The CEA defines "commodity" broadly, and includes within the definition "all services, rights, and interests […] in which contracts for future delivery are presently or in the future dealt in […]".("Commodity Exchange Act," 1936) It has been the consistent stance of CFTC that "Bitcoin and other virtual currencies are encompassed in the definition and properly defined as commodities".("In the Matter of: Coinflip, Inc., d/b/a Derivabit, and Francisco Riordan," 2015) This was similarly propounded by the Court in CFTC v. McDonnell.("Commodity Futures Trading Comm'n v. McDonnell," 2018) In the latter case, the court held that "[v]irtual currencies are "goods" exchanged in a market for a uniform quality and value. They fall well-within the common definition of "commodity" as well as the CEA's definition of "commodities" as "all other goods and articles ... in which contracts for future delivery are presently or in the future dealt in."("Commodity Futures Trading Comm'n v. McDonnell," 2018) CFTC oversees the "futures, options and derivatives contracts" involving a commodity.(LabCFTC, 2017) Cryptocurrency which is used in a derivatives contract falls under the CFTC's jurisdiction. CFTC's jurisdiction is also invoked if there is "fraud or manipulation involving a virtual currency traded in interstate commerce".(LabCFTC, 2017) More importantly, even though CFTC has the jurisdiction to regulate "derivative products" it generally has no power to monitor "spot or cash market exchanges and transactions" concerning virtual currencies.(LabCFTC, 2017)

Early 2013, "Financial Crimes Enforcement Network" (FinCEN) through a Guidance Note FIN-2013-G001, on the "Application of FinCEN's Regulations to Persons Administering, Exchanging, or Using Virtual Currencies" announced the applicability of the "Bank Secrecy Act" (BSA) to business entities and undertakings participating in the cryptocurrency ecosystem. (Department of the Treasury Financial Crimes Enforcement Network, 2013) The Note stated that a "user of virtual currency" does not constitute a Money Service Business (MSB). However, "an administrator or exchanger [of virtual currency] is an MSB" and is subjected to MSB regulations of registration, reporting, and recordkeeping. (Department of the Treasury Financial Crimes Enforcement Network, 2013) In 2014, IRS issued Notice 2014-21 on virtual currencies and clarified that virtual currencies are treated as property for tax purposes, and therefore "[g]eneral tax principles applicable to property transactions apply to transactions using virtual currency". (Internal Revenue Service, 2014) Virtual currencies are not treated as currencies that could "generate foreign currency gain or loss" for taxation purposes. (Internal Revenue Service, 2014)

There is no unified approach between federal and state regulations. This has led to uncertainties and "concerns from market participants over [compliance] with the patchwork of regulation".(Sonksen, 2021) The US Congress has not issued any legislation thus far on cryptocurrencies. Nevertheless, Congress has impelled government agencies to "coordinate to ensure they do not work at cross purpose".(Joint Economic Committee, 2018) With four varying classifications of cryptocurrencies, namely "commodity, security, currency and property", the cryptocurrency landscape may not be favourable for investors and entrepreneurs.(Joint Economic Committee, 2018) In the case of "Commodity Futures Trading Comm'n v. McDonnell", the Court provided nine possible alternatives for cryptocurrency regulation, namely (i) no regulation; (ii) partial regulation by way of "criminal law prosecutions of Ponzi–like schemes by the Department of Justice, or state criminal agencies, or civil substantive suits based on allegations of fraud"; (iii) regulation by CFTC; (iv) regulation by SEC; (v) regulation by FinCEN; (vi) regulation by IRS; (vii) regulation by "private exchanges"; (viii) state regulations; (ix) a combination of any of the 8 possible alternatives (as described above).("Commodity Futures Trading Comm'n v. McDonnell," 2018) In furtherance of the complexity in adopting a unified approach at the federal level, there are different state regulations on cryptocurrencies. Several states in the US have either proposed and/or enacted legislation concerning cryptocurrency, whilst other states have not addressed the crypto market. In relation to the states that have proposed and/or enacted legislation on cryptocurrency, differing approaches have been adopted. As mentioned, several states have enacted enabling laws to become a "crypto-friendly" state, whilst states like Maryland and Hawaii have adopted a cautious approach by issuing warnings regarding investments in cryptocurrencies.(Dewey, 2021) An overview is provided of the states in the US that have been progressively enacting regulations on cryptocurrencies.

i. Colorado

In 2018, the Division of Banking issued an "Interim Regulatory Guidance on Cryptocurrency and Colorado Money Transmitters Act". (Colorado Department of Regulatory Agencies, 2018) The aim of its issuance is to outline whether an entity partaking in the business of "buying, selling and/or facilitating the transfer" of cryptocurrency has to be licensed under the "Money Transmitters Act" (MTA) as a money transmitter.("CO Rev Stat § 11-110," 2018) The MTA aims to regulate the transmission of money (ie legal tender). However, in Colorado, cryptocurrencies are not recognized as legal tenders. The direct transmission of cryptocurrency between one individual to another is not subjected to licensing. (Colorado Department of Regulatory Agencies, 2018) On the contrary, the "presence of fiat currency during a transmission may be subject to licensure".(Colorado Department of Regulatory Agencies, 2018) The license may also be required when an entity is engaged in (a) buying and selling of cryptocurrencies for fiat currency; (b) transfer of cryptocurrency to another customer within the virtual currency exchange and (c) transfer of fiat currency through the mode of cryptocurrency. (Colorado Department of Regulatory Agencies, 2018) In March 2019, the "Cryptocurrency Exemption Colorado Digital Token Act" was enacted which provides "limited exemptions from the securities registration and securities broker-dealer and salesperson licensing requirements for persons dealing in digital tokens". ("S.B.19-023, 73rd Leg. Sess. (Col) ", 2019)

ii. New York

In 2015, the New York Department of Financial Services ("DFS") set out its virtual currency regulation under the Financial Services Law of New York.("23 NY Comp Codes Rules and Regs §," 2015) Pursuant to 23 NYCRR 200.3(a), to conduct a "Virtual Currency Business Activity", a license is required.("23 NY Comp Codes Rules and Regs §," 2015) The regulatory framework, known as BitLicense, is the first all-encompassing framework in the US. This is a progressive regulation as it ensures regulated access of virtual currencies. The "Virtual Currency Business Activity" provided under 23 NYCRR 200.2(q) is defined as "conduct of any one of the following types of activities (1) receiving virtual currency for transmission or transmitting virtual currency[…] (2) storing, holding, or maintaining custody or control of virtual currency on behalf of others; (3) buying and selling virtual currency as a customer business; (4) performing exchange services as a customer business; or (5) controlling, administering, or issuing a virtual currency".("23 NY Comp Codes Rules and Regs §," 2015) The regulatory framework provides for consumer protection and anti-money laundering safeguards. ("23 NY Comp Codes Rules and Regs §," 2015)

DFS has acknowledged that some business entities may face difficulties in obtaining licenses during the application process which can consume significant time and resources in order to comply with the regulatory requirements outlined in the regulation. DFS was created to "encourage, promote and assist banking, insurance, and other financial services institutions to effectively and productively locate, operate, employ, grow, remain, and expand in New York state."(Department of Financial Service, n.d.) To meet these objectives, DFS proposed a conditional BitLicensing Framework to allow a new player to collaborate and engage with an authorized BitLicense holder or a holder of "New York limited purpose trust charter" for support and services consisting of "structure, capital, systems, personnel, or any other support needed" during the term of the conditional license.(Department of Financial Service, n.d.) DFS envisages that the entity requesting a Conditional License will in due course endeavour to obtain a full BitLicense.

iii. Wyoming

By the passing of SF0111, W.S. 39-11-105(b)(vi)(A) is amended to incorporate virtual currencies, as being exempted from property taxation.("SF0111, 64th Leg., Budget Sess (Wyo)," 2018) Virtual currencies are defined to include a "digital representation of value" that is used as a "medium of exchange, unit of account or store of value" and is not recognized as a legal tender.("SF0111, 64th Leg., Budget Sess (Wyo)," 2018) Under the "Wyoming Money Transmitters Act" (WMTA), any individual or business undertaking that is carrying out a business of money transmission must be licensed under the WMTA. By the enactment of HB0019, virtual currencies are exempted from the WMTA.("H.B. 0019, 64th Leg., Budget Sess (Wyo)," 2018) This exemption allows entities to buy, sell, issue, or take "custody of payment instruments or stored value in the form of virtual currency", or receive virtual currency to be transmitted to a location within or outside the US. ("H.B. 0019, 64th Leg., Budget Sess (Wyo)," 2018)

Wyoming also enacted H.B. 70, known as the "Utility Token Bill". It states that a person who develops and sells open blockchain tokens is exempted from specified securities and money transmission laws provided the developer or seller meets specified requirements. The specified requirements are as follows: (a) the developer or seller of the token must file a "notice of intent with the secretary of state"; (b) the purpose of the blockchain token is for consumptive purposes only "which shall only be exchangeable for, or provided for the receipt of, goods, services or content[…]"; (c) the token is not sold as a "financial investment" to the initial buyer by the developer or seller of the token. ("H.B. 0070, 65th Leg., Gen. Sess. (Wyo)," 2018) This is not in line with the position adopted by the "Federal Securities and Exchange Commission" that regards tokens as potential securities offerings. (Higgins, 2018)

Wyoming in 2019 passed HB0001 relating to the creation of a blockchain task force. ("H.B. 1, 65th Leg., Gen. Sess. (Wyo.)," 2019) Besides that, a bill on digital assets was enacted which (a) classifies digital assets under existing laws; (b) specifies that digital assets are property under the "Uniform Commercial Code"; (c) authorizes security interest in digital assets; (d) establishes "opt-in framework" for banks to provide "custodial service" and specifies standards and procedures for such service; and (e) clarifies the jurisdiction of Wyoming in relation to digital assets. ("S.F. 125, 65th Leg., Gen. Sess. (Wyo)," 2019)

Besides that, in 2020, Wyoming enacted bills on blockchain and cryptocurrency. HB 0027 established a "Select Committee on Blockchain, Financial Technology and Digital Innovation Technology". ("H.B. 27, 65th Leg., Gen. Sess. (Wyo)," 2020) It sets out the role of the select committee "to develop and introduce legislation as necessary to promote blockchain, financial technology, and digital innovation". ("H.B. 27, 65th Leg., Gen. Sess. (Wyo)," 2020)

In 2021, Wyoming enacted SF0038 allowing the recognition of decentralized autonomous organization ("DAO") as a limited liability company, allowing the company to be wholly or partly run or managed algorithmically through smart contracts. The Bill also provides for the formation, articles of organization, operating agreements, smart contracts, management, standards of conduct, membership interests, voting rights, the withdrawal of members, and dissolution. ("S.F. 38, 66th Leg, Gen. Sess. (Wyo)," 2021) The bill takes effect in 2021. This is a pertinent enactment as it permits the incorporation of DAOs as a limited liability company which is a company structure where the members of the company are not held personally liable for liabilities incurred by the DAO.

iv. Ohio

Ohio is the first state in the US that provides business entities with the option to pay taxes using cryptocurrency.(Phillips, 2018) John Mandel, the then Treasurer of Ohio stated that "We're doing this to provide Ohioans more options and ease in paying their taxes and also to project Ohio's leadership in embracing blockchain technology."(Phillips, 2018)

v. Vermont

In 2017, Vermont amended its money transmission legislation to incorporate virtual currencies where companies are now permitted to hold virtual currencies as investments, but only "to the extent of outstanding transmission obligations received by the licensee in identical denomination of virtual currency". ("H.B. 182, Gen. Assemb., Reg. Sess. (Vt.)," 2017) In furtherance to that, the legislation sets out the definition of virtual currency where virtual currency can be defined as a stored value that: "(A) can be a medium of exchange, a unit of account, or a store of value; (B) has an equivalent value in money or acts as a substitute for money; (C) may be centralized or decentralized; and (D) can be exchanged for money or other convertible virtual currency". ("H.B. 182, Gen. Assemb., Reg. Sess. (Vt.)," 2017)

From the discussion above, the regulatory framework in the US in relation to cryptocurrency lacks consensus and is piecemeal. It is pertinent to adopt a standardized definition of cryptocurrency to hinder "jurisdictional issues" and other associated risks resulting from the lack of consistency.(McKinney Jr et al., 2020) A proper regulatory framework that delineates the responsibilities of government agencies can prevent users or participants of cryptocurrencies from attempting to "evade the regulator by becoming camouflaged in the current ambiguity of a definition and government authority".(McKinney Jr et al., 2020) Business entities and undertakings may struggle to understand whether cryptocurrencies would fall within the jurisdiction of CFTC, SEC, or other government agencies, leading to confusion.(McKinney Jr et al., 2020) The lack of consensus can exacerbate risks and weaken the protection of investors. In furtherance to that, states in the US have not adopted a uniform approach to cryptocurrency.

CONCLUSION AND RECOMMENDATIONS

The countries in the first category have embraced common regulatory measures by the legalization of cryptocurrencies and the adoption of a proactive regulatory scheme. Besides that, Gibraltar, Switzerland, Singapore, and Malta have introduced comprehensive industry-specific regulations, while Estonia has adopted partial regulations in regulating cryptocurrencies. Countries in the second category have adopted a relatively proactive approach towards regulating cryptocurrencies and are in the midst of augmenting cryptocurrency regulations. On the other hand, India, amongst other countries have adopted a regressive approach towards the regulation of cryptocurrencies.

There remain an array of issues surrounding cryptocurrencies that can undermine "consumer and investor protection, market integrity, money laundering, terrorism financing, tax evasion, and the circumvention of capital controls and international sanctions". (Hamil, 2018; Zharova & Lloyd, 2018) It has been stated that "[c]ryptocurrencies have become a combination of a bubble, a Ponzi scheme and an environmental disaster".(Bank for International Settlements, 2018) Differences in the legal and regulatory landscapes, such as the banning of cryptocurrencies by several jurisdictions and the adoption of a proactive regulatory landscape by others have resulted in "regulatory arbitrage" where business entities have shifted their operations to countries with friendlier regulations.(Nabilou, 2019) Countries and international standard-setting organizations should adopt a consistent regulatory approach to promote transparency and market integrity of cryptocurrency exchanges which may hinder regulatory arbitrage. (International Monetary Fund & Monetary and Capital Markets (MCM) Department, 2018)

Scholar Nabilou has identified the decentralized indirect regulation as a more suitable approach in regulating cryptocurrencies, instead of a centralized direct regulation built on "command-and-control". (Nabilou, 2019) By the adoption of an indirect regulation, the rules enacted by regulators are transformed into principles and/or standards to be implemented by financial institutions, known as "surrogate regulators".(Nabilou, 2019) Therefore, under this approach, "central banks and other banking and payment regulators would regulate the entities or intermediaries enabling the interface and interaction between cryptocurrencies and fiat currency in cryptocurrencies schemes with the bidirectional flow".(Nabilou, 2019) Given the decentralized nature of cryptocurrencies and various innovative use cases that can be developed upon them, the command-and-control approach seems inefficient and inflexible, leading to the possibility of hampering future innovations.(Nabilou, 2019) Instead, "light-touch" regulation may be a better regulatory approach with the constantly emerging and evolving nature of cryptocurrencies. (Nabilou, 2019) The "hard-touch regulatory approach" or "overregulation" of cryptocurrencies might be unfavourable to the industry's landscape as it may deter investors from investing and may affect the volatility and stability of the crypto market.(Nabilou, 2019; Shanaev et al., 2020) A balance has to be established by regulators, where on one hand, consumers have to be protected against the idiosyncratic risks attached to cryptocurrencies, and on the other hand, promote innovative freedom of cryptocurrencies.

In the US, Federal agencies such as the SEC, CFTC, FinCEN, and IRS have clarified their policies in relation to virtual currency transactions. Nevertheless, the disparate approaches taken by the agencies in the US towards the treatment of cryptocurrencies are partly due to the versatility of cryptocurrencies which have consequentially resulted in uncertainties for business entities. It is pertinent to ascertain which agency should have the "primary authority over shaping regulations". (Sonksen, 2021) Several states in the US have clarified their approach regarding the legality of cryptocurrencies and the application and enforcement of legislation surrounding cryptocurrencies. With the ever-changing landscape of cryptocurrency markets, the regulatory regime is likely to evolve and emerge to address issues relating to taxation and financial crime.

1. Should the Regulatory Agencies Work Towards Coordinating Efforts to Effectively Regulate Cryptocurrencies?

As described above, the users of cryptocurrencies fall within the realm of various regulatory agencies with disparate "jurisdictional reach, enforcement priorities, budgets, and leadership".(McGill et al.,

2018) The lack of consensus on jurisdiction and enforcement procedures might deter business entities and investors from investing in cryptocurrencies. Scholar Bessemer recognized the peculiarity of regulatory agencies in "relinquishing their power or cooperating in an effective manner" to reach a consensus on a proper regulatory framework of cryptocurrencies.(Bessemer, 2019) The designation of a central and independent regulatory agency solely addressing cryptocurrency might be a better fit to resolve the inconsistencies surrounding cryptocurrencies.(McKinney Jr et al., 2020)

2. Should Congress Define and Classify Cryptocurrencies?

Based on recommendations by scholars, Congress should step in to first define and classify cryptocurrency. A cautious approach to the "legal categorization of cryptocurrencies" has to be adopted as the determination of such categorization may prompt a multitude of legal implications. (Nabilou, 2019) Congress should also specify the federal regulatory agency that is responsible and accountable for providing regulatory oversight of the crypto market.(Bessemer, 2019; Massad, 2019) It is pertinent to put forth a suitable legal definition and construct for cryptocurrencies that can be espoused and implemented in the legal landscape.(Bessemer, 2019) Besides that, providing certainty as to which regulatory agency has jurisdiction over cryptocurrency can eliminate uncertainties in the crypto market.(Bessemer, 2019) Congress can enact legislation to confer authority on the regulatory agency to "regulate the offering, distribution and trading of crypto-assets".(Massad, 2019) In furtherance to that, Congress can utilize the principle-based approach by setting out central principles that have to be regulated by the agency. (Massad, 2019) It can include principles concerning "risk management", prevention of fraudulent activities, and "procedure for reporting and monitoring crypto-transactions", amongst others. (Bessemer, 2019; Massad, 2019) The regulatory agency that is given the mandate to regulate and implement the central principles can then issue specific regulations.(Massad, 2019) The regulatory framework has to be all-encompassing and complete, to include all possible cryptocurrency use cases.(Bessemer, 2019) This might be an effective approach in light of the objective to develop a coordinated, unified, and comprehensive framework to be applicable to crypto markets.

FUTURE RESEARCH DIRECTIONS

In this chapter, the author has adopted a descriptive method of examining the regulatory approach of cryptocurrency in various countries. For purposes of future research, a comparative analysis of regulatory efforts can be conducted, including providing an overview of the weaknesses and strengths of the regulatory approaches by each country.

REFERENCES

Anti-Money Laundering Act of 10 October 1997, (1997).

Anti-Money Laundering Council. (2014). *Warning Advisory on Virtual Currencies.* http://www.amlc.gov. ph/2015-12-09-07-34-10/2015-12-14-04-11-34/request-for-amla-training/2-uncategorised/60-warning-advisory-on-virtual-currencies

Artemov, N. M., Arzumanova, L. L., Sitnik, A. A., & Zenin, S. S. (2017). Regulation and Control of Virtual Currency: To be or not to be. *J. Advanced Res. L. Econ.*, *8*, 1428.

Autoriti Monetari Brunei Darussalam. (2017). *Public to Exercise High Caution with Cryptocurrencies.* https://www.ambd.gov.bn/

Autoriti Monetari Brunei Darussalam. (2018). *Autoriti Monetari Brunei Darussalam Reiterates Position on Cryptocurrencies.* https://ambd.gov.bn/

Bangko Sentral ng Pilipinas. (2017). *BSP Circular No. 944.* https://www.bsp.gov.ph/Regulations/Issuances/2017/c944.pdf

Bank for International Settlements. (2018). *Annual Economic Report.* https://www.bis.org/publ/arpdf/ar2018e.pdf

Bessemer, C. (2019). Cryptocurrency: Legality and Role within US Financial Institutions. *Syracuse J. Sci.Tech. L.*, *36*, 3.

Blakstad, S., & Allen, R. (2018). *FinTech Revolution: Universal Inclusion in the New Financial Ecosystem.* Springer International Publishing. https://books.google.com.my/books?id=0_VeDwAAQBAJ

Brank, L., Dunaev, P., & Korotkova, E. (2021). *Russian Laws Advance Framework for the Use and Regulation of Digital Financial Assets and Currency.* https://www.jdsupra.com/legalnews/russian-laws-advance-framework-for-the-9925457/

Buchanan, K. (2019). *Regulatory Approaches to Cryptoassets in Selected Jurisdictions-Indonesia.* https://www.lawscopelibrary.com/admin/articles/regulatory-approaches-to-cryptoassets-in-selected-jurisdictions/cryptoasset-regulation.pdf

Buttigieg, C. P., & Efthymiopoulos, C. (2019). The regulation of crypto assets in Malta: The virtual financial assets act and beyond. *Law Financial Markets Review*, *13*(1), 30–40.

Buttigieg, C. P., Efthymiopoulos, C., Attard, A., & Cuyle, S. (2019). Anti-money laundering regulation of crypto assets in Europe's smallest member state. *Law Financial Markets Review*, *13*(4), 211–227.

Chokor, A., & Alfieri, E. (2021). Long and short-term Impacts of Regulation in the Cryptocurrency Market. *The Quarterly Review of Economics and Finance.*

Clayton, J. (2017). *Statement on Cryptocurrencies and Initial Coin Offerings.* https://www.sec.gov/news/public-statement/statement-clayton-2017-12-11

CO Rev Stat § 11-110, (2018).

CodeC. (2015). https://www.economica.vn/Content/files/LAW%20%26%20REG/91_2015_QH13%20Civil%20Code.pdf

Código Orgánico Monetario, Y. Financiero. (2014). http://www.pge.gob.ec/documents/Transparencia/antilavado/REGISTROOFICIAL332.pdf

Cohen, J. (2019). *Cryptocurrency Regulations in Mainland Southeast Asia.* https://www.tilleke.com/wp-content/uploads/2019/09/Cryptocurrency-Regulations-in-Mainland-Southeast-Asia_0.pdf

Colorado Department of Regulatory Agencies. (2018). *Interim Regulatory Guidance Cryptocurrency and the Colorado Money Transmitters Act.* Author.

Commissioner for Revenue. (2018). *Guidelines on the Income Tax Treatment of transactions or arrangements involving DLT Assets.* https://cfr.gov.mt/en/inlandrevenue/legal-technical/Documents/Guidelines%20-DLTs%20Income%20tax.pdf

Commodity Exchange Act, (1936).

Commodity Futures Trading Comm'n v. McDonnell, F. Supp. 3d 287 (Dist. Court, ED New York 2018).

Cumming, D. J., Johan, S., & Pant, A. (2019). Regulation of the crypto-economy: Managing risks, challenges, and regulatory uncertainty. *Journal of Risk Financial Management, 12*(3), 126.

Dalmia, V. P. (2020). *India: RBI ban on banks' crypto deals quashed.* https://globalbankingregulation-review.com/pro/content/cryptocurrency-verdict-imai-vs-rbi

Department of Financial Service. (n.d.). *Virtual Currency Businesses: Request for Comments on a Proposed Framework for a Conditional BitLicense.* https://www.dfs.ny.gov/apps_and_licensing/virtual_currency_businesses/gn/req_comments_prop_framework#_edn1

Department of the Treasury Financial Crimes Enforcement Network. (2013). *Application of FinCEN's Regulations to Persons Administering, Exchanging, or Using Virtual Currencies.* https://www.fincen.gov/sites/default/files/shared/FIN-2013-G001.pdf

Dewey, J. (2021). *Blockchain & Cryptocurrency Regulation – USA.* https://www.globallegalinsights.com/practice-areas/blockchain-laws-and-regulations/usa

Directive, No. 10/CT-TTg, (2018). http://ssc.gov.vn/ssc/faces/en/enlinks/endetail/investor/investoralert/enchitiet167?dDocName=APPSSCGOVVN162121076&_afrLoop=66504322089922874&_afrWindow-Mode=0&_afrWindowId=gflldph6f_51#%40%3F_afrWindowId%3Dgflldph6f_51%26_afrLoop%3D66504322089922874%26dDocName%3DAPPSSCGOVVN162121076%26_afrWindowMode%3D0%26_adf.ctrl-state%3Dgflldph6f_79

Ellul, J., Galea, J., Ganado, M., McCarthy, S., & Pace, G. J. (2020). Regulating Blockchain, DLT and Smart Contracts: a technology regulator's perspective. *ERA Forum, 21*(2), 209-220. doi:10.1007/s12027-020-00617-7

European Securities and Markets Authority. (2017). *ESMA alerts firms involved in Initial Coin Offerings (ICOs) to the need to meet relevant regulatory requirements.* https://www.esma.europa.eu/sites/default/files/library/esma50-157-828_ico_statement_firms.pdf

Federal Act on the Adaptation of Federal Law to Developments in Distributed Ledger Technology, (2020).

Federal Council of Switzerland. (2018). *Legal framework for distributed ledger technology and blockchain in Switzerland: A n overview with a focus on the financial sector.* https://www.newsd.admin.ch/newsd/message/attachments/55153.pdf

Federal Department of Finance. (2012). *Circular No. 36: Commercial securities trading.* Author.

Federal Law No. 259-FZ on Digital Financial Assets and Digital Currencies, (2020).

Financial Market Infrastructure Act of 19 June 2015, (2015).

Financial Services (Distributed Ledger Technology Providers) Regulations, (2020).

Garcia, J., & Garcia, J. (2021). Blockchain & Cryptocurrency Regulation 2021 - Gibraltar. *Global Legal Insights*. https://www.globallegalinsights.com/practice-areas/blockchain-laws-and-regulations/gibraltar

Gibraltar Financial Services Commission. (n.d.). *Distributed Ledger Technology Regulatory Framework (DLT framework)*. https://www.fsc.gi/dlt

Governor of Bank Indonesia. (2016). *Bank Indonesia Regulation Number 18/40/PBI/2016 Concerning Operation of Payment Transaction Processing*. http://intr.insw.go.id/files/ecommerce/7.%20Regulation%20of%20BI%20No%2018.40.PBI.2016%20on%20Concerning%20the%20implementation%20of%20payment%20transaction.pdf

Gürcan, B. (2019). Various Dimensions and Aspects of the Legal Problems of the Blockchain Technology. *Comparative Law Working Papers, 3*(1).

Ha, T. L. D., Lee, C., & Cho, S. (2021). VCG Auction Mechanism based on Block Chain in Smart Grid. *International Conference on Information Networking*.

Haeberli, D., Oesterhelt, S., & Wherlock, A. (2021). *Blockchain & Cryptocurrency Regulation 2021 – Switzerland*. https://www.globallegalinsights.com/practice-areas/blockchain-laws-and-regulations/switzerland

Hamil, J. (2018). *Bitcoin is a 'bubble' and cryptocurrency trading relies on 'finding the greater fool', Bank of England governor Mark Carney warns*. https://metro.co.uk/2018/03/02/bitcoin-bubble-cryptocurrency-trading-fools-says-bank-england-governor-mark-carney-7356044/

H.B. 0019, 64th Leg., Budget Sess (Wyo), (2018).

H.B. 0070, 65th Leg., Gen. Sess. (Wyo), (2018).

H.B. 1, 65th Leg., Gen. Sess. (Wyo.), (2019).

H.B. 182, Gen. Assemb., Reg. Sess. (Vt.), (2017).

H.B. 27, 65th Leg., Gen. Sess. (Wyo), (2020).

Higgins, S. (2018). *SEC Chief Clayton: 'Every ICO I've Seen Is a Security'*. Retrieved June 30, 2021 from https://www.coindesk.com/sec-chief-clayton-every-ico-ive-seen-security

HM Government of Gibraltar. (2020). *Gibraltar Regulator Refreshes Jurisdiction's Distributed Ledger Technology Regulation - 631/2020*. https://www.gibraltar.gov.gi/press-releases/gibraltar-regulator-refreshes-jurisdictions-distributed-ledger-technology-regulation-6312020-6206

Hofverberg, E. (2019). *Regulatory Approaches to Cryptoassets in Selected Jurisdictions-Denmark*. https://www.lawscopelibrary.com/admin/articles/regulatory-approaches-to-cryptoassets-in-selected-jurisdictions/cryptoasset-regulation.pdf

Hughes, S. D. (2017). *Cryptocurrency Regulations and Enforcement in the US*. Academic Press.

In the Matter of: Coinflip, Inc., d/b/a Derivabit, and Francisco Riordan, WL 5535736 (2015).

Income Tax Act (1949).

Indonesia, K. P. R. (2019). *Bappebti Terbitkan Empat Peraturan Aset Kripto dan Emas Digital*. http://bappebti.go.id/resources/docs/siaran_pers_2019_02_18_gpfdzt8b_id.pdf

Inland Revenue Authority of Singapore. (2020). *IRAS e-Tax Guide: Income Tax Treatment of Digital Tokens*. https://www.iras.gov.sg/irashome/uploadedFiles/IRASHome/e-Tax_Guides/etaxguide_CIT_Income%20Tax%20Treatment%20of%20Digital%20Tokens.pdf

Internal Revenue Service. (2014). *IRS Notice 2014-21*. https://www.irs.gov/pub/irs-drop/n-14-21.pdf

International Monetary Fund, & Monetary and Capital Markets (MCM) Department. (2018). *Global Financial Stability Report, April 2018: A Bumpy Road Ahead*. International Monetary Fund. https://books.google.com.my/books?id=_K4ZEAAAQBAJ

Internet and Mobile Association of India v. Reserve Bank of India CPSC58 (SC 2020).

Ji, J. Z. K., Wang, R., Chen, B., & Dai, C. (2018). Energy Efficient Caching in Backhaul-Aware Ultra-Dense Cellular Networks. *Proceedings - IEEE 2018 International Congress on Cybermatics: 2018 IEEE Conferences on Internet of Things, Green Computing and Communications, Cyber, Physical and Social Computing, Smart Data, Blockchain, Computer and Information Technology, iThings/GreenCom/CPSCom/SmartData/Blockchain/CIT 2018*.

Joint Economic Committee. (2018). *H. Rept. 115-596 - Report of the Joint Economic Committee Congress of the United States on the 2018 Economic Report of the President Together with Minority Views*. https://www.congress.gov/congressional-report/115th-congress/house-report/596/1

Kasprzyk, M. (2018). Comparative Review of Regulatory Framework of Virtual Currency (Cryptocurrency) In Selected Countries. *Review of European Comparative Law Working Papers*, 35(4), 7–26.

LabCFTC. (2017). *A CFTC Primer on Virtual Currencies*. https://www.cftc.gov/sites/default/files/idc/groups/public/documents/file/labcftc_primercurrencies100417.pdf

Lacity, M. (2020). Crypto and Blockchain Fundamentals. *Arkansas Law Review*, *73*, 363.

Law on the State Bank of Vietnam. (2010). https://sites.google.com/a/ecolaw.vn/luat-tieng-anh/1-bo-luat-luat/-law-on-the-state-bank-of-vietnam

Malta Financial Services Authority. (2018a). *Virtual Financial Assets Framework - Frequently Asked Questions*. https://www.legal500.com/developments/wp-content/uploads/sites/19/2019/03/MFSA-VFARFAQs-24.10.18.pdf

Malta Financial Services Authority. (2018b). *Virtual Financial Assets Rulebook - Chapter 1*. https://www.mfsa.mt/wp-content/uploads/2019/02/VFAR_Chapter1_FINAL.pdf

Massad, T. G. (2019). It's Time to Strengthen the Regulation of Crypto-Assets. *Economic Studies at Brookings*, 34-36.

McGill, D. H., Sauter, B. J., & Barnes, B. D. (2018). Cryptocurrency Is Borderless—but Still Within the Grip of US Regulators. *International Law Practicum, 31*(1), 11. https://www.huntonak.com/images/content/5/3/v2/53787/international-law-practicum-nysba.pdf#page=11

McKinney, R. E. Jr, Baker, C. W., Shao, L. P., & Forrest, J. Y. (2020). Cryptocurrency: Utility Determines Conceptual Classification despite Regulatory Uncertainty. *Intell. Prop. Tech. LJ, 25*, 1.

Medina, A. F. (2020). *Cambodia Launches Digital Currency: Key Features.* https://www.aseanbriefing.com/news/cambodia-launches-digital-currency-key-features/

Ministry of Finance. (n.d.). *Draft Banning of Cryptocurrency & Regulation of Official Digital Currency Bill, 2019.* https://prsindia.org/billtrack/draft-banning-of-cryptocurrency-regulation-of-official-digital-currency-bill-2019

Moalem, D., & Probst Larsen, K. (2020). *The Virtual Currency Regulation Review: Denmark.* https://thelawreviews.co.uk/title/the-virtual-currency-regulation-review/denmark#footnote-016

Monetary Authority of Singapore. (2019). *"Payment Services Bill" - Second Reading Speech by Mr Ong Ye Kung, Minister For Education, On Behalf of Mr Tharman Shanmugaratnam, Deputy Prime Minister and Minister-In-Charge of The Monetary Authority of Singapore on 14 Jan 2019.* https://www.mas.gov.sg/news/speeches/2019/payment-services-bill

Monetary Authority of Singapore. (2020). *A Guide to Digital Token Offerings.* https://www.mas.gov.sg/-/media/MAS/Sectors/Guidance/Guide-to-Digital-Token-Offerings-26-May-2020.pdf

Money Laundering and Terrorist Financing Prevention Act (2017).

Nabilou, H. (2019). How to regulate bitcoin? Decentralized regulation for a decentralized cryptocurrency. *International Journal of Law and Information Technology, 27*(3), 266–291.

Nakamoto, S. (2008). Bitcoin: A peer-to-peer electronic cash system. *Decentralized Business Review*, 21260.

National Bank of Cambodia. (2018). *Joint Statement between The national Bank of Cambodia, the Securities and Exchange Commission of Cambodia and the General-Commissariat of National Police.* Author.

No. 80/2016/ND-CP Decree, (2016). https://vanbanphapluat.co/decree-no-80-2016-nd-cp-amend-governments-decree-101-2012-nd-cp-on-non-cash-payments

NY Comp Codes Rules and Regs §, (2015). https://govt.westlaw.com/nycrr/Browse/Home/NewYork/NewYorkCodesRulesandRegulations?guid=I7444ce80169611e594630000845b8d3e&originationContext=documenttoc&transitionType=Default&contextData=(sc.Default)&bhcp=1

Office of Assistant to Deputy Cabinet Secretary for State Documents & Translation. (2018). *Bank Indonesia Warns All Parties Not to Sell, Buy, or Trade Virtual Currency.* https://setkab.go.id/en/bank-indonesia-warns-all-parties-not-to-sell-buy-or-trade-virtual-currency/

Payment Services Act 2019, (No. 2 of 2019).

Payment Services (Amendment) Act 2021, (No. 1 of 2021).

Peraturan, B. P. P. B. K. N. (2019). *5 Tahun 2019 Tentang Ketentuan Teknis Penyelenggaraan Pasar Fisik Aset Kripto (Crypto Asset)*. Di Bursa Berjangka.

Philippines: Where, How, and What you can buy for bitcoins. (2018). https://medium.com/kriptapp/philippines-where-how-and-what-you-can-buy-for-bitcoins-4e6e28fb71d4

Phillips, K. (2018). *Ohio Becomes The First State To Allow Taxpayers To Pay Tax Bills Using Cryptocurrency*. https://www.forbes.com/sites/kellyphillipserb/2018/11/26/ohio-becomes-the-first-state-to-allow-taxpayers-to-pay-tax-bills-using-cryptocurrency/?sh=77791f056b04

Prevention of Money Laundering and Funding of Terrorism Regulations (2018).

Prodent, L. (2021). *Vietnam to Start Regulating Cryptocurrencies*. https://www.aseanbriefing.com/news/vietnam-to-start-regulating-cryptocurrencies/

Quintais, J., Bodó, B., Giannopoulou, A., & Ferrari, V. (2019). Blockchain and the law: A critical evaluation. *Stanford Journal of Blockchain Law Policy, 1*.

Republic of Estonia Financial Intelligence Unit. (2020). *Estonia fully transposes the European Union money laundering directives*. https://fiu.ee/en/news/estonia-fully-transposes-european-union-money-laundering-directives

Republic of Estonia Tax and Customs Board. (2021). *Taxation of private person's virtual currency/cryptocurrency earnings*. https://www.emta.ee/eng/private-client/declaration-income/other-income/taxation-private-persons-virtual

Reserve Bank of India. (2013). *Press Release: RBI cautions users of Virtual Currencies against Risks*. https://www.rbi.org.in/scripts/BS_PressReleaseDisplay.aspx?prid=30247

Reserve Bank of India. (2017a). *Press Release: Reserve Bank cautions regarding risk of virtual currencies including Bitcoins*. https://www.rbi.org.in/scripts/BS_PressReleaseDisplay.aspx?prid=42462

Reserve Bank of India. (2017b). *Press Release:RBI cautions users of Virtual Currencies*. https://www.rbi.org.in/scripts/BS_PressReleaseDisplay.aspx?prid=39435

Reserve Bank of India. (2018). *Prohibition on dealing in Virtual Currencies (VCs)*. https://rbidocs.rbi.org.in/rdocs/Notification/PDFs/NOTI15465B741A10B0E45E896C62A9C83AB938F.PDF

Rizzo, P. (2014). *Bolivia's Central Bank Bans Bitcoin*. https://www.coindesk.com/bolivias-central-bank-bans-bitcoin-digital-currencies

Rubio, M. (2020). *Cryptocurrency: The Complete Blockchain Guide for Beginners to Make Money and Passive Income (Understand Ethereum, Blockchain, Smart Contracts, Icos)*. Martzel Rubio. https://books.google.com.my/books?id=53LgDwAAQBAJ

SF0111. 64th Leg., Budget Sess (Wyo), (2018). https://legiscan.com/WY/text/SF0111/id/1753980

Sahoo, P. K. (2017). Bitcoin as digital money: Its growth and future sustainability. *Theoretical Applied Economics, 24*(4).

S.B. (2019). *19-023, 73rd Leg*. Sess.

Schwinger, R. A. (2018). *Cryptocurrencies held subject to US federal securities laws.* https://www.nortonrosefulbright.com/en-ug/knowledge/publications/b9789fd9/cryptocurrencies-held-subject-to-us-federal-securities-laws

SEC v. WJ Howey Co, 328 US 293 (Supreme Court 1946).

Securities and Exchange Commission. (2017). *Report of Investigation Pursuant to Section 21(a) of the Securities Exchange Act of 1934: The DAO.* Author.

S.F. 125, 65th Leg., Gen. Sess. (Wyo), (2019).

S.F. 38, 66th Leg, Gen. Sess. (Wyo), (2021).

Shanaev, S., Sharma, S., Ghimire, B., & Shuraeva, A. (2020). Taming the blockchain beast? Regulatory implications for the cryptocurrency Market. *Research in International Business and Finance, 51,* 101080.

Singh, U. P. (2021). *Indian Cryptocurrency Saga: Regulation And IP Protection.* https://www.mondaq.com/india/fin-tech/1084772/indian-cryptocurrency-saga-regulation-and-ip-protection

Sonksen, C. (2021). Cryptocurrency Regulations in ASEAN, East Asia, & America: To Regulate or Not to Regulate Notes. *Wash. U. Global Stud. L. Rev., 20,* 171.

State Bank of Vietnam. (2017). *Dispatch No.5747/NHNN-PC.* Author.

United States v. Zaslavskiy, 2018 WL 4346339 (2018).

Virtual Financial Assets Act (2018).

Weinstein, J., Cohn, A., & Parker, C. (2019). *Promoting innovation through education: The blockchain industry, law enforcement and regulators work towards a common goal.* https://www.acc.com/sites/default/files/resources/vl/membersonly/Article/1489775_1.pdf

Zharova, A., & Lloyd, I. (2018). An examination of the experience of cryptocurrency use in Russia. In search of better practice. *Computer Law & Security Review, 34*(6), 1300–1313.

Chapter 6
The Legality of Smart Contracts in a Decentralized Autonomous Organization (DAO)

Andasmara Rizky Pranata
University of Malaya, Malaysia

Pardis Moslemzadeh Tehrani
ⓘD https://orcid.org/0000-0001-9698-8698
University of Malaya, Malaysia

ABSTRACT

This chapter discuss the legality of smart contract in a decentralized autonomous organization (DAO). The regulation framework of blockchain is developing rapidly with many countries such as Malta and Estonia utilizing and allowing the use of blockchain. While many researchers have discussed the legality of smart contract, its relation to DAO as one of blockchain's applications is rarely discussed. There are three issues discussed in this chapter: the definition of DAO, the definition of smart contract, and the legality of smart contract in DAO. Each country has their own legal threshold of a contract's legality, but there are generally five elements in a legal contract, namely offer and acceptance, consideration, intention, certainty, and completeness. It is possible for the smart contract to fulfil the five legal elements of a contract. As there are different regulations in different countries, there may have been different elements to the law. In conclusion, the legality of smart contracts, like blockchain itself, depends on who uses it, where it is used, and how it is used.

INTRODUCTION

The world has been through a very rapidly changing technology improvement. One of the most discussed recent technology breakthroughs is Decentralized Autonomous Organization (DAO), an organization that is decentralized and autonomous. DAO is a type of application that can be made in blockchain. Hsieh (2018) defined DAO as a "novel form of organizing", by noting the ability of the DAO codes to

DOI: 10.4018/978-1-7998-7927-5.ch006

have a better corporate governance and its potential to be a better form of organization. A research by Kondova and Barba (2019) stated that DAO is an organization with functions similar to that of a company except that it is running on blockchain, which retaining blockchain's features such as autonomous and decentralized. The autonomous feature in DAO is shown in how the company process is taking action. There are still real people inside of DAO, including the token or shareholder, but the execution of the decision taken based on consensus of the them is done in full autonomous.

The legality of DAO itself is still unclear in most countries and whether it complies to the legal framework is unclear, and one of the many problems are the definition (Chohan, 2017). Jentzch (2017) stated the dependency of DAO on how it is used, where it is used, and who uses it. This indirectly clarifies the various kinds of DAO as well as its definitions. In discussing the definition of DAO, there are a few important aspects. The first is its mechanism as it helps in creating understanding on how it works. The second is the difference between DAO and virtual company. The last one is to discuss the examples of existing and newer DAOs, to completely understand how DAO has evolved and how it is used in the present time. DAO is built by utilizing smart contract, which is a code programmed that can automatically execute the contract in it after the pre-determined terms are met (Sadiku, Eze, and Musa, 2018).[1] Smart contract is made in blockchain and thus retain blockchain's features (Gilcrest and Carvalho, 2018). Just like DAO, there are no set definition of smart contract, moreover the set consensus is on the legality of smart contract (Syllaba, 2020).

As more and more DAO emerges and smart contract is utilized, there is a need to explore the legality of smart contract uses in DAO. To do that, there are some issues that need to be addressed. The first is, like DAO, which is to determine the definition of smart contract and the technical aspect for making the smart contract. The second issue is to address the issue in the uses of smart contract as a contract in general in order to get idea on how it will work in DAO. Following the second issue, this research aims to discuss the importance of smart contract and how it is utilized in DAO. Lastly, it also discusses the legal framework of smart contract and whether it fulfills the criteria of a legal contract. The discussion in this chapter will proceed by discussing two big issues, and those are the definition of DAO and the legality of smart contract. The definition of DAO varies from the uses of DAO, and the various forms of DAO make it harder to discuss the legality of smart contract. Thus, to discuss the legality of the smart contract in DAO, a common understanding on the definition of DAO is needed. Therefore, the first subchapter will discuss on the definition of DAO, followed by the important issues that will support the definition consisting of its mechanism, the difference between DAO and virtual company, and the examples of DAO. The next subchapters will discuss deeply on the issues of smart contract such as its definition, the technical aspect and the issues in the uses of smart contract, and the importance of smart contract to DAO. Finally, the discussion can proceed to the legal framework of smart contract, which allows these discussions to support the discussion on the legality of smart contract used in DAO. The objective of this chapter is to have an understanding in the legality of smart contract uses in DAO. Achieving this objective will contribute more to the advancement of research on smart contract and DAO in general.

THE DEFINITION OF DAO

DAO runs on a blockchain, a technology that is also called as Distributed Ledger Technology (DLT) (Walch, 2017). Hüllman (2018) described blockchain as a distributed ledger with immutable data, meaning that the data stored in blockchain ledger will stay unchangeable and be a trustable source regarding any transaction and changes done in the ledger. Not only immutable, blockchain is also irreversible (Gudkov, 2018). It means that the things added on the blockchain cannot be undone (Bruyn, 2017). These two are the most notable features of blockchain that also exist in DAO. It can be imagined as a ledger that cannot be erased or tampered with. It does not necessarily mean that the information is right or wrong, but whatever done in the chain will still be there and remain unchanged.

In a book by Drescher (2017), it is explained that blockchain is executing this function in a similar way to a witness in court. A witness in a court can attest to what they know, see, or heard regarding the case. This is the same case with blockchain, only that it will be more than one witness each time. The more people attest to the transaction, the more credible it is, and DAO can utilize this feature.

There are many definitions of DAO. One of the earliest definitions of it is stated in the white paper by Jentzch (2017), stating that DAO is "automated organizational governance and decision-making." The research also stated that, the DAO code that he made for his white paper can be used by individuals or corporate that will work without using the traditional corporate structure (Jentzch, 2018).

The definition of DAO set by Allen and Overy LLP (2016) defined DAO as an organization runs on blockchain, that works autonomously and contain some aspects of corporate governance. DAO in its basic form is a community with sets of guidelines that have been agreed with many possibilities of function and its basic principles is the voice of the majority (Allen & Overy LLP, 2016). Specifically, any changes and decision taken in a DAO must be done after the majority approval of the said change and decision.

Metjahic (2018) in her paper has discusses specifically on the predecessor of DAO. She stated the DAO as a general partnership or at least a joint venture that should be regulated as either of them. Metjahic (2018) stated that, the DAO in the US has fulfilled the three criteria for a union to be considered as a partnership which are "(1) the co-owners share property or ownership; (2) the co-owners share in gross returns; and (3) and the courts presume a person who shares in profits to be a partner." Based on this, Metjahic (2018) stated that "The DAO, and other decentralized organizations are likely general partnerships in the United States".

Oren's (2018) research on the other hand, is more detailed in terms of legal status and definition of DAO, which stating DAO as decentralized. In other word, it has no one party controlling the organization, and it is autonomous, because it is run by codes made before the organization is completely made. DAO can then be classified as an organization that practically run by itself by just following what has been ruled out in the codes. Initially, DAO is made possible because of smart contract, a contract made in a decentralized format (in this case: blockchain), its immutable feature, and able to execute the agreed terms automatically after the parties fulfill the required terms inside the contract (Hsiao, 2017).

DAO Mechanism

According to Jentzsch (2017), the making of DAO requires several steps which starts with the creation phase. The first principle of making DAO is that to do anything, it needs ether as its fuel.[2] To make DAO, a person needs to make the DAO code and put it in the blockchain. The person just then needs to submit the ether to the DAO's smart contract address, and it will automatically give DAO token proportionally to the ether given. This is how basic transaction commonly works in DAO. The other aspect of DAO, however, is not that much different from the aspect of blockchain mechanism.

In blockchain, and DAO consequentially, there are many ways to preserve the data. The most common way, is to have a confirm and secure procedure that is very similar to the way we do transfer via bank services, only without intermediaries (Reyes, 2017). There are public key and private key in the blockchain. The public key is similar to a bank account number, which is also signified the address to the blockchain wallet. The private key is a confirmation code that will be required every time a person want to do a transaction, which is also similar to a password that only the user knows. Unlike traditional company where the involvement of people in the company usually made by written contract with the exact term, the involvement of the stakeholders in DAO is written in one long ledger of smart contracts. In fact, everything that happens in DAO will be written in the long ledger list, making it immutable. Thing that made these effects possible is the smart contract in blockchain. There are articles associating DAO with the term virtual company.[3]

DAO and Virtual Company

Virtual company or organization itself has many different definitions. One of them is that virtual company is an alliance of different individual or group, combining their assets, capacity, and information to accomplice their common goals (Nami, 2008). According to the researcher, "a virtual organization is always a form of partnership" and there are a few basic principles of human interaction that is important to this type of partnership including "Fairness; Trust; Integrity; Competency; Open Communication; Balance of rewards; Self Interest of both partners" (Nami, 2008). This is quite different in DAO as most of those principles can be accommodated by the code and the smart contract.

Another definition of virtual company is simply identified through a temporary cooperation between companies in the form of a network structure (Rautenstrauch, 2002). The researcher also mentioned that there is also a degree of decentralization of competencies, which there are no organization that is higher than the other in this structure. There a few specific characteristics in virtual company (Bejleri and Fishta, 2017):

1. The nature of virtual company does not need many assets since it can be accommodated through the network;
2. It is flexible as most of the work is fulfilled by doing outsourcing and has extended service range with the help of internet;
3. They require few capital assets to function but still need high fund allocation to information technology to tend the network and direct relationship with the stakeholders;
4. The goal is a long-term partnership instead of a short-term goal.

Bejleri and Fishta (2017) stated that the very important point about virtual company is that, traditional and physical constraints such as delivery time or supply management is still a big challenge in the virtual company. There are a few things that can be discussed regarding the difference of DAO and virtual company based on the above definition and characteristics of each.

First of all, the definition of virtual companies by researcher such as Nami (2008) and Rautenstrauch (2002) stated that virtual company means an alliance or partnership between companies. As discussed in the last subchapter, DAO stands as its own entity with its own purpose and while DAO has the possibility to consist of many organizations, its fundamentally different than the virtual company for DAO can only made it possible as only one entity (Faqir, Arroyo, and Hassan, 2020). Next, regarding the characteristics of virtual company, most of them are possible to be seen in DAO. The first characteristic explains that a company that is part of the virtual network will be able to lessen the burden of assets storage as it is possible to accommodate each other through the network. To be more exact, it is possible for blockchain, as one of the main uses of blockchain is to handle assets management (Metjahic, 2018). It is not, however, a characteristic apparent only in DAO, but also in any other blockchain application.

The second characteristic explains that virtual company has some flexibility regarding the workers inside of the community. Again, it is possible in DAO, but with certain restrictions in who can be active in the organization. A person has to had a coin (shares) inside of the DAO first in order to be considered as the active member of the organization who can then work inside. It is possible to employ workers doing outsourcing but it usually done for certain work that requires physical world attention only, like how the DAO operates (Reyes, 2017). The third characteristics also relatively a possible situation in using DAO. Every new technology means new updates, possibly new hardware to accommodate the software changes, and other technological changing. The last characteristic stated that the goal is long term partnership instead of short term one. However, a time constraint is never be the important aspect of DAO. A DAO can be made for certain purposes or for a long-time partnership. Its purpose is always depended on DAO's stakeholder's decision (Jentzsch, 2017).

Discussing by the characteristics, there are many similarities between what is called a virtual company and DAO. Essentially, a DAO is a type of virtual company. The definition discussed by Bejleri and Fishta (2017), Rautenstrauch (2002), and Nami (2008) explained virtual company as a set of networks to manage a cooperation between organizations or business. While DAO as a company or organization defines establishing DAO as one entity with its specific purposes, which is also possible to be a partnership of people. To understand more, it is important to discuss the examples of DAO that has existed.

Examples of DAO

Aragon.org

Aragon.io is one of the largest DAO platforms, providing a free and open-source platform for people to make and manage their own DAO (Faqir, Arroyo, and Hassan, 2020). It is a very unique platform to let people experience DAO. In a rough draft of Aragon Network, Izquierdo (2017) explained that the Aragon network is a dApp in Ethereum blockchain that is managed using the token where the stakeholders can do transaction in it with minimal risk, which may come from both technical aspect or human ill intention. The name Aragon may mean two things, which signify a platform for people to offer DAO software as its service and a DAO named Aragon Governance. What will be discussed next is the DAO version, Aragon Governance.

Izquierdo (2017) listed several issues that he wanted to face in the making of Aragon. There are subjective breaches, software bugs, and reward systems.[21] The issue with subjective breaches is the subjectivity in human relationship. Whether the relationship between the stakeholders is managed by the code or not, there may still be conflict between the human behind the code. The second one is the software bugs, where Izquierdo aims to make a system that is easier to be fixed. The last one is the reward system to reward the stakeholders that is contributing to the DAO.

Technically, Aragon works like DAO, where every decision will be decided by voting and has a very friendly user interface to ease the people that is not very familiar with common blockchain interface.[4] This opens the possibility for wider range of people to use DAO. The mechanism on how DAO work is exactly as discussed in the previous section. In Figure 2.1, it is the Aragon Governance DAO as its own entity, where the decision is made by voting and is passed or rejected by the total voting in a certain frame of time. It is also the example of smart contract that has been passed around in Aragon DAO.

Figure 1. Aragon interface and examples of smart contract

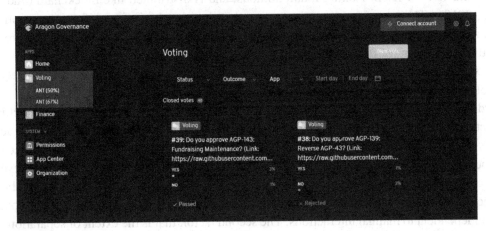

Decentraland DAO

Decentraland DAO is a very unique type of DAO. According to the white paper on Decentraland, it is a virtual reality platform where the user can buy and sell digital land and the basic is a digital real estate initially called Metaverse (Ordano, Meilich, Jardi, and Araoz, 2017). By buying a piece of "land", the user can access Decentraland DAO to make applications, real estate contract, content, and marketplace while the whole experience will be in a decentralized environment where the "land owner" is the one who decides how things run in the Decentraland DAO.[5] To make it even more interesting to the user, the user can customize their looks in the world.[6]

The notable feature in Decentraland is that it created a whole virtual land where the main currency is the ether, the cryptocurrency of Ethereum, which can be seen as a way to imagine the other world of currency, which is unlike now where fiat money controlled by the government is the main currency. As with Aragon, the way it works is still within the same principle of DAO mechanism, where the user puts in some cryptocurrency to the DAO to get proof of ownership of that particular DAO. Then, all the decision within the platform will be decided by voting appropriately between all the shareholders in DAO.

Thus, from this example and the discussion above, the definition of DAO clarifies it as an organization. It is evident that most companies or organizations that is categorized as DAO is established as its own entity with its own purposes that is usually go toward the development of blockchain and DAO especially. Hence, this chapter has concluded the definition of DAO as an organization build on blockchain that operate as an independent and decentralized organization.

THE DEFINITION OF SMART CONTRACT

Smart contract is a mechanism that allows people from all over the world to collaborate without meeting each other with a high degree of trust in the blockchain network. In its basic form, a smart contract is similar to complex codes arranged to represent the terms and condition for an agreement and the command to execute the said terms when the conditions are fulfilled. There are various elements of smart contract such as a code run in blockchain; part of a software/program; once it is created, it is self-performed and self-sufficient making it autonomous; and is distributed like blockchain (Sadiku, Eze, and Musa, 2018).[7] There are many sources stating that the most basic form of a smart contract is as simple as a code in vending machine[8]. Bourque and Tsui (2014) also explained that, there are actually levels to the "smartness" of the smart contract measured by three factors namely, the level of automation; the extent of separation between the contract's terms and its coded version; and who gets to keep the control of the contract.

According to the first factor, the higher the level of automation, the "smarter" the contract is. To be more exact, according to Syllaba (2020), a key difference in smart contract and other similar automatic contract is the element of autonomous found in smart contracts that runs on blockchain. Because it is autonomous, it is possible for the smart contract to execute the contract without any outside or even inside interference once the contract is encoded.[9] Syllaba (2020) basically stated that more automation to the contract equals to less manual interaction needed by the coded contract and it results in the contract being more independent to manual interactions. The second factor, that is the extent of separation between the terms and the actual code hinted that the less the difference between the contract terms agreed by the parties and the actual coded contracts, the "smarter" the contract is (Bourque and Tsui, 2014). The researchers also discussed that there are actually practices of an electronic contract which does not reflect the actual agreement between the party.[10] The more the difference is between the two, the less smart it is.

The third factor is basically who gets to keep control of a contract. In a situation where the smart contract is distributed using a blockchain network, it allows more freedom to the people to choose to enter the contract or modified it until there is an agreement to both parties. In many instances such as found in e-commerce, the merchant held more control regarding the contract thus leading it to be non-negotiable. This differs with the level of smartness of the smart contract in blockchain, that prioritize the willingness of both parties to make the contract that suits for both or more parties (Bourque and Tsui, 2014). Hence, to differ it to other kind of contract which is not as "smart", smart contract discussed in this chapter will be only those that runs on blockchain as that is the main focus of this chapter (Syllaba, 2020). A smart contract with such criteria is able to be distributed like the blockchain and is mostly known for its use in Ethereum (Sadiku, Eze, and Musa, 2018). Though so, Durovic and Lech (2019) explained that a smart contract, while can be found in blockchain, is actually different and able to stand independently. It is important to note that the two is a different thing and each have their own characteristics.

Durovic and Lech (2019) also stated that, for a smart contract to be recognized as a contract, it requires a "blend between code and natural language". Currently, such thing is possible. It is a common misunderstanding nowadays claiming that the smart contract is only a smart contract when it is a bunch of code that not everyone can interpret. There are at least 4 forms or types of smart contract, which are the contract is entirely written in code; the contract is written in code but a natural language version is provided; a combination of both; and a contract written in natural language with "encoded payment mechanism" (Smart Contracts Alliance, 2018). The first three form of smart contract is made by encoding natural language and the last one is an automated payment system. This particular statement may lead to an easier acceptance of smart contract in the public eye.

Another misconception in smart contract is that, people tend to relate smart contract with Artificial Intelligence (AI) (De Caria, 2019), while the two have their own different concept. AI is a system that accumulates information that will be processed to be an intelligence that can be executed by a system (Grewal, 2014). In short, what make a program to be considered an AI is the specific thinking process and possibility to learn from it. Smart contract is considered smart not because it has the ability to think by itself like AI does, but because it has the ability to automatically execute the agreement because the code that was written beforehand is already set certain rules and terms to execute the said contract (Grewal, 2014).

The previous two paragraphs on the misunderstanding and misconception of smart contract are trying to contribute into a discussion by separating what kind of program that can be included in the definition of smart contract and vice versa. First of all, there is no restriction that limit smart contract's form to only have one form. What matters is that there is still a code made in blockchain that retains the feature such as self-executing and self-sufficient. The second is that smart is inequal to the ability to think for itself. What is considered smart in smart contract is the ability to self-execute and self-sufficient after the code has been established or the smart contract has been made.

To have more discussion regarding the definition of smart contract and what differs it from traditional contract, the next subchapter will discuss about the technical aspect of the smart contract and how is it specifically used in blockchain.

THE TECHNICAL ASPECT OF SMART CONTRACT

It has been explained and simply discussed in the previous section about the technicality of blockchain and smart contract. The details can be a bit different. There a few steps to making the smart contract, which are: identifying agreement; setting the conditions; encoding the business terms; processing the code/contract to be encrypted; waiting for the contract execution; and the last one is network updates (Smart Contract Alliance, 2018). The first step is to identify the agreement to be put in the smart contract. In this step, the parties must identify themselves, deciding on the subject and object of the agreement, and then agreeing on the business process. The object of the agreement can be many things including funds, transferal of rights, and even house or other assets (Mohanta, Panda, and Jena, 2018). This is the same aspect as it is with traditional contract, but with different mechanism.

The second step is to set the condition for the contract. This step means that the parties included in this agreement will decide within themselves the terms and conditions of the contract. This condition can be many things such as payment of a certain fee to the other party, stock prices, and even weather conditions (Mik, 2017). Though so, the researcher also stated that condition such as stock prices and weather condition represent the harder time to make sure the correctness of the contract as it is outside of the blockchain realm and is another type of complexion in using the smart contract (Elfstrom 2018). The third step is to encode the terms that has been set by the parties. This particular step is the deployment of the smart contract to the blockchain. It works by one of the parties that initiate a special transaction execution, which will assign a unique label or address to the contract to allow the contract to be uploaded in the blockchain (Durovich and Lech 2019). According to Hsiao (2017), there is always an additional party in a smart contract, known as the computer system. It is not only the people must be able to understand the contract, it is also important for the computer to understand the contract as it will be the one that executes the terms inside of the contract.

The next step is to see through the contract's execution. The ease of execution in the use of smart contract is one of the main reasons to choose smart contract over traditional contract. The execution of the smart contract is autonomous once the conditions that were set in the contract is completed. For example, a smart contract is made between Steph and his basketball coach with the condition that when Steph has finished the basketball practice with him (detected by a fingerprint, other coaches, or other method to make sure), then a payment of $30 from the coach's account will be moved to Steph's account. This condition will then make sure the coach's money can only be moved when Steph goes to practice and Steph can only get the payment after he finished the practice. With the smart contract, whether the money has been moved or not will be easily proved, as it leads to the transparency of every contract execution.

The last step is the network updates. This is a very important step toward the completion of the smart contract. This step is needed to update all the blockchain user where the smart contract is used and a transaction based on the smart contract is happened. As mentioned before, blockchain eliminate unnecessary party and all the update in the blockchain ledger will be recorded in the each of the user's computer. The blockchain is as true as its users' database and that is why this process is very important.

As of now, skipping a step could mean either it is not fully a smart contract yet or there is a possibility of an error down the roads. After discussing the above theories and understanding the steps that make the smart contract works, it can be concluded that the definition of the smart contract is a contract made in code resides in a blockchain that has the ability to self-execute and very self-sufficient. The next subchapter will discuss the possible issue that may arise in using the smart contract in order to create full understanding upon the subject matter.

THE ISSUE IN SMART CONTRACT

With all the advantages of smart contract mentioned in the above subchapter, it does not mean that smart contract has no disadvantage. There are some issues in implementing the smart contract. According to Elfstrom (2018), contract has a freedom of format and is only needed to fulfill some essentials of a contract in order to be considered a binding agreement. This means that the format of the contract does not really matter as long as the "contract" fulfilled all the essentials needed for it to be recognized as a contract under the law. According to Hullman (2018), the smart contract has some issues. For example, the immutability element in the smart contract also means that the contract is wrongly made, and it is irreparable (Jetnzsch, 2017). There are also other issues such as the difficulty of translating the legal language, the interpretation of the code, how to ensure the assimilation of the network and real life, as well as party's anonymity issue.

The first issue is the use of legal language in the smart contract. The previous subchapters explained the fact that the smart contract has multiple form, but still, the basic form of code is written in the blockchain. This means that before making the other forms of smart contract, there is still a process of translating the legal terms that is used in traditional contract to produce the code. According to Mik (2017), there is a certain set of difficulty in translating the legal language, which is very unique that maybe some words have different meanings depending on the context of the documents (Elfstrom, 2018). The second issue is how to interpret the language used in code to the natural language. According to Hsiao (2017), there is a very complex exchange in commercial use of contract, and smart contract can be rigid, not very flexible in its use and further argue that there may be situation where the parties actually choose to have a certain level of ambiguity in the contract.[11] The use of natural language allows this ambiguity instead of the direct approach by smart contract.

Essentially, for the first and second issue, smart contract user can try to solve it by making a separate document that support the real meaning of the contract. As explained in the previous subchapter, there are various forms of smart contract including one where there is both version of smart contract: coded and natural language. The third issue is ensuring the self-execution of the smart contract in the real world. The assimilation of smart contract and the "real world" is still facing some technical challenges, particularly on how to detect if the terms and conditions are fulfilled in the case where it happens in the real world and the self-execute are functioned in the real world (Elfstrom, 2018). The fourth issue is the party's anonymity which may result in lack of protection to the smart contract's users (Smart Contract Alliance, 2017). As in blockchain, it is possible for smart contract to be made while the parties are anonymous. The smart contract users are identified by their public keys that work as address and creating a public key normally does not need the person's actual identities, hence leading to the creation of an anonymous system in the smart contract (Linoy, Stakhanova, and Matyukhina, 2019). What anonymity brings is uncertainty of the parties' condition or identity. The point is that there are still many adjustments for the smart contract to be incorporated in people's daily life. The discussion on the next subchapter will discuss the aspects of smart contract that has been discussed and important in DAO.

IMPORTANCE SMART CONTRACT AND HOW IT IS USED IN DAO

In the previous subchapters, there are already many functions of smart contract discussed. Some of them are particularly important in making and operating. The first being the smart contract is a code run in blockchain. It means that smart contract retains many of blockchain's system and advantages, which can be found in its immutable feature. When there is any attempt to change the recorded activity in smart contract, what will happen instead is a new record will be made (Walker, 2019) which according to Gilcrest and Carvalho (2018), it provides "an uncensored source of truth" and also made an easy path to retrace all the changes in the smart contract. Secondly, smart contract is having an ability to self-execute. This means that smart contract can act as a code that will give several benefits that limit outside party's interference, make the transaction happened within the DAO be more transparent, and allows automation of the terms to be happened in the smart contract (Bourque and Tsui, 2014). Reyes (2017) stated that the self-executing factor would help by ensuring the compliance by the parties once the terms in the contract is fulfilled.

The third is its self-sufficient ability, which making it autonomous, able to run without constant maintenance by the creator. According to Wright and Fillipi (2015), self-sufficient is an ability for the DAO[12] to independently accumulate capital as long as they receive "sufficient funds". Reyes (2017) stated that this function is reflected in Plantoid, a metal flower runs on DAO code that can move and being self-sufficient, able to move and do activities independently as long as it has the necessary fuel, bitcoin.[13] Lastly, it is regarding the decentralization of smart contract, which is align with DAO's basic idea on a decentralized autonomous organization. Basically, traditional company works with an exact hierarchy or chain of command. The basic concept of DAO, however, is exactly to erase the said hierarchy system in order to ensure a better and more indiscriminative way to run the company. Such things are possible with the application of smart contracts (Metjahic, 2018). Subliminally, these show the importance and how smart contract in DAO. After understanding the aspect that made smart contract irreplaceable in DAO, the next subchapter will discuss the legal framework of smart contract and supports the next discussion regarding the legality of DAO itself.

THE LEGAL FRAMEWORK OF SMART CONTRACT

From the previous subchapters, the current researchers obtain the definition of smart contract as a contract made in code resides in a blockchain with the ability to self-execute that retains blockchain's features such as immutability, decentralized, and self-sufficient. However, there is still an inquiry regarding the ability of a smart "contract" to be considered a legally binding "contract". Some scholars actually introduced the terms Legal Smart Contract and discussed further on the basis of such smart contract known as "Ricardian Contract".[14] It introduces a system to automize the contract in which its cryptography can be read by both humans and machines, keeping the intention of the parties while making the contract. As a smart legal contract, it creates its own legal clauses that examine "the variety of legal consequences" (Six, Ribalta, Herbaut, and Salinesi, 2020). This is another possibility of form that can be taken by the smart contract.

But ultimately, it is important to see whether a smart contract is actually a contract according to the current legal system. According to Elfstrom (2018), contract has a freedom of format and only needed to fulfill some essentials of a contract to be considered a binding agreement. This means that the format of the contract does not really matter as long as the "contract" has fulfilled all the essentials needed for it to be recognized as a contract under the law. MacMillen and Stone (2004) discussed that, generally in UK, there are at least 5 elements in a legal contract. These 5 elements will determine whether the agreement between the parties is a legally binding contract or not, regardless the forms of the contract. The 5 elements are identified as Offer and Acceptance; Consideration; Intention; Certainty; and Completeness.

Malaysia with the same system of common law has similar elements with the UK which are proposal, acceptance, consideration, intention to create legal relations, capacity, and consent. (Malaysia Contract Act, 1950). As Malaysia had the root of common law from UK, there is not much difference from the UK with exception of an added elements like capacity and consent. To get a clearer vision on the legal framework of the smart contract, it is better to use essence of the elements that present from the two above. The following elements will be discussed in the next subchapter: offer and acceptance, consideration, intention to create legal relation, certainty, and completeness. These 5 elements will be posited as the current researchers' benchmark regarding the criteria of a legal binding contract. How these elements are seen in the smart contract perspective will be the main discussion in the next subchapters.

Offer and Acceptance

The first and second elements are often included as one. An offer is a feat done by a party that gives the other party a legal chance so that they can engage in a contract (Corbin, 1916). Initially, offer is an action that initiate the making of a contract because essentially, a contract is a promise and an offer is stating a party as willing to make the promise. What is commonly misunderstood is that, an offer is not the same as a statement of intention and the difference falls in the willingness of the party, and giving a statement of intention signifies a party that intends to engage in a contract, not willing to (Elfstrom, 2017). However, giving an offer means that a party is willing to engage in a contract, for example, to sell a house. The difference is in the motive of the party is only identified through the intend to do or actually willing to do.

An acceptance is a feat to an offer that will be the sign that both parties are ready to move with the offer of making an agreement (Malaysia Contract Act, 1950). An acceptance can be communicated by words or conduct and can only valid upon communication. An acceptance must be differentiated from a counter-offer. An acceptance is when the party accepts the offer without adding or changing anything to the offer. Should such things happen, it will be a counter offer, annihilating the initial offer. Below is how offer and acceptance connected generally in terms of the making of a contract:

Figure 2. Offer and acceptance

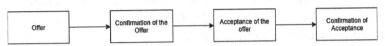

The first thing to start an agreement is an offer. Once the offeror is sure about the object he/she wanted to offer, a confirmation of the offer is needed to make sure that the object or other elements offered would not change midways of the agreements without the consent of both parties. It is also important so that the other party/s get the correct information regarding the offer. The next step is for the other party to accept the offer made by the offeror. Said acceptance must then be confirmed again by the other party to the offeror, ensuring the understanding of the offeror that the other party has accepted the offer.[15] None of this step may be absent to confirm the offer and acceptance has been done by the parties. With the current technology improvement, it is easier to communicate the offer or communicate an acceptance. That holds even more true in the making of smart contract in DAO since most of the steps are done online, which also means that every offer, counter-offer, and the acceptance are recorded to a certain extends, which making easier for the party to backtrack or reconsider after a counter offer was done.

Even so, has smart contract fulfilled the required elements of offer and acceptance? To a certain extends, an offer and acceptance procedure has been established in a smart contract. As explained in the previous subchapter on how the smart contract works, the first and second step are to identify the agreement and set the conditions in the smart contract. These steps can be considered an offer and acceptance part of the smart contract and they are essential for the making of smart contract. Without the confirmation of both party regarding the terms and conditions of the contract, a smart contract cannot be deployed.

In the making of smart contract, a party will communicate the offer and if it is accepted, both are agreeing to make the code to the smart contract and will then adjusts it to fit the offer accepted. Without the acceptance and confirmation from both parties, the code cannot be deployed, meaning the contract is not in effect and the offer holds no value as a contract.[16] The key discussion in this subchapter is determined through the smart contract that has offer and acceptance as the elements of being a legal binding contract.

Consideration

Consideration is something or some action to fill in as the price of a promise made in a contract. One of the importance of consideration is to determine whether a contract is legally binding, enforceable, and resulted from an exchange of offer and acceptance (Elfstrom, 2018). According to Weitzenböck (2012), a consideration must be adequate, equal, and reasonable to the object or action offered in a contract or a promise and without consideration, a contract or a promise cannot be considered a binding contract and cannot be enforced. To add more to the definition, Atiyah (1971) stated that a consideration is either a merit to the side offered and/or a loss to the other side. The points in the two definitions determined through two general criteria of a consideration namely, something or some action that is adequate, equal, and reasonable to the offer; and a merit to the offeror party and/or a loss the other party.

However, Atiyah (1971) further stated that most of the time, a court would not be asking whether a consideration is reasonable or is of equal value to the offer, as it would focus on whether there is or there is not a consideration. Most of the time, it is not about the content of consideration, but the existence of the consideration itself. It can be said that a consideration can also act as an assurance that the accepting party will proceed with the agreement or the contract.

Figure 3. Simple example of consideration

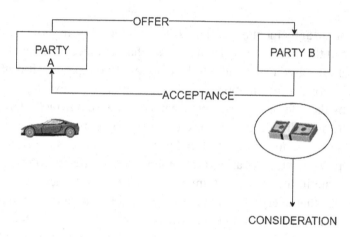

Above in the figure is a very simple example of a consideration. It can be seen from the figure above that Party A made an offer to sell a car to Party B, and after acceptance, the money will be moved from Party B to Party A. The money is the element that being called a consideration. It is something that will be a loss to the Party B (as Party B moves the money from his possession) and a gain to Party A (as he will get the money from Party B). It can also be inferred from the above illustration that it is not discussed whether the money is equal to the car, but of whether there is an actual consideration to the offer given by Party A.[17] Does consideration part of the smart contract? The simple answer would be yes. According to Smart Contracts Alliance (2018), a set of conditions can be put in smart contract's coding steps. This includes the insertion of consideration in a contract. Initially, it is possible as DAO has the ability to put consideration in smart contract. In fact, the exchange of consideration is one of the most important pieces in using smart contract. Smart contract's function and self-execution are made to ensure that the exchange of the consideration is executed.

Intention to Create Legal Relations

This element is very important to the English Law. Making a contract means the parties intent to engage a legal relation with legal consequences, rights and obligations of the parties upon entering the contract. Without a presentation of such intention, a contract that is even already supported by the consideration may not be an enforceable contract (Macmilen and Stone, 2004). Ultimately, this requirement is important to differentiate a contract and just an intention in the domestic and social agreements. For example, in an agreement between friends or family members, that usually is said an act without any intention to create a sue-able contract.

Once again, smart contract in blockchain already has a mechanism to make sure the intention to create legal relations exists in both parties, and particularly fulfilling the need of parties' special code to create the contract. If one party does not provide their specific code, it means that there is no intention to be bound by the code, then the contract will not be made, let alone enforceable. Hence, this mechanism will prove the intention to create legal intention by every party.

Certainty

Certainty is a relatively simpler element between all of the other elements. Basically, there is a need for a contract to utilize a specific mechanism that will support the terms in the contract (Elfstrom, 2018), such as a date of the contract's execution or a specific mechanism to execute the contract's terms. This to prevent an agreement made in an unclear manner that provides no clarity to the parties regarding how the agreement will played out. The certainty aspect is similar to what Miller, Comfort, and Stold (2001) had discussed as clear unequivocal language. According to them, it is very important for the writing in the contract to be expressed clearly and avoided any meaning other than the intended meaning that pressed on the importance of a contract being clear, certain, precise and exact. There should not be any subliminal meaning to the words or sentences used in the contract. Such certainty is very important for a smart contract. To use a smart contract, both parties need to clearly expressed how the contract will played out from beginning to the end of the contract, from the first offer up to the completion of the contract. Due to the use of code in the smart contract, the parties must be very clear about the terms in the contract (Bourque and Tsui, 2014). This shows the possibility for a smart contract to provide certainty and clarity regarding the agreements made in smart contract.

Completeness

Completeness is always an element that is always discussed regarding the legality of a contract, and in fact, most of the researches stated that there is no way a contract is ever truly complete. In fact, there is no need for a contract to be perfectly complete. The incompleteness of contract will be covered by the existing law (Crasswell, 2005). Kosnik (2014) stated that a contract actually needs to be flexible in order to give rooms for adapting any future unforeseen circumstances and at the same time still comprehensive competent to set necessary boundary as a legal contract. Ultimately, a complete contract means that it contains all the important elements that is needed according to the contract law. For example, a contract must contain Offer and Acceptance, Consideration, Intention to Create Legal Relation, Certainty, as well as general elements in the UK contract law for this chapter. Generally, it is possible, as discussed in above subchapters, that smart contract completely presents all the elements of a contract, which making it not totally complete but does present the ability to cover all the elements needed in a contract.

FUTURE RESEARCH DIRECTIONS

The research world on blockchain, DAO, and smart contracts is still very limited. Almost everything seems new and there will always be more things to discover, especially regarding the legal aspects of the topic. Even discussing the definitions will bring forth new things into discussion. What is more important in the future is still to discuss more on the legal aspects of the field as a legal recognition means more opportunity to let the field expand. As the regulation in each country differs, it may be better in the future where it could make a more focused research on how each country's regulation reacts to smart contract and DAO.

CONSCLUSION

In conclusion, currently, it is not feasible for a smart contract to actually replace the whole system of contract-making for various reasons that stated in the above subchapters, and it is not the purpose of the creation of smart contract. The whole point of smart contract is to ease the transaction in blockchain and act as a form of contract that can be more trusted with its system. DAO works exactly like other apps in blockchain. It created and works with using a cryptocurrency used in the blockchain. The big difference of DAO and traditional company is that, the mechanism in DAO made it possible to operate without third party and physical interference. Discussing by the characteristics, there are many similarities between what is called a virtual company and DAO. However, DAO and virtual company are different where virtual company is a set of networks made by existing organizations or companies to create a cooperation or link, while DAO can work as its own as a standalone company or organization.

There are 2 examples of DAO used in this chapter namely, Aragon.org and Decentraland. Both are relatively the new DAOs that are still operating currently. Aragon as DAO is made with the purpose of supporting other blockchain-related projects. Decentraland acts as a virtual reality realm where the user can buy to own or sell its virtual land.

Essentially, Decentraland is also an organization of its own with the similar mechanism to blockchain that revolves around by utilizing smart contract and cryptocurrency as the activities' general fuel. Based on the discussion, the definition of DAO is an entity build on blockchain that operates as an independent and decentralized organization. Smart contract is a contract made with code in blockchain that has the ability to self-execute and very self-sufficient after the code has been established or the smart contract has been made. An important aspect to understand about smart contract is that there is no restriction that limits smart contract's form to only has one form and the term smart is inequal to the ability to think for itself. A few important steps to making the smart contract include identifying agreement; setting the conditions; encoding the business terms; processing the code/contract to be encrypted; waiting for the contract execution; and the network updates.

There are still some issues in smart contract uses in general. For example, how the immutability element in the smart contract also means that should the contract is wrongly made, it is irreparable.[9] There are also other issue such as the difficulty of translating the legal language, the interpretation of the code, and how to ensure the assimilation of the network and real life. Generally, this issue did not directly affect the legality status of smart contract but instead impacting the experience in using the smart contract. There are various ways about the essentiality of smart contract in DAO. The first is that smart contract made it possible for DAO to run in blockchain as due to the code that can be designed to make

DAO and it also retains many of blockchain's system and advantages that is crucial in DAO. The second is that smart contract is able to self-execute, and will automate the terms' execution. The third one is self-sufficient which makes DAO able to be autonomous, able to run without constant maintenance or interference by any party once it is deployed. The last one is the decentralization of smart contract, which supports the idea of DAO on a decentralized autonomous organization that will erase the hierarchy and centralized system of traditional company.

The elements of contract that is used to determine the legal framework of smart contract are offer and acceptance, consideration, intention, certainty, and completeness. It is possible to consider smart contract as a legally binding contract because it fulfilled all the elements of a legally binding contract. As a contract, it records all the thing and is better than the traditional contract in the aspect of transparency as the contract cannot just be changed without the willingness of both parties, thus able in minimizing the possibility of fraud or deception. While DAO's legality is still arguable in most countries, the existence of smart contract seems to be clearer. Depends on where it is used, smart contract that is used in DAO can be legal. It can be interpreted that, there are no definite form of a contract in most of laws. There are however certain elements that works as a requirement to the contract. Smart contract then can be considered legal as long as it has fulfilled the requirements, which it can in most case. In other words, it may not be necessary for a country to make a new contract law to regulate the smart contract as smart contract undoubtedly can fit into the current regulation of legal contracts.

REFERENCES

Allen & Overy LLP. (2016). *Decentralized Autonomous Organization*. Retrieved from Allen & Overy LLP website: https://www.allenovery.com/en-gb/global/news-and-insights/publications/decentralized-autonomous-organizations

Atiyah, P. S. (1971). *Consideration in Contracts: A Fundamental Restatement*. Australian National University Press Canberra.

Bejleri, E., & Fishta, A. (2017). Toward Virtual Business. *Mediterranean Journal of Social Sciences*, *8*(3), 275–280. doi:10.5901/mjss.2017.v8n3p275

Bourque, S., & Tsui, S. F. L. (2014). A Lawyer's Introduction to Smart Contracts. *Scientia Nobilitat Reviewed Legal Studies*, 4–23.

Bruyn, A. S. (2017). *Blockchain, an Introduction*. University Amsterdam.

Chohan, U. W. (2017). The Decentralized Autonomous Organization and Governance Issues. SSRN *Electronic Journal*, (April). doi:10.2139/ssrn.3082055

Corbin, A. L. (1916). Offer and Acceptance, and Some of the Resulting Legal Relations. *The Yale Law Journal*, *26*(169), 169–206.

Crasswell, R. (2005). Contract Law: General Theories. Encyclopedia of Law and Economics, (3), 1–24.

De Caria, R. (2019). The Legal Meaning of Smart Contracts. *European Review of Private Law*, *6*, 731–752. www.bis.org/cpmi/publ/d137.pdf

Drescher, D. (2017). Blockchain Basics: A Non-Technical Introduction in 25 Steps. APRESS. doi:10.1007/978-1-4842-2604-9

Durovic, M., & Lech, F. (2019). The Enforceability of Smart Contracts. *Italian Law Journal, 5*(2), 493–512.

El Faqir, Y., Arroyo, J., & Hassan, S. (2020). An overview of Decentralized Autonomous Organizations on the Blockchain. *Proceedings of the 16th International Symposium on Open Collaboration*, 1–8. 10.1145/3412569.3412579

Elfstrom, A. L. (2018). *Blockchain organizations: Decentralized Autonomous Organizations and the Law*. University of Gothenburg.

Gilcrest, J., & Carvalho, A. (2018). Smart Contracts: Legal Considerations. *2018 IEEE International Conference on Big Data (Big Data)*, 3277–3281. 10.1109/BigData.2018.8622584

Grewal, D. S. (2014). A Critical Conceptual Analysis of Definitions of Artificial Intelligence as Applicable to Computer Engineering. *IOSR Journal of Computer Engineering, 16*(2), 9–13. doi:10.9790/0661-16210913

Grigg, I. (2004). The Ricardian contract. *Proceedings - First IEEE International Workshop on Electronic Contracting, WEC 2004*, (September), 25–31. 10.1109/WEC.2004.1319505

Gudkov, A. (2017). Control on Blockchain Network. *Nova Law Review, 42*, 353.

Hsiao, J. I.-H. (2017). "Smart" Contract on the Blockchain-Paradigm Shift for Contract Law? *US-China Law Review, 14*(10), 685–694. doi:10.17265/1548-6605/2017.10.002

Hsieh, Y.-Y. (2018). *The Rise of Decentralized Autonomous Organizations: Coordination and Growth within Cryptocurrencies*. The University of Western Ontario.

Hüllmann, T. A. (2018). *Are Decentralized Autonomous Organizations the Future of Corporate Governance*. Otto Beisheim School of Management., doi:10.13140/RG.2.2.34344.88327

Izquierdo, L. C. J. (2017). *Aragon Network; a Decentralized Infrastructure for Value Exchange*. Retrieved from https://www.chainwhy.com/upload/default/20180705/49f3850f2702ec6be0f57780b22feab2.pdf

Jentzsch, C. (2017). *Decentralized Autonomous Organization to Automate Governance*. Retrieved from Slock.it website: https://lawofthelevel.lexblogplatformthree.com/wp-content/uploads/sites/187/2017/07/WhitePaper-1.pdf

Kondova, G., & Barba, R. (2019). Governance of Decentralized Autonomous Organizations. *Journal of Modern Accounting and Auditing, 15*(8), 406–411. doi:10.17265/1548-6583/2019.08.003

Kosnik, L.-R. (2014). Determinants of Contract Completeness: An Environmental Regulatory Application. *International Review of Law and Economics, 37*, 198–208. doi:10.1016/j.irle.2013.11.001

Linoy, S., Stakhanova, N., & Matyukhina, A. (2019). Exploring Ethereum's Blockchain Anonymity Using Smart Contract Code Attribution. *15th International Conference on Network and Service Management, CNSM 2019*. 10.23919/CNSM46954.2019.9012681

MacMillen, C., & Stone, R. (2004). Elements of The Law of Contract. University of London. doi:10.1201/9781003029250-6

Metjahic, L. (2018). Deconstructing the DAO: The Need for Legal Recognition and the Application of Securities Laws to Decentralized Organizations. *Cardozo Law Review*, *39*, 1541.

Mik, E. (2017). Smart Contracts: Terrminology, Technical Limitations and Real-World Complexity. *Law, Innovation and Technology*, *9*(2), 269–300. doi:10.1080/17579961.2017.1378468

Miller, L. K., Comfort, P. G., & Stoldt, G. C. (2001). Contracts 101: Basics and Applications. *Journal of Legal Aspects of Sport*, *11*(1), 79–89. doi:10.1123/jlas.11.1.79

Mohanta, B. K., Panda, S. S., & Jena, D. (2018). An Overview of Smart Contract and Use Cases in Blockchain Technology. *International Conference on Computing, Communication and Networking Technologies 2018*. 10.1109/ICCCNT.2018.8494045

Nami, M. R. (2008). Virtual Organizations: An Overview. *International Conference on Intelligent Information Processing*, 211–219.

Ordano, E., Meilich, A., Jardi, Y., & Araoz, M. (2017). *Decentraland: White Paper*. Academic Press.

Oren, O. (2017). ICO's, DAO'S, and the SEC: A Partnership Solution. *Columbia Business Law Review, hs*(2), 617–657.

Rautenstrauch, T. (2002). *The Virtual Corporation: A strategic option for Small and Medium sized Enterprises (SMEs)*. Association for Small Business and Entrepreneurship.

Reyes, C. L. (2017). Conceptualizing Cryptolaw. *Nebraska Law Review*, *96*(2).

Sadiku, M. N. O., Eze, K. G., & Musa, S. M. (2018). Smart Contracts: A Primer. *Journal of Scientific and Engineering Research*, *5*(5), 538–541.

Six, N., Ribalta, C. N., Herbaut, N., & Salinesi, C. (2020). A Blockchain-Based Pattern for Confidential Pseudo-anonymous Contract Enforcement. *3rd International Workshop on Blockchain Systems and Applications*.

Smart Contracts Alliance. (2018). Smart Contracts: 12 Use Cases for Business & Beyond. In *Chamber of Digital Commerce* (Vol. 56). Retrieved from http://digitalchamber.org/assets/smart-contracts-12-use-cases-for-business-and-beyond.pdf

Syllaba, O. (2020). Internet Smart Contracts: Are They Really Smart? *Common Law Review, 16*, 19–22. Retrieved from https://heinonline.org/hol-cgi-bin/get_pdf.cgi?handle=hein.journals/comnlrevi16&section=9

Walch, A. (2017). The Path of the Blockchain Lexicon (and the Law). *Boston University Review of Banking & Financial Law*, (36).

Walker, C. (2019). *Immutability, Friend or Foe: An Analysis of Smart Contracts Against the Fundamentals of Contract Law*. Academic Press.

Weitzenböck, E. M. (2012). *English Law of Contract: Consideration*. Norwegian Research C enter for Computers and Law.

WrightA.De FilippiP. (2015). Decentralized Blockchain Technology and the Rise of Lex Cryptographia. doi:10.2139/ssrn.2580664

ENDNOTES

[1]   Sadiku mentions a bit differently. The exact sentences used in the article was: (1) solely electronic nature; (2) software implementation; (3) increased certainty; (4) conditional nature; (5) self-performance; (6) self-sufficiency. Meanwhile, Mohanta, B. K., Panda, S. S., & Jena, D. (2018). An Overview of Smart Contract and Use Cases in Blockchain Technology. International Conference on Computing, Communication and Networking Technologies 2018, (October). https://doi.org/10.1109/ICCCNT.2018.8494045 stated as such: smart contract is machine readable code run on blockchain platform • Smart contracts are part of one application programs • Smart contracts are event driven program • Smart contracts are autonomous, and once created no need to monitor • Smart contracts are distributed. This statement is the essence of both researches.

[2]   The cryptocurrency of Ethereum, a blockchain where DAO can run as an application.

[3]   For example, the one by Chavez in 2016. Chavez-Dreyfuss, G. (2016). "Virtual company may raise $200 million, largest in crowdfunding." Retrieved from https://br.reuters.com/article/us-blockchain-crowdfunding-idUSKCN0Y82LI

[4]   https://client.aragon.org/#/. The voting mechanism as shown in figure 1

[5]   https://dao.decentraland.org/en/

[6]   Interestingly, the user can even choose to vote what kind of wearable items are allowed or not.

[7]   Smart Contracts: A Primer. *Journal of Scientific and Engineering Research*, 5(5), 538–541. Sadiku mentions a bit differently. The exact sentences used in the article was: (1) solely electronic nature; (2) software implementation; (3) increased certainty; (4) conditional nature; (5) self-performance; (6) self-sufficiency. While Mohanta, B. K., Panda, S. S., & Jena, D. (2018). An Overview of Smart Contract and Use Cases in Blockchain Technology. International Conference on Computing, Communication and Networking Technologies 2018, (October). https://doi.org/10.1109/ICCCNT.2018.8494045 stated as such: smart contract is machine readable code run on blockchain platform • Smart contracts are part of one application programs • Smart contracts are event driven program • Smart contracts are autonomous once created no need to monitor • Smart contracts are distributed. This statement is the essence of both researches.

[8]   Due to the same analogy: if a then b, as discussed in earlier chapters.

[9]   According to Syllaba, the contract in a vending machine is easily disrupted by a single party (which is usually the owner). But with smart contract, once it is employed, it is not possible for only one side to change the contract.

[10]   Which is found often in an electronic contract within an e-commerce mechanism

[11]   Though so, I personally feel conflicted about this since one of the functions of smart contract is used to eliminate the ambiguity and ascertain certainty to a contract.

[12]   Enabled by the smart contract

[13]   Reyes. Pg. 1. It is a really interesting "robot-like" structure. Reyes stated that the planetoid can dance upon receiving a donation. The purpose of the Plantoid is to raise fund until its sufficient

to create new Plantoid by letting the token holder to select and commission artist or other parties that will be responsible to build a whole other Plantoid which means it can reproduce.

14 Six, Ribalta, Herbaut, and Salinesi (2020) cite the article by: Grigg, I. (2004). The ricardian contract. *Proceedings - First IEEE International Workshop on Electronic Contracting, WEC 2004,* (September), 25–31. https://doi.org/10.1109/WEC.2004.1319505.

15 Generally, there are various discussion regarding how the confirmation of the offer and confirmation of the acceptance is confirmed.

16 The smart contract actually made it easier to track on which promises need to be kept or not. Usually, without paper, it will be hard to keep on track on the promises in a contract. Using a smart contract is also an easy way to identify the real party and reducing the possibility of fraud and deception as the smart contract can only be made by the specific account key that is very discreet.

17 The reason for the and/or loss status on merit and loss is that it is generally accepted that only a loss to the accepting party is needed. In her book, Atiyah (1971) stated that "The reason for this doubt is principally the rule, or supposed rule, that consideration must move from the promisee. If the promisee need tosupply the consideration to the promisor, and if the promisor must benefit by the consideration, there must be few cases indeed in which the promise will be enforceable without detriment to the promisee".

Chapter 7
Blockchain Technology in China's Digital Economy:
Balancing Regulation and Innovation

Poshan Yu
https://orcid.org/0000-0003-1069-3675
Soochow University, China

Ruixin Gong
Independent Researcher, China

Michael Sampat
Independent Researcher, Canada

ABSTRACT

Compared with the traditional industrial economy, the Chinese digital economy uses brand-new production factors and production organization methods to bring changes to human society and promote the transformation of the economy. This chapter aims to explore the practical problems of adopting blockchain technology in China's digital economy and study how different cities (managed by various local governments) enhance their unique financial technology ecosystem's economic performance and promote RegTech policy in order to improve the digital economy under the central government's institutional setting. This chapter in turn analyzes the recent cases of blockchain in China's financial industry, compares the application and development of the latest financial technology related policies in major cities, and demonstrates how these regulations can promote the development of blockchain technology in the transformation of China's digital economy.

INTRODUCTION

The Chinese financial technology (FinTech) industry is booming with the solid support of underlying technologies such as big data, artificial intelligence, cloud computing, blockchain, etc. Thanks to

DOI: 10.4018/978-1-7998-7927-5.ch007

tremendous technological reforms, FinTech has transformed the dynamics of the traditional financial industry, which greatly enhances financial inclusiveness in China. Accordingly, the innovative regulatory technology (RegTech) mechanism should be adopted to coordinate with the FinTech market ecology. The diversity of blockchain applications leads to different regulatory attitudes towards specific branch application fields.

The comprehensive regulatory framework of blockchain in the Chinese FinTech industry has been gradually established in recent years. Blockchain, an increasingly applicable technology in the FinTech industry, has been tested with trial and error by numerous FinTech companies in China. Moderate regulation is required for the healthy and sustainable development of blockchain. Fundamentally, the regulatory framework of blockchain in China is made up of 1) rigid laws and regulations; 2) the flexible regulatory sandbox mechanism. The regulatory sandbox is also known as the FinTech innovative regulation pilot, acting to compensate for the lag associated with financial regulation and the costly process of legislation. Moreover, although the rigid laws and regulations can be applied to practical blockchain services and products in the FinTech industry, they are of little direct applicability. On the other hand, the normative documents can be used for regulating blockchain applications more directly. Thus, the effectiveness of laws and regulations on the blockchain is sometimes below regulators' expectations. This necessitates the operation of the regulatory sandbox as it provides experimental spaces for innovative blockchain with synchronized regulation. Through this combination of rigid and flexible regulation methods, the blockchain regulatory framework is gradually improving its overall efficiency and effectiveness.

The FinTech innovative regulation pilot (regulatory sandbox) is very important to balancing regulation and innovation. The pilot is implemented in 9 cities (areas) with various regional characteristics. Supply chain finance is emphasized in Beijing and Xiong'an New Area's piloting blockchain projects. In Shenzhen and Guangzhou, Greater Bay Area cross-border RMB payment and SME financial inclusiveness are highlighted. Three rural problems (agriculture, countryside, and farmers) and related intelligent banking services are the focus of the blockchain application in the pilot of Chengdu and Chongqing. While for Shanghai, Suzhou, and Hangzhou, the Yangtze River Delta credit chain establishment and e-commerce related blockchain services are strongly promoted in the FinTech innovative pilot. However, the highlights included can only represent partial characteristics of blockchain applications in the Chinese FinTech industry. Meanwhile, the effectiveness of the regulatory sandbox mechanism in China can hardly be assessed due to the limited implementation period. Further follow-up research should be undertaken to assess the feasibility of the nationwide promotion of innovative FinTech regulation.

THE REGULATORY FRAMEWORK OF BLOCKCHAIN IN CHINESE FINTECH INDUSTRY

The blockchain regulation framework in China consists of two parts. One is the rigid laws and regulations targeted at absolute prohibition in fields of blockchain, namely, peer-to-peer (P2P) lending, initial coin offering (ICO), and cryptocurrency. The other part is the flexible regulatory mechanism for blockchain-related FinTech enterprises, the FinTech innovative regulation pilots in selected cities (Chinese version of Regulatory Sandbox), which are implemented under the guidance of the "FinTech development plan" issued by the People's Bank of China.

According to the China financial stability report released by The People's Bank of China (2020), China's FinTech regulation is based on the following principles:

1.   The rigid bottom line of financial security must not be violated, based on the existing laws and regulations, departmental rules, and basic standards. The bottom line of innovation should be clearly defined;
2.   Set flexible boundaries. Balance financial security and efficiency. Use information disclosure, public supervision and other methods to allow the public to participate in financial technology governance. Create an ideal development environment for financial technology innovation;

The overall idea is that based on adhering to the bottom line of financial security, the Chinese government is trying to promote the rational and innovative development of blockchain in the financial technology industry. The next part will first explain China's rigid financial bottom line.

The Rigid Laws and Regulations for Blockchain-Related FinTech Application Area

Strictly Forbidden Areas: Cryptocurrency, ICO, and P2P Lending

Cryptocurrency is strictly forbidden in China, due to high volatility in pricing, ease of manipulating the price mechanism, and the anonymity of transactions. Speculative attacks on the cryptocurrency market will disrupt the stability of the financial system and anonymity will induce terrorist financing, money laundering, tax evasion and other cyber-criminal activities.

Under the control of some institutional investors, the price of virtual currency once soared hundreds of times overnight, which attracted a large number of individual investors, according to Disparte (2018). The large sum of funds absorbed disturbed the normal financial ecology and destroyed wealth. There are moral risks and responsibility shirking caused by imperfect trading systems in cryptocurrency markets; the digital wallet of investors can be hacked. These inevitable risks are considered by regulators in banning cryptocurrency in China.

For the same reasons, ICOs are also banned in China. Given the lack of industry certification and evaluation mechanisms for financing projects, and the incomplete disclosure of ICO project information, Chinese ICO projects will mislead immature investors and affect the entire financial market. Table 1 demonstrates the policies related to cryptocurrency and ICO.

Table 2 shows the policies about P2P lending in China.

Since the fall of 2018, the P2P online lending market problematic platform loans have been issued frequently (Yu et al., 2021). The repeated outbreak of risks in the P2P online lending market has reduced investors' confidence in the P2P industry with a significant impact on the healthy development of the industry.

Laws and Regulations on Other Blockchain Application Areas in the Chinese FinTech Industry

The regulatory environment is under deepening reform, with FinTech seeking a balanced transition. FinTech has broadened the channels for traditional financial business, provided diversified business forms, however, it also brought fast-spreading, complicated, hard-to-identify financial risks, including technical risk, credit risk, information disclosure risk, etc. FinTech undoubtedly has impacted the

Table 1. Some important policies related to cryptocurrency and ICO in China

Prohibition Field	Policy	Authority	Issue Date	Main contents
Cryptocurrency and so-called virtual currency	Notice on preventing bitcoin risks	People's bank of China, Ministry of industry and information technology, China Banking Regulatory Commission, China Securities Regulatory Commission China Insurance Regulatory Commission	December 3, 2013	1. Bitcoin is a specific virtual commodity, which does not have the same legal status as currency and cannot and should not be circulated and used as currency in the market. Bitcoin transaction is regarded as an internet commodity trading behavior, the public have the freedom to participate at their own risk. 2. All financial institutions and Payment institutions shall not price products or services with bitcoin, buy or sell bitcoin or act as central counterparties, underwrite insurance business related to bitcoin or include bitcoin into the scope of insurance liability, or provide customers with other services related to bitcoin directly or indirectly. 3. The major bitcoin trading platforms shall be filed with the telecommunications regulatory authorities in accordance with the law.
	Tips on preventing the risks of bitcoin and other so-called virtual currencies	National Internet Finance Association of China	September 13, 2017	1. Bitcoin and other so-called "virtual currencies" have increasingly becoming tools for money laundering, drug trafficking, smuggling, illegal fund-raising and other illegal and criminal activities. Investors should keep vigilant and report to the police immediately when they find clues of illegal and criminal activities. 2. There is no legal basis for the establishment of various so-called "currency" trading platforms in China. 3. All association members shall obey industry self-discipline rules, strictly abide by national laws and regulations, not participate in any centralized transactions related to the so-called "virtual currency" or provide services for such transactions, and actively resist any illegal financial activities.
	Notice on preventing speculation risk of virtual currency transaction	Payment & Clearing Association of China, National Internet Finance Association of China and China Banking Association	May 18, 2021	1. Virtual currency is a specific virtual commodity, which is not issued by the monetary authority and has no monetary attributes such as legal compensation and compulsion. 2. Financial institutions, Payment institutions and other association members shall not carry out business related to virtual currency. 3. Consumers should raise awareness of risk prevention and guard against property and rights losses. 4. Strengthen the self-discipline reguation of association members in participation of any business activities related to virtual currency
ICO (Initial Coin Offering)	Announcement on preventing financing risks of Initial Coin Offering	People's Bank of China, Office of the Central Cyberspace Affairs Commission, the Ministry of industry and information technology, the State Administration for Industry and commerce, the China Banking Regulatory Commission, the China Securities Regulatory Commission and the China Insurance Regulatory Commission	September 4, 2017	1. Prohibits the Initial Coin Offering (ICO) and clarifies the essence of ICO is unauthorized illegal public financing behavior, which is suspected of illegal sale of token notes, illegal issuance of securities, illegal fund-raising financial fraud, pyramid schemes and other illegal criminal activities. 2. Any platform shall not engage in the exchange business between legal tender, token and "virtual currency", shall not buy or sell token or "virtual currency" as a central counter party, and shall not provide pricing, information intermediary and other services for token or "virtual currency".

traditional regulatory framework. A flexible and targeted regulatory framework shall be designed and implemented for FinTech, to improve the timeliness and coverage of regulation.

In China, the preliminary multi-level FinTech regulatory framework has been established, covering laws, administrative regulation, industry self-regulation, enterprises' internal control, and social supervision (Xiao, 2017).

The Laws and Administrative Regulations

Laws and administrative regulations are peremptory and highly effective. Their applicable provisions are critical, focusing on personal information, network security, civil infringement, and economic criminal activities.

Firstly, it is crucial to demonstrate the hierarchy of laws in the Chinese context.

At the level of law, there are 1) common laws, which are generally applicable, such as the criminal law and the civil code; 2) special laws, which are targeted at particular legal problems.

Table 2. Some important policies about P2P lending in China

Prohibition Field	Policy	Authority	Issue Date	Main Contents
P2P lending	The Implementation Plan for Special Rectification on Risks in Internet Finance(the 'rectification plan')	the General Office of the State Council	April 12,2016	The P2P online lending platform shall not set up a pool of funds, shall not grant loans, shall not raise funds illegally, shall not raise funds, shall not provide a guarantee for itself, shall not mislead lenders, and shall not conduct offline marketing
	Notice on Standardizing and Rectifying Cash Loan Business	Leading group for special rectification of Internet financial risks and leading group for special rectification of P2P online loan risks	December 1,2017	1.It is forbidden for P2P platform to deduct interest, service charge, management fee, deposit from loan principal, and set high overdue interest, overdue fine, fine, etc; 2.It is not allowed to match the funds of banking financial institutions to participate in P2P network lending; 3.It is not allowed to provide down payment loan, real estate off-site financing and other loan matching services for house purchase financing; 4.It is not allowed to provide loan matching business without designated purpose
	Opinions on classified disposal and risk prevention of online lending institutions	Leading group for special rectification of Internet financial risks and leading group for special rectification of P2P online loan risks	December 19, 2018	1.Adhere to the principle of P2P enterprises' exit as the main direction of work. Except for some strictly compliant operating entities, other P2P enterprises shall exit as much as possible. 2. Increase the intensity and speed of rectification of illegal and non-compliant P2P companies.

Figure 1. The hierarchy of laws in China

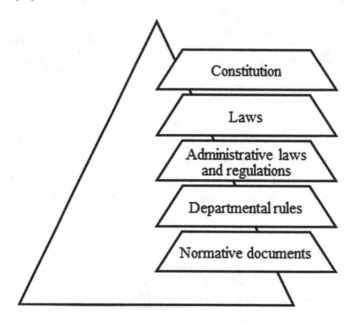

The related legal provisions in China's civil code and criminal law can be seen in Table 3. In The Civil Code, articles of protection of privacy and personal information, as well as legal data and virtual property often involve blockchain, as information and virtual property play paramount roles in the life cycle of blockchain application. In the Criminal Law, the crime of property violation is probably applicable in regulating blockchain-related companies, especially illegal fundraising, unauthorized stock issuing, and personal information infringement.

Table 3. Some common laws related to the application of blockchain in financial technology

Legal norm: Common Law	The Civil Code	Chapter 6: Privacy and personal information protection
		A127: Provision on legal data and virtual property
	Criminal Law	A175 Crime of usurious loan
		A176 Crime of illegally absorbing public deposits
		A179 Crime of issuing stocks, corporate bonds or corporate bonds without authorization
		A192 Crime of fraud in fund raising
		A225 Crime of illegal business operation
		A253 Crime of infringing citizens' personal information
		A286 Crime of refusing to perform the obligation of network information security management
		A287 Crime of illegal use of information network; Crime of aiding information network criminal activities

Meanwhile, the special legislation for blockchain is essential in the legal framework of blockchain. Related special laws are shown in Table 4. However, these special laws are from the technological perspective. More legislation should be established for blockchain in the FinTech application scenarios, i.e., the protection of financial consumers' property rights and personal information while involved in blockchain-related FinTech services and products.

Table 4. Some special laws related to the application of blockchain in financial technology

Legal Norm: Special Law	The cybersecurity law
	Electronic commerce law
	Electronic signature law
	The decision of the Standing Committee of the National People's Congress on strengthening the protection of network information
	Standardization law
	Securities law
	Cryptography law
	Anti-unfair competition law
	Anti-money laundering law
	Advertising law

Table 5. Regulation in the age of digitalization in China

Administrative regulations	*Measures for banning illegal financial institutions and illegal financial business activities*
	Measures for the administration of Internet information services
	Regulations on the administration of credit reference industry
	Regulations on security protection of computer information system
Departmental regulations	PBC: *Measures for the implementation of the protection of the rights and interests of financial consumers*
	Cyberspace Administration of China: *Regulations on management of blockchain information service*
Normative documents	General office of CPC and The State Council: *Opinions on promoting the healthy and orderly development of mobile Internet*
	PBC, CBIRC, CSRC: *Guidance on improving the supervision of systemically important financial institutions*
	CBIRC: *Opinions on promoting rural commercial banks to stick to their positioning, strengthen governance and enhance financial service capacity*
	CBIRC: *Notice on further improving the quality and efficiency of financial services for small and micro enterprises in 2019*
	CBIRC: *Notice on further strengthening intellectual property pledge financing*
	CBIRC, PBC, Development and Reform Commission, MIIT, Ministry of Treasury: *Notice on temporarily delaying repayment of principal and interest for loans of small, medium and micro enterprises*
	PBC and other 7 ministries and commissions: *Opinions on standardizing the development of supply chain finance to support stable circulation and optimization and upgrading of supply chain industry chain*
Judicial explanation	The Supreme People's Court: *Provisions on Several Issues concerning the trial of cases by Internet courts* (stipulates the authentication of e-certificate blockchain)

In terms of laws, not only has the existing legislation been implemented, but some supporting regulatory guidelines have also come into effect to promote the healthy function of the FinTech industry in China. This has focused especially on the emerging business modes, such as retail banking services, online loan and finance (including P2P and ICO), cloud computing platforms, digital currency, asset management and Internet insurance, etc.

However, due to the high-speed evolution and development of blockchain and financial technology applications, as well as the inherent lag of legislation, the current regulatory system still lacks pertinence and comprehensiveness. It still needs to follow the development of the industry to supplement and improve response time, promote the healthy development of the blockchain industry, and improve the predictability and certainty of relevant compliance work.

As for administrative regulation, the focus is more on flexibility and inclusiveness in the Internet era, as well as inheritance laws and reasonable traditional financial regulation. Based upon Xiao (2017), efforts are made in:

1. Market entry and functional supervision, meaning all FinTech businesses and activities should come under the scope of regulation.
2. The enhancement of regulatory consistency and penetration, comprehensively assessing and regulating the FinTech businesses.
3. The particular protection for the FinTech consumers, ensuring consumers' right to know, right to free choice, right to property security and right to reimbursement.

The administrative regulations of blockchain are established by the State Council, which are aimed at regulating illegal financial business activities and non-compliant internet services.

Among the departmental rules, the *"Regulations on the management of blockchain information services"* deserves mention. Issued by the Cyberspace Administration of China, it is the most direct and comprehensive regulation for blockchain technology at present. It is the most important and direct legal compliance basis and norm for blockchain developers and operators (Table 5).

By simply comparing the numbers of normative documents and other laws and administrative regulations, one conclusion can be made that normative regulations established by financial regulatory authorities and related ministries play a greater role in the regulatory framework. They are more targeted (Deng, 2019), operable and comprehensive in FinTech industry regulation, although the normative documents of ministries and financial regulatory departments are of low legal ranking in China.

Industry Self-Regulation, Enterprise Internal Control and Social Supervision on Blockchain

The industry self-regulation, enterprise internal control, and social supervision provide alternative regulation channels on blockchain application in the Chinese FinTech industry, which is less mandatory compared to laws and administrative regulations but with higher standards on the self-discipline of related subjects and the effectiveness of public supervision.

For industry self-regulation, the National Internet Finance Association of China (NIFA) was formally established in March 2016 to strengthen the formulation and implementation of industry standards and self-discipline rules (Tian, 2016). Industry self-regulation is a bridge between market entities' self-discipline and regulations, which translates industrial consensuses and practices into written rules. Moreover, it fills in the gap of detailed self-regulation on specific issues of blockchain services and products.

From the perspective of enterprise internal control, the practitioners, especially the emerging business entities, have been enhancing the awareness of risk control, compliance management, and emergency response.

In terms of social supervision, the exclusive reporting information platform for Internet finance is under operation, facilitating the supervision from institutions and the public on illegal behaviors of the Internet financial industry through such a centralized platform.

Table 6. Diverse regulation channels of FinTech industry

Regulation Channel	Regulations (Platforms)
Industry Self-Regulation	National Internet Finance Association of China (NIFA) *Proposal for Healthy Development of Internet Finance Industry* *NIFA Member Self-Discipline Convention* *Measures for the administration of self-discipline and punishment* *Self-discipline Convention on overdue debt collection of Internet Finance (On Trial)* *Self-discipline Convention on marketing and publicity activities of Internet financial institutions (On Trial)* *Publicity mechanism of the out-of-contact member of NIFA*
FinTech Enterprises' Internal Control	Enterprises' Awareness of Risk Prevention and Control, Compliance Operation Emergency Response, And Other Internal Control
Social Supervision	China Internet Finance Reporting Platform

To conclude, the regulatory framework of blockchain in the Chinese digital economy is in gradual perfection, with the mandatory laws, administrative regulations and the self-disciplined rules as well as the public supervision. The comprehensive framework provides solid support for the healthy and sustainable development of blockchain.

The Trend of Digitalized Regulation on Blockchain

Moreover, regulatory authorities actively attempt to digitalize regulation. In terms of FinTech supervision, the People's Bank of China is vigorously promoting the construction of a digital central bank, intending to upgrade the financial service of PBC, supported by cutting-edge technology (Su, 2020). China Banking and Insurance Regulatory Commission (CBIRC) has concentrated on comprehensive regulation of banking services and products in the financial market through a centralized and unified electronic report and information registration platform (China Securities News, 2019), paving the way for information sharing and data interconnection. Meanwhile, the China Securities Regulatory Commission (CSRC) has stepped up in the construction of a central regulatory and monitoring information platform (People's Daily, 2015), which comprehensively strengthened the capacity of market risk monitoring and abnormal transaction behavior identification. The National Internet Finance Association of China (NIFA), the industry's self-regulating organization, is committed to building a comprehensive service platform and monitoring mechanism for Internet finance (Zhou and Pang, 2016), by sufficiently utilizing big data, AI and other high-tech to improve the real-time risk monitoring and the accuracy of early warning, as well as providing timely and reliable statistics and information for industry supervision and self-discipline.

FLEXIBLE REGULATORY BOUNDARY FOR BLOCKCHAIN INNOVATION IN FINANCIAL INDUSTRY - THE REGULATORY SANDBOX MECHANISM (FINTECH INNOVATIVE REGULATION PILOT)

In August 2019, the People's Bank of China (PBC) issued the *"FinTech Development Plan (2019-2021)"*, *The FinTech 3-year plan* emphasizes that timely application and sharing of technological achievements should be promoted through piloting, to upgrade the overall competitiveness of Chinese FinTech industry chain, to explore FinTech regulation tools that are in sync with the international RegTech practices (Wu, 2019).

The FinTech development plan (2019-2021) pays special attention to the role of regulation, to promote the transformation of China's FinTech from the 1.0 era to the 2.0 era. Particularly in strengthening regulatory coordination, enhancing the penetration and prudence of regulation, innovating regulatory mechanisms, accelerating the formulation, monitoring, analysis, and evaluation of basic regulatory rules, and enhancing the professionalism and unity of financial supervision, according to The People's Bank of China (2019, August 23).

Moreover, the financial regulatory authority is targeted at encouraging fundamental, universal and key technology R&D with essential application in FinTech pilot projects, providing a feasible policy framework and operative mode in establishing the "regulatory sandbox" with Chinese characteristics. The regulatory sandbox was initiated by the Financial Conduct Authority (FCA) in the UK (Financial Conduct Authority, 2015). It provides testing grounds for emerging business models that are not protected by current regulation or supervised by regulatory institutions. The growing need to develop regulatory frameworks for emerging business models makes regulatory sandbox imperative in the FinTech innovation process. The purpose of the sandbox is to adapt regulatory compliance to the growth and pace of the most innovative companies, in a way that does not smother the FinTech industry with rigid rules but also protects financial consumers' interests.

This attempt aspires to guide licensed financial institutions to create a safe, inclusive and open atmosphere for the FinTech industry under the requirement for compliance and consumer safeguard mechanisms. The FinTech innovative regulation pilot ("regulatory sandbox") is a solid step in bringing the development of FinTech in line with international RegTech experience.

The PBC officially launched the FinTech innovative regulation pilot (the Chinese version of Regulatory Sandbox) in December 2019, (The People's Bank of China, 2019) with Beijing being the first pilot city. At present, after two rounds of expansion in regional scope, the pilot is implemented in 9 cities (districts), including Beijing, Shanghai, Chongqing, Shenzhen, Xiong'an New Area, Hangzhou, Suzhou, Chengdu and Guangzhou, among them are 4 tier-one cities, 4 new tier-one cities and 1 state-level new area, according to The People's Bank of China (2020, April 27).

The pilot has aided efforts to create a prudent and inclusive FinTech regulatory tool by using a flexible framework including information disclosure, product publicity, and social supervision. This ultimately constructs a FinTech regulation model with professionalism, unity and penetration.

China's FinTech innovative regulation pilot is still in the early stage of development. The pilot cities possess qualifying features, that is, those with a more prosperous economic and financial environment.

Not only the four tier-one cities with the strongest economic strength are covered, namely, Beijing, Shanghai, Guangzhou, Shenzhen, but also the cities (areas) with enormous potential in the local FinTech industry, viz Hangzhou, Suzhou, Chongqing, Xiong'an New Area, and Chengdu.

As of writing, 86 projects in nine cities (areas) are selected for pilots. Among them,

Figure 2. The regional distribution of FinTech innovative regulation piloting projects
Data Source: Provincial Branches of The People's Bank of China

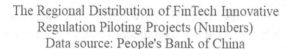
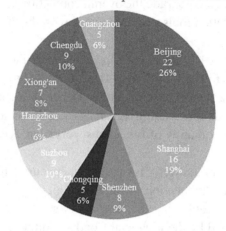

Beijing has carried out three rounds of pilot projects, with 22 covered, accounting for 26% of the total projects, followed by Shanghai with 16 projects, Suzhou and Chengdu with 9 projects each, Shenzhen with 8 projects, Xiong'an New Area, Chongqing, Hangzhou, and Guangzhou (Figure 2).

As for the types of FinTech innovative regulation pilot projects, except Beijing's because the first round of FinTech projects are not finalized, the others can be divided into two categories: financial services and technological products. As seen in the bar chart below, the distribution of projects in Beijing, Shanghai, Chongqing, Hangzhou, Xiong'an New Area, and Chengdu is relatively balanced. The pilot projects in Shenzhen and Guangzhou are more inclined to financial services, while those in Suzhou tend to give more priority to technological products.

The FinTech innovative regulation pilot takes applications. Once the applicant is selected by the provincial capital branches of PBC, the branches publicize the *"Statement on FinTech innovative application"* on the official website. The document involves the following four aspects.

To a certain extent, China's FinTech innovative regulation pilot absorbs the international experience of the "regulatory sandbox" initiated by the UK's FCA, popularized in Singapore, Australia, and other countries with mature financial markets. The content of the "Statement on FinTech innovative application" in Chinese pilots shares many similarities with the information disclosure of the regulatory sandbox mechanism.

Figure 3. The category distribution of FinTech innovative regulation piloting projects in each city (or area)
Data Source: Provincial Branches of The People's Bank of China

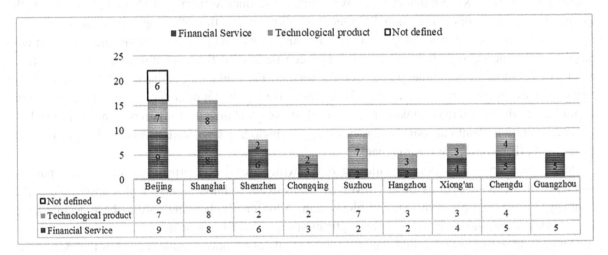

	Beijing	Shanghai	Shenzhen	Chongqing	Suzhou	Hangzhou	Xiong'an	Chengdu	Guangzhou
□ Not defined	6								
▨ Technological product	7	8	2	2	7	3	3	4	
■ Financial Service	9	8	6	3	2	2	4	5	5

Table 7. Contents of the "Statement on FinTech Innovative Application" published on the provincial branches of The People's Bank of China

Basic Informantion and Service Information of the Projects
- Name, Category (financial service or technological product), Application institution, Descripition on technological application, Function introduction; Statement on innovativeness, Expected effect and scale, Service channel, time, Target customers and Protocol.

Legal Compliance and Technological Security Assessment
- Assessment agency, Assesment time, Term of validity, Assessment conclusion and material.

Risk Prevention and Control & Reimbursement Measures
- Key risk points, Measures of risk control, Reimbursement and exit mechanism, Contingency plan, etc.

Complaint Response Mechanism
- Channels of institutional complaints and self-descipline complaints

Table 8. Comparison of the differences between China's pilot financial technology innovation regulation and the UK's regulatory sandbox

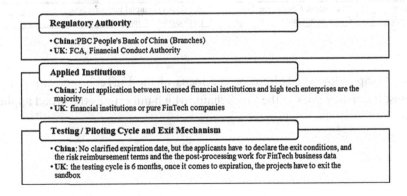

Regulatory Authority
- **China**:PBC People's Bank of China (Branches)
- **UK**: FCA, Financial Conduct Authority

Applied Institutions
- **China**: Joint application between licensed financial institutions and high tech enterprises are the majority
- **UK**: financial institutions or pure FinTech companies

Testing / Piloting Cycle and Exit Mechanism
- **China**: No clarified expiration date, but the applicants have to declare the exit conditions, and the risk reimbursement terms and the the post-processing work for FinTech business data
- **UK**: the testing cycle is 6 months, once it comes to expiration, the projects have to exit the sandbox

There are distinctive disparities in the maturity of financial markets, political regimes, and regulatory objects between the UK's regulatory sandbox (Financial Conduct Authority, 2015) and China's FinTech innovative regulation pilot. The main differences are illustrated in the following perspectives:

In China, most of the pilot projects are jointly applied by financial institutions and high-tech enterprises. The increasingly tight cooperation between traditional financial institutions and high-tech enterprises demonstrates the integration of these sectors. The regulatory authority gives more priority to the licensed financial institutions in FinTech innovative regulation pilot application because of their comparative advantages in risk-taking and comprehensive reimbursement regimes. Among licensed financial institutions, banks account for the vast majority, including large state-owned banks, commercial banks, and urban (rural) commercial banks.

Meanwhile, financial services entities such as payment service enterprises, insurance companies, and other financial institutions are also involved. Mainstream technologies are highly applicable to the banking industry i.e., big data, AI, and blockchain. Additionally, banking entities have accumulated large-scale data resources, improving the application scenario of high-techs.

Another difference is that, unlike the centralized regulatory sandbox implemented by the FCA in the UK, China's pilot FinTech innovation regulation is carried out by the provincial branches of the People's Bank of China. This has the characteristics of decentralization and regional diversity so typical of the FinTech industry.

There are strong regional characteristics in the projects entering the FinTech innovative regulation pilot, which indicates that the pilot is well-targeted at serving the national strategy of building a regional development focus. The following part will explain this in detail.

Table 9. Some key points of FinTech innovative regulation pilot in different regions

Pilot Cities (Areas)	Regional development strategy	Key points of FinTech innovative regulation pilot
Beijing	Coordinated Development of the Beijing-Tianjin-Hebei Region (BTH)	Supply chain finance
Xiong'an New Area (Heibei Province)		
Shanghai	Yangtze River Delta (YRD) Integration Development	Regional credit chain establishment
Suzhou		
Hangzhou		E-commerce
Shenzhen	Guangdong-Hong Kong-Macao Greater Bay Area (GBA)	Financial inclusiveness for Small-and-Micro Enterprises
Guangzhou		Cross-border payment (Between Mainland China and Hong Kong Special Administrative Region, Macao Special Administrative Region)
Chengdu	Chengdu & Chongqing Two Cities Economic Circle	Rural area financial inclusiveness
Chongqing		Intelligent banking service

The word cloud map below sheds light on the focus of the FinTech innovative regulation pilot in China. The greatest frequency goes to the blockchain, which underlines the broad application of blockchain in FinTech.

Figure 4. Word cloud map (Authors)

BLOCKCHAIN INNOVATION HIGHLIGHTS IN CHINESE FINTECH INNOVATION REGULATION PILOT WITH REGIONAL CHARACTERISTICS

Beijing and Xiong'an New Area: Supply Chain Finance

Table 10. Supply chain finance

> **Demand side of supply chain finance**
> - Medium, small and micro-sized enterprises
>
> **Supply chain finance service provider**
> - Financial institutions: Banks, factoring agencies, micro-credit companies, trust comanies and fund companies; capital investment institutions; guarantee compies and insurance companies.
> - Fintech service providers: Fintech operation platform
> - Platform service providers: Supply chain management service companies; logistics service provider; industrial internet
> - Supply chain core enterprises: Key enterprises
>
> **Supply chain fiance infrastructurer builder**
> - Informationized infrastructure suppliers
> - Other infrastructure suppliers
> - Industry association, research institutes

Beijing has accumulated the best scientific research institutions and numerous headquarters of high-tech companies in China. Thus, the leadership in FinTech R&D is in doubt. China has the potential to catch up to cutting-edge high techs. Furthermore, the gathering of authoritative media fuels blockchain R&D in the public and private sectors. Beijing, with its high-density population, is an ideal place for the promotion of inclusive finance. *Beijing FinTech development plan (2018-2022)* paves the way for the FinTech innovative regulation pilot. Xiong'an New Area is constructed under the national strategy of Coordinated Development of the Beijing-Tianjin-Hebei Region in 2017 (Administrative Commission of Zhongguancun Science Park, 2018).

One emphasis of Beijing and Xiong'an New area's FinTech innovative regulation pilots is supply chain financing (Table 10). In recent years, supply chain finance has been encouraged by several policies at the national level. On July 9, 2019, the China Banking and Insurance Regulatory Commission (CBIRC) issued the *"Guidance of the general office of CBIRC on promoting the supply chain financial serving the real economy."* This requires that bancassurance institutions rely on the core enterprises in the supply chain to provide a package of comprehensive financial services such as financing, settlement, and cash management for the upstream and downstream enterprises of the supply chain. In September 2020, the PBC, the Ministry of Commerce, the Ministry of Industry and Information Technology and other eight Ministries and Commissions issued the *"Opinions on standardizing the development of supply chain finance to support the stable circulation, optimization and upgrading of the supply chain and industry chain."*(Ministry of Industry and Information Technology et al., 2020) This required financial institutions and enterprises to strengthen information sharing and collaboration, and improve the online and digital level of supply chain financing. It has become a programmatic document for the development of China's supply chain finance. In 2021, the government work report mentioned "innovating the mode of supply chain finance" for the first time, (The State Council, 2021) which means that the development of supply chain finance has become a national strategy.

Supply chain finance is a comprehensive financial model that regards the core enterprises and their related upstream and downstream enterprises in the supply chain as a whole, relying on the core enterprises to provide financial services or products to the upstream and downstream enterprises in China. Through the supply chain financial service platform, financial institutions can integrate business and capital flow, and other information. With the blessing of Internet technology, they can accurately match financial resources and provide efficient and low-cost financial services for small and mid-size enterprises (SMEs), to reduce their financing pressure.

Despite supply chain finance, Xiong'an has its feature of green innovation in area development (Xinhua News Agency, 2021). Through this reform of payment, settlement, and other traditional financial scenarios, a novel financial ecology has emerged in Xiong'an new area with a high level of inclusiveness.

Blockchain has laid down the foundation of the smart city. The new area explores the application of blockchain in the integration of government affairs, data sharing, and cross-chain interaction. The government together with FinTech enterprises have successively built the blockchain platform for dynamic forestry fund regulation, the blockchain management platform for land requisition and relocation funds, and the blockchain system for construction engineering funds (Li, 2020).

One of the FinTech innovative regulation pilot projects is related to the blockchain information system of resettlement fund management. Through the system, the encrypted data of contract information and relevant personal information of the acquisition and relocation are obtained and stored on the chain. After the level-by-level approval of the smart contract inspection, the land resettlement fund is transferred from the government's financial special account to the residents' account. This is promising in improving administrative efficiency, fund allocation, and supervision during the land resettlement process. Besides, Xiong'an New Area is setting up a blockchain-based digital currency wage payment platform.

All these attempts have played an effective role in ecological environment management, residential demolition and relocation, construction fund management, and central bank digital currency pilot projects.

Shenzhen and Guangzhou: Greater Bay Area's Cross Border RMB Payment and SME Financial Inclusiveness

On February 18, 2019, the CPC Central Committee and the State Council issued the *"Outline of Development Planning for Guangdong, Hong Kong and Macao Bay Area."*(CPC Central Committee and State Council, 2019) Hong Kong, Macao, Guangzhou and Shenzhen are the core engines of regional development under the Greater Bay Area (GBA) initiative.[1]

Driven by the institutional settings of the GBA, the region is aimed at reconstructing as a dynamic world-class cluster of cities, an international technological innovation center, a crucial pillar of The Belt and Road Initiative, and a demonstration area for the deep cooperation among mainland China, Hong Kong and Macao.

Figure 5. The Guangdong-Hong Kong-Macao Greater Bay Area (GBA)
Map Source: GBA Cities, n.d.

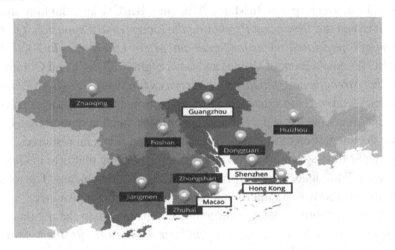

Shenzhen, as the pioneer in reform and opening-up, considers the application of blockchain in the financial field a priority, relying on the characteristics of local large-scale technology enterprises and an innovation-inclusive city. Guangzhou grasps the major strategic opportunity of digital "new infrastructure" and provides multiple application opportunities for blockchain.

Cross-border RMB payment and settlement is one highlight of the pilot projects. Many experts regard blockchain as the new infrastructure in the digital finance era. In December 2020, the Digital Currency Research Institute of the People's Bank of China signed a strategic cooperation agreement with UnionPay (China UMS, a subsidiary of China UnionPay) to jointly study the innovative application of online and offline payment scenarios in the digital RMB pilot, thus promoting the construction of the digital RMB ecosystem (China News, 2020).

RMB cross-border payment will bring greater convenience to tourists travelling between mainland China, Hong Kong and Macao. It provides an alternative payment option for people who need to make cross-border RMB transactions. Hong Kong has an edge in financial infrastructure, especially its multi-currency and multi-level platform. The cross-border RMB payment in the FinTech regulatory sandbox will further enhance the interconnection between Hong Kong and mainland China, especially the GBA.

It expands the two-way channels of cross-border RMB funds circulation. Additionally, the central bank's digital currency is being vigorously promoted, promising to accelerate the process of RMB internationalization.

Small-and-Micro Enterprises (SME) are also aided by blockchain as it deepens the financial inclusiveness in China, especially for medium-sized, small, and micro-sized companies. Among the 86 projects, 11 are linked with medium-sized and small-and-micro enterprises, mainly for the convenience of loaning, financing, bill circulation, and intelligent finance. This is particularly highlighted in Guangdong province. The introduction of FinTech narrows the Macmillan Gap[2], the universal problem of modern SMEs and micro enterprises' lack of financial resources, particularly long-term shortages. In recent years, to alleviate the problem of information asymmetry faced by small and micro enterprises, while also enhancing data productivity, financial institutions have reformed with the empowerment of FinTech. This has mainly occurred in credit product design, fundraising, customer acquisition strategy, credit approval, risk pricing, transaction & payment, and post-credit management.

Policy departments have realized the outstanding capacity of FinTech for the upgrading of financial services for small-and-micro enterprises. In March 2020, the CBIRC (China Banking and Insurance Regulatory Commission) issued the *"Notice on Promoting the Incremental Expansion, Quality Improvement and Cost Reduction of Financial Services for Small and Micro Enterprises in 2020"* (CBIRC, 2020a), and in June, the PBC (People's Bank of China) and other eight Ministries and Commissions issued the *"Guidance on Further Strengthening the Financial Services for Small and Micro Enterprises."* (PBC et al., 2020) Both policies focus on core values of optimizing the credit mode of small and micro enterprises by using FinTech and improving the supply chain capability of small and microloans. In addition, these policies strengthen the integration of industry development and financial resources.

Yue Xin Rong, the SME credit information and financing docking platform in Guangdong province, has involved 20 cities, 67888 financing enterprises, and 12649 bank branches. The total finance amount has been 1419.9 billion for SMEs and micro-enterprises in Guangdong province.[3]

At the same time, the authorities have made adaptive adjustments to the regulatory policies for the digitalization of financial services. For example, *"the Interim Measures for the Management of Internet loans of commercial banks,"* (CBIRC, 2020b) regularize remote bank account opening, non-contact financial services, and Internet loan business. These regulatory attempts provide more flexibility at the boundary of financial digitalization.

The key to improving financial services for small and micro enterprises, as well as deepening financial inclusiveness, is mechanism innovation. Supported by the government's policy orientation toward the digital economy and FinTech, the integrated development of technology, business scenarios, and finance has created a new model of customer acquisition, risk control, and business profit for small and micro-enterprises. The strategic deployment, organizational structure, and credit culture of banks are also altering, particularly the upgrading of credit supply chains for small and micro-companies.

Chengdu and Chongqing: Three Rural Problems (Agriculture, Countryside, and Farmers) and Related Intelligent Banking Services

One emphasis of China's financial inclusiveness is the application of blockchain in rural areas, concerning agriculture, countryside, and farmers. This is stressed in the 2020 CPC Document No.1, especially in Chongqing and Chengdu, the provincial capital of Sichuan (Dong and Jing, 2020). In 2020, Sichuan had the greatest amount of value added to the primary industry of 555.6 billion yuan, ranking first country-wide (Sichuan Provincial Bureau of Statistics, 2021).

Figure 6. Ranking of provinces by the added value of China's primary industry
Data source: Provincial Statistical Bulletin of National Economic and Social Development in 2020

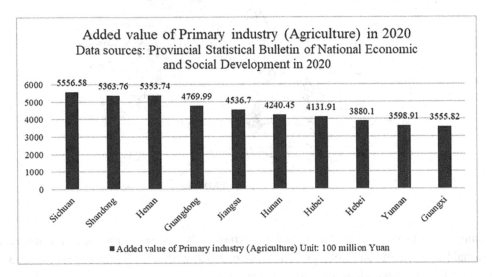

Chengdu and Chongqing play crucial roles in Chinese agriculture and are steadily progressing agricultural modernization. Thus, the focus of FinTech piloting here is on rural financial inclusiveness. Chongqing develops characteristic projects, such as intelligent banking services, digital mobile banking services, and agriculture-related credit services based on multi-party learning technology. This supports Chongqing's local dialect, enhances the universality of FinTech application, and helps with poverty alleviation. Among the five projects related to the rural theme, two are related to Chengdu and Chongqing local dialect intelligent banking services. It is well-known that the penetration rate of the Sichuan dialect is relatively high nationwide. So, the promotion of banking services in the Sichuan dialect provides more convenience for customers regardless of knowledge level and age group.

Another important advantage of blockchain is supply chain finance in rural areas. Based on blockchain technology, financial institutions form the big database of agriculture-related upstream and downstream enterprises to better utilize the dynamic fund pool. Moreover, blockchain can be used to investigate the future cash flow processes of small-and-micro agricultural enterprises as well as verifying the data related to business operations and accounts receivable. These all aim to deepen rural-area financial inclusiveness, for the small-and-micro enterprises in rural areas, as well as narrow the gap in development level between urban and rural areas, striving ultimately for a fair and prosperous society.

Shanghai, Suzhou and Hangzhou: Yangtze River Delta Credit Chain Establishment and E-Commerce

The National strategy of regional integration development of the Yangtze River Delta (YRD) was proposed by President Xi Jinping at the China International Import Expo (CIIE) in November 2018. *Outline of*

Figure 7. The Yangtze River delta region
(Zhang et al., 2011)

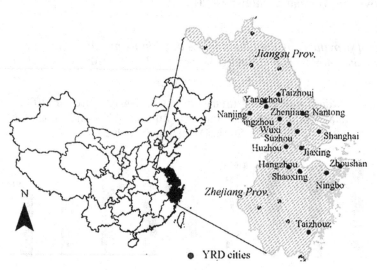

Regional Integration Development Plan of Yangtze River Delta has been implemented since December 2019 (National Development and Reform Commission, 2019) within the 9 pilot cities (areas), 3 of which are located in YRD (i.e. Shanghai, Suzhou and Hangzhou).

Shanghai is often seen as the flagship of FinTech in mainland China. Particularly, it advances the Shanghai Pilot Free Trade Zone.[4] It is the first mover in the clustering of R&D talents and distinctive technological innovation parks. Meanwhile, the regulatory and business environment is well-established, with the first financial court in China (Shanghai Pudong Government, 2018). The Shanghai Intellectual Property Court can also provide a solid guarantee for FinTech IP protection. With its strong financial foundation, relatively sophisticated financial infrastructure, and comprehensive categories of financial institutions, Shanghai stands as the FinTech leader in the YRD synergy effect, according to Xinhua News Agency (2014).

Suzhou is a city developed by the economic radiation effect of Shanghai. It is in the first batch of the 5G network and central bank digital currencies pilot cities in China with the first blockchain Industrial Development Cluster area in Jiangsu province (Suzhou Daily, 2021). Hangzhou, described by President Xi as a city with innovation and dynamics (Xi, 2016), is particularly well-known for its prosperous e-commerce industry supported by the government's innovation and startup policy.

FinTech innovated the current credit practices. During the pandemic, the traditional offline financial business was almost in stagnation, while the online financial business has been actively transformed in the direction of digital, intelligent, and non-contact financial services. Credit in the pandemic era

Figure 8. The operation process of the credit chain

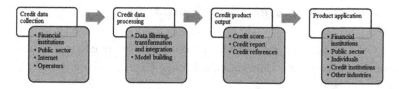

Figure 9. The Peking University digital financial inclusion index of China
(*Guo et al., 2020*)

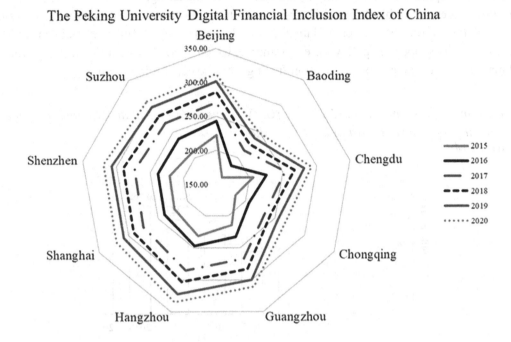

emphasized the business-to-business market, especially corporate financial services based on supply chain, trade chain, and industrial chain (Geng, 2020).

In the interest of risk avoidance, the incorporation of blockchain in the credit system facilitates the establishment of a comprehensive data pool based on decentralized distributed ledger technology. With the assistance of big data, the process of risk assessment and credit evaluation of customers is more convenient, reliable, and speedy. Blockchain's "hard-to-tamper" quality made information distortion less possible, which may reduce the risk of bad debts to some extent.

Since 2020, under the guidance of the People's Bank of China and Nanjing Branch, exploration of blockchain in the field of credit reference and the YRD credit reference chain has been carried out.

It builds an application platform including regulators, credit reference institutions, financial institutions, and other entities, realizing the whole-process cross-regional credit integration service, and storing real-time certificates on the chain, to make credit query records, authorization certificates, and credit data reliable and traceable. This truly realizes the sharing and co-regulation of credit data. The YRD credit chain application platform provides a convenient and efficient remote joint credit inquiry service for financial institutions through the data collaboration of local credit institutions.

By the end of December 2020, 11 cities in Jiangsu Province, Zhejiang Province, Anhui Province and Shanghai have joined the YRD credit chain, with 7.89 million enterprises, 8.62 million credit reports and 83.05 million credit information. At present, 65 financial institutions have used the YRD credit chain for inquiry, with 523 enterprises eligible for loans totalling 1.28 billion yuan (Ye, 2021).

The operation of the YRD credit chain hopefully breaks the "data isolation" of the medium, small, and micro-sized enterprises. The integration of the credit investigation chain in YRD paves the way for data sharing and intercommunication of local credit agencies by the utilization of blockchain and big data. Moreover, this application of blockchain credit chain effectively broadens the financial channel for businesses and promotes high-quality financial resource clustering.

One special scenario of blockchain in Hangzhou is the application of e-commerce in Hangzhou.

Among all the piloting cities (areas), Hangzhou has the highest digital financial inclusion index. This is mainly due to its supporting policy for e-commerce, which encourages entities in the private sector toward mass entrepreneurship and innovation fueling Chinese economic growth.

Figure 10. Annual gross merchandise volume (GMV) transacted on Alibaba's retail marketplaces in China from the financial year 2014 to 2021 (in billion yuan)
Data Source: Alibaba

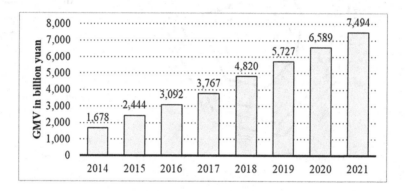

For instance, Alibaba, the pioneer of the Chinese e-commerce market, demonstrates the potential of digital trade, triggering the boom in e-commerce in Zhejiang province. As an emerging internet city, Hangzhou has performed well in blockchain patent application, relying on its active innovation and industrial foundation, with many high-tech enterprises investing a large number of R&D funds in blockchain represented by Alibaba.

Blockchain facilitates cross-border payment in e-commerce. The distributed ledger technology, featured in convenient, secure, and cost-saving transactions, enables users to complete cross-border remittance under a decentralized payment mechanism, which continuously breeds potential market space in the international e-commerce market. The government continuously promotes supportive policy in cross-border e-commerce, as is illustrated in the *Implementation opinions of Hangzhou Municipal Government on accelerating the development of cross border E-commerce,*(Hangzhou Municipal Government, 2019) especially in the cultivation of entities, brands, and talents and the construction of the industrial park, warehouse, and logistics infrastructure in e-commerce. Yiwu Cross-border Index outperformed other indexes, which shows that international e-commerce plays an outstanding role in the Chinese e-commerce industry.

2 out of 5 projects in Hangzhou's FinTech innovative regulation pilot are related to the payment and logistics applications in e-commerce.

The facilitation of cross-border payment and settlement provides convenience for domestic e-commerce enterprises and merchants but also advances the transformation towards digital trade. In addition, blockchain plus e-commerce make it possible for consumers to verify the authenticity of online shopping goods by blockchain's application in traceability, upgrading consumption experience, ideally rejuvenating domestic demand. As for customs, traceability can be used to identify smuggling and contraband

Figure 11. Yiwu e-commerce development index
Data source: Ministry of Commerce of PRC

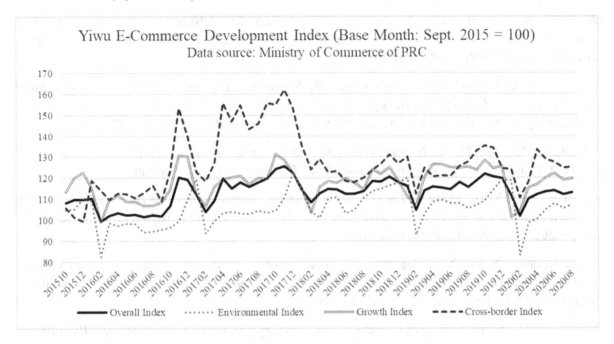

goods. Moreover, banks can confirm the authenticity of credit applicants through traceability. Therefore, the quality of the logistics and e-commerce industries are destined to enter a new stage in Hangzhou, Zhejiang Province and ultimately the whole of China.

CONCLUSION

Based upon the previous discussion, this chapter has investigated the regulatory framework of the Chinese blockchain industry. The framework is composed of two parts, the rigid laws and regulations and the flexible regulatory sandbox mechanism balancing regulation and innovation. Meanwhile, the chapter also gives a special glimpse of the regional characteristics among the FinTech innovative regulation pilot in the 9 cities (area). The chapter sets forth the recent developments in blockchain in China's financial industry, comparing the application and development of the latest financial technology-related policies in major cities, and elaborating how these regulations can promote the development of blockchain technology in the transformation of China's digital economy. The application of blockchain technology is an irresistible trend. The question now becomes, how to find a proper approach to balance regulation, competition, and innovation to strengthen the efficiency of the digital economy in China. More research will surely help to address the issue.

REFERENCES

Administrative Commission of Zhongguancun Science Park. (2018, November 9). *Notice on printing and distributing the Beijing Fintech Development Plan (2018-2022).* Available at: http://zgcgw.beijing. gov.cn/zgc/zwgk/ghjh/179396/index.html

CBIRC. (2020a, Mar.31). *Notice on Promoting the Incremental Expansion, Quality Improvement and Cost Reduction of Financial Services for Small and Micro Enterprises in 2020.* Available at: http:// www.cbirc.gov.cn/cn/view/pages/govermentDetail.html?docId=896876&itemId=878&generaltype=1

CBIRC. (2020b, Jul.17). *The Interim Measures for the Management of Internet loans of commercial banks.* Available at: http://www.gov.cn/xinwen/2020-07/17/content_5527714.htm

China News. (2020, December 9). *The Digital Currency Research Institute of the People's Bank of China signed a strategic cooperation agreement with UnionPay.* Available at: http://www.szzg.gov.cn/2020/ szzg/gzdt/202012/t20201209_5478980.htm

China Securities News. (2019, December 3). *CBIRC: Encourage insurance companies to conduct data docking with third-party credit reference institutions and various big data institutions.* Available at: http://ddcredit.dandong.gov.cn/zh/News_18951.html

CPC Central Committee and State Council. (2019, February 18). *Outline of Development Planning for Guangdong, Hong Kong and Macao Bay Area.* Available at: http://www.xinhuanet.com/politics/2019-02/18/c_1124131474.htm

Deng, Y. (2019, November 5). *Overview of current laws and compliance of blockchain: Young but not undependable.* Available at: https://lvdao.sina.com.cn/news/2019-11-05/doc-iicezuev7236612.shtml

Disparte, D. A. (2018, July 21). Beware Of Crypto Risks - 10 Risks To Watch. *Forbes.* Available at: https://www.forbes.com/sites/dantedisparte/2018/07/21/beware-of-crypto-risks-10-risks-to-watch/?sh=f8cef5c5f17f

Dong, J., & Jing, X. (2020, Feb. 5). 2020 CPC Document No. 1 Announced Two Key Tasks. *The Xinhua News Agency.* Available at: http://www.gov.cn/xinwen/2020-02/05/content_5474860.htm

Financial Conduct Authority. (2015, November). *Regulatory Sandbox.* Available at: https://www.fca. org.uk/publications/documents/regulatory-sandbox

GBA Cities. (n.d.). *Guangdong-Hong Kong-Macao greater Bay area - Gba cities.* https://www.bayarea. gov.hk/en/about/the-cities.html

Geng, J. (2020, Mar). Recognition of B-end Business of Digital Bank Under the Epidemic. *Fudan Financial Review.* Available at: https://fisf.fudan.edu.cn/ffr/content/292

Guo, F., Wang, J., Wang, F., Kong, T., Zhang, X., & Cheng, Z. (2020). Measuring China's digital financial inclusion: Index compilation and spatial characteristics [in Chinese]. *China Economic Quarterly,* *19*(4), 1401–1418.

Hangzhou Municipal Government. (2019, Oct. 31). *Implementation opinions of Hangzhou Municipal Government on accelerating the development of cross border E-commerce*. Available at: https://z.hangzhou.com.cn/2019/hzsrmzfgb/content/content_7645608.html

Li, R. (2020, December 28). Two blockchain scenario application platforms have been built in the Xiong'an area of Hebei free trade zone. *Beijing Daily*. Available at: http://ie.bjd.com.cn/5b5fb98da0109f010fce6047/contentApp/5b5fb9d0e4b08630d8aef954/AP5fe9de40e4b02f6bb4131f12.html

Ministry of Industry and Information Technology. the People's Bank of China, Ministry of Justice, Ministry of Commerce, State Owned Assets Supervision and Administration Commission, State Administration of market supervision and administration, CBIRC, State Administration of Foreign Exchange. (2020, September 18). *Opinions on standardizing the development of supply chain finance to support the stable circulation, optimization and upgrading of the supply chain and industry chain*. Available at: http://www.gov.cn/zhengce/zhengceku/2020-09/22/content_5546142.htm

National Development and Reform Commission. (2019, Nov). *Regional Integration Development Strategy of Yangtze River Delta*. Available at: https://www.ndrc.gov.cn/gjzl/csjyth/201911/t20191127_1213169.html

PBC (People's Bank of China). (2020, Jun.1). *Guidance on Further Strengthening the Financial Services for Small and Micro Enterprises*. Available at: http://www.gov.cn/zhengce/zhengceku/2020-06/02/content_5516693.htm

People's Daily. (2015, February 8). *CSRC: Using big data analysis to crack down on "rat trading" cases*. Available at: http://www.ce.cn/xwzx/xinwen/yw/201502/08/t20150208_4541771.shtml

Shanghai Pudong Government. (2018, Aug. 21). Shanghai Financial Court Officially Established. *Pudong News*. Available at: http://www.pudong.gov.cn/shpd/news/20180821/006001_7f36d025-0463-4204-8f63-11f86864e35f.htm. Official website: http://www.shjrfy.gov.cn/jrfy/gweb/index.jsp

Sichuan Provincial Bureau of Statistics. (2021, Mar.14). *Statistical bulletin of national economic and social development of Sichuan Province in 2020*. Available at: http://tjj.sc.gov.cn/scstjj/tjgb/2021/3/14/c64ac94ca86c4714adaf117789e47073.shtml

Su, S. (2020, May 19). The PBC has proposed "digital central bank" construction for four consecutive years, and financial digital transformation is urgent. *Securities Daily*. Available at: http://epaper.zqrb.cn/images/2019-04/19/A2/A2.pdf

Suzhou Daily. (2021, Jan.5). *Suzhou digital economy and digital development promotion conference are held*. Available at: http://www.suzhou.gov.cn/szsrmzf/szyw/202101/f6c44ccfc91740c0be40d3e384faa8c0.shtml

The People's Bank of China. (2019, August 23). *The People's Bank of China issued the development plan of FinTech (2019-2021)*. Available at: http://www.gov.cn/xinwen/2019-08/23/content_5423691.htm

The People's Bank of China. (2019, December 5). *The People's Bank of China Launched the FinTech Innovative Regulation Pilot*. Available at: http://www.pbc.gov.cn/goutongjiaoliu/113456/113469/3933971/index.html

The People's Bank of China. (2020, April 27). *The People's Bank of China Expands the FinTech Innovative Regulation Pilot in cities (districts) including Shanghai.* Available at: http://www.pbc.gov.cn/goutongjiaoliu/113456/113469/4014870/index.html

The People's Bank of China. (2020, November 7). *The People's Bank of China issues China's financial stability report (2020).* Available at: http://www.gov.cn/xinwen/2020-11/07/content_5558567.htm

The State Council. (2021, March 5). *Government Work Report.* Available at: http://www.gov.cn/guowuyuan/zfgzbg.htm

Tian, A. (2016, March 25). National Internet Finance Association is officially established. *China Daily.* Available at: http://www.cac.gov.cn/2016-03/25/c_1118478823.htm

Wu, Y. (2019, August 22). The People's Bank of China proposed the Fintech Three-year Development Plan. *The Xinhua News Agency.* Available at: http://www.gov.cn/xinwen/2019-08/22/content_5423531.htm

Xi, J. (2016, Sep.3). A new starting point for China's development and a new blueprint for global growth——Keynote speech at the opening ceremony of G20 Business Summit. *Xinhua News Agency.* Available at: http://www.gov.cn/xinwen/2016-09/03/content_5105135.htm

Xiao, X. (2017, December 6). Ten characteristics of FinTech in China. *China Times.* Available at: https://www.chinatimes.net.cn/article/72955

Xinhua News Agency. (2014, September 1). *The Decision of the Standing Committee of the National People's Congress on the establishment of intellectual property courts in Beijing, Shanghai and Guangzhou.* Available at: http://www.npc.gov.cn/npc/c12489/201409/9d38b14721f44b35817082f371afb76a.shtml

Xinhua News Agency. (2021, March 29). *Green, innovation and intelligence: decoding the high standard and high-quality development of Xiong'an New District.* Available at: http://ie.bjd.com.cn/5b165687a010550e5ddc0e6a/contentApp/5b16573ae4b02a9fe2d558fa/AP6061ce2fe4b0b87b-6752b7e3.html

Ye, Y. (2021, Jan. 29). "Yangtze River Delta credit chain application platform" realizes the interconnection of enterprises' credit information, with 7.89 million enterprises on the chain. *Suzhou Daily.* Available at: http://www.subaonet.com/2021/szyw/0129/157360.shtml

Yu, P., Hu, Y., Waseem, M., & Rafay, A. (2021). Regulatory Developments in Peer-to-Peer (P2P) Lending to Combat Frauds: The Case of China. In A. Rafay (Ed.), Handbook of Research on Theory and Practice of Financial Crimes (pp. 172-194). IGI Global. doi:10.4018/978-1-7998-5567-5.ch010

Zhang, H., Uwasu, M., Hara, K., & Yabar, H. (2011). Sustainable Urban Development and Land Use Change—A Case Study of the Yangtze River Delta in China. *Sustainability, 3*(7), 1074–1089. doi:10.3390u2071074

Zhou, Y., & Pang, D. (2016, July 15). NIFA: Accelerate the construction of Internet financial statistical monitoring and risk early warning system. *Financial Times.* Available at: https://finance.sina.com.cn/roll/2016-07-15/doc-ifxuapvw2010011.shtml

ENDNOTES

1   Core Cities include Hong Kong, Macao, Guangzhou and Shenzhen. The rest areas are key node cities including Zhaoqing, Foshan, Dongguan, Zhongshan, Jiangmen, Zhuhai and Huizhou. Map Source: https://www.bayarea.gov.hk/en/about/the-cities.html

2   Macmillan Gap, available at: https://www.finansleksikon.no/en/Eng_Finance/M/Macmillan_Gap.html

3   The information is obtained from Yue Xin Rong's website (https://finance.gzebsc.cn/)

4   Shanghai Free Trade Zone. Website: www.china-shftz.gov.cn

Section 2
Technical Challenges of the Blockchain in Addressing Regulatory Framework

Chapter 8
Blockchain Applications in the Energy Industry

Soheil Saraji
University of Wyoming, USA

Christelle Khalaf
University of Wyoming, USA

ABSTRACT

The current energy transition from a fossil-fuel-based economy to a zero-carbon has significantly accelerated in recent years, as the largest emitters have committed to achieving carbon-neutral goals in the next 20-30 years. The energy industry transition is characterized by modernization through digital technologies, increased renewable energy generation, and environmental sustainability. Blockchain technology can play a significant role in providing secure digital distributed platforms facilitating digitization, decarbonization, and decentralization of the energy systems. Several promising blockchain applications in the energy sector are under research and development, including peer-to-peer energy trading; carbon monitoring, management, and trading; and IoT-enabled electric grid management. However, several challenges are slowing down the commercialization of these applications, including outdated legislation and regulations, slow pace of adaptation from the traditional energy industry, and risks associated with the new, untested technology.

INTRODUCTION

This chapter begins with a summary of technological advances and paradigm shifts in the blockchain industry over the past two decades. To illustrate, recent advancements in technology enable interoperability between different blockchains, which negates the earlier view of a general-use blockchain network, thus, actualizing a world with multiple specialized interconnected blockchains. In addition, this chapter discusses the impact of emerging blockchain commercialization on different industries, especially the energy industry. To facilitate this discussion, we provide a brief overview of the global energy transition and its disruptive impacts on the traditional fossil fuel industry. Further, we explore the role that block-

DOI: 10.4018/978-1-7998-7927-5.ch008

chain technology could play in this transition towards more sustainability. Finally, the chapter examines current implementations, use-cases, and potential futuristic blockchain applications in the energy industry. We explore select applications in detail. In summary, this chapter aims to advance knowledge of these pertinent topics, given that blockchain is expected to have a foundational role in the future of the internet.

BACKGROUND

Overview of the Global Energy Transition

The current energy transition from a fossil-fuel-based economy to a zero-carbon one, which effectively began in the early 2000s, has significantly accelerated in recent years, as the largest emitters have committed to achieving carbon-neutral goals in the next 20-30 years. To illustrate, the United States (U.S.) pledged U.S. carbon neutrality by 2050 (Biden, 2020), while China aims to go carbon neutral by 2060 (AP, 2020). In addition to national-level commitments shaping policy, market dynamics have pushed major oil producers to shift capital towards solar and wind as exhibited, for example, by BP's plan to increase its investment in low-carbon energy 10-fold to $5 billion a year by 2030, taking its renewable-energy capacity to 50 gigawatts (GW), from 2.5 GW in 2019 (McFarlane, 2020). Globally, fuel importing countries have been faster to transition compared to fuel exporting countries. However, the gap between average Energy Transition Index scores for countries in the top quartile and the rest is narrowing, reflecting a growing global consensus on the priorities and speed of the energy transition (World Economic Forum, 2020). Figure 1 illustrates the Energy Transition Index by country. This index is scored on a scale from 0 to 100 with the goal of benchmarking countries on the performance of their energy system, as well as their readiness for transition to a secure, sustainable, affordable, and reliable energy future. Key parameters included in index calculations range from measures of fossil fuel dependency to investment in new energy infrastructure as well as political commitment.

The energy transition has been effectively motivated by increases in emissions. In the Paris agreement, countries concerned with the current trend in carbon emissions set a goal to limit global warming to well below 1.5 ° Celsius compared to pre-industrial levels. However, a look at the global carbon emission trends over the last three decades reveals that the growth has been exponential (Figure 2). Most importantly, the contribution of the Energy Sector (shown in dark blue and green colors in Figure 2) is responsible for more than half of the total carbon emissions. Therefore, achieving the goal of the Paris agreement requires an urgent and immediate restructuring of the energy industry. This means a faster pace of transition from fossil fuels to renewable energy, developing and integrating new carbon capture utilization and storage (CCUS) schemes into our current energy sources, moving towards decarbonized power systems, and eventually achieving net-zero carbon energy production by 2050 (IRENA, 2018).

This Global Energy Transition, which is well underway, has two main driving forces: the emergence of renewables as alternatives to fossil fuel-based energy, and the growth of electric-based technologies, like battery-powered vehicles for transportation (Wood-Mackenzie, 2018). Currently, the power and transportation sectors account for 70% of global coal demand, 50% of global oil demand, and upwards of 30% of global gas demand (Wood-Mackenzie, 2018). Meanwhile, renewables (mainly solar and wind) currently account for 7% of the global power market (Wood-Mackenzie, 2018). Globally, unsubsidized wind and solar projects have become more cost effective than projects reliant on fossil fuel technologies. As a result, more systems are now integrating renewables (Wood-Mackenzie, 2018). It is expected that the

Figure 1. Index scores reflect a global consensus on energy transition.
(Note: Figure created by authors using data from World Economic Forum (2020) retrieved from http://www3.weforum.org/ docs/WEF_Fostering_Effective_Energy_Transition_2020_Edition.pdf)

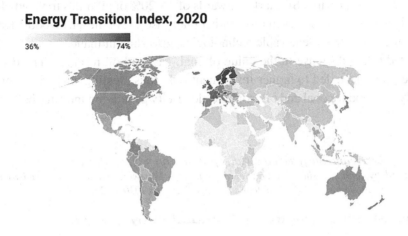

Figure 2. Global GHG emission per type of gas and emission source
(EC-JRC, 2019).

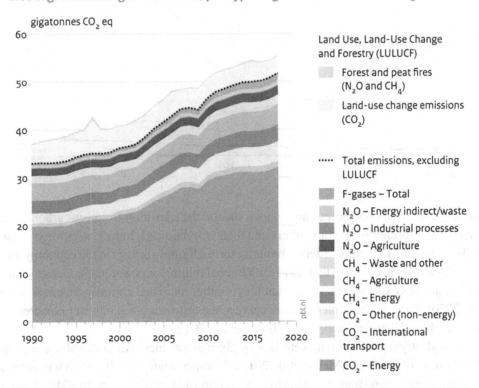

point of singularity, which marks the end of this transition and the start of a new phase of energy system evolution, will be reached by 2035 (Wood-Mackenzie, 2018). By then, close to 15-20% of global power needs will be met by solar or wind. Similarly, upwards of 15-20% of all miles traveled globally by cars, trucks, buses, and bikes will use electric motors rather than gasoline or diesel. (Wood-Mackenzie, 2018).

In sum, the competition from renewable technologies, government mandates, and a shift in demand have all contributed to the decrease in the value of coal, gas, and oil reserves. The decrease in price, profits, and share prices have led to higher investment risk, thus creating challenges for the fossil fuel economy. Notably, demand for coal and oil from the electricity generation industry has steadily declined (Figure 3).

Figure 3. The share of coal and oil-fired electricity production has steadily declined over the last decade. (Note: Figure produced by authors using data retrieved from https://ourworldindata.org/electricity-mix#:~:text=In%20 2019%2C%20almost%20two%2Dthirds,and%20nuclear%20energy%20for%2010.4%25.)

Global Share of Electricity Production by Source

Beyond the impact on companies and balance sheets, the transition to lower-carbon sources of energy adversely impacts energy-sector workers and their communities. In fact, workforce impacts extend beyond laid-off workers to their broader community through ripple effects in the economy. Studies from Appalachia to Australia have found that, as a result of coal mining or power plant operation closures, surrounding communities experience a significant loss of other retail and commercial employment (Carley & Konisky, 2020). Further, the depletion of fiscal revenue following coal industry closures often leaves communities reeling (Haggerty et al., 2018; Jolley el al., 2019).

The energy industry transition is characterized by digitization, increased renewable energy generation, and environmental sustainability (Megha et al., 2019). A modernization of all sectors within the industry is required, from generation and transportation to consumption and management. In addition, an accounting framework that facilitates international transactions, as postulated in Article 6.2 of the Paris Agreement is vital (Paris Agreement, 2015). Therefore, blockchain technology can play a significant role in providing secure digital distributed platforms facilitating digitization, decarbonization, and decentralization of the energy systems (Megha et al, 2019; Brilliantova & Thurne, 2019). Further, blockchain has a wide range of applications at the intersection of energy and sustainability, including green certificates, carbon credit markets, peer-to-peer and bulk energy trading, smart microgrids, smart cities, etc. The inherent characteristics of blockchain, e.g., transparency, are in line with the key attributes required in a registry system as enumerated in Article 6.2 of the Paris Agreement (Paris Agreement, 2015).

In terms of sustainability, blockchain technology's biggest challenge remains the use of energy-intensive mining operations required to secure the network in a 'Proof of Work' consensus mechanism (Baker, 2021). In fact, blockchains currently account for 0.58% of global electricity consumption, whilst Bitcoin mining alone consumes almost as much energy as the entire U.S. federal government (Baker, 2021). However, the new generation of blockchains adapted new energy-efficient consensus mechanisms such as variations of 'Proof of Stack' that allow sustainable operation of blockchain networks (i.e., Ethereum 2.0, Cardano, Polkadot) (Jiang et al, 2021). As these efforts intensify, energy-efficient blockchains will become more mainstream in the coming decade.

Recent Advances in Blockchain Technology

Blockchain technology is based on a distributed immutable ledger that is validated and agreed upon by the parties that participate in its operation. The foundations for blockchain are rooted in the ability to achieve a consensus of distributed parties, a problem that has been solved since the early 1980s (Lamport et al., 1982). Redundant, consensus-backed systems have existed in mission-critical spaces for decades, but technology limitations meant that the implementation overhead made these systems impractical and cost-ineffective until the late 2000s. The collapse of the financial markets exposed trust-based issues related to double-spending, which formed the impetus for Satoshi's seminal work to leverage peer-to-peer distributed systems to generate computational proof of chronologically ordered transactions (Nakamoto, 2008).

Since then, blockchain has evolved from a decentralized network to secure cryptocurrencies into a foundational technology, enabling next-generation secure digital ecosystems with applications in various industries. Since the inception of the Bitcoin network, attempts were made to modify the base code to expand its capabilities and functionality (Buterin, 2016). These efforts faced limited success due to rigid code script and the unwillingness of the community to modify the network beyond Satoshi's vision. In 2015, a new concept was introduced by Vitalik Buterin, presenting a generalized blockchain network enabled by a virtual machine to execute costume computer codes (Buterin, 2016). This new blockchain network, called Ethereum, brought the paradigm of World Computer to light. The premise was to create a Turing-complete distributed computing system capable of running immutable pieces of codes called Smart Contracts. Since then, there has been massive adaptation of Smart Contract-enabled blockchain platforms with many networks currently under development. This technology facilitated the emergence of Decentralized Autonomous Organizations (DAOs), companies fully or partially governed by the code on the blockchain. In fact, the state of Wyoming (United States) has recently announced legislation that recognizes DAOs as a legal company with similar protections to LLCs (Governor Gordon, 2021).

Currently, experts are less convinced that blockchain will evolve into a "world computer" due to several inherent limitations in blockchain, including computational expenses for participating nodes, block size limitations, scalability issues, etc. Another paradigm that gained traction shortly after the Ethereum whitepaper considers blockchain as the foundation for the future of the internet, or Web 3.0 (Wood,

2016). In this paradigm, blockchain technology is envisioned as the base layer (protocol layer) of the new internet replacing current protocols such as TCP/IP, HTTP, SMPT, etc. (Monero, 2016). This technology allows for a more secure and autonomous user experience as they are allowed to own their data and monetize it. This is in direct contrast with the current model of the internet (Web 2.0), where the most value is captured and reaggregated on top at the application layer (see Figure 4a). In this model, there are thin protocols and fat applications from an economic valuation perspective. This relationship is reversed in the blockchain application stack: "fat" protocols and "thin" applications (Figure 4a) (Monero, 2016).

Figure 4. Paradigm of blockchain as the enabling technology for Web 3.0
(Monero, 2016; Wood, 2016).

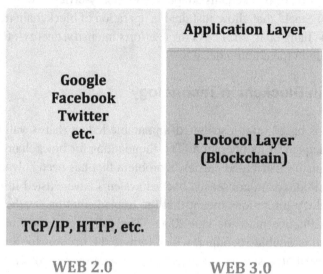

One of the most important recent development in blockchain technology is "Interoperability". Interoperability is the ability of a source blockchain to change the state of a target blockchain (or vice-versa), enabling users to transfer their assets from a blockchain to another or build cross-blockchain decentralized applications (Belchior, 2021). There are different ways of implementing interoperability ranging from relays, side-chains, blockchain of blockchains, bridges, and blockchain-agnostic protocols (Nuzzi, 2019). Interoperability between blockchains solves one of the fundamental challenges of this technology (i.e., scalability) and allows for specialization (Belchior, 2021). These new developments led to yet another major paradigm shift in the space, negating the earlier view that one generalized blockchain network wins it all and becomes the most adapted network, rendering the remaining blockchain networks into "ghost networks". In this new paradigm, the future will be the world of interoperable specialized blockchains (Figure 4b), allowing the distribution of computational load and value creation among many blockchains. This will naturally lead to specialization and the formation of micro-ecosystems around each discipline. This seems to be the current paradigm providing a mental model for what blockchain technology could become. However, we are at the early development stages of this new technology. Only the future will tell whether this paradigm will win, or perhaps new paradigms will emerge and take this technology in an unpredictable direction.

THE ROLE OF BLOCKCHAIN IN THE ENERGY INDUSTRY

With the developing recognition that blockchain is one of the newest, most disruptive additions in many different markets from financial services to healthcare, the interest in potential energy applications has grown significantly. The impact of emerging blockchain commercialization on energy industries includes recording and tracking data exchanges, utilizing a distributed system to verify transactions, providing secure accounting systems, improving energy efficiency, allowing shared governance of electricity, facilitating the startup process for financial companies, reducing overhead costs, increasing energy security, boosting climate actionability, and enhancing international energy competitiveness (Omezzine & Schleich, 2019). Whether renewable or not, the energy sector can benefit greatly from the emerging applications currently under development. Blockchain can make it possible to track low-carbon energy and certificates from origin through every stage until transaction, transform the way parties across a value chain interact, and create transactive energy within both renewable and nonrenewable energy businesses.

In the following subsections, the impact and current applications of blockchain technology within the energy sector are reviewed. An example of a related commercial project is discussed under each subsection. A more comprehensive list of commercial project and startup companies related to these applications are provided in Table 1. At the end, the benefits, challenges, and risks of blockchain applications in the energy sector are discussed.

Peer-to-Peer Energy Trading

Peer-to-peer trading is one of the early, universal blockchain applications regarding decentralized energy transmission, widely considered to be a viable solution for the future. Peer-to-peer, or P2P, is a direct energy trade structure that includes a group of participants, i.e., generators, consumers, and prosumers (Soto et al., 2021). The direct energy trade structure encourages trade between consumers and prosumers without intermediating conventional energy suppliers, typically within a local grid network (Zhang et al., 2018). Figure 5 provides an example illustrating how blockchain can be used as a next-generation energy management technique. In addition to trading, peer-to-peer allows energy generated to be stored, exported, and sold. Peer-to-peer trading contains sub-applications, including wholesale trading and utility trading, each following the same basic principles.

A successful example of peer-to-peer energy trading is the Brooklyn Microgrid project (Papajak, 2017). Brooklyn Microgrid, implemented by LO3 Energy, is a demonstration project where citizens can buy and sell locally produced solar electricity from one another. The project started in early 2015, and in April 2016, the first community activity took place when three residents of President Street in Park Slope participated in the first-ever peer-to-peer energy transactions (Papajak, 2017). The project started first on a private blockchain to remove intermediaries and facilitate peer-to-peer transactions. In 2020, following the success of the Brooklyn Microgrid project, LO3 Energy released its open-source blockchain solution for utilities called Pando.

Utility Trading

"In general, electricity power providers are usually large and complex organizations that generate their energy from power plants, solar farms, and various other energy sources. An opportunity exists here to utilize blockchain to provide shared, immutable data between the actual utility providers using a shared

Table 1. A list of commercial applications and projects implementing blockchain technology in the energy industry.

No.	Company/Project	Category	Description	Location	Status / Implementation Date
1	Brooklyn Microgrid https://www.brooklyn	Peer-to-Peer	Decentralized peer-to-peer energy trading for private owners of solar panels	United States	2015 (ongoing)
2	Electron https://electron.net/about-us/	Peer-to-Peer	P2P Trading Platform	United Kingdom	2015 (ongoing)
3	Enerchain https://enerchain.ponton.de/	Peer-to-Peer	P2P Trading Platform	Europe	2017 (ongoing)
4	P2P – Smart Test https://www.p2psmartest-h2020.eu	Peer-to-Peer	Advanced control and ICT for P2P	Finland, UK, Spain, and Belgium	2015 (ongoing)
5	Lition https://lition.de	Peer-to-Peer	Energy provider with a blockchain based peer2peer energy trading solution	Germany	2017 (ongoing)
6	Nori https://nori.com	Carbon Credits	Carbon Removal marketplace for farmers	United States	2017 (Ongoing)
7	XELS https://www.xels.io	Carbon Credits	Blockchain-based carbon offset platform	Japan	2018 (Ongoing)
8	ClimateTrade https://climatetrade.com	Carbon Credits	Environmental offsetting platform	Spain	2017 (Ongoing)
9	AirCarbon https://www.aircarbon.co	Carbon Credits	Blockchain-based carbon trading platform	Singapore	2019 (Ongoing)
10	Carbon Grid Protocol http://carbongrid.io	Carbon Credits	Develops an economic framework to reward blockchain networks and DApps for offsetting their carbon footprint	Singapore	2018 (Ongoing)
11	Reneum https://reneum.com	Renewable Certificates	Digitizing & democratizing the market for RECs	Singapore	2018 (Ongoing)
12	Power Ledger https://www.powerledger.io/	Renewable Certificates	Encourage tracking and trading of renewable energy, flexible services, and environmental commodities	Australia	2018 (operational)
13	WePower https://wepower.com/	Renewable Certificates	Power purchase concept of tokens to buy, sell, trade (renewable)	Estonia	2016 (operational)
14	Efforce https://efforce.io/	Renewable Certificates	Web-based platform leveraging blockchain (including tokens) to encourage global energy efficiency	Malta	2018 (operational)
15	Greeneum Network https://www.greeneum.net/	Renewable Certificates	Blockchain solutions for a green energy market (green certificates and carbon credits)	Israel	2018 (operational)
16	Energy Web https://www.energyweb.org	Distributed Electricity	An open-source enterprise blockchain platform tailored to the retail energy sector	United States	2019 (ongoing)
17	LO3 Energy https://lo3energy.com	Distributed Electricity	Develop and deploy open-source decentralized technologies	United States	2019 (ongoing)
18	WePower https://wepower.com	Distributed Electricity	A transparent platform on which consumers could monitor energy prices and adapt and diversify their energy portfolio off of their predictions.	Estonia	2016 (ongoing)
19	Iberdrola https://www.iberdrola.com	Distributed Electricity	A major Spanish electricity utility blockchain to prove that power supplied and consumed is 100% renewable.	Spain	2019 (ongoing)
20	Electron https://electron.net	Distributed Electricity	Create local flexibility markets in the energy grid	United Kingdom	2015 (ongoing)
21	Share&Charge https://shareandcharge.com/innovation/	IoV/IoME	An organization that enables open innovation for a better EV charging	Switzerland	2016 (ongoing)
22	MotionWerk https://motionwerk.com	IoV/IoME	Blockchain-based solution for EV charging, transaction, and data sharing.	Germany	2018 (ongoing)
23	Amo https://www.amo.foundation	IoV/IoME	A blockchain platform connecting cars, people and service providers	Korea	2017 (ongoing)
24	DAV https://dav.network	IoV/IoME	a decentralized, peer-to-peer transportation network.	Switzerland	2017 (ongoing)
25	Chorus Mobility https://www.chorus.mobi	IoV/IoME	Blockchain solutions for the Future of Transportation, aiming to transform Urban Mobility and Improve Traffic with Micro Payments for Connected and Autonomous Vehicles.	United States	2017 (ongoing)
26	Bitlumens https://www.bitlumens.com	e-IoT	Facilitating the scaling of green technologies to off grid communities	Switzerland	2017 (ongoing)
27	Drone Energy https://droneenergy.com/	e-IoT	Make energy grids more efficient	United States	2018 (ongoing)

continued on following page

Table 1. Continued

No.	Company/Project	Category	Description	Location	Status / Implementation Date
28	Hdac https://www.hdactech.com	e-IoT	A subsidiary of Hyundai Corporation, plans to use blockchain and IoT to automate energy sector	Korea	2019 (ongoing)
29	Ockham https://www.ockam.io	e-IoT	Integrate identity management, trust, and interoperability between energy connected devices	United States	2019 (ongoing)
30	Atonomi https://atonomi.io	e-IoT	Provides IoT developers and manufacturers with an embedded solution to secure devices with blockchain-based immutable identity and reputation tracking.	United States	2017 (ongoing)
31	Ondiflo https://www.ondiflo.com	Data Management	fully automate the Procure-to-Pay process for fluid hauling and deliver enforceable automation via Blockchain	United States	2017 (ongoing)
32	BlueNote https://bluenote.world/	Data Management	Increase quality and veracity of energy consumption and data	Singapore	2017 (ongoing)
33	Megavatio Control SL https://mvcontrol.com/	Data Management	Improve transparency on energy origins and data from creation to consumption	Spain	2011 (ongoing)
34	Lition https://lition.de	Data Management	Connect energy producers and consumers directly to reduce costs and regulate data	Liechtenstein	2017 (ongoing)
35	Bittwatt https://bitwatt.io	Data Management	Data-driven price optimization for B2C energy supplier	Germany	2017 (ongoing)
36	Vakt https://www.vakt.com/	Commodity Trading	Commodity-focused blockchain platform aiming to digitalize post-trade management processes	United Kingdom	2018 (ongoing)
37	Komgo https://www.komgo.io/	Commodity Trading	Digitalize commodity trading in finance sector	Switzerland	2018 (ongoing)
38	DLT Ledgers https://dlt.sg/	Commodity Trading	Commodity trading finance	Singapore	2018 (ongoing)
39	TradelX https://tradeix.com/about/	Commodity Trading	Futuristic plastform for trade and working capital initiatives	Dublin	2017 (ongoing)
40	Contour Blockchain https://www.contour.network/	Commodity Trading	Digitalize trade and trade finance	Singapore	2016 (ongoing)
41	OpenPort https://openport.com/	Supply-Chain Management	Connect shippers and carriers directly to reduce cost, improve performance, drive and optimize the supply chain	Asia	2015 (ongoing)
42	OriginTrail https://origintrail.io/	Supply-Chain Management	Data exchange protocol for interconnected supply chains	Slovenia	2011 (ongoing)
43	SkuChain https://www.skuchain.com/	Supply-Chain Management	Security and Visibility for the global supply chain	United States	2014 (ongoing)
44	Syncfab https://syncfab.com/	Supply-Chain Management	Purchase order management, capacity, and order tracking	United States	2007 (ongoing)
45	everLedger https://everledger.io	Supply-Chain Management	Provide transparency in global supply chain using blockchain	United Kingdom	2015 (ongoing)

blockchain ledger" (Braithwaite, 2020). Distributed ledger technology offers distinct benefits to utility providers, as blockchain can process, validate, and secure the data from numerous network elements and devices at the power systems' grid edge. In addition, energy providers can utilize the blockchain to create a system for transactions of critical distribution data" (Braithwaite, 2020)

In practice, utilities can leverage blockchain to apply automated billing for consumers and distributed generators (Indigo Advisory Group, 2017) as well as to decentralize energy systems and microgrids (Burger et al., 2016). This technology can potentially improve operations if used for communications of smart devices, data transmission, and/or storage. In addition, blockchain can assist in grid management while safeguarding privacy and data. Coupled with artificial intelligence techniques, this technology can be used to identify consumer energy patterns and consequently tailor energy products (Burger et al., 2016).

Wholesale Trading

Wholesale electricity trading allows the trade and purchase of energy between the generators and retailers. Wholesale trading typically includes third-party intermediaries such as brokers, exchanges, trading

Figure 5. A peer-to-peer trading model comprises four main actors: consumers, prosumers, an electric company, and an energy sharing coordinator. The difference between prosumers and consumers is that prosumers generate and consume electricity, and consumers only consume. Between prosumers and consumers, there is an exchange of energy and money represented by the trading arrows and the energy arrows. A prosumer can sell electricity to a consumer or to another prosumer. The entire negotiation process is carried out using a platform that functions as an energy exchange coordinator. The trading arrows in one direction represent that the consumer can only receive energy from the energy sharing coordinator. The bidirectional trading arrows represent that prosumer can buy and sell electricity to the energy sharing coordinator
(Soto et al., 2021).

WEB 3.0 (2020)

agents, price reporters, banks, regulators, and logistic providers within the mass-energy markets (Andoni et al., 2019). These intermediaries are critical for the process, ensuring manual post-processing and increased communications, in order to consolidate information that is held separately by each part of the transaction. Blockchain has the potential to circumvent the need for these intermediaries by integrating the trade lifecycle and reducing transactional and operational costs through disintermediation and automation of post trade reconciliation.

To illustrate, we examine Ponton Enerchain, a software company headquartered in Hamburg, Germany. This company has been focused since 2000 on the standardization and automation of business processes in the wholesale energy market. They started piloting a project in 2017 with a consortium of 44 energy trading firms with the goal of building a blockchain based software to allow for peer-to-peer energy trading in the European electricity market. In 2019, Enerchain 1.0 was launched, the first blockchain based distributed trading infrastructure that enables OTC energy trading in power and gas products (Merz, 2019).

Figure 6. Flow diagram showing the proposed carbon credit ecosystem on a blockchain (Saraji & Borowczak, 2021).

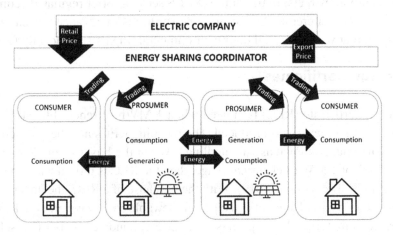

Carbon Credit Markets

Blockchain technology provides a safe, reliable, efficient, convenient, open, and inclusive platform that is uniquely suited for implementing Carbon Credit Markets. The immutable cryptographically-secured distributed ledger on the Blockchain allows for reliable issuance and tracking of carbon credits. Public blockchains are easily accessible to small and medium-sized enterprises, reducing the entry threshold for the carbon trading market. Furthermore, the information provided by companies is transparent and accessible to everyone. Recently, free automated market makers (AMMs) have been developed on blockchains, allowing for the trading of digitized assets directly on the Blockchain without intermediary and minimal algorithmic fees. This provides the infrastructure required to create a digital carbon credit ecosystem and engage all interested stakeholders.

One proposed scheme is shown in Figure 6 (Saraji & Borowczak, 2021). In this scheme, different stakeholders involved are "Generators" of carbon credit (i.e., wind farms, tree-planting operations, CO_2 sequestration projects, etc.) and "Consumers" of carbon credit (i.e., carbon emitters or polluters of any kind such as the energy industry) as well as other stakeholders such as regulators, concerned citizens, and validators. "Validators" are an essential part of this ecosystem. They are accredited, globally distributed, technically competent consultants incentivized to parameterize appropriately and onboard projects to an open architecture marketplace that matches interested parties generating and retiring carbon credits.

The carbon credits will be transferred to the Blockchain by converting them into digital tokens distributed to carbon credit generators after properly validating their projects. Buyers and sellers of carbon credit will use a decentralized exchange platform on Blockchain to trade Carbon credits. The price will be determined by market dynamics driven by supply and demand. The Carbon Tokens would be retired via a "buy and burn" model by sending the given Carbon Tokens to a smart contract or defined blockchain address whose private key is not known by any party and can be visible to the collective of validators as well as regulators or other stakeholders. The companies and individuals who successfully burn their Carbon Tokens will be issued non-fungible tokens as a carbon removal certificate.

XELS, a startup based in Japan, is tackling climate change by increasing participation and transparency in carbon markets. XELS has launched its blockchain platform and eponymous digital asset. The startup's tokenized offset credits, which exist on an immutable public ledger, are designed to boost transparency and participation in carbon markets. In the future, XELS seeks to offer regulated "compliance" credits in addition to voluntary offset credits. In addition, the startup is in advanced discussions with several Japanese corporations that wish to curtail their environmental impact significantly (XELS, 2021).

Renewable Energy Certificates

A Renewable Energy Certificate (REC) is created when 1 MWh of renewable energy (such as water, solar, wind, biomass, or geothermal) is produced. The resulting RECs may be sold separately and apart from the electricity in what is known as "unbundling." When the buyer of the REC uses the credit to demonstrate an "offset" of 1 MW of electrical usage, then the REC is retired and can no longer be used by any other power user" (Deatherage, 2019). With the purchase of a REC, the buyer is adopting the renewable attributes of the specified amount and type of renewable energy generation. RECs are tradeable, non-tangible energy commodities. The suppliers of RECs are mandated by law to disclose the quantity, type (water, solar, wind, etc.), and geographical source of the certificates (Bonneville Environmental Foundation, 2016).

The renewable energy certificate (REC) market, in particular, can be revolutionized using blockchain technology. The recording of transactions between electric generation suppliers and electric distribution companies can be automated and easily accessed with this new technology. Blockchain produces an easy-to-understand ledger, graphical user interface, and generates data that is easily extractable to be used by other, preexisting enterprise-level software. Lastly, and perhaps most importantly, the blockchain can include all the critical data points required by law in the United States for REC generation, registration, and recording (Spinnell, 2018).

For instance, Reneum Institute (a not-for-profit company headquartered in Singapore) aiming to attract global climate capital for new renewable energy developments using blockchain technology. By digitizing and democratizing the RECs market, Reneum aims to create liquidity and stability as a global, digital marketplace. They will facilitate the commodity exchange of renewable energy certificates, opening up a global market to support the sustainability targets of companies, governments, and non-for-profits worldwide. Therefore, providing a solution to a fragmented, complex, and opaque system involved in registering and issuing green energy credits (HSV, 2020). The conceptual workflow of Reneum is as follows (HSV, 2020): (a) connecting the smart meters of renewable energy producers directly to the blockchain to verify and validate the provenance of the energy and issue RECs tokens. (b) Use smart contracts to automatically execute the sale of RECs, allowing for global trading in a fully transparent and secure manner. (c) tokens may then be purchased for fiat currency by a corporate buyer and retired from circulation directly in the platform to ensure tracking compliance. (d) this will allow project developers to realize a revenue stream from the growing demand for renewable energy in markets around the world, incentivizing green growth and development in clean energy. The other similar applications ate listed in the table below.

Integrated Distributed Electricity Network

Integrated distributed electricity networks consist of small-scaled operations that provide trackable, transparent transactions at lower costs (Braithwaite, 2020). The network makes use of information technology and management technology to relate larger, more complex devices and systems (Cioara et al., 2020). "Digital technologies like blockchain are creating new options for streamlining and simplifying paper processes, and for disrupting long-established business models" (Fraenkel, 2018). "Decentralized management and coordination of energy systems are emerging trends facilitated by the uptake of the Internet of Things and Blockchain, offering new opportunities for more secure, resilient, and efficient energy distribution. Even though the use of distributed ledger technology in the energy domain is promising, decentralized smart grid management solutions are in the early stages. Smart grids coordinate the requirements and capabilities of all grid operators, generators, end-users, and electricity market stakeholders. A smart grid network encompasses numerous connected IoT devices, which can react to electricity grid signals by adjusting their power consumption accordingly, as and when required. Battery storage is seen as being a key ingredient in helping to maintain this grid stability and pricing flexibility, soaking up excesses during periods of high energy production and returning it to the grid when demand outstrips supply" (Cioara et al., 2020). "Blockchains could assist in network management of decentralized networks, flexibility services or asset management. Blockchains could achieve integrated flexibility trading platforms and optimize flexible resources, which might otherwise lead to expensive network upgrades. As a result, blockchains might also affect revenues and tariffs for network use" (Andoni et al., 2019).

A good example is Energy Web Foundation. Energy Web (EW) is a global nonprofit organization accelerating a low-carbon, customer-centric electricity system by unleashing the potential of open-source, decentralized technologies. In 2019, EW launched the Energy Web Chain, an open-source enterprise blockchain platform tailored to the retail energy sector. This platform aims at providing services and integrating a wide range of distributed energy resources. There are a variety of projects and initiatives that have launched since the inception of this platform by EW, including a decentralized finance crowdfunding platform to accelerate energy access in sub-Saharan Africa (Energy Web, 2021a), energy market exchanges to accelerate the development of renewable energy projects in fragile, energy-poor countries (Energy Web, 2021b), a platform for decentralized lifecycle battery asset management (Energy Web, 2021c), etc.

Internet of Vehicles (IoV) / Internet of Mobile Energy (IoME)

Electric vehicles (EVs) are significant drivers of the global energy transition, and their use is expected to grow steadily in the next 15 years (Wood-Mackenzie, 2018). EVs emerge as new unconventional and highly disruptive participants in the grid that can add significant benefit and flexibility (Jurdak & Dorri, 2021). These vehicles are conventionally viewed as energy consumers that are charged at charging stations to support their movement. EVs' charging and discharging behavior have a significant impact on the power system stability and power market operation (Huang et al., 2021). For example, the electricity exchange between EVs and the power grid, wireless charging among EVs, and EV route optimization based on the availability of vehicles and static charging stations, are new challenges that need to be addressed (Jurdak & Dorri, 2021). Blockchain has attracted tremendous attention as a potential solution to many of these challenges due to its salient features, including decentralization, security, anonymity, auditability, and transparency (Jurdak & Dorri, 2021; Sharma, 2018).

Share&Charge is a Switzerland foundation building a decentralized blockchain protocol for electric vehicle charging (O'Brien, 2019). The goal is to create more seamless and intelligent networks of charging stations to facilitate the adoption of electric vehicles and the use of more sustainable energy. They believe that blockchain's transparency helps build trust among different players, allowing users to make authenticated payments and access more charging stations. For instance, a startup company adapting the

Share&Charge principles, MotionWerk, has developed a decentralized protocol for electric vehicle charging, transaction, and data sharing (Garcia, 2018). In a pilot project in the U.K. in 2018, Share&Charge noted that drivers of electric vehicles still needed to have several different accounts of services to use the array of charging stations in the country (O'Brien, 2019). With Share&Charge powering the apps of different partners, customers could charge and pay across different systems using a single account. In addition, the Share&Charge Foundation wants to create better information and incentives to encourage people to charge at different times to avoid overloading the electric grid at peak times (O'Brien, 2019).

Energy Internet of Things (e-IoT)

Internet of things (IoT) comprises various mechanical devices and sensors, which are connected to each other through a gateway (Muhanji et al., 2019). With the rapid development of wireless sensor networks, smart devices, and traditional information and communication technologies, there is tremendous growth in the use of IoT applications and services in our everyday life (Pal et al., 2021). Recent research has shown that decentralization in IoT access control may overcome limitations of traditional centralized access control models such as single point failure, reliance on trusted third parties, internal attack, and central leak (Song et al., 2021). Blockchain can provide a secure, distributed, and anonymous framework for IoT devices, enabling secure access and data management. Recently, the energy Internet of Things (e-IoT) has been proposed as an energy management solution in modern energy grids (Muhanji et al., 2019). In the modern digital energy grid of the future, all devices that consume electricity are internet-enabled and, consequently, can coordinate their energy consumption with the rest of the grid in or near real-time (Muhanji et al., 2019). In addition, the integration of blockchain-enabled IoT technology into the smart electricity grid will promote the decentralized generation, transmission, distribution, and management of energy (Muhanji et al., 2019).

An example is Bitlumens, a startup company specializing in electro-distribution. They leverage blockchain and IoT to positively change rural areas across the globe (Ritz, 2018). They produce IoT-ready systems consists of several devices, including a solar panel, a battery, a LED light, several electrical outlets, and a whole host of various sensors. Bitlumens chose four locations in Latin America as the initial testing ground for its project: Escuintla in Guatemala, Valle Department in Honduras, Chinandega in Nicaragua, and Guarumal in Panama (Ritz, 2018). The selection criteria were based on the history of electricity shortages, telecommunication infrastructure in place, and an inflation rate below 10% for the cryptocurrency system to work properly (Ritz, 2018). The initial batch of clients for the service were women from remote villages in Guatemala. They were given the opportunity to lease equipment for gathering solar energy and pay it back in installments with a cryptocurrency.

Energy Data Management

Concerning data management, the blockchain supports technology and can perfectly manage all data collected through electricity meters and facilitate real-time consumption monitoring. In addition, it provides the ability for consumers to securely share subsets of data to the market results in more efficient data management. Furthermore, blockchain offers the possibility to give consumers control over their energy sources, as being an immutable ledger, this offers real-time and secure updates of their used energy. The global energy markets have experimented with several tests in this space, including blockchain infrastructure connected to water meters that can trace flows and identify issues in need of repair (Braithwaite, 2020).

An example is Ondiflo, a Texas-based startup that leverages sensor data and blockchain technology to fully automate conversations between humans, devices (IoTs), and business systems in the oil field. For example, by using blockchain, they provide visibility to tank levels and locations, operators can provide truckers with the ability to manage dispatch and scheduling better. Also, by providing transparency to all movements, the trucker provides the operator with the benefit of planning and risk avoidance (AWS Admin, 2019).

Commodity Trading

Commodity trading typically relies on traditional documentation and written records to process and accomplish a transaction (Fraenkel, 2018). "Commodity trading systems built on decentralized ledgers provide the required security, immutability, and real-time view of pricing and transaction status" (Braithwaite, 2020). Replacing expensive proprietary systems can open the door to a wider variety of market participants (Braithwaite, 2020). Applying blockchain technology to commodity trading would be cheaper, more efficient, provide more security, and rapidity than existing proprietary systems. The benefits of blockchain in commodity trading is that it can eliminate the slow adaptability of large-scale proprietary systems which is one of the major limiting factors. The unique advantage for this use case in the commodity and energy trading market is creating an ecosystem that encompasses the start-to-finish transaction life cycle, in essence, a private blockchain network. Finally, this results in potential cost savings coupled with improving processes more efficiently (Braithwaite, 2020) Commodity trading within specifically the energy sector includes, but is not limited to, commodities of crude oil, natural gas, gasoline, and heating products.

The most prominent example is Vakt, an enterprise-level blockchain platform specializing in modernizing and digitizing commodity markets, creating a secure, trusted ecosystem powered by blockchain, smart contracts, and machine learning. It aims to alter the post-trade lifestyle by connecting the trading parties and the participants. Vakt has major investors in the oil and energy markets such as BP, Shell, Saudi Aramco, and more (Vasey, 2019).

Supply-Chain Management

Blockchain is a potentially disruptive technology for the design, organization, operations, and general management of supply chains. Blockchain's ability to guarantee the reliability, traceability, and authenticity of the information, along with smart contractual relationships for a trustless environment, all portend a significant rethinking of supply chains and supply chain management (Esmaeilian et al., 2020). Blockchain has the potential to advance supply chain processes and supply chain management towards sustainability. "Blockchain plays a particularly important sustainability role. Four main Blockchain capabilities can support sustainable supply chains: (1) they help reduce the product recall and rework due to its tracking capabilities; (2) they make it easy to trace the actual footprint of products and determine the accurate amount of carbon tax that each company should be charged; (3) they facilitate recycling behavior by incentivizing individuals to participate in deposit-based recycling programs; (4) they improve the efficiency of emission trading schemes by reducing fraud and improving the fidelity of the system" (Esmaeilian et al., 2020).

Everledger is a blockchain-based startup aimed at tracking and protecting items of value. The team has built a platform that brought greater transparency to the open market places and global supply chain—by ensuring that the asset's authenticity is secured and stored among all industry participants. By involving major certification houses around the globe, they have successfully developed digital thumbprints to protect diamonds, art, wine, metals, and minerals (Altoros, 2017). In coordination with a grant from the United States Department of Energy, Everledger is now tracking products with lithium-ion batteries by registering them with immutable records on the blockchain for greater security, privacy, and traceability. By validating the collection and responsible recycling of these batteries, the supply of critical metals and minerals is ensured for years to come.

BENEFITS, CHALLENGES, AND RISKS OF BLOCKCHAIN IN ENERGY

The advantages that public blockchains can provide the energy sector are numerous and can potentially outweigh the challenges and risks. Blockchain data are essentially unchangeable, highly reliable, providing fault tolerance and strong integrity (Tuefel et al., 2019). Since anyone can generate blocks, create, and keep copies, an attack on one or more nodes does not impact the entire network (Tuefel et al., 2019). Notably, blockchains do not require an intermediary. As the technology supplies prosumers easy access to the energy market, this technology delivers clear, quantitative power straight to consumers (Tuefel et al., 2019). Although decentralization can provide many benefits such as fraud prevention, faster transaction times, and no single point of failure, the traditional blockchain involves weaknesses as well (Tuefel et al., 2019).

To make the blockchain applicable and feasible in the energy sector, it is crucial to reduce or eliminate barriers to deploy the technology (Tuefel et al., 2019). The most significant obstacles against blockchain energy commercialization are legal and regulatory issues, as these issues include contract law, energy law, data protection, liability, consumer rights, and sovereignty (Tuefel et al., 2019). These issues generally stem from the capability to access and view most, if not all, of the data on the public blockchains. In sum, countries and localities need to adopt regulatory frameworks to ensure different economic agents can leverage blockchain and capture its benefits in various applications. For instance, it is uncommon for regulatory frameworks to allow consumer to consumer electricity trading. As such, new laws and frameworks are required to reverse some of the strict regulations in the electricity market.

Other barriers that blockchain presents are scalability and electricity. To illustrate, the electricity costs and expenditures of blockchain are colossal and dependent on the number of participants. The quality of the network tends to decrease as the number of users increase (Tuefel et al., 2019). Maintaining the speed of the network while protecting its integrity of the network is a key concern (Tuefel et al., 2019). However, as discussed earlier in Section 3, there are solutions for converting modern blockchains to energy-efficient networks. These solutions are expected to be fully implemented in the next five years.

The logistics of blockchain usage have also become hurdles when discussing the compatibility of different technologies and private key management or user identity (Tuefel et al., 2019). For example, blockchain innovation in e-mobility applications face significant challenges since blockchains are inherently public ledgers. Information about location and movement of EV users would need to be anonymised to protect their privacy and the systems have to be tamper-proof, to prevent the endangering of the safety of EV users (Andoni el al., 2019).

Lastly, the energy network could become vulnerable to distributed-denial-of-service (DDoS) attacks, unknown vulnerabilities in algorithms or their implementation, attacks targeting the number of nodes of a blockchain, and lack of ability to employ changes to the deployed blockchain (Tuefel et al., 2019). If failures do occur, it is near impossible to determine who is responsible for the errors in a public block-chain (Tuefel et al., 2019). These issues have been under research and development, and solutions to address these concerns are currently being developed.

SUCCESS AND FAILURE OF BLOCKCHAIN APPLICATIONS IN ENERGY

Internal and external factors could impact the current implementations of blockchain technology within the energy sector. The leading expected cause of success and failure of use cases are funding, design, and stakeholders (Disparte, 2019). Since blockchain commercialization is still in the early stages of de-velopment and exploration, funding is crucial to sustaining the applications long enough to produce an impact within the energy sector. Successful companies and applications have a track record of optimizing transactions, securing a source of energy, pursuing one united goal or mission, sharing information, and being transparent in their efforts. Upon adoption of blockchain technology, reducing risks and fulfilling commercial and technical constraints prior to widespread action has been the most beneficial (Disparte, 2019). Companies and applications that fail typically do not demonstrate a long-term plan, clear lack of vision or understanding, defined direction or focus, or lack of upkeep and advancements once the project is undergoing (Disparte, 2019). Often social, organizational, or market coordination issues are present, forcing stakeholders' interests, tradeoffs, and activities to become unaligned (Disparte, 2019). These applications start at a very early stage of play, possess low-capacity models which lack scalability, and require algorithmic or computationally intense burdens (Disparte, 2019). In addition to the representative characteristics of successful blockchain applications, it is important to note that these applications typi-cally occurred in prominent countries capable of ongoing research, understanding, and drive to develop solutions to known and unknown problems (Disparte, 2019).

CONCLUSION

Blockchain technology is in the early stages of research, implementation, development, and commer-cialization. Much research and discussion have been conducted on the emerging possibilities of this technology in the energy industry. In combination with the current global energy transition, this trend provides a unique opportunity to disrupt the traditional energy sector. Blockchain technology can provide a secure digital platform facilitating digitization, decarbonization, and decentralization of energy systems. The promising applications for commercialization in the near future include peer-to-peer energy trading, carbon monitoring, management and trading, and IoT-enabled electric grid management. However, more research and development are required to better understand how to securely scale this technology for mass adaptation in energy. There is also a crucial need for implementing pilot projects to demonstrate the benefits of blockchain in the real world while minimizing the potential adverse impacts of failure. The notable challenges that may negatively impact the adaptation of Blockchain technology in energy are outdated legislation and regulations, slow pace of adaptation from the traditional energy industry, and risks associated with the new, untested technology.

ACKNOWLEDGMENT

The authors would like to thank the Grand Challenge Initiative, Provost Strategic Investment Fund, and Office of Research and Economic Development at the University of Wyoming for their financial support.

REFERENCES

Admin, A. W. S. (2019). Ondiflo is using Blockchain to Revolutionize Oil and Gas Industry. *AWS Startups Blog*. https://aws.amazon.com/blogs/startups/ondiflo-is-using-blockchain-to-revolutionize-the-oil-and-gas-industry/

Altoros. (2017). A Close Look at Everledger - How Blockchain Secures Luxury Goods. *Medium*. https://medium.com/altoros-blog/a-close-look-at-everledger-how-blockchain-secures-luxury-goods-5c3447d07373

Andoni, M., Robu, V., Flynn, D., Abram, S., Geach, D., Jenkin, D. P., McCallum, P., & Peacock, A. (2019). Blockchain Technology in the Energy Sector: A Systematic Review of Challenges and Opportunities. *Renewable and Sustainable Energy Reviews*, *100*, 143-174. doi:10.1016/j.rser.2018.10.014

AP. (2020). *China, top global emitter, aims to go carbon-neutral by 2060*. Retrieved from https://apnews.com/article/climate-climate-change-paris-xi-jinping-emissions-reduction-7a4216a-d4026090adb8d600fab210406

Baker, J. (2021). Blockchain and Sustainability: Oxymoron or Panacea? *Forbes*. https://www.forbes.com/sites/jessibaker/2021/05/25/blockchain-and-sustainability-oxymoron-or-panacea/?sh=6bfcca239af9

Belchior, R., Vasconcelos, A., Guerreiro, S., & Correia, M. (2021). *A Survey on Blockchain Interoperability: Past, Present, and Future Trends*. arXiv:2005.14282

Biden, J. (2020). *The Biden plan for a clean energy revolution and environmental justice*. Retrieved from https://joebiden. com/climate-plan

Bonneville Environmental Foundation. (2016). *What Are Renewable Energy Certificates (RECs)?* http://www.b-e-f.org/learn/what-are-renewable-energy-certificates/

Braithwaite, C. (2020). *Blockchain in Energy Markets*. lisk.com/blog/research/blockchain-energy-markets.

Brilliantovaa, V., & Thurne, T. W. (2019). Blockchain and the future of energy. *Technology in Society*, *57*, 38–54. doi:10.1016/j.techsoc.2018.11.001

Burger, C., Kuhlmann, A., Richard, P., & Weinmann, J. (2016). *Blockchain in the energy transition a survey among decision-makers in the German energy industry*. https://shop.dena.de/fileadmin/denashop/media/Downloads_Dateien/esd/9165_Blockchain_in_der_Energiewende_englisch.pdf

Buterin, V. (2016). *A Next Generation Smart Contract and Decentralized Application Platform*. Ethereum White Paper.

Carley, S., & Konisky, D. M. (2020). The justice and equity implications of the clean energy transition. *Nature Energy*, *5*(8), 569–577. doi:10.103841560-020-0641-6

Cioara, T., Pop, C., Zanc, R., Anghel, I., Antal, M., & Salomie, I. (2020). Smart Grid Management Using Blockchain: Future Scenarios and Challenges. *19th RoEduNet Conference: Networking in Education and Research (RoEduNet)*. 10.1109/RoEduNet51892.2020.9324874

Deatherage, S. (2019). Mutually Evolving Technologies: Blockchain, Renewable Energy, and Energy Storage. *American Bar Association*. www.americanbar.org/groups/business_law/publications/blt/2019/12/evolving-tech/

Disparte, D. A. (2019). Why Enterprise Blockchain Projects Fail. *Forbes Magazine*. www.forbes.com/sites/dantedisparte/2019/05/20/why-enterprise-blockchain-projects-fail/?sh=4f649a7d4b96

Energy Web. (2021a). Bebat Launches EasyBat, an Open-Source, Decentralized Solution for Battery Lifecycle Management. *Medium*. https://medium.com/energy-web-insights/bebat-launches-easybat-an-open-source-decentralized-solution-for-battery-lifecycle-management-281f2ace61e9

Energy Web. (2021b). Energy Web and Energy Peacg Partners Annouces Peace Reneable Energy Credit (P-REC) Digital Marketplace Platform. *Medium*. https://medium.com/energy-web-insights/energy-web-and-energy-peace-partners-announce-peace-renewable-energy-credit-p-rec-digital-6295ea233218

Energy Web. (2021c). ENGIE Energy Access and Energy Web Announce DeFi Crowdfunding Platform to Help Scale Solar, Mini Grids in Sub-Saharan Africa. *Medium*. https://medium.com/energy-web-insights/engie-energy-access-and-energy-web-announce-defi-crowdfunding-platform-to-help-scale-solar-mini-2142029ad84f

Esmaeilian, B., Sarkis, J., Lewis, K., & Behdad, S. (2020). Blockchain for the Future of Sustainable Supply Chain Management in Industry 4.0. *Resources Conversation & Recycling*, *163*, 105060. doi:10.1016/j.resconrec.2020.105064

European Commission Joint Research Centre (EC-JRC)/Netherlands Environmental Assessment Agency (PBL) (2019). Emissions Database for Global Atmospheric Research (EDGAR), release EDGAR v5.0 (1970 - 2015) of November 2019. Author.

Fraenkel, M. (2018). Blockchain for Commodities: Trading Opportunities in a Digital Age. *Trading Opportunities in a Digital Age | S&P Global*. www.spglobal.com/en/research-insights/featured/blockchain-for-commodities-trading-opportunities-in-a-digital-age

Garcia, H. (2018). TheCrypto Emobility Company. *Medium*. https://medium.com/motion-werk/the-crypto-emobility-company-5223bfd81e29

Governor Gordon. (2021). *State of the State address, March, 2*. https://governor.wyo.gov/media/news-releases/2021-news-releases/governor-gordon-celebrates-states-resilience-lays-out-vision-to-address-w

Haggerty, J. H., Haggerty, M. N., Roemer, K., & Rose, J. (2018). Planning for the local impacts of coal facility closure: Emerging strategies in the US West. *Resources Policy*, *57*, 69–80. doi:10.1016/j.resourpol.2018.01.010

HSV. (2020). Reneum Collaborate with Energy Web & Will Host the Companies Blockchain Enabling Aggregation with Other Brokers. *Medium*. https://hsvgts.medium.com/reneum-becomes-an-energy-web-affiliate-will-host-the-companies-blockchain-enabling-aggregation-a216fc16c6b9

Huang, Z., Li, Z., Lai, C. S., Zhao, Z., Wu, X., Li, X., Tong, N., & Lai, L. L. (2021). A Novel Power Market Mechanism Based on Blockchain for Electric Vehicle Charging Stations. *Electronics (Basel)*, *10*(3), 307. doi:10.3390/electronics10030307

Indigo Advisory Group. (2017). *Blockchain in energy and utilities use cases, vendor activity, market analysis*. https://www.indigoadvisorygroup.com/blockchain

IRENA. (2018). *Global Energy Transformation: A roadmap to 2050*. International Renewable Energy Agency.

Jiang, S., Jakobsen, K., Jaccheri, L., & Li, J. (2021). *Blockchain and Sustainability: A Tertiary Study*. IEEE.

Jolley, G. J., Khalaf, C., Michaud, G., & Sandler, A. M. (2019). The economic, fiscal, and workforce impacts of coal-fired power plant closures in Appalachian Ohio. *Regional Science Policy & Practice*, *11*(2), 403–422. doi:10.1111/rsp3.12191

Jurdak, R., Dorri, A., & Vilathgamuwa, M. (2021). A Trusted and Privacy Preserving Internet of Mobility Energy. *IEEE Communications Letters*, *59*(6), 89–95. doi:10.1109/MCOM.001.2000754

Lamport, L., Shostak, R., & Pease, M. (1982). The Byzantine Generals Problem. *ACM Transactions on Programming Languages and Systems*, *4*(3), 387–389. doi:10.1145/357172.357176

McFarlane, S. (2020). BP Bets Future on Green Energy, but Investors Remain Wary. *The Wall Street Journal*. Retrieved from https://www.wsj.com/articles/bp-bets-future-on-green-energy-but-investors-remain-wary-11601402304#:~:text=The%20deal%20is%20part%20of,investment%20in%20solar%20business%20Lightsource

Megha, S., Lamptey, J., Salem, H., & Mazzara, M. (2019). *A survey of blockchain-based solutions for Energy Industry*. arXiv:1911.10509.

Merz, M. (2019, May 20). *Enerchain 1.0 is live!* https://enerchain.ponton.de/index.php/articles/2-uncategorised/37-enerchain10live

MoneroJ. (2016). *Fat Protocols*. https://www.usv.com/writing/2016/08/fat-protocols/

Muhanji, S. O., Flint, A. E., & Farid, A. M. (2019). eIoT: The Development of the Energy Internet of Things in Energy Infrastructure. Springer.

Nakamoto, S. (2008). *Bitcoin: A Peer-to-Peer Electronic Cash System*. Bitcoin White Paper.

Nuzzi, L. (2019). *Interoperability in the Age of Siloed Blockchains Pt.1*. https://medium.com/digitalassetresearch/interoperability-in-the-age-of-siloed-blockchains-pt-1-4d7393fbf420

O'Brien, C. (2019). Startup of the Week: Share&Charge Foundation. *Medium*. https://innovator.news/startup-of-the-week-share-charge-foundation-359425b226c6

Omezzine, F., & Schleich, J. (2019). The Future of Blockchain According to Experts in the Energy Sector. *The Conversation*, *5*(Mar). theconversation.com/the-future-of-blockchain-according-to-experts-in-the-energy-sector-111780

Pal, S., Dorri, A., & Jurdak, R. (2021). *Blockchain for IoT Access Control: Recent Trends and Future Research Directions*, arXiv:2106.04808

Papajak, U. (2017). Can the Brooklyn Microgrid project revolutionize the energy market? *Medium.* https://medium.com/thebeammagazine/can-the-brooklyn-microgrid-project-revolutionise-the-energy-market-ae2c13ec0341

Paris Agreement. (2015). *Paris agreement.* Report of the Conference of the Parties to the United Nations Framework Convention on Climate Change (21st Session, 2015: Paris). https://unfccc.int/files/meetings/paris_nov_2015/application/pdf/paris_agreement_english_.pdf

Ritz, N. (2018). Bitlumens: A New Energy Powered by IoT and Blockchain Technology. *Medium.* https://medium.com/@nina.d.ritz/bitlumens-a-new-energy-powered-by-iot-and-blockchain-technology-483cd212a6

Saraji, S., & Borowczak, M. (2021). *A Blockchain-Based Carbon Credit Ecosystem.* University of Wyoming, Whitepaper. www.uwyo.edu/research/advancing-research-and-scholarship/a-blockchain-based-carbon-credit-ecosystem.pdf

Sharma, V. (2018). An Energy-efficient Transaction Model for the Blockchain-Enabled Internet of Vehicles (IoV). *IEEE Communications Letters.*

Song, L., Ju, X., Zhu, Z., & Li, M. (2021). An access control model for the Internet of Things based on zero-knowledge token and blockchain. *Journal of Wireless Communication Network*, *105*(1), 105. Advance online publication. doi:10.118613638-021-01986-4

Soto, E. A., Bosman, L. B., Wollega, E., & Leon-Salas, W. D. (2021). Peer-to-Peer Energy Trading: A Review of the Literature. *Applied Energy*, *283*, 116268. Advance online publication. doi:10.1016/j.apenergy.2020.116268

Spinnell, J. J., & Zimberg, D. M. (2018). *Renewable energy certificate markets: blockchain applied.* Energy System Engineering Institute, Lehigh University.

Teufel, B., Sentic, A., & Barmet, M. (2019). Blockchain Energy: Blockchain in Future Energy Systems. *Journal of Electronic Science and Technology*, *17*(4), 100011. doi:10.1016/j.jnlest.2020.100011

Vasey, G. M. (2019). *VAKT, Blockchain, Consortia and Solving Industry Problems.* https://www.ctrm-center.com/blog/opinion/vakt-blockchains-consortia-and-solving-industry-problems/

Wood, G. (2016). *Polkadot: Vision for a Heterogeneous Multi-chain Framework.* Polkadot Whitepaper.

Wood Mackenzie. (2018). *Thinking Global Energy Transitions: the what, if, how, and when.* https://www.woodmac.com/news/feature/global-energy-transition/

World Economic Forum. (2020). *Fostering Effective Energy Transition.* Retrieved from http://www3.weforum.org/docs/WEF_Fostering_Effective_Energy_Transition_2020_Edition.pdf

XELS. (2021). *Award-Winning Carbon Broker to Assist XELS With Offset Procurement and Strategy.* https://www.prnewswire.com/news-releases/award-winning-carbon-broker-to-assist-xels-with-offset-procurement-and-strategy-301281322.html

Zhang, C., Wu, J., Zhuo, Y., Cheng, M., & Long, C. (2018). Peer-to-Peer Energy Trading in a Microgrid. *Applied Energy, 220,* 1–12. doi:10.1016/j.apenergy.2018.03.010

ADDITIONAL READING

Anisie, A., & Boshell, F. (2020). *The Benefits of Peer-To-Peer Electricity Trading for Communities and Grid Expansion.* Energy Post, November 13. https://energypost.eu/the-benefits-of-peer-to-peer-electricity-trading-for-communities-and-grid-expansion/

Brink, S. (2021). *How Can Blockchain Support the Energy Transition?* Shell Global, 13 Jan., https://www.shell.com/energy-and-innovation/digitalisation/news-room/blockchain-building-trust-to-enable-the-energy-transition.html

Buterin, V. (2021), The Limits to Blockchain Scalability, Blogpost, https://vitalik.ca/general/2021/05/23/scaling.html

Deign, J. (2018). *Battery Storage Comes to the Blockchain.* Greentech Media, 6 Apr., https://www.greentechmedia.com/articles/read/battery-storage-comes-to-the-blockchain

Dutsch, G., & Steinecke, N. (2017). Use Cases for Blockchain Technology in Energy & Commodity Trading. *PWC,* July, https://www.pwc.com/gx/en/industries/assets/blockchain-technology-in-energy.pdf

Ellsmoor, J. (2019). *Blockchain Is The Next Big Thing For Renewable Energy.* Forbes Magazine, 11 June, https://www.forbes.com/sites/jamesellsmoor/2019/04/27/blockchain-is-the-next-big-thing-for-renewable-energy/?sh=144c4b6d48c1

Hafner, M., & Tagliapietra, S. (Eds.). (2020). *The Geopolitics of the Global Energy Transition.* Springer. doi:10.1007/978-3-030-39066-2

Khalili, S., Disfani, V., & Ahmadi, M. (2021). Impact of Blockchain Technology on Electric Power Grids – A case study in LO3 Energy, arXiv:2106.05395.

Kulagin, V. A., Grushevenko, D. A., & Kapustin, N. O. (2020). Fossil Fuels Markets in the 'Energy Transition' Era. *Russian Journal of Economics, 6*(4), 424–436. doi:10.32609/j.ruje.6.55177

Mika, B., & Goudz, A. (2020). Blockchain-Technology in the Energy Industry: Blockchain as a Driver of the Energy Revolution? With Focus on the Situation in Germany. *Energy Systems, 12*(2), 285–355. doi:10.100712667-020-00391-y

Rao, A. (2020), Accelerating Energy Transition with Blockchain Technology. *IFPEN,* 21 Jan., https://www.ifpenergiesnouvelles.com/article/accelerating-energy-transition-blockchain-technology

Chapter 9
Cryptocurrency and Blockchain:
The Future of a Global Banking System

Namrata Dhanda

Amity University, Lucknow, India

ABSTRACT

As the technologies are evolving day by day, they are able to rejuvenate any sector either individually or by incorporating other technologies. There are many prominent sectors in the market such as healthcare, education, entertainment, business, information technology, retail, etc. Every sector has its own set of profits and consequences, but apart from all, the banking or finance sector is the only sector that provides dynamicity to all other sectors and helps them to generate maximum revenue from their principal investment. In this chapter, the authors are focusing on the traditional and modern ways of banking, currencies such as cryptocurrency like Bitcoin, Ethereum, Litecoin, and how the modern currency will change the transaction procedure in the global banking system, creating an amalgamation of such currency with a current transaction system with the role of technology such as Blockchain in the betterment of the global banking system making the system fully decentralized, distributed, transparent, fast, immutable, and efficient.

INTRODUCTION

With the advancements in technology in almost every area, things are much better now as compared to the previous time. There are many prominent sectors such as education, healthcare, retail, manufacturing industry, finance, transportation, supply chain, food and beverages, travel, defence, entertainment etc, which have benefitted and grown substantially in the global market. To determine the efficiency of each sector, it is important to evaluate individual sectors based on some standard parameters like target audience, approach and strategies followed, workflow, inputs and outputs, profits and consequences, various types of impacts, and financial flow, etc. Among these parameters, financial flow is one of the key parameters and plays a major role in every sector. It is used to provide dynamicity to any sector because it is directly related to the finance system that deals with transactions and is used to forecast the revenue of the sector. By understanding the importance of financial flow, every sector is looking for

DOI: 10.4018/978-1-7998-7927-5.ch009

the safest and secure environment and is ready to adopt new technologies that will provide a safe and efficient environment for transactions to take place. In 2021, the financial system is adopting modern ways of banking by introducing new types of currencies and banks such as cryptocurrency and crypto banks and also utilizing emerging technologies such as Blockchain, IoT, cloud computing, etc.

To understand how Blockchain and cryptocurrency will give an impact on the global banking system, one needs to have a thorough idea of the banking system and how the traditional and modern banking system work. Also one must identify the need of using Blockchain technology in banking sector and how cryptocurrencies are rejuvenating the entire banking system. The bank is the financial institution run by centralized governing bodies in any country. The bank is responsible for any transaction between two or more parties whether they are directly connected or independent to each other. In the Indian banking system, there are five types of banks available such as a central bank, commercial bank, investment bank, cooperative bank and postal bank. The services provided by the banks are retail banking, personal banking, commercial banking, investment banking, credit or debit, online banking, loan provider, insurance handler, mutual funds, etc. There are three key components of the banking system such as capital, deposit, and loans. Initially, when the idea of the banking system was introduced, people were transferring money from one account to the other. This idea is then growing with some prominent features such as cash deposit, flexibility as per the users, convenience, providing better options as per the customers, one governing body, zero interruption, etc. As the population is growing so rapidly, these advantageous features became drawbacks of the traditional banking system because of lack of resources, poor customer service, failure in management, poor interest rate, a wide range of banking charges, and connectivity issues, etc. These are the reason for the transformation of the banking system and a new type of banking system was introduced that came to be known as digital banking or Crypto banking. Crypto banking is based on Blockchain technology and from this originated a new type of currency called cryptocurrency that spanned the market. Figure 1 depicts the countries where Blockchain utilization is the highest. These countries are the USA, UK, Singapore, Switzerland, Japan, China, UAE, Sweden, Estonia, and Malta.

Figure 1. Countries using blockchain technology

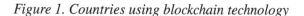

In this chapter, we intend to give a brief understanding of the banking system and its structure, the role of Blockchain in the banking sector, facts and figures associated with Blockchain, recent work in Blockchain, profits, and consequences of the digital banking system, Blockchain consensus mechanism, and other protocols. A study of cryptocurrency, decentralized control of cryptocurrency, exchange, and authorization, a finite supply of currency, pros and cons of cryptocurrency, availability statistics, bitcoin transaction procedure, crypto transactions procedures, future scope and lastly some questionnaires with the conclusion will also be a part of this chapter.

BACKGROUND

With the amalgamation of Blockchain technology and cryptocurrency in the finance sector, researchers highlight the three universal factors of concern that is the processing of data, storage of data, and security of data. Blockchain technology can provide all three services under one roof called Blockchain as a service (BaaS). The BaaS works in a similar way as one of the pillars of the Cloud-Services does i.e., Software as a Service (SaaS). The BaaS works for the Management and Operations of Organizations working on Blockchain Applications. BaaS can act as a spark in the spreading of the Blockchain Spectrum. The Major Functions of Baas are management of Bandwidth, Requirement of Hosting, Data Security, etc., (Zheng et al., 2019). BaaS acts like a catalyst and motivates people to adopt Blockchain technology by providing the necessary resources and infrastructure required to run Blockchain applications. In the banking system several processes are performed in parallel such as debit, credit, loan, investment, trading, payments either online or offline, cheque clearance, etc. BaaS acts as a facilitator for performing such operations and maintaining the consistency of the system. The work of few researchers in the domain of Blockchain and Supply Chain is depicted below. Researcher (Kabra et al., 2020) suggested a concept of mudra chain that is similar to the Blockchain and is used to clear cheques in a hassle-free manner. The researcher proposed a QR-based algorithm that uses the concept of a digital signature on cheques and also proposed an OTP-based algorithm that promotes automatic cheque clearance. Researcher (Davydov & Pitaikina., 2020) discussed the concept of Blockchain to overcome the issues in traditional methodology so that the digital economy increases. For that researcher took the help of bitcoin. Like the supply chain, the banking system is following the process chain and at each step, all the previously performed steps should be synchronized. For that researcher, (Fosso et al., 2020) proposed a systematic review of Blockchain technology to understand the core concepts of the supply chain.

The finance sector is dealing with tons of transaction every single minute. In order to make sure that all the transactions work independently and efficiently, a methodology was proposed that understands the transactional cost of each transaction between two parties and provided an improved economical technique of start-up funding (Ahluwalia et al., 2020). The concept of the letter of credit was proposed to provide more dynamicity to international trade (Chang et al., 2020). To understand the voting system and public interest during market research a conceal decentralized system was proposed (Sudhakaran et al., 2020; Cahill et al., 2020). A framework was proposed that can be used to analyze cryptocurrency such as bitcoin to understand the market scenario while working in the finance sector (Akar.S & Akar.E., 2020; Janssen et al., 2020). To perform all the operations legitimately the researcher (Wamba, S. F., & Queiroz, M. M., 2020) discussed the supply chain concepts, benefits, challenges, and future research opportunities to make the system better and efficient. The Role of Blockchain in the Banking Industry is very crucial nowadays. Blockchain follows three principles namely Transparency, Immutability, and Decentralization. If these three principles are applied successfully to a Banking System, then it can be made more secure. As Decentralization leads to the Removal of the Central Authenticator, the addition of the Immutability concept removes the fabricated data in a single administrator scenario. If

Anonymity is followed then, the banking industry can be made more secure. The old solutions of the Banking Industry are somehow responsible for the new issues of Banking Industry. The Blockchain has the capability to solve these issues if applied in a correct manner. ICICI Bank is already applying this Blockchain Technology (Hughes et al., 2019; Hassani et al., 2018). The next section depicts the diverse forms of Banking Systems.

BANKING SYSTEM

To understand the banking system, one should know the term 'bank'. A bank is a financial institution that works closely with various sectors such as healthcare, education, retail, defence, manufacturing, information technology, travel, food industry, and finance sector itself for the betterment of the social and business economics of the society. In the banking system, one can perform operations such as deposit and withdraw money in various forms such as cash and other digital forms. These operations are called transactions. Nowadays, there are many ways of transaction like through debit and credit card, cash transaction, Cheques, RTGS, Net banking, digital payment such as BHIM UPI, Google pay, Phone pay, etc., digital wallet like PAYTM, cryptocurrency like bitcoin, Ethereum, Ripple, Litecoin, etc. The banking system is used to provide financial stability to the country.

There are two kinds of services provided by the bank:

- Retail banking services like saving account, fixed deposit, mutual funds, credit card, debit card, personal loan, chequebook, ATM card, real-time gross settlement, national electric fund transfer, etc.
- Commercial banking services like business loan, capital raising, term loan, credit services, cash, and risk management, etc.

The banking sector can help the national economy by providing services such as the issue of money, settlement and netting of payments, credit intermediation, quality improvement of credit, asset-liability, and maturity, and money creation and destruction. In India, only the Reserve Bank of India has the governing rights over the entire banks present in the Indian banking ecosystem. In the Indian banking system there are various types of banks available as per the needs of banking such as public sector, regional rural banks, private sector banks, Local area banks, small financial banks, payment banks, foreign banks, cooperative banks, and urban cooperative banks. The most prominently used ones include Retail banking, Business banking, Co-operative banking, Private banking, and Investment banking.

Traditional Banking Structure

Traditional banking mainly is surrounded by two things like bank and user. It provides limited coverage to its customers. It does not contain any marketing tools for the betterment of the customers as well as the bank itself. It promotes a lengthy process that takes a lot of time. In traditional banking, there was a lack of full commitment to the transactions and promotes lots of paperwork. The main drawback of traditional banking was that if a person wants to perform any transaction, then every time, he/she has to go to the bank and carry cash all the time. Figure 2 shows the traditional banking practices. To overcome the loopholes of the traditional banking system, the modern banking system was introduced.

Figure 2. Traditional banking structure

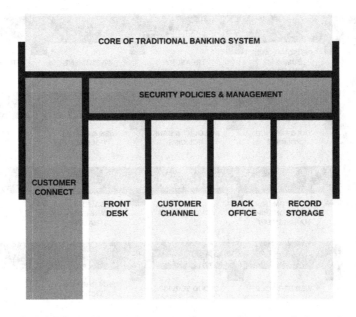

Modern Banking Structure

To eliminate the limitations of the traditional banking system, modern practice of banking was introduced. This banking is associated with a lot of benefits such as - flexibility to the users by making user-friendly policies, existence of separate sales and marketing tools for the betterment of bank and the users, deduction of lengthy processes, paperless work, no requirement to carry cash all the time and even no need to visit the bank for every task. Nowadays the banking system is more technology oriented and uses tools and technologies such as cloud computing, Blockchain, IoT, Big Data, CRM tools, machine learning, artificial intelligence, deep learning, image processing, data analytics, etc. to understand and serve the modern system. These services of the bank can be divided into two broad categories - front end working and back end working. Based on the working, its further categorizes into departments like sales, marketing, technology, management, public dealing, and advertising, etc. In modern banking, there is a collaborative work of every department. Figure 3 is showing the modern structure of banking.

BLOCKCHAIN AND ITS ROLE IN THE BANKING INDUSTRY

In the global banking sector, the Blockchain is used to provide a platform where a number of parties come together and perform certain operations such as sharing of data, updation of data, transactions etc., without any trustworthy central governing body. By providing space to individual stockholders, they carry their ledgers and perform operations such as payment operations, clearance and settlement, fundraising, security, trade, finance and credit, and loans, etc. over the Blockchain business network. Figure 4 demonstrates the areas where is applied in the finance sector.

Figure 3. Modern banking structure

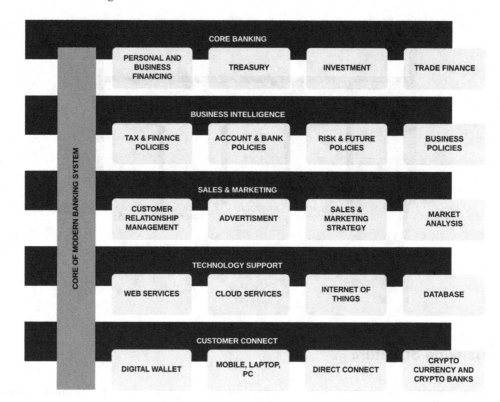

Blockchain: Facts and Figures

As everyone knows that Blockchain is a technology that is based on a decentralized and distributed mechanism where every single entity has its own ledger to store the specific information related to that particular entity. For a transaction between two parties, both parties can have their own set of ledgers and after the transaction is completed, both the parties will update their ledgers and all the associated parties will also update their ledgers. There are a massive number of facts and figures of Blockchain, some of which are discussed here.

- The Blockchain solution will reach around $11.7 billion by 2022 worldwide.
- The global market of Blockchain will generate revenue of around $20 billion by 2024.
- There are more than 42 million Blockchain wallet users present worldwide.
- Blockchain can reduce the infrastructure cost of the bank by around 30%.
- Blockchain technology banking firms can save up to $12 billion per year.
- More than 90% of American and European banks are using Blockchain technology for the betterment of the banking system on a global scale.
- In last year the banking sector invested almost $552 million in Blockchain technology.
- More than 55% of the healthcare industries are using Blockchain.
- IoT devices will reach up to $60 billion by 2021, and hence Blockchain usage will also increase.

Figure 4. Areas of blockchain usage in banking

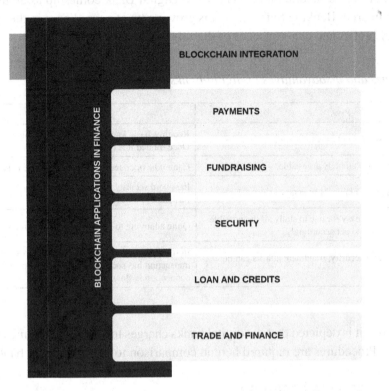

Blockchain: Recent Work

There are a large number of advantages of Blockchain technology like it maintains trust, provides transparency, execution time is less, has better vision, impressive security policies, complex mathematical rules, etc. but to make the technology stable and extendable in front of a growing market, it is important to make some suitable changes for the betterment of the entire technology at regular intervals like constant updating of versions, platforms, the user interface, functionality, security policies, processing mechanisms, etc. Here, there are a few updates that were visible by the end of 2020.

- China launched the digital currency of the Chinese central bank called CBDC in 2020.
- Facebook launched LIBRA as a cryptocurrency with limited functionality in 2020.
- Ethereum 2.0 is in progress and was launched by the end of 2020.
- Better interoperability between the Blockchain makes the entire process more prominent.
- Lightning network and open financial ecosystem available.

Advantages and Drawbacks of Digital Banks

Nowadays, most of the banking services can be performed online without any need of visiting the bank. Any kind of service be it transfer of funds from one account to other, depositing money, viewing account statements for a particular duration can be performed at the click of button and from any location where there is Internet connectivity. All these services can be performed on any Internet enabled device like a desktop, laptop, or even a mobile phone. The Term Digital Bank comes up as an umbrella term that consists of all the Internet Banking Services that is growing up at a rapid pace in the entire world. Here in Table 1, the key profits and consequences of digital banks has been shown.

Table 1. Advantages and disadvantages of digital banks

Pros	Cons
Digital banking is very simple and easy to operate.	Requires basic knowledge of the technology and GUI being used. Once trained it is easy to operate.
Location is not a constraint. Remotely accessible.	Cannot be operated in areas where there is lack of net connectivity.
Most of the operations are available 24 hours.	Password security is a must. It should be kept privately. If mishandled it can result in great loss.
Through digital banking it is easy for one to study all the possible options and plans available and act accordingly.	Quite annoying to receive continuous promotional mails.
Since there is multiple level security, fraudulent attacks can be prevented.	In some cases, the user may not come to know whether the transaction has successfully completed or aborted if the net connection is slow.

In the above table, it is depicted that the digital banks charges low fees and requires no physical location. Less Mails or Procedures are required here in comparison to the non-digital banks.

Blockchain: Consensus Protocols

Consensus Protocols form the backbone of Blockchain network. Though there is no centralized authority to validate the transactions in Blockchain yet every transaction is secure and verified. This is because of the implementation of Consensus Protocol. In Consensus algorithm, all the peers in a distributed network are able to reach a common agreement about the present state of the distributed ledger. This is how the implementation of Consensus algorithms builds trust among a number of unknown peer nodes. The consensus protocol ensures that every new block that is added to the Blockchain is the unique version of the truth that is agreed upon by all the nodes in the Blockchain. In the Blockchain there are many consensus algorithms Some of the consensus algorithms are proof of work, proof of stake, and delegated proof of stake. The various types of Blockchain Consensus protocols are:

1. **Proof of Work (PoW):** In this the Consensus algorithm is used to select the miner for the next block. Here, The Miners solve mathematical puzzles to gain the power so that they can add blocks in the Blockchain (Kiayias & Zindros., 2019). The node that first solves the mathematical puzzle is given the opportunity to mine the next block.

2. **Proof of Stake (PoS)** (Li et al., 2017): It is most commonly used substitute of PoW. Here instead of investing computational time and resources to solve the puzzle, validators invest in coins of the system and lock some of their coins at stake. This is a reward based mechanism to reach a particular conclusion or agreement. Validators will be validating the block by putting a bet on the block if they think it could be added to the chain. Based on the number of correct blocks added to the chain the validators will be rewarded. The validator that receives the maximum number of rewards is selected to generate the next block.

3. **Delegated Proof of Stake (DPoS)** (Fan & Chai., 2018): In this algorithm, users can either vote themselves or can delegate their responsibility to vote on their behalf. A list of witnesses is selected who are designated to create the blocks by verifying the transactions. If all the transactions within a block are verified they get a reward that is shared with all who have voted for that witness. However, the block is said to have been missed if the witness fails to verify all the transactions in the block in a given time frame.

4. **Proof of Capacity (PoC)** (Zheng et al., 2018): In this the generation of the next block is based on the validator that has the maximum amount of hard disk space.

5. **Proof of Elapsed Time (PoET)** (Chen et al., 2017): It is implemented in permissioned Blockchain networks. Each and every validator gets a chance to create their own block. All the validators in the network do so after waiting for a random amount of time. The created blocks are then broadcast in the network after appending the waiting time to it. The block with the least wait time is the winner and is added to the Blockchain.

6. **Byzantine fault tolerance (BFT)** (Stifter et al., 2019): Since in a permissionless decentralized Blockchain system the participants can communicate with each other in an uncontrolled manner which could at times be malicious. In order to control such malicious or hardware failures there need to be some mechanism to arrive at a proper consensus for which we can apply this algorithm. The following are the rules to reach to some decision:
   a. The nodes reach to some output in which case the algorithm terminates.
   b. The majority of the nodes agree to the same output value which leads to agreement.

7. **Practical Byzantine fault tolerance (PBFT)** (Hao et al., 2018): This algorithm ensures that the client receive accurate responses for the requests that they have raised and also abides safety. The condition for executing this algorithm is that out of n nodes there could be at maximum only (n-1)/3 faulty nodes. Secondly, the algorithm does not delay by more than time t. t is basically the difference in time when the message was sent by the sender and when it was received by the destination.

8. **Proof of Activity (PoA)** (Liu et al., 2019): It works by imbibing in itself the goodness of PoW and PoS algorithms. The mining process starts in the same way as the PoW algorithm with each miner making its best attempt to find the block with its computational power. Once the block is retrieved it switches to the PoS algorithm with the retrieved block containing the header along with the address of the miners reward.

9. **Proof of Burn (PoB)** (Gourisetti et al., 2019): In this technique instead of investing time in hardware, the validators are required to burn coins by transmitting them to addresses in such a way that they cannot be retrieved. The more is the number of coins burnt by a validator the better are the chances of that validator generating the next block.

10. **Proof of weight (PoW)** (Alam., 2019): In this algorithm each user is assigned weight depending on the amount of cryptocurrencies he is holding.

11. **Directed acyclic graph (DAG)** (Bencic & Zarko., 2018): In such kind of cryptocurrency mechanism each vertex can be thought of as a transaction. There are no blocks in this algorithm. There a number of transactions instead those are built on top of one another.

CRYPTOCURRENCY

Cryptocurrencies are a kind of digital currency run by private bodies or organizations for digital exchange or financial swap. These types of currencies are not governed by any national bodies but they should be treated as an alternative currency based on a decentralized mechanism. The most preeminent available cryptocurrency is bitcoin. It is the most popular and widely used all over the globe. At the time of writing this paper, one bitcoin equals to $9330.29 USD, market capitalization $170,143,009,565 USD, volume $31,944,341,320 USD, circulating supply 18,188,825 BTC, and maximum supply 21,000,000 BTC. In Figure 5, is shown the vertical graph that depicts the growth of cryptocurrency users, no. of currencies introduced, and the average price of bitcoin yearly.

Figure 5. Digital currency growth rate

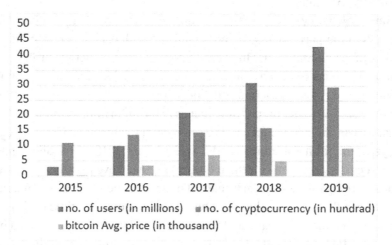

This type of currency uses cryptographical techniques or complex rules to perform the encryption and decryption operations to provide a secure environment to the financial swaps. These complex rules are based on mathematical theories that are impossible to crack. These mathematical theories are also identifying the cryptocurrency users and after the identification, it allows users to participate in the transaction procedures. Cryptocurrency is the type of currency that uses cryptographic functions to perform financial transactions between two or more entities in an internet-oriented environment. It uses Blockchain technology to make sure that all transactions must be decentralized, fully transparent, and immutable. The most prominent feature of this currency is that there is no centralized authority meaning to say there is independence from the centralized governance. This type of currency can be easily transferable between the two or more parties through their public and private key. The following are the features of Cryptocurrency.

1. Decentralized Control

Cryptocurrencies are completely free from any central authority; it is working on a decentralized concept. That means every single entity related to the transaction system should have an independent ledger and when anything happens between two ledgers, it will automatically update the information to all the ledgers simultaneously. To perform a transaction successfully, one must solve the cryptographic puzzle. A person who is solving the puzzle is called a miner and the procedure of solving the puzzle is called mining.

2. Exchanged Through Authorized Currencies

Cryptocurrency can be exchanged or purchased by performing exchange through authorized currencies. There are thousands of cryptocurrencies that are available in the market with different exchange rates. This type of currency is available only in online mode hence it is very sensitive towards hacking but the chances of hacking are very minimal.

3. Finite Supply

These types of currencies are bound within the standard supply of the currency that is after performing mining a certain number of times, it is not possible to mine it further. On the other side, centralized banks are free to generate currencies as per the user requirements under some circumstances. The constraint of finite supply makes cryptocurrency constitutionally declined.

Profits and Cons of Cryptocurrecy

Like anything cryptocurrency also has sets of benefits and drawbacks. The working of cryptocurrency transactions is free from political interference and centralized governance that makes it more prominent and efficient. All the transactions can be taken over the internet that makes the transaction procedure a bit risky. There are sets of pros and cons discussed in Table 2.

Table 2. Pros and cons of cryptocurrency

Pros	Cons
Support true value	Regulation poverty
Zero governance monopoly	Tax intersection
Personal policies	Higher dryness and manipulation
Robust protection	Not changeable often
No financial punishment by the government	Refund constraint
Not cost-effective	Financial loss sometimes

Cryptocurrencies: Availability in the Market

Currently, there are several cryptocurrencies such as Bitcoin, Ethereum, Ripple, Litecoin, Monero, Ethereum classic, Dash, Augur, NEM; waves, etc. that are available in the market. Here in Table 3, we are showing some currency statistics. The table represents the statistics of cryptocurrency concerning the available supply, volume, and market capture.

In Figure 6 the current prices of the currency in USD are shown.

Table 3. Popular cryptocurrency statistics

Cryptocurrency	Available Supply	Volume	Market Capture
Bitcoin	18,183,300	21,653,172,580	155,650,117,212
Ethereum	109,441,095	8,962,440,894	18,205,672,475
Ripple	43,675,903,665	1,449,084,008	9,867,443,720
Litecoin	639,43,099	3,234,808,868	3,580,548,937
Monero	174,17,051	438,90,454	1,112,379,060
Ethereum classic	1163,13,299	1,622,143,485	1,056,499,671
Dash	92,88,176	1,037,614,192	1,029,770,034
Augur	110,00,000	341,74,561	1579,22,078
NEM	89,999,99,999	88,15,157	3614,70,873
Waves	1009,73,464	562,86,227	878,11,877

Figure 6. Price variation chart of cryptocurrency

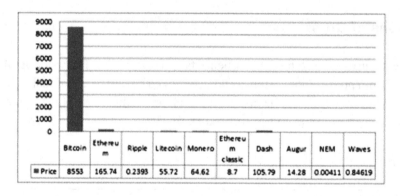

	Bitcoin	Ethereum	Ripple	Litecoin	Monero	Ethereum classic	Dash	Augur	NEM	Waves
Price	8553	165.74	0.2393	55.72	64.62	8.7	105.79	14.28	0.00411	0.84619

BITCOIN TRANSACTION PROCEDURE

To understand the cryptocurrency transaction procedure in a better way, we must know two things: the working of the Blockchain mechanism and the core of cryptocurrency. Let us create a scenario where ROB wants to send 'X' bitcoin to LAURA's account. Then first both the users should have a proper valid bitcoin account. In the very first step, we should have transaction details that stores the information of a sender, receiver, and how much amount a sender is going to send to the receiver's account. Then these transaction details are passing to a hashing algorithm. In bitcoin, we are using a secure hash algorithm (SHA-256). The outcome of SHA-256 is then passed to a signature algorithm with the receiver's private key, that is used to identify the receiver uniquely and the output will be distributed across the Blockchain network so that we will get the right information of the receiver among the available users in the Blockchain network. This can be performed by the public key of the users. During the process, those who are involved in checking whether the transaction is valid or not are called "miners". Once it is verified by the miners, values of every user's ledger are updated and 'X' bitcoin is successfully transferred to

LAURA's account from ROB account. Figure 7 is showing the transaction procedure in the Blockchain and Figure 8 is showing the transaction between ROB and LAURA's account.

Figure 7. Transaction procedures in blockchain

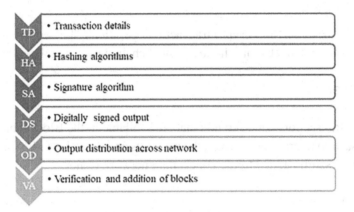

Figure 8. Bitcoin transaction

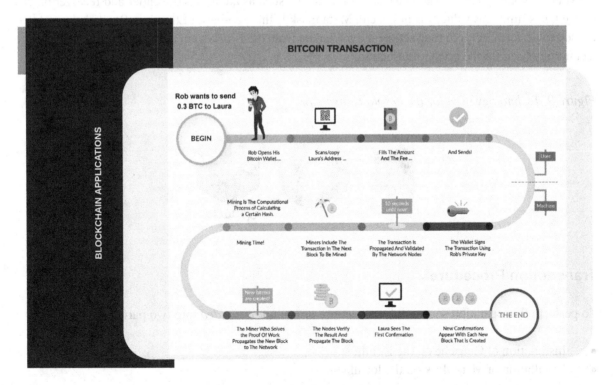

Crypto Transaction on Localhost

Perform crypto transaction operations like deposit and send through crypto wallet on Localhost.

General Statement

In the localhost environment, perform crypto transaction operations like deposit and send from one account to another account, add blocks into the local Blockchain network and get the transaction details.

Procedural Statement

While performing the transaction, add accounts that are available in the Blockchain network to a crypto wallet, perform transaction operations between the accounts and then check the transaction details back whether a block is successfully added to the Blockchain network or not.

Technology Used

Here, the authors have used two Ethereum Blockchain tools named Ganache and MetaMask on the localhost. Ganache is an Ethereum Blockchain tool that is used to install a personal local Blockchain network on your system so that one can see the details such as addresses of sender and receiver blocks created, gas limit, gas value, gas price, etc. Meta mask is the web-based Ethereum Blockchain tool that is used to perform a crypto transaction and fetch data from the Blockchain network. Figure 9, shows the technology used for the crypto transaction.

Figure 9. Technology used for the crypto transaction

Transaction Procedure

To perform this operation successfully, the entire procedure is *divided* into two parts:

- Installation of Ganache on the localhost.
- Installation of MetaMask on the localhost.

The Procedure of Ganache Installation

It is following four commands such as:

- Git clone https://github.com/trufflesuite/ganache.git
- Cd ganache
- Npm install
- Npm start

Once installation is completed open Ganache. It will provide ten accounts with 100 ethers and the initial block created and added to the Blockchain network is zero. So, there are no transaction logs.

The Procedure of Installation of MetaMask

It is following simple steps such as:

- Open Chrome browser and search MetaMask.
- Add chrome extension of MetaMask.
- Set password and next.
- Once the installation is completed, open the MetaMask. It will provide one main network, four test networks and two custom networks with an account having zero ether.

Now, to perform a transaction, we first need to add an account from Ganache to MetaMask. For that go to Ganache and get the key of an account that is to be imported and then open MetaMask and click on import account and put that account key into the private key box and then click import. By doing this one can add as many accounts to MetaMask as he desires. Finally, this is the time to transfer ethers from one account to other. So, select an account and then choose any operation either deposit or send. After that just click on that and select another account where one has to transfer the amount and then fill the amount that has to be transferred. Also select the transaction rate like slow, medium or fast and click on confirm. All the transaction details are automatically available on the Ganache and one block of a transaction is successfully added to the Blockchain network.

RESULT

The given Figure 10 shows the Ganache after successful installation on localhost. This contains ten accounts with hundred ethers each. Initially, there was no transaction. So, the block count is zero, and the rest of the things such as gas limit, gas price, network ID, RPC server, mining status, account address, and account key.

Figure 11, shows the MetaMask after installation on localhost (chrome browser). This contains a single account along with one main network, four test networks and two custom networks.

Figure 12, shows the fast transaction of 50 ethers from account 3 to account 1 excluding transaction charges.

Figure 13 shows the fast transaction of 50 ethers from account 3 to account 1 including 0.000168 ether transaction charges.

Figure 14 shows the details of Account 3 after deduction of 50.000168 ethers.

Figure 15, demonstrates the status of Account 3 on the ganache Blockchain network with the balance ether.

Figure 10. Ganache after installation

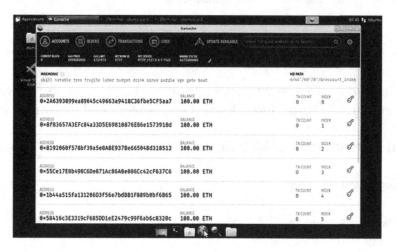

Figure 16 shows the transaction history between Account 3 and Account 1.

By seeing the above transaction results, we found that the transaction was completely decentralized because there was no central governing body and the transaction can take place independently. It is immutable because after successful transaction through MetaMask, details were automatically updated on the Ganache Blockchain network very fast because for every transaction there were three options with their respective transaction fees. These things are making the transaction process more secure and efficient.

Figure 11. MetaMask after installation

Figure 12. Transaction from account 3 to account 1

Figure 13. MetaMask before a transaction

Figure 14. MetaMask after the transaction

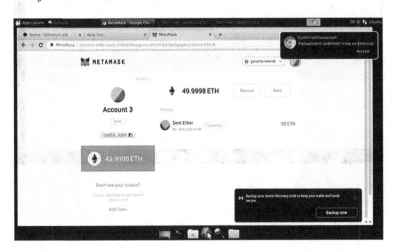

Figure 15. Transaction history on Ganache Blockchain Network

Theoretical Implications

The theoretical implications spotlighted the back-end processing of the transaction. For this crypto transaction, the Ethereum tool is used. So, here in Figure 17, shows the theoretical implications of the performed transaction.

Figure 16. Transaction history between Account 3 and Account 1

Figure 17. Theoretical implications of crypto transaction through Ethereum

HASHING ALGORITHM	ETHASH	MERKLE PATRICIA TREE	META DATA STRUCTURE
START STATE	NEW GENESIS BLOCK	PUBLIC	ADMISSION
REPLICATION	POSSIBLE	PEER TO PEER	TYPE
SMART CONTRACT	TURING COMPLETE	UNILAYER	MODEL
TRANSACTION SYSTEM	POSSIBLE	UNSTRUCUTRE	STRUCTURE
NATIVE TOKEN	POSSIBLE	OPEN SOURCE	CODEBASE
---	INFLATIONARY	YES	UNIQUE SCRIPTING LANGUAGE
ISSUANCES	NO ISSUANCES	ECDSA BASED	DIGITAL SIGNATURE SCHEME
CONSENSUS ALGORITHMS	PROOF OF WORD	ACCOUNT BASED	OWNERSHIP MODEL
---	---	FULL	PROFITS OF TRANSPARENCY

CHALLENGES IN ADOPTION OF BLOCKCHAIN

Blockchain technology is a topic of interest in almost all sectors both in India and across the world (Dhanda & Garg., 2021). The main reason for recognition of Blockchain in India is governance. Transparency in governance is the main objective and in order to achieve it the auditability characteristic of Blockchain can be utilized. The first currency that brought about a revolution in banking sector in many parts of the world was Bitcoin. India is still a bit hesitant about its adoption but in the near future Bitcoin or the other crytocurrencies are going to span the market. The anonymous nature of the Blockchain will be the main feature that will lead to its adoption. Apart from the several advantages that Blockchain possesses there are certain prominent challenges that are slowing down it adoption:

1. As the number of users increases, the network speed decreases which results in increase in the transaction fees. Thus scalability is an issue.
2. Standard rules across the globe need to be setup for the adoption of naive technology that comes up in the market. Such rules are gradually built over a period of time.
3. The third important challenge is security and privacy. Blockchain is an open platform which is accessible to all users in the network. This is why it is said to possess the property of transparency. At the same time, it should maintain the privacy of its users.

REGULATORY AND LEGAL ASPECTS OF BLOCKCHAIN

The number of users of cryptocurrency in India is estimated to be 15 Million. The objective is form a set of rules and regulations to replace currency by crypto assets. However at present there is no fixed set of rules or framework to govern cryptocurrecies. It is still in the evolving stage. In April 2018, Reserve Bank of India had issued an order that none of the entities related to it must encourage the use of any kind of virtual currency. A similar statement was also issued by the finance ministry later in 2018. Further in 2019 the Government was stricter towards non usage of cryptocurrency and also set up a punishment in the form of imprisonment for 10 years for any person found involved in these cryptocurrencies. However, a revolution came about in 2020 when the Supreme Court opposed RBIs order and permitted the banks for transactions involving cryptocurrency. The government is still in the process of making digital currency more prominent as it wants to keep in pace with the upcoming technologies like Blockchain. According to the statement of RBI Governor Shaktikanta Das the time has come to leverage its applications while at the same time strengthening the digital infrastructure.

KEY DISCUSSIONS

1. How Blockchain technology is impacting the global banking system by changing landscapes?

In the past, it has been seen that banks acted as middle entities between the two parties while performing a transaction or financial operations. Because of the unavailability of the ledger, it was difficult to trace every single detail efficiently. Through Blockchain, every single entity is having its own ledger which will be updated right after the successful transaction. The trustworthy agreement between the two makes the entire transaction procedure faster, cheaper, more conceal, and prominent.

2. What are the key profits of Blockchain in the financial swap?

Through Blockchain technology, we get an ample number of benefits over the traditional methodologies like it provides better security by avoiding the single point failure, provides better transparency, establishment of trust, better programmability, better concealment policy, and better interoperability that increases the overall performance while performing a transaction. In Figure 18, we are show the profits of the usage of Blockchain technology in the banking sector.

3. How to reduce the Blockchain scalability problem in the banking environment?

SegWit is the protocol used to overcome scalability problem and to make sure Blockchain applications run smoothly over the Blockchain business network. In the Blockchain network, there are thousands of transactions that can be performed within a second. This protocol helps to reduce the slowdown impact on the transaction. SegWit stands for segregated witnesses or signatures. The idea of using this protocol is to isolate the signature from the transaction data so that the transaction process will run faster. There are several benefits of SegWit like capacity increase, increase transaction speed and increase malleability.

4. What is the role of crypto-economics?

Figure 18. Profits of blockchain in the financial system

Crypto-economics involves combining the participant of the Blockchain network with cryptographic mechanisms and economics. It solves the participation problems during the transaction. It is used to promote faster peer-to-peer connections or transactions in the Blockchain business network. It also includes complex mathematical problems such as hash algorithms that can be solved by miners to perform mining procedures.

5. How to perform technical quality assurance by using Blockchain in the banking system?

To get technical quality assurance in the Blockchain business network, parabolic SAR is used. SAR stands for stop and reverse. This is used to promote short trades over long trades. It is very helpful to understand market trends and insights. The limitation of this is that it is not very useful during the consolidation period. It will generate false signals in case of unclear trends.

CONCLUSION

Through spotlighting the impact of Blockchain and cryptocurrency on the global financial system, we found that digital currency is the absolute future of the financial system because of traditional banking lacks trustworthiness, transparency, security, robustness, speed, and efficiency. By seeing the statistics shared above and the market analysis, we also found that complex mathematical rules are more advantageous and useful in a consensus mechanism. There are several consensus algorithms and protocols available that are helpful to justify the authenticity of the transaction procedure between two bodies. During the time of research, there are almost 2700 cryptocurrencies present, 35 million users using cryptocurrencies, total revenue of Blockchain market is 3 billion approximately and will be 14 billion by 2024 and the global market of Blockchain technology will reach 60k million approximately by 2025 and more than 60% of banks are already using Blockchain. The rate of usage of Blockchain technology, crypto wallet, and currencies is still increasing. By seeing the exceptional growth rate of such technology there will surely be a huge impact on the financial sector and the entire sector will become more prominent and efficient in terms of customers, services, and revenue.

REFERENCES

Ahluwalia, S., Mahto, R. V., & Guerrero, M. (2020). Blockchain technology and startup financing: A transaction cost economics perspective. *Technological Forecasting and Social Change*, *151*, 119854. doi:10.1016/j.techfore.2019.119854

Akar, S., & Akar, E. (2020). Is it a New Tulip Mania Age? A Comprehensive Literature Review Beyond Cryptocurrencies, Bitcoin, and Blockchain Technology. *Journal of Information Technology Research*, *13*(1), 44–67. doi:10.4018/JITR.2020010104

Alam, T. (2019). IoT-Fog: A communication framework using blockchain in the internet of things. *International Journal of Recent Technology and Engineering*, *7*(6).

Benčić, F. M., & Žarko, I. P. (2018, July). Distributed ledger technology: Blockchain compared to directed acyclic graph. In *2018 IEEE 38th International Conference on Distributed Computing Systems (ICDCS)* (pp. 1569-1570). IEEE. doi:10.2139srn.3638991

Cahill, D. G., Baur, D. G., Liu, Z. F., & Yang, J. W. (2020). I am a Blockchain too: How does the market respond to companies' interest in Blockchain? *Journal of Banking & Finance*, 105740. doi:10.1016/j.jbankfin.2020.105740

Chang, S. E., Luo, H. L., & Chen, Y. (2020). Blockchain-Enabled Trade Finance Innovation: A Potential Paradigm Shift on Using Letter of Credit. *Sustainability*, *12*(1), 188. doi:10.3390u12010188

Chen, L., Xu, L., Shah, N., Gao, Z., Lu, Y., & Shi, W. (2017, November). On security analysis of proof-of-elapsed-time (poet). In *International Symposium on Stabilization, Safety, and Security of Distributed Systems* (pp. 282-297). Springer. 10.1007/978-3-319-69084-1_19

Davydov, D., & Pitaikina, I. (2020). Blockchain Technology Is Changing the Innovation Aspect in the Digital Economy. In Avatar-Based Models, Tools, and Innovation in the Digital Economy (pp. 103-112). IGI Global. doi:10.4018/978-1-7998-1104-6.ch006

Dhanda, N., & Garg, A. (2021). Revolutionizing the Stock Market With Blockchain. In Revolutionary Applications of Blockchain-Enabled Privacy and Access Control (pp. 119-133). IGI Global.

Fan, X., & Chai, Q. (2018, November). Roll-DPoS: a randomized delegated proof of stake scheme for scalable Blockchain-based internet of things systems. In *Proceedings of the 15th EAI International Conference on Mobile and Ubiquitous Systems: Computing, Networking and Services* (pp. 482-484). 10.1145/3286978.3287023

Fosso Wamba, S., Kala Kamdjoug, J. R., Epie Bawack, R., & Keogh, J. G. (2020). Bitcoin, Blockchain and Fintech: A systematic review and case studies in the supply chain. *Production Planning and Control, 31*(2-3), 115–142. doi:10.1080/09537287.2019.1631460

Gourisetti, S. N. G., Mylrea, M., & Patangia, H. (2019). Evaluation and demonstration of Blockchain applicability framework. *IEEE Transactions on Engineering Management, 67*(4), 1142–1156. doi:10.1109/TEM.2019.2928280

Hao, X., Yu, L., Zhiqiang, L., Zhen, L., & Dawu, G. (2018, May). Dynamic practical byzantine fault tolerance. In *2018 IEEE Conference on Communications and Network Security (CNS)* (pp. 1-8). IEEE.

Hassani, H., Huang, X., & Silva, E. (2018). Banking with Blockchain-ed big data. *Journal of Management Analytics, 5*(4), 256–275. doi:10.1080/23270012.2018.1528900

Hughes, L., Dwivedi, Y. K., Misra, S. K., Rana, N. P., Raghavan, V., & Akella, V. (2019). Blockchain research, practice and policy: Applications, benefits, limitations, emerging research themes and research agenda. *International Journal of Information Management, 49*, 114–129. doi:10.1016/j.ijinfomgt.2019.02.005

Janssen, M., Weerakkody, V., Ismagilova, E., Sivarajah, U., & Irani, Z. (2020). A framework for analysing Blockchain technology adoption: Integrating institutional, market and technical factors. *International Journal of Information Management, 50*, 302–309. doi:10.1016/j.ijinfomgt.2019.08.012

Kabra, N., Bhattacharya, P., Tanwar, S., & Tyagi, S. (2020). Mudrachain: Blockchain-based framework for automated cheque clearance in financial institutions. *Future Generation Computer Systems, 102*, 574–587. doi:10.1016/j.future.2019.08.035

Kiayias, A., & Zindros, D. (2019, February). Proof-of-work sidechains. In *International Conference on Financial Cryptography and Data Security* (pp. 21-34). Springer.

Li, W., Andreina, S., Bohli, J. M., & Karame, G. (2017). Securing proof-of-stake Blockchain protocols. In *Data Privacy Management, Cryptocurrencies and Blockchain Technology* (pp. 297–315). Springer. doi:10.1007/978-3-319-67816-0_17

Liu, Z., Tang, S., Chow, S. S., Liu, Z., & Long, Y. (2019). Fork-free hybrid consensus with flexible proof-of-activity. *Future Generation Computer Systems, 96*, 515–524. doi:10.1016/j.future.2019.02.059

Stifter, N., Judmayer, A., & Weippl, E. (2019). Revisiting practical byzantine fault tolerance through Blockchain technologies. In *Security and Quality in Cyber-Physical Systems Engineering* (pp. 471–495). Springer. doi:10.1007/978-3-030-25312-7_17

Sudhakaran, S., Kumar, S., Ranjan, P., & Tripathy, M. R. (2020). Blockchain-Based Transparent and Secure Decentralized Algorithm. In *International Conference on Intelligent Computing and Smart Communication 2019* (pp. 327-336). Springer. 10.1007/978-981-15-0633-8_32

Wamba, S. F., & Queiroz, M. M. (2020). *Blockchain in the operations and supply chain management: Benefits, challenges and future research opportunities*. Academic Press.

Zheng, W., Zheng, Z., Chen, X., Dai, K., Li, P., & Chen, R. (2019). Nutbaas: A Blockchain-as-a-service platform. *IEEE Access: Practical Innovations, Open Solutions, 7*, 134422–134433. doi:10.1109/AC-CESS.2019.2941905

Zheng, Z., Xie, S., Dai, H. N., Chen, X., & Wang, H. (2018). Blockchain challenges and opportunities: A survey. *International Journal of Web and Grid Services, 14*(4), 352–375. doi:10.1504/IJWGS.2018.095647

Chapter 10

An Analysis on the Terms and Conditions of the Clickwrap Agreement and the Benefits of Maintaining the Click Wrap Agreement in Cloud Computing

Dhiviya Ram

University of Malaya, Malaysia

ABSTRACT

One of the most unique forms of contracting is apparent in cloud computing. Cloud computing, unlike other conventional methods, has adopted a different approach in the formation of binding contract that will be used for the governance of the cloud. This method is namely the clickwrap agreement. Click wrap agreement follows a take it or leave it basis in which the end users are provided with limited to no option in terms of having a say on the contract that binds them during the use of cloud services. The terms found in the contract are often cloud service provider friendly and will be less favourable to the end user. In this article, the authors examine the terms that are often found in the cloud computing agreement as well as study the benefit that is entailed in adopting this contracting method. This chapter has undertaken a qualitative study that comprises interviews of cloud service providers in Malaysia. Hence, this study is a novel approach that also provides insight in terms of the cloud service provider perspective regarding the click wrap agreement.

INTRODUCTION

Non-negotiability is the key characteristics of this type of contract. However, it is seen that there has been greater negotiability in the recent to allow the end users to communicate their interest to the providers (Alistair Maughan, Christopher D. Ford, and Scott W. Stevenson, 2014). Nonetheless, it is also mentioned in the same scholarly article that if one demands for negotiability in the contract to ensure their interest

DOI: 10.4018/978-1-7998-7927-5.ch010

and wants are heard, the cloud is not the infrastructure for such demands (Alistair Maughan, Christopher D. Ford, and Scott W. Stevenson, 2014). Hence, it can be seen despite the increase in the negotiability, the general mind set is practicing a non-negotiability practice in the cloud agreement and condoning the concept of relinquishing negotiation power that an end user might have in a regular contract. Before undertaking the study on the terms and condition and legal issues underlying it, this article will look at the process of the whole contract and how this contract is communicated to the end users. Furthermore, this study will also include the study on local providers that will deepen the analysis of this agreement as well as assist us in the understanding of the reason behind adopting the clickwrap agreement. This rule can also be applied in the smart contracts found in Blockchain system. It is said that an application of smart contracts running on a permissioned distributed ledger (essentially a private blockchain where only credentialed participants are allowed to read and write) to managing tenant and service accounts in a cloud computing data center. (Sambit Nayak, Nanjangud C Narendra, Anshu Shukla, 2018)

BACKGROUND: NATURE OF THE CLOUD CONTRACT

An ordinary contract in the ordinary world often a written and the contract is passed from the offeror to offeree. Upon the concluding the contract, neither part could withdraw their offer nor acceptance as the contract has already been formed. The contract is concluded upon the signature of the offeree which expresses acceptance of the offer. A contract can also be verbally concluded without being in a written form. However, the standard form contract is different from a conventional contract despite have a face-to-face meeting. One would come across such contracts in many circumstances that involves sale and purchase. Nonetheless, it is also noted that in such contract, the consumers are presented a take it or leave it basis contract (*similar to the clickwrap agreement as mentioned before*) and this contract are rarely understood by the consumers. Hence, despite having a face-to-face meeting, it is said that terms and condition are left unread. This is because consumers consistently fail to read their standard terms. This failure undermines market pressure to provide mutually beneficial terms (Robert a. Hillman & Jeffrey j. Rach.insri, 2002).

The failure to obtain mutually benefitting terms is due to various factors. Some of the factors are as the following. Firstly, this contract often entails terms and condition that is not understandable to the consumer. These terms are also, at most of the time, communicate in small bold print which reduces the consumers interest in perusing the contract that they are binding by. Moreover, the consumers also rarely look at the contract as a major deciding factor in their purchase because in most circumstance the consumer/buyer would have made up their mind on their purchase before being handed the contract. The deciding factor often relies on the reasonableness of the price, quality as well weighing whether the purchase is indeed worth the money paid. Thus, majority of the consumer are more inclined to ensure that they have received a good bargain rather than focusing on the small bold prints present during the purchase. The contracts are also often lastly placed thus leaving behind a risk of unconscionable terms being present in the signed contract. The consumer also underestimates the adverse risk that maybe present in the contract. The question therefore lies on how the courts decide on the enforceability of such contracts. The current legal approach adopts a similar approach to what was illustrated by Karl Llewellyn's (Professor Karl Llewellyn, 1994) vison that the law should create a presumption of assent which was referred to as a blanket assent recognized that businesses generally compete to offer reasonable goods and services to consumers, and assumed that businesses, better than judges, could determine the "particular set of terms that 'fits' the practical problems and needs that arise... in carrying out the transactions.' "Blanket assent" is regarded as a valid assent to contract despite the fact the consumers do not understand the terms stated. The basis of the assent lies in the fact that the contract is valid as long as the consumer is able to apprehend that he will be bound by the terms and conditions in the contract. Thus, the court limit their interference to only getting involved when there is a presence unconscionable and unfair terms in the said contract. Such rights are vested upon the courts in various act and one of it is the **United Kingdom Unfair Contract Terms Act 1977** which deals with contracts that includes unconscionable terms in the contracts. The Section 3 of the act states that a party cannot contract terms against the other party in the following situations.

(a)When himself in breach of contract, exclude or restrict any liability of his in respect of the breach; or

(b)claim to be entitled—

(i)to render a contractual performance substantially different from that which was reasonably expected of him, or

(ii)in respect of the whole or any part of his contractual obligation, to render no performance at all, except in so far as (in any of the cases mentioned above in this subsection) the contract term satisfies the requirement of reasonableness. (Unfair Contract Terms Act 1977 S(3))

A reasonable term shall have been a fair and reasonable one to be included having regard to the circumstances which were, or ought reasonably to have been, known to or in the contemplation of the parties when the contract was made. The reasonableness is often based on the knowledge of the parties, whether they are made aware of the terms, bargaining power and many more (Aneela Akbar, 2011). If the party seek to prove that the term is valid, the party bears the burden to prove the reasonable in the terms.

In such circumstance, the affected party are allowed a remedy pursuant to situation that has arisen. The court can choose to disregard to give effect to the terms but can also deem the whole contract void.

The above shows the situation in where courts choose to interfere in arrangement between the parties. It often relates to unfairness of the contract and how the other party choose to take advantage of the privilege that is present to him in deciding the terms of contract. This shows that generally if one holds the right to decide on a term, it is common for such right to abused and used against another contracting party. Thus, unfair term in a contract should not be of any surprise in a contact that has terms which are set with no room for negotiations.

THE CLICKWRAP AGREEMENT AN ENFORCEABLE CONTRACT

This is a common lingering confusion that exists and has not been clarified by many studies. Many studies that were started on the literature review has embarked on the enforceability of the clickwrap agreement but has failed to explain how the use of the word "agreement" in Cloud Contract should not be mistaken for what is commonly regarded as an agreement. The nature of this agreement is important as it determines whether such an agreement is binding and enforceable to the other party. Nonetheless, firstly, it is important to understand the distinction between a contract and an agreement.

A contract is a voluntary agreement between two or more parties that the court will be able to enforce. The rights of obligation that arises from the terms of the contract are only valid to the contracting parties and will not be subjected to any other party outside the contract. An agreement, on the other hand, is an arrangement between two or more parties that is not enforceable by law. It is often done in an informal manner and can be distinguished from an ordinary contract. An agreement also lacks the characteristics of a contract which are namely offered, acceptance and consideration. focus on whether the plaintiffs had reasonable notice of and manifested assent to the clickwrap agreement.

Thus, based on the enforceability of the Clickwrap Agreement, it is clear that it is indeed a contract. It also satisfies the criteria needed to prove a contract being Offer, Acceptance, and Consideration. All this element is easily found in a clickwrap agreement which shall suffice to deem it a contract. It is also safe to assume that the Clickwrap Agreement is an electronic standard form contract because as it shares similar characteristics such as non-negotiability and the take it and leave it basis that prominently present in both types of contracts.

CLASSIFICATION FOUND IN CLICKWRAP AGREEMENT AND ITS SIMILARITY WITH SMART CONTRACT IN BLOCKCHAIN TECHNOLOGY

The contract in cloud computing do not differ as much conceptually to ordinary contract that we face in our daily lives. In fact, it is safe to say that the click wrap agreement in cloud computing infrastructure is actually a standard form contract. Clickwrap agreement is a type of contract that is widely used with software licenses and online transactions in which a user must agree to terms and conditions prior to using the product or service. This is particularly used in the cloud world for various reason which will be discussed later in this study. Likewise, with standard form contracts, the click wrap agreement is flawed with discrepancies and legal issues which often arises due the nature cloud computing as the non-negotiability of the cloud contract. Furthermore, it is vital to analyse the process of conclusion of the clickwrap agreement and the steps taken during this process.

The parties of cloud contract are the cloud service providers (CSP) as well as the client of the cloud provider whom are often regarded as end user consisting of entities or even individuals. As mentioned earlier in a click wrap agreement does not give room for negotiation or customization of the contract and the client are often left in a take it or leave it basis. Thus, clients are often stuck in a dilemma where in order to enjoy the services provided in the cloud, they would have to agree to the terms of the contract. Similarly, in Blockchain Technology, smart contracts self-execute the stipulations of an agreement when predetermined conditions are triggered. The parties "sign" the smart contract using cryptographic security and deploy it to a distributed ledger, or blockchain. Hence, the contract would be concluded without any negotiation or what would otherwise be seen in a traditional contract. (Reggie O'Shields,2017). The end users often enter in the contract with the provider without modification and solely adhering to the contract that is set by the cloud service provider. There are very few providers who are willing negotiate on the terms set despite the fact that in some circumstance the end user consist of a large company (Carlos A. Rohrmann & Juliana Falci Sousa Rocha Cunha, 2015). In most cases, the cloud service providers often consist of a large entity who is well equipped with professionals and experts that will be required. However, it should not be mistaken that a smaller entity will not be capable of providing cloud services. Small entity which has the infrastructure and the necessary resources will be capable of engaging in cloud services. Nonetheless, generally cloud computing providers often comprises of large multinational companies who are equipped with manpower and expertise that can run the cloud services and hand the required services to the end user according to their demands and needs (Carlos A. Rohrmann & Juliana Falci Sousa Rocha Cunha, 2015). Hence, this chapter will be drawing the analogy in the discrepancy's fount in the smart contract in Blockchain Technology by analysing and examining the clickwrap contract.

LEGAL ISSUES IN RELATION TO CLICKWRAP CONTRACT

Upon learning the types of contracts that are involved in the cloud and the distinctive nature of both the types of the contracts. This explanation has allowed to comprehend the various type of contract and the clickwrap contract is distinct in comparison to the normal contracts. Hence, upon perceiving the different types of Cloud Computing, the study shall proceed with the legal issues that surrounds Clickwrap Contract. There are no regulatory issues that may arise due to cloud contract per se, but it can be improved and even eliminate as much as possible with a well drafted contract that exhibits characteristics that protects the end user/data user.

First, it is in relation to data privacy, which was given utmost importance in the newly legislated regulation being the European Union General Data Protection Regulation (herein referred to as EUG-DPR/GDPR). The new regulation gives respect to the data of the end users while also requiring the data controller to give due care to the rules and regulations set by the processor, eg service providers (Carlos A. Rohrmann & Juliana Falci Sousa Rocha Cunha, 2015). This is monitored to regulate and maintain the privacy whilst allowing the flexibility for the service provider in updating their services for the end user. The cloud contract will illustrate the type of privacy that is being accorded between the end user and the cloud provider. Hence, the cloud contract plays a major role in terms of maintaining privacy in cloud computing.

Moreover, it is also important for the data to be served and not accessible to any unauthorised access and such access can lead to the end user to suffer enormous detriment monetarily as well as it may affect one's reputation. An example of such situation can be seen in the availability of data of personal health record that can tarnish someone's name and reputation upon being exposed to an unauthorised third party. Hence, when the data that is being handled is sensitive and may cause serious damage to the end users, it is advisable for the contractual obligation to set certain clauses that assert the confidentiality of the information stored (ENISA, 2009). This clause may be named special care clause which would accord higher level security for such personal data. It is said that in most cases, the end user would require a minimum level of protection. However, in cases where the data involves sensitive information should be significant higher.

Furthermore, cloud servers also involve user that are located in other countries and may not necessarily be confined to where the service provider is located. Hence in such circumstances, the cloud providers are situation in different countries or under different jurisdiction (OECD, 2014). The new regulation prohibits any form of data transfer to a country that fails to satisfy the adequate protection (with a few exceptions) (General Data Protection Regulation (GDPR), 2016/679). Thus, in such cross-border transfer, it is advantageous that there is an additional term in the contract that states the level of protection, the method of handling the data allows a cleared and better administration of such transfer while allowing the flexibility the cloud mechanism required (Pardis Moslemzadeh and Sabaruddin, Johan Shamsuddin and Ramanathan, Dhiviya, 2018).

Moreover, there is also an issue that is raised because of processor and sub-processor agreement. A sub processor is typically a third party hired by the processor to delegate their current job according to the extent that is set by these processors (Oracle, 2019). There may be many extraneous reasons behind delegating the job which often relates to where the expertise lies. Article 3(e) (General Data Protection Regulation (GDPR), 2016/679) has defined sub processor as a processor engaged by the data importer or by any other sub processor of the data importers personal data exclusively intended for processing activities to be carried out on behalf of the data exporters after the transfer in accordance with data exporters instruction (General Data Protection Regulation (GDPR), 2016/679). There is persisting issue regarding whether cloud providers fall under data controller or data processor. Many providers have chosen to negate from being bound by liabilities that they out to bear according to the role they play (Pardis Moslemzadeh Tehrani, Johan Shamsuddin Bin Hj Sabaruddin, Dhiviya AP Ramanathan. 2017). A clear and accurate contract will help to elevate this issue by distinguishing the unique character and characteristics of each part in a cloud whilst also specifying the responsibility that ought to be borne by each entity/individual.

Finally, there is an issue of exercising the data users right. Data user, being the sole proprietor of the data stored, should have exclusive right to their data. In a cloud setting, often this right is also an exercised by the data controller. Hence, the mere categorizing of them as cloud processor should not exclude their responsibility. A clear contract can specify the responsibility that is attached with such rights. Based on this, it can be seen that there are many issues that can be resolved by ensuring that the cloud contract terms attempt to prevent the above legal issue. However, in reality, the terms are also used as a method to avoid responsibility and liability, thus not curbing the legal issue that surround the cloud computing. Upon learning the issues of the cloud and how the cloud contract can help to resolve the issues, the following section will look on the clickwrap agreement and terms that are found in the clickwrap agreement that may contribute to legal issues mentioned above.

TERMS AND CONDITION OF CLICK WRAP CONTRACT

Similar to an ordinary contract, the clickwrap agreement comprises of terms and condition which often left unread and unnoticed by the end during the process of assenting to the contract. The terms and condition will often be provided in a separate webpage from the acceptance page and often does not require the end user to read through the terms before accepting it. There are often several forms that is comprised in the Terms and Conditions of a cloud infrastructure. The terms and condition incorporate a number of forms that ranges from being short to lengthy complexed documents (Carlos A. Rohrmann & Juliana Falci Sousa Rocha Cunha, 2015).

Firstly, the terms and condition will compose of the terms of services. This is referred to as Service Level Agreement. It is safe to say that this document is the core of the agreement and this article will majorly discuss on this document. In this document, the relationship between the cloud service providers and the customers are stated. It also asserts the legal issues, jurisdiction and many more. Service Level Agreement (SLA) specifies the level of service the provider aims to deliver together with the process for compensating customers if the actual service falls short of that. SLA functions as a guarantee to the cloud customer that a sufficient level of services will be provided by the provider. This is specifically intended to regain confidence of the end user on the services that they have subscribed to (Abdallah Ali Zainelabden A. IBRAHIM, Dzmitry Kliazovich, Pascal Bouvry, 2016). However, this agreement has faced criticism as it is difficult to assess whether the services are provided with due quality. Some of the criticism includes the burden of proof being heavily placed on the end user to when there is a breach of agreement (Pankesh Patel, Ajith Ranabahu, Amit Sheth, 2009). Furthermore, the cloud contract also comprises of the Acceptable Use Policy (AUP). AUP is a document details the permitted (or in practice, forbidden) uses of the service. This will include the restriction places by service provider to the end user in the manner they are allowed to enjoy the service thus setting a limitation on unfair usage that may be detrimental to the provider. Finally, in the cloud contract, there is also Privacy policy which consist of document that outlines what the public cloud provider can, and can't, do with the personally identifiable information (PII) that the cloud user might share in the process of contracting the service. The importance of this document increases in circumstances where the data handled is sensitive in nature. In most circumstances, the end user will be presented with all four (including the terms and condition) documents when they are faced with the contract of the Cloud. However, there are instances where the documents may overlap with one another. This can particularly be seen in AUP where it often overlaps with Privacy Policy in the cloud contract (Kevin Buck, Diane Hanf, and Daniel Harper, 2015).

Nonetheless, as a whole, the objective of all the documents will be satisfied despite the unclear distinction between these documents. This contract also can change quickly and the ever-changing nature of the terms of this contract could cause problems. It is ideal in such circumstances for the cloud service providers to adopt a method that will notify the end-users on the changes that have been made to terms that were previously agreed upon. Notification will usually be done through their verified email addresses. However, certain cloud providers dismiss themselves from being obliged to notify the end-user on any change of the terms and conditions. This change, however, is meant to promote flexibility in the cloud infrastructure and to allow the terms to accommodate the evolving technology. However, it is opined that notification is necessary to remove the unjust amendment of terms and to allow the end-user to consider whether such an amendment may cause them to terminate the contract as a whole. Due to the fact that providing notification may not necessarily be done compulsorily, many end user are unaware with the of the change of the terms. Hence, the end user is unable to weigh in the impact of the change of the term and whether it would be advisable for them to end the contract which may or may not result in a termination charge. Many banks, credit card companies and social media sites have adopted the approach that notifies their customers of the changes made (Robert McLelland, Yvette Hackett, Grant Hurley, Daniel Collins, 2014). However, they may only notice that changes have been made in the previously agreed terms and leave the room for their clients to discover the nature of the changes and their potential impact on them (Robert McLelland, Yvette Hackett, Grant Hurley, Daniel Collins, 2014). Thus, it is preferable for the cloud service providers to notify their clients of the changes made to maintain a healthy relationship between the cloud services providers and their clients.

CONSENT IN CLOUD COMPUTING CONTRACT

The contract between the end-user and service will come into effect upon assenting to the contract[1]. The contract shall be effective until the expiration date of the last of the Cloud services purchased by the Customer, with each Party being entitled to withdraw, to be notified to the other party according to what has been agreed upon. Upon the termination of the Contract, in most circumstances, the services will be discounted and any surcharge that is paid will be refunded to end-users.

It should be noted that often the problem does not arise from the formation of this contract. One would rarely come across a circumstance where the end-user wishes to dispute the formation of the contract. However, the dispute arises when the end-user is of the opinion that certain terms that were contained in the contract have been unfairly inserted and thus leaving the end-user at the losing end in certain situations. This occurs solely because the terms are not negotiated in a clickwrap contract and often the end-users omit from reading the details of the contract. The understanding is also limited as the end-user often are unfamiliar with the terminology adopted by the cloud service provider due to its technicality.

One of the main unjust plead by the end-user is the cloud provider's avoidance of liability through the means of this kind of contract. Thus, to understand this aspect of cloud computing the terms of the contract should be analyzed in detail. However, it should be noted that this behavior is expected and generally perceivable based on the overall responsibility borne by the cloud providers. Often, the providers are seen as a large entity that goes all its way to avoid and negate any form of liability that could be placed on them. Although one may say that it is only natural for one to avoid its liability, one should not condone such behavior that can cause severe damages to the end-user and also prevent the end-user from seeking damages. Moreover, it also appears that an entity that can negate its liability to its fullest and it is often held not accountable for the data stored in their control, it is highly possible for the level of security and care to plummet due to this lack of responsibility. Hence, it is best to possibly monitor and ensure that providers do not act irresponsibly and choose not to provide the necessary care that the end-user requires solely because they are able to avoid being liable and accountable for any mishap that occurs in the cloud infrastructure.

CONTRACTUAL TERMS AND THE RISKS

This article will omit the discussion on ordinary clauses that does not cause legal issues and merely focus on terms that serves as a problem in the eyes of the law. Hence, we will describe the terms that are often found in the cloud contract and how the inclusion of such terms can result detrimental to the end user. Thus, based on this subsection, one will be able to comprehend the legal issues in the clickwrap contract and study pros of cons of adopting such terms in the contract.

Although the clickwrap contract is usually regarded as cloud friendly and one sided, it should also be noted that the contract does not only comprises of terms that discharge the cloud provider from responsibility but also protect the cloud provider from unacceptable behaviour from the end user. These terms are justified since the cloud provided do not want to be held liable to the illicit behaviour of the cloud user. Such circumstances can be seen in the case of L'Oréal SA and others v eBay International AG and others (L'oreal Sa And Others V Ebay International Ag And Others [2009]) where in this case, counterfeit products were sold in the cloud platform. The claimant being a manufacturer and supplier of high-quality product brought a claim against eBay that they are jointly liable for infringement of trademark that was committed by one of their selling in the cloud platform. Despite the fact eBay has indirectly facilitated the infringement of the trademark, the courts held that they are not jointly liable for the infringement because eBay is not under a legal duty to prevent the infringement. The courts held that the mere intention to profit is insufficient to deem the defendant as a joint tortfeasor. However, the cloud providers are not always lucky to avoid liability in these circumstances.

In the case of Twentieth Century Fox Film Corp v Newzbin Ltd [2010], in deciding whether the provider is a joined tortfeasor, the judge considered the case in detail to know whether the provider being Newzbin Ltd has facilitated with the infringement of the copyright of the claimant. Hence it has said that having the mere knowledge of the infringement is insufficient to deem the Newzbin as a joint tortfeasor. The level of involvement and the participation in committing the tort is the determining factor of whether the provider has committed an infringement. In this case, Kitchin J found that, the site was structured in such a way as to promote infringement by guiding members to infringing copies of films and providing them with the means to download infringing copies at the click of a button (via the NZB facility) and so concluded that the defendant had procured and engaged in a common design with its premium members to infringe the claimants' copyrights. Thus, based on both this cases it can be seen that although the infringing content were not directly used by the provider, they can be held liable for the end user's infringement. Hence, this is rationale behind using such a clause to prevent further liability. However, does mere insertion of that clause allow the provider to negate the liability which would otherwise be placed upon them? Based, on the case of Twentieth Century, it is clear that in deciding whether the provider is a joint tortfeasor, the involvement in the wrongdoing was observed.

Thus, to prevent such unduly circumstances from occurring, the cloud providers have specified the end users acceptable use when they enjoy the cloud services offered by the provider. These terms are usually found separately outside the terms condition and it is commonly referred to as Acceptable Use Policy (AUP). An example of acceptable use of policy can be seen in Dropbox who has included a separate tab for clauses in relation to acceptable use. Dropbox has specified that it prohibits;

Table 1.

> • probe, scan, or test the vulnerability of any system or network;
> • breach or otherwise circumvent any security or authentication measures;
> • access, tamper with, or use non-public areas or parts of the Services, or shared areas of the Services you haven't been invited to;
> • interfere with or disrupt any user, host, or network, for example by sending a virus, overloading, flooding, spamming, or mail-bombing any part of the Services;
> • access, search, or create accounts for the Services by any means other than our publicly supported interfaces (for example, "scraping" or creating accounts in bulk);
> • send unsolicited communications, promotions or advertisements, or spam;
> • send altered, deceptive or false source-identifying information, including "spoofing" or "phishing";
> • promote or advertise products or services other than your own without appropriate authorization;
> • abuse referrals or promotions to get more storage space than deserved;
> • circumvent storage space limits;
> • sell the Services unless specifically authorized to do so;
> • publish or share materials that are unlawfully pornographic or indecent, or that contain extreme acts of violence;
> • advocate bigotry or hatred against any person or group of people based on their race, religion, ethnicity, sex, gender identity, sexual preference, disability, or impairment;
> • harass or abuse Dropbox personnel or representatives or agents performing services on behalf of Dropbox;

Source: Dropbox Acceptable Use Policy

Furthermore, PTC Inc., a computer software and services company founded in 1985 which is headquartered outside of Boston, Massachusetts also have provided a detailed acceptable use policy which consist of 4 pages. In this Acceptable use policy that was drafted by the cloud provider. It can be seen that the policy was subcategorised into several paragraphs namely prohibited activities, security violation, customer responsibility, AUP enforcement and notice and reporting. In comparison to the Dropbox's acceptable use policy, PTC is seen to be more detailed in their policy. Dropbox have generalised any breach in a simple term that reads "violate the law in any way, including storing, publishing or sharing material that's fraudulent, defamatory, or misleading; or violate the privacy or infringe the rights of others" (Dropbox Acceptable Use Policy) where else the PTC have provided a non-exhaustive list of the type of security violation that is prohibited. However, most of the prohibited activities that was listed by PTC does fall under the general term that was listed by Dropbox.

In contrast it can be seen that certain providers have adopted a more unconventional approach that describes the acceptable use of policy. These providers have exercised the use of laymen terms in their policy to make it easily understandable to the general public who more often than not, do not understand the legal jargon an ordinary policy entail. An example can be seen in the Flickr, an image and video storing host, that have taken such unconventional method in their AUP. This policy falls under their community guideline and is seen in a separate tab along with the terms and privacy policies. Such terms include captions such as "Play nice" (Flicker Guidelines) and "Don't be creepy" (Flicker Guidelines) which specifies that the end user has to respect the privacy of other end user whilst enjoying their services. They also stress the importance of following these guidelines by stating that "if one can't abide by our Community Guidelines as outlined above, maybe Flickr isn't for them" (Flicker Guidelines). This proves that the host is serious about ensuring the guideline are followed religiously by the end user and will not tolerate act that deviates from the said terms. Ultimately, all of these providers mentioned above share similar objective in ensuring that the end user does not have a run in the law whilst using their cloud services Due to cases such as Twentieth Century Fox Film Corp v Newzbin Ltd [2010], providers are required to be more cautious in ensuring that the end users do not use the interface to commit a crime. Based on the observation made on the above and several other cloud providers, it is apparent that the policy, although worded in a different manner, is aimed to ensure compliance with the laws and regulations of the specific countries in the governing use of the Internet (PTC Acceptable Use Policy for Cloud Services).

THE TROUBLING TERM IN THE CONTRACT

One of the terms that give rise to a legal issue is in relation to the data preservation of the data stored in the clickwrap contract. Data preservation occurs when the end user has decided to end the clickwrap contract with the provider and cloud has decided to preserve the data for a grace period upon the termination. Although it is clear to the end user that ending a contract entails inability to use the cloud services, it is unsure to them what occurs to the data that was formerly stored in the cloud. Importance should be placed for such data as it still requires adequate privacy and security to be accorded despite ending the contract. Before embarking on the terms of the cloud providers pertaining to their right to preserve date, one should perceive the intended purpose of practicing data preservation.

The main purpose of maintaining and preserving a data is mainly to ensure that the data is not deleted improper or mistakenly. This grace period allows the end user to retract and recover any data that could be permanently deleted otherwise. However, concern have arisen on whether there would be an actual erasure of data. Many articles have since been published that regards data preservation as one of the dangers of storing data in a cloud. Articles have gone as far as describing as zombie data which "comes to haunt you" despite deleting the specific data years ago (Fahmida Y. Rashid, 2017). An example can be seen when the issue in terms of Dropbox have recently resurfaced where Dropbox bug kept users' deleted files on its servers for more than six years (Allie Coyne, 2017). This is despite the fact the new General Data Protection Regulation has introduced the right to be forgotten in terms of the personal data stored in the cloud. This is found in Article 17 of the General Data Protection Regulation where it states that "the data subject shall have the right to obtain from the controller the erasure of personal data concerning him or her without undue delay and the controller shall have the obligation to erase personal data without undue delay" (General Data Protection Regulation, 2016/679) However, before entering into the details of the new regulation, we would analyze what is the common terms that are found amongst the cloud providers in terms of data preservation. It is said that most of the cloud providers fall into three broad categories in the aspects of dealing with customer information following the end of the relationship between them and the customer (Bradshaw, Simon and Millard, Christopher and Walden, Ian, 63/2010). Firstly, are the set of providers that have asserted that they will preserve the data of the customers for a fixed period of time upon the termination of the contract. Salesforce has stated that the data will be made available to the end user 30 days after the termination of contract. However, after the 30 days period, Salesforce is under no obligation to maintain provide any the end user's data and will thereafter delete or destroy all copies of your data in our systems or otherwise in our possession or control, unless legally prohibited (Salesforce Master Subscription Contract). This term can also be seen in Dropbox where it is said to save deleted and previous versions of files for a specific period of time in case you want to recover them. After, however, the period of the time has lapsed, the deleted files will be deleted and "purged" (Dropbox) from their system thus giving no option for recovery. The specific period listed by Dropbox for their basic subscription is 30 days upon the termination of contract. However, ironically, Dropbox was also accused of storing data that were deleted 6 years ago in their system due to a certain bug that has hindered the deletion process. Hence, it brings a suspicion that whether an actual deletion is actually done upon the lapse of the specific period mentioned in their terms of services.

The second set of providers on the other hand has opted for an immediate deletion upon the end of the relationship between the cloud providers and end users. Apple in their MobileMe product have stated that all data stored will be deleted immediately upon the termination of the end user's account. However, such a method of deletion can give rise to other legal one of such as if the termination of contract was subsequently deemed ineffective. Such a situation will lead to cloud providers to compensate the data loss of the end user due to their mistake of data deletion. Furthermore, in the UK, Section 3 of Computer Misuse Act 1990 (Computer Misuse Act [1990]) has made it illegal any unauthorised acts with intent to impair, or with recklessness as to impairing, operation of computer, etc (Computer Misuse Act [1990]). Hence, an improper deletion of the data can lead to the provider being liable for the above provision. Apple has since moved away from such draconian deletion has amended their data deletion provision in the iCloud which is a software that replaced MobileMe. iCloud has stated that upon the termination of the Account, the end user may lose all access to the Service and any portions thereof, including, but not limited to, your Account, Apple ID, email account, and Content. However, they have specified that the deletion of information and data stored in the account will only be done after a period of time (iWork. com Public Beta Terms of Service). This period of time is not specified in the contract thus bring to the third set of providers which are regarded as the hybrid approach (Bradshaw, Simon and Millard, Christopher and Walden, Ian, 63/2010).

This hybrid approach can be said to be a vague approach that does not provide any specification on the actual date of deletion but rather a general term that allows the provider to delete according to their standard of procedure and convenience. An example can be seen in Google Drive where no clear specific time was provided in terms of use as to period of the data retention. The Google Drive have however mentioned different frame times for different form of datums for example where cookies will be deleted after 18 months and the complete deletion of the data from their ´server takes around 2 months"

(Google Privacy Policy). The data retention policy has mainly focused on the reason behind such preservation. Microsoft SQL Azure Databased have also used a similar approach where it stated that "Upon the expiration of the term or any termination or cancellation of this contract, your rights to access or use the Services immediately cease, and you must promptly remove from the Services any data, software programs or services (if any) used in connection with your access to or use of the Services. If you do not remove such data, software programs or services from the Services, we reserve the right to remove them in accordance with our normal business practices for the Services." (Microsoft Azure Privacy Policy). Since data deletion is a serious aspect it should be noted that such a hybrid approach does not compensate the concerns an end user may have in regards to the data preservation.

In the recent General Data Protection Regulation, it was stated in Article 17 of the GDPR that "the data subject shall have the right to obtain from the controller the erasure of personal data concerning him or her without undue delay and the controller shall have the obligation to erase personal data without undue delay" (General Data Protection Regulation, 2016/679). One of the grounds that apply is "that the personal data are no longer necessary in relation to the purposes for which they were collected or otherwise processed". Despite the fact that this attempt does help to eradicate the fear of unwanted storing of deleted data, the reasoning that was provided by providers such as Google Drive should serve as a purpose of storing the data for a longer period. Moreover, a lot of problems were said to be associated with the Article 17 (General Data Protection Regulation, 2016/679). Some of the problems are, the end user being the data controller, may not be able to contact the relevant parties (Cesare Bartolini, Lawrence Siry, 2016). Furthermore, the providers might have different grounds for the lawfulness of the data processing, so the erasure request might not be effective toward them even if it is for the original controller (Cesare Bartolini, Lawrence Siry, 2016). Moreover, as mentioned in before, due to ambiguity of the controller and processor that still exist in the Cloud, it is unclear how much of control the providers may have in terms of its data (Cesare Bartolini, Lawrence Siry, 2016).

Hence based on this, it can be seen that a proper answer has yet to have be obtained for the problems in regard to the data preservation. The cloud does appear to preserve some form of data retention to prevent any unauthorised erasure. Despite the fact that the main objective of the data retention is to ensure unapproved data deletion, retention of data for a non-specific time has caused fear among the general public. It has also averted people from subscribing to a cloud for dismay that the data will not be deleted. Furthermore, the level of privacy and security that is accorded to such data is also ambiguous and uncertain since it is unclear on even the existence of such deleted data. Furthermore, it also should be noted that most if not all, cloud providers have retained a discretion to vary the terms of the cloud contract. In other words, most of the cloud contract is subject to change and it applicable to all their available client.

Clickwrap contract comprises of general terms and condition that can be subject to change according to the cloud provider. It has been described as a floating contract as it the terms are ever changing, and the contract allows a variation of the agreed terms if the cloud provider is of the opinion that it would be suitable for their services for such change of terms. In general contract, change of term or also known as contract modifications occurs when both parties agree and consent for such modification occurs. However, variation of terms in the cloud contract does not require the consent of the end user. The main reason for allowing the terms to be changed is due to the evolving nature of the services that will cause inconvenience if it is tied down by a rigid contract. Although the intention of allowing the change of contract is for the advantage of those who enjoy the services, it cannot be denied that the ability to vary the terms has caused concerns to the end users.

The unfairness in the cloud contract can be seen in this aspect where it can be seen that the cloud contract is clearly cloud provider friendly and is more advantageous to the providers. This is because, due to the fact that the cloud provider reserves the rights to vary the contract, it is only the end user who is bound by the terms of the contract. The cloud provider, on the other hand, hold the power to change the terms thus having no liability to stick by the terms of contract. Based on the observation, it can be seen that there are two types of approach that the cloud providers have adopted in withholding the power to change the terms. Firstly, are those providers who will notify the client on the change of terms.

This can be seen in the Apple iCloud where it was stated that "Apple reserves the right at any time to modify this Contract and to impose new or additional terms or conditions on your use of the Service, provided that Apple will give you 30 days' advance notice of any material adverse change to the Service or applicable terms of service." (iCloud Terms and Conditions). They have also stated that they would refrain from making any adverse change unless required to do so. Facebook also follows a similar approach of notifying the client before the change is brought to effect to allows their users to review of the change of terms (Facebook Terms of Services) .

The second type are providers who states that notification will not be brought to the end user in the event of change of terms. This can be seen in Rackspace, a cloud computing company that is based in US, where they have stated that "Rackspace may, without notice to the end user, at any time amend these Terms and any other information contained on this website." (Rackspace Terms of Use). However, they have stated that the new version of the contract can be found in their website. Nonetheless, it is unlikely that the end user will be aware of such changes if the provider merely posted a revised terms and condition in their webpage. There are also several providers that makes no mention on variation of terms in their terms and condition (Bradshaw, Simon and Millard, Christopher and Walden, Ian, 63/2010).

Continued usage of the cloud by the end user upon the change of terms and services amounts to an acceptance of the changed term. In spite of that, if the end user does not agree to the terms and condition, the client is only left with the option of deleting or terminating the contract thus deleting their account with the cloud provider. This is a classic example of the "take it and leave it basis attitude that is found in this click wrap contract.

Furthermore, the terms of the cloud contract also consist of the limitation of warranties and liabilities which all cloud providers embark in to avoid and minimize the damage the provider is liable for. First and foremost, most of the contracts by the cloud providers have excluded implied warranties that they may bear to the end users in terms of their services. For example, Gmail has specified that Google nor its suppliers or distributors makes any specific promises that they would warrant any mishap that may have occurred as a result of their services hence excluding all warranties to the extent permitted by the law (Google Terms of Services). Dropbox have, on the other hand, extended their exclusion of warranties to state that this term will apply regardless of whether or not Dropbox or any of its affiliates has been warned of the possibility of such damages (Dropbox Privacy Policy). In spite of that, it appears that Dropbox have been negligent in circumstance where they have been warned that there would unduly repercussions. Nonetheless, Dropbox remains affirmative to disclaim the warranty to the extent permitted by the law. Despite the difference in wording and how the terms are phrased, most if not all cloud providers aim to disclaim any form of express or implied warranties that the service provided will be fit for purpose or merchantable. A similar route is dealt in tackling with liabilities that may have risen from the cloud providers and caused damages to their customers.

There are two types of liability which is direct and indirect liability. Indirect liability are generally excluded by the cloud provider. In a cloud contract, "direct liability" is defined as liability that arise from losses to the customers relating to the loss or compromise of data hosted on the Cloud Services. This can be seen in Facebook where the liability "shall be limited to the fullest extent permitted by applicable law, and under no circumstances will we be liable to you for any lost profits, revenues, information or data, or consequential, special, indirect, exemplary, punitive or incidental damages arising out of or related to these Terms or the Facebook Products, even if we have been advised of the possibility of such damages" (Facebook Terms of Services) . Thus, Facebook have denied any form of liability that may have arisen except for those that should be borne by the applicable law. These terms appear to negate the responsibility that should be down to the customers to maintain and preserve their data. Hence, this is one of the main reasons of concern for the end user who chooses to store important personal data in the cloud computing infrastructure.

Furthermore, notwithstanding the fact the cloud provider have denied almost all of the warranties and liabilities as permitted by law, the cloud provider has also limited the amount of damages that they will be held liable for circumstance that they cannot exclude liability. For example, Rackspace have specified that they will limit their liability to 12 months of the fee of their paid services. Other free providers, on the other hand have remain silent on the limitation of liability but have denied indirect and direct liability. This seems to suggest that the deny all liability whatsoever that may rise in their relationship with their customer.

Despite the fact that the attitude of the cloud provider is to ensure that they are not liable, they did not fail to include an indemnification terms that excludes from any damages payable as a result of their customer's action. These can be widely seen in both paid and free services. Facebook for example have stated that "If a third party brings a claim against us related to your actions, content or information on Facebook, you will indemnify and hold us harmless from and against all damages, losses, and expenses of any kind (including reasonable legal fees and costs) related to such claim" (Facebook Terms of Services). Hence this clause places the liability of the end user to pay for the damages caused by their action whilst also negating any form of liability from the cloud provider.

Based on this, it can be seen that the general approach of the Cloud Providers is to ensure that the provider will be excluded of any liability and warranty that may otherwise rise as a result of their role. The main purpose of the drafting of the terms and condition is to ensure that they will not be liable for damages. However, one should ponder that whether the act of drafting a cloud provider friendly that avoids liability and warranty to be placed to big enterprises and reverting the burden to cloud consumers who consist of smaller enterprises and even individual is indeed the right approach to governing cloud computing. Since clickwrap contract does not provide room for negotiation, the end user can either take the contract as it is and agree to terms of the contract or leave the services by disagreeing to the contract. It is clear from the above discussion that cloud provider does have an upper hand in the contract and the end user is on the losing end. In spite of that, there also many benefits that can be seen as a result of this clickwrap contract. To deepen the understanding further an interview was conducted amongst cloud providers located primarily in Malaysia. The following subsection will discuss the findings that was derived from the interview.

FINDINGS FROM THE INTERVIEW CONDUCTED WITH THE CLOUD PROVIDERS

Pursuant to the study conducted, an interview was conducted to allow a in depth analysis on the issue in question. The interview was conducted primarily through email and phone calls. At initial stages, twenty cloud providers who either provides or maintains a cloud server in Malaysia, was approached to help in assisting in the study of the cloud contract. However, only eight cloud providers responded to the queries asked in the interview. This may be because most the cloud providers do not have their own legal team and is often unclear with their own terms and conditions. Hence, this makes them incapable of answering the questions asked required in the interview. However, this subsection will be based on the results obtained from the eight providers that have responded to the interview. There were four question that were presented for the purpose of this study. The following are the question that were asked during this interview;

- Are the terms in your contract subject to change?
- If your contract is indeed subject to change, do you notify your client on the terms that have been subjected to change?
- Do you allow your end user to negotiate on your terms and condition?
- Briefly explain the benefits of maintaining a click wrap contract to govern your services.

Most of the question has yes or no variable except for the last two question that are left open ended for the interviewee to allow them to explain the answers in their own words.

Seven interviews were conducted through telephone conversation and one was obtained through email. The interviews that were conducted through phone conversation lasted for a duration of five to ten minutes. The person interviewed are from the technical support teams or from the sales department. The reason behind choosing this institution is because most of them involve dwell solely or majorly on cloud services and also manages other companies' clouds.

This survey is a novel approach to deepen the study on this area. Prior study has based their findings merely on the analysis of the terms and condition that were usually found in the website of the cloud provider. In spite of the fact such a study will be able to understand the nature of cloud contract, one will not be able to perceive the intention of the cloud and the reason behind the adoption of the cloud contract and its terms. The survey will also assist in developing ideas and solution that is present in the cloud contract. Thus, this survey will be able to provide reasoning on the nature of the cloud contract whilst also allowing the cloud provider to provide insights on the cloud contract. The question that was posed to the cloud providers are mainly in regard to terms of contract and the benefits of maintaining of maintaining a click wrap contract.

As mentioned earlier, eight enterprises who focusses mainly on cloud were interviewed for this study. The enterprises are;

- G-Asia Pacific
- Yeah Host
- Net on Board
- Rapid Cloud
- Exabytes

- Integrated Global Solutions (IGS)
- RockSoft Sdn. Bhd.
- SKALI Cloud

The following are the findings obtained from the interview conducted with the enterprises mentioned above.

Skali Cloud is a cloud provider that is said to offer flexibility and ability to scale up the capability according to the need of the customer (Skali Cloud). The provider has promised to offer cost efficiency by allowing their customers to buy the exact capacity they would require. The provider also promises a "peace of mind" of running on a professionally managed infrastructure. However, during the interview, the provider did profess that the terms of the contract that governs the relationship between the client and cloud provider is subject to change. The provider stated during the interview that such changes will be notified to the client. It is also mentioned in their terms and condition that any change of terms of contract will be notified 30 calendar days before any alteration takes effect (Skali Cloud Terms of Service). Most of the cloud providers have mentioned that the change on the terms of the contract will be notified to the client. Nevertheless, three of the eight cloud providers namely Yeah Host, Exabytes and Rapid Cloud have asserted that changes to the terms of the contract will not be informed to the customer.

Yeah Host have stated distinctly in the terms of their services that they "reserves the right to change, edit, or update the policies contained in these terms without notice" (Yeah Host Terms) Rapid Cloud on the other hand remains silent in their terms whether the end user will be informed if there is a material change. Furthermore, Exabytes have stated in their change of their terms will only be notified when there is a material change (Exabytes Terms). What amounts to a material change still remains ambiguous thus not providing clarity on the instances where the end user will be notified of the variation of the terms.

In reference to whether the providers policy on allowing negotiation of the terms of the contract, four of the providers being Skali Cloud, Rock soft, Net on Board and G Asia Pacific have stated during the interview that they allow their customer to negotiate the terms of the contract. They have mentioned that they would like to promote flexibility and also tailor their services according to the end users. Two other cloud providers being Yeah Host and Rapid Cloud on the other hand have mentioned that the negotiation will be based on the end user. Yeah Host have also asserted that this negotiation is to allow leniency in their contract whilst also accommodating the needs of their customers. In spite of that, the other providers being Exabytes, IGSB and Rapid cloud have affirmed that negotiation is not allowed and thus upholding the terms of contract that is drafted by these providers.

Moreover, to understand the reasoning of maintaining the click wrap contract, the interviewee was also asked on the benefits that is entailed in such a contract that is fixed by the cloud provider. Most of the provider have stated that it assists them internal governance. IGSB have stated that such an contract will allow the provider to be better prepared in understanding the terms that would comprise in the contract. Hence it will be easier to respond to a breach of the contract. Exabytes, has also mentioned that varying terms will only give rise to confusion to the providers in governing their services. Rocksoft was also of the same opinion as Exabytes despite stating they would allow negotiation with end user for the terms of the contract. Majority of the providers have also specified that it is time saving and it requires less resources in maintaining a click wrap contract. Net on Board stated that a click wrap contract that is drafter by the cloud provider allows them to prevent any abuse by the end user that can affect the cloud provider. Yeahhost have stated that maintaining a click wrap contract is meant to benefit both the end user and the cloud provider. However, the interviewee has failed to clarify how such a contract will benefit the end user.

The following subsection will illustrate and in-depth discussion on the benefits that a click wrap contract incorporate. It is vital to comprehend the pros and cons of a particular system before reaching a conclusion on it. Hence, the benefit of the click wrap contract should not be disregarded as it plays a significant role in the discussion of the click wrap contract. Many scholarly articles and materials have shunned away from the discussion of the benefits of the click wrap contract and have confined their opinion on the legal complication that it has given rise to. Hence, to refrain from making similar mistake, the discussion below will illustrate the advantages of the click wrap contract

CONCLUSION

The above discussion has examined the terms that is often found in a cloud contract and the legal issues that may arise as a result of it. Most of these circumstances shall also be applicable for smart contract in Blockchain Technology. As mentioned above, advantage is also an important factor in any discussion. Thus, to provide a thorough discussion in this article, this subsection will discuss on the advantages of the click wrap contract. Generally, most of the benefit will be in favour of the provider who is the drafter of the contract. However, there also certain advantages enjoyed by the end user due to the governance through click wrap contract.

One of the main advantages for any provider is that the end user is denied access to the services offered by the provider until he or she assents to the click-wrap terms and conditions (Adam Gat, 2002). Despite being coercive in nature, such approach does facilitate the governance of the services offered. This is also expressed by the cloud provider who has participated in interview. Moreover, the cloud providers have also specified that click wrap contract consumes lesser time and is more efficient. It is clearly impractical, if not impossible, and it would be significantly inefficient for a provider to separately negotiate terms, bargain, and enter into contracts with each and every consumer on an individual basis (Adam Gat, 2002). For cloud providers, disallowing negotiation can reduce legal liabilities and other risks and warranties that may be otherwise be borne (W. Kuan Hon, Christopher Millard & Ian Walden, 2012). It has also been noted that some even large cloud provider does not comprise of an adequate legal team to allow negotiation and deal with users' requests to change terms (W. Kuan Hon, Christopher Millard & Ian Walden, 2012). G Asia Pacific, one of the providers who was interviewed for the purpose of this study have mentioned that they do not comprise of a legal team and depend on their external lawyer to manage the terms of the contract. In spite of that, the end user will also profit from a reduced subscription fee which would other be much higher if negotiation is allowed for all cloud contracts (W. Kuan Hon, Christopher Millard & Ian Walden, 2012).

Such contract is generally thought to be a form of adhesion contract. It is said to lay a beneficial part in the economy. It is said that the terms that are found in a click wrap contract does provide economic benefit as it provides certainty as to how and where a future dispute will be litigated (Kaustuv M. Das, 2002). The cloud provider can also determine the fees according to the liability that it has given thus allowing a lower price for contract that contains limited liability. Despite the fact that click wrap contract provides benefit in terms of commerce, a balance should be prevalent in ensuring that unfair terms are not included that may affect the privacy and the security of the personal data in the cloud infrastructure.

REFERENCES

Akbar, A. (2011). *Exclusion Clauses and the Reasonableness Test*. https://www.lawdit.co.uk/news/473/10/Exclusion-Clauses-and-the-Reasonableness-Test

Bartolini, C., & Siry, L. (2016). The right to be forgotten in the light of the consent of the data subject. *Computer Law & Security Review, 32*(2), 218–237. doi:10.1016/j.clsr.2016.01.005

Bradshaw, S., Millard, C., & Walden, I. (2010). Contracts for Clouds: Comparison and Analysis of the Terms and Conditions of Cloud Computing Services. *Queen Mary School of Law Legal Studies*. https://ssrn.com/abstract=1662374 doi:10.2139/ssrn.1662374

Buck, K., Hanf, D., & Harper, D. (2015). *Cloud SLA Considerations for the Government Consumer Case Number 15-2504 J*. https://www.mitre.org/sites/default/files/publications/pr_15-2504.pdf

Coyne, A. (2017). Dropbox 'inadvertently' kept users' deleted files for up to 7 years. *IT News*. https://www.itnews.com.au/news/dropbox-inadvertently-kept-users-deleted-files-for-up-to-7-years-448676

Das. (2002). *Comment, Forum-Selection Clauses in Consumer Clickwrap and Browsewrap Agreements and the "Reasonably Communicated"*. Academic Press.

Dropbox Acceptable Use Policy. (n.d.). https://www.dropbox.com/privacy#acceptable_use>

ENISA. (2009). *Benefits, risks and recommendations for information security*. https://resilience.enisa.europa.eu/cloud-security-and-resilience/publications/cloud-computing-benefits-risks-and-recommendations-for-information-security

Flicker Guidelines. (n.d.). https://www.flickr.com/help/guidelines

Gat, A. (2002). *Electronic Commerce — Click-Wrap Contracts The Enforceability Of Click-Wrap Agreements*. https://edisciplinas.usp.br/pluginfile.php/2056275/mod_resource/content/1/enforceability%20of%20clickwrap%20%28Adam%20Gatt%29.pdf

Google Privacy Policy. (n.d.). https://policies.google.com/privacy

Hon, Millard, & Walden. (2012). Negotiating cloud contracts: Looking at clouds from both sides. *Stan. Tech. L. Rev., 79*.

iWork.com Public Beta Terms of Service. (n.d.). https://www.apple.com/legal/iworkcom/en/terms.html

L'oreal Sa And Others V Ebay International Ag And Others [2009] EWHC 1094 (Ch), [2009] RPC 21

Maughan, A., Ford, C. D., & Stevenson, S. W. (2014). *Negotiating Cloud Contract*. https://media2.mofo.com/documents/141217negotiatingcloudcontracts.pdf

McLelland, R., Hackett, Y., Hurley, G., & Collins, D. (2014). *Agreements between Cloud Service Providers and their Clients: A Review of Contract Terms*. <https://www.girona.cat/web/ica2014/ponents/textos/id210.pdf>

Meiklejohn, A. M. (1994). Castles in the Air: Blanket Assent and the Revision of Article 2. *Washington and Lee Law Review*. https://scholarlycommons.law.wlu.edu/cgi/viewcontent.cgi?article=1602&context=wlulr

Nayak, Narendra, & Shukla. (2018). *Saranyu: Using Smart Contracts and Blockchain for Cloud Tenant Management Salesforce Master Subscription Agreement*. https://www.salesforce.com/content/dam/web/en_us/www/documents/legal/salesforce_MSA.pdf

O'Shields, R. (2017). *Smart Contracts: Legal Agreements for the Blockchain*. https://scholarship.law.unc.edu/cgi/viewcontent.cgi?referer=&httpsredir=1&article=1435&context=ncbi

OECD. (2014). *Cloud Computing: The Concept, Impacts and the Role of Government Policy*. OECD Digital Economy Papers, No. 240, OECD Publishing. doi:10.1787/5jxzf4lcc7f5-en

Oracle. (2019). *Data Processing Agreement for Oracle Cloud Services*. https://www.oracle.com/us/corporate/contracts/data-processing-agreement-011218-4261005.pdf

Patel, Ranabahu, & Sheth. (n.d.). *Service Level Agreement in Cloud Computing*. Knoesis Center, Wright State University.

Rackspace Terms of Use. (n.d.). https://www.rackspace.com/information/legal/websiteterms

Rashid, F. Y. (2017). *Don't get bit by zombie cloud data*. https://www.infoworld.com/article/3190131/security/dont-get-bit-by-zombie-cloud-data.html

Robert a. Hillman & Jeffrey j. Rach.insri, N.Y.U. Law (2002) Standard-Form Contracting In The Electronic Age. NYU Law Review. http://www.nyulawreview.org/sites/default/files/pdf/NYULawReview-77-2-Hillman-Rachlinski.pdf

Rohrmann & Cunha. (2015). Some legal aspects of cloud computing contracts. *Journal of International Commercial Law and Technology*.

Scoca, Uriarte, & De Nicola. (2018). *Smart Contract Negotiation in Cloud Computing*. Academic Press.

Skali Cloud. (n.d.). http://skalicloud.com/v4/wp-content/uploads/2013/10/SKALICloud-Leaflet.pdf

Tehrani, bin Sabaruddin, & Ramanathan. (2017). *The problem of binary distinction in cloud computing and the necessity for a different approach: Positions of the European Union and Canada*. Academic Press.

Tehrani, P. M., Sabaruddin, J. S., & Ramanathan, D. (2018). Cross border data transfer: Complexity of adequate protection and its exceptions. *Computer Law & Security Review, 34*(3), 582-594. http://support.ptc.com/WCMS/files/164830/en/Acceptable_Use_Policy_Cloud_Services_Eng_Jan_2015_2.pdf

Twentieth Century Fox Film Corporation And Another V Newzbin Ltd [2010] [2010] EWHC 608 (Ch) *Unfair Contract Terms Act 1977* S(3)

Yeah Host Terms. (n.d.). https://www.yeahhost.com.my/terms

Zainelabden, Kliazovich, & Bouvry. (2016). *16th IEEE/ACM International Symposium on Cluster, Cloud, and Grid Computing*. https://ieeexplore-ieeeorg.ezproxy.um.edu.my/stamp/stamp.jsp?tp=&arnumber=7515740

ENDNOTE

[1]   In these circumstances, clicking the tab 'I agree' at the end of the terms and agreement presented.

Chapter 11
Bitcoin Prediction Using Multi–Layer Perceptron Regressor, PCA, and Support Vector Regression (SVR):
Prediction Using Machine Learning

Aatif Jamshed

(iD) https://orcid.org/0000-0003-3152-6147

ABES Engineering College, Ghaziabad, India

Asmita Dixit

ABES Engineering College, Ghaziabad, India

ABSTRACT

Bitcoin has gained a tremendous amount of attention lately because of the innate nature of entering cryptographic technologies and money-related units in the fields of banking, cybersecurity, and software engineering. This chapter investigates the effect of Bayesian neural structures or networks (BNNs) with the aid of manipulating the Bitcoin process's timetable. The authors also choose the maximum extensive highlights from Blockchain records that are carefully applied to Bitcoin's marketplace hobby and use it to create templates to enhance the influential display of the new Bitcoin evaluation process. They endorse actual inspection to check and expect the Bitcoin technique, which compares the Bayesian neural network and other clean and non-direct comparison models. The exact tests show that BNN works well for undertaking the Bitcoin price schedule and explain the intense unpredictability of Bitcoin's actual rate.

INTRODUCTION

For a long time, bitcoin price prediction has been a hot topic of study. Bitcoin (Nakamoto, 2008), as a pioneer in the blockchain monetary revolution, plays a significant role in the overall cryptocurrency

DOI: 10.4018/978-1-7998-7927-5.ch011

market capitalization. As a result, the machine learning and data mining communities are very interested in being able to forecast bitcoin price fluctuations and share experiences to better understand what causes bitcoin instability and how to better evaluate associated risks in the cryptocurrency sector. To forecast the bitcoin stock market price, several academics used machine learning algorithms and social media sentiment analysis.

Bitcoin has fallen in recent months, dropping by more than half from its April high of over $35,000. The price of bitcoin is still much higher than it was when it began its most recent surge in October, a bull run that propelled the entire crypto market to a whopping $1.5 trillion before plunging. As per the prediction, bitcoin will supplant the US dollar as the dominant form of global finance by the year 2050, according to a panel of cryptocurrency experts, putting the bitcoin price at just over $66,000 by the end of 2021.

Bitcoin price prediction is done mainly by Neural Network (Multi-Layer Perceptron Regressor), PCA, and Support Vector Regression (SVR). The value of Bitcoin fluctuates similarly to that of a stock, but in a different way. A variety of algorithms are employed to anticipate stock market prices using stock market data. However, the factors that influence Bitcoin are not the same. As a result, it is vital to forecast Bitcoin's value in order to make sound investing decisions. Unlike the stock market, the price of Bitcoin is not affected by business events or interfering governments. As a result, we believe that leveraging machine/deep learning technology to anticipate the price of Bitcoin is very important.

Bitcoin is fruitful figure money brought into the monetary market dependent on its exceptional convention and Nakamoto's precise auxiliary particular (Nakamoto, 2008). In contrast to existing monetary forms with national banks, Bitcoin intends to accomplish total decentralization. Members in the Bitcoin showcase assemble trust connections through the development of blockchain-dependent on cryptography systems utilizing hash capacities. Intrinsic attributes of Bitcoin(Amjad et al.,2017) got from Blockchain advancements have prompted assorted research premiums in the field of financial matters as well as in cryptography and AI.

Bayesian Neural Networks

A modified multi-layer perceptron (MLP) for Bayesian neural systems, which is a general term for ANNs in AI. Across various implementations, programs have been successful, such as Image recognition, concept recognition, common language use, and money-related scheduling. It gets realized that much successful to speak to the intricate time arrangement than the customary straight models(Matta et al.,2015), i.e., autoregressive and moving normally, and so on. The structure of a BNN is developed with various handling units grouped into three classifications: an info layer, a yield layer, and at least one shrouded layer. In particular, neural systems containing beyond what one shrouded layer can explain the selective OR (XOR)

the issue, which can't be tackled by a solitary layer perceptron. Not quite the same as a solitary layer perceptron, which must be directly isolated, they take care of XOR issues by introducing backpropagation calculations and concealed layers(McNally et al.,2018). The concealed layer mapping the first information to another space changes the information that can't be straight isolated into directly distinguishable information.

Loads of a BNN must be learned between the input hidden layer and the covered-up yield layer. Backpropagation alludes to the procedure where loads of shrouded layers are balanced by the mistake of concealed layers spread by the blunder of the yield layer. An enhancement strategy called the delta rule

Figure 1. Multi-layer perceptron regressor
Source: https://www.chegg.com/homework-help/questions-and-ansThe authors

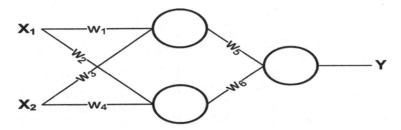

is utilized to limit the contrast between an objective worth and yield esteem when inferring the back-propagation calculation. When all is said in done, BNNs limit the total of the accompanying mistakes, EB, utilizing the backpropagation calculation and delta rule.

As a method to avoid overfitting, Bayesian neural networks are helpful for addressing issues in areas where data is sparse. Molecular biology and medical diagnostics are two examples of applications (areas where data often come from costly and difficult experimental work).

Bayesian Neural Networks (BNNs) is a kind of neural network that uses posterior inference to control overfitting. In a wider sense, the Bayesian approach employs statistical methods to ensure that every-thing, including model parameters, is assigned a probability distribution (Weights and biases in neural networks). Variables that can accept a particular value in programming languages will provide the same outcome every time you access that variable.

Let's start with a basic linear model that predicts the output based on the weighted sum of a set of input characteristics.

- Bayesian neural networks are helpful for preventing overfitting when addressing issues in areas where data is sparse. Molecular biology and medical diagnostics are two examples of applications areas where data often come from costly and difficult experimental work).
- Bayesian networks are very helpful.
- They can improve outcomes for a wide range of jobs, but scaling to big issues is very challenging.
- When dealing with data from unknown targets, BNNs enables you to automatically compute an error associated with your predictions.

It enables you to calculate the degree of uncertainty in forecasts, which is useful in areas like medicine.

Principal Component Analysis

In fact, a central part can be characterized as a straight mix of ideally weighted watched factors. The yield of PCA is these central segments, the quantity of which is not exactly or equivalent to the number of unique factors. Less, in the event that when the article wishes to dispose of or decrease the measure-ments in our dataset. The PCA has some helpful properties which are recorded underneath. The PCA is basically the straight blend of the first factor, the load's vector(Dyhrberg,2016; Bouri et al.,2017) in this mix is really the eigenvector discovered which thusly fulfils the standard of least squares. Henceforth, the PCA is symmetric. As the author move from the first to the last PCA, so the variation in the PCs

Figure 2. Bayesian neural networks (BNNs)
Source: https://miro.medium.com/max/1400/1*ozBVCzy6acVfLuSESiyeBw.png

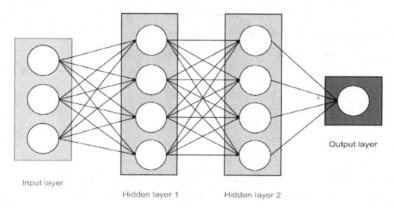

declines, the significance. Furthermore, in some cases, the less significant PCA is useful for recurrence, recognition of anomalies, etc.

Figure 3. Principal component analysis
Source: https://en.wikipedia.org/wiki/Principal_component_analysis/media

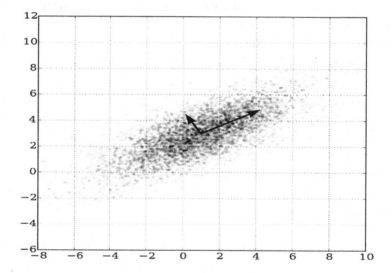

PCA is a method for decreasing the dimensionality of such datasets, improving interpretability while minimising information loss. It does this by generating new uncorrelated variables that optimise variance in a sequential manner. PCA is an adaptive data analysis method because it simplifies finding new variables, the principal components, to solving an eigenvalue/eigenvector problem, and the new variables are determined by the dataset at hand, not a priori. It's adaptable in another way, too, since multiple versions of the method have been created for different data kinds and architectures.

BACKGROUND

With the use of Long Short Term Memory(LSTM)(Mc. Nally et al.,2018)brought the idea of the Bayesian Optimized Recurrent Neural Network(RNN). The outcome is an error rate of 8% and precision 52%. Another work (Chen et al.,2019) uses Random Forest, XGBoost, Quadratic Discriminant Analysis, Vector Support, and LSTM to predict Bitcoin's pricing interval statistics. Looking the same A preliminary examination of the relevance of the sample dimension in machine learning techniques may be considered in our Bitcoin price prediction research. With the use of The min-max standardization, Adam optimization, windows min-max standardization, and other deep learning networks and techniques (Jiang et al.,2020) found the exactness of the results. The used data was from the last 24 hours to forecast the price of Bitcoin for the upcoming one-hour period. A number of models were tested and discovered that the Multi-Layer Perceptron (MLP) is not suitable for the forecasting the current trend due to a lack of available memory, whereas When the previous memory and the Gated Recurrent Network (GRU) are taken into consideration, the Long Short Term Memory (LSTM) gives the most accurate prediction.

In another article the concept of Machine Learning and sentiment analysis is used to predict the price direction of Bitcoin in USD. (Raju et al.,2021) Using sentiment analysis and supervised machine learning methods, the relationship between Bitcoin price movements and emotions in tweets was examined. In order to construct a prediction model, supervised learning experiments were performed on a number of machine learning methods. ARIMA models are hard to work with owing to their inherent complexity. To then use long-term memory cells Recurrent Neural Networks (RNNs) (LSTM) are used. Evaluations are done for the predictability of bitcoin price and sentiment analysis of bitcoin tweets to traditional methodology with the use of long short-term memory (LSTM) models to bitcoin pricing (ARIMA). LSTM (with a single feature) has a lower RMSE (Root-mean-square error) than the ARIMA model, demonstrating that single feature LSTM is more accurate.

Several other research studies the author carried out late to demonstrate Bitcoin's time arrangement as an alternative market variable with explicitly specialized guidelines. The total unpredictability measure Autoregressive Conditional Heteroscedastic (GARCH) is conducted to analyse the timetable of Bitcoin costs (Dyhrberg,2016; Katsiampa,2017). A variety of accurate or prudent characteristics studies and Bitcoin expense portrayals allude to their strengths as a money-related utility. Such exploratory locations are around observable characteristics (Bariviera et al.,2017; Chu et al.,2015), Bitcoin's loss according to the principle of the competitive market (Urquhart,2015; Nadarajah,2017) supportive capacity (Dyhrberg,2016; Bouri et al.,2017), Bitcoin's abstract air pockets (Cheah,2015), linking bitcoin with search data for example.

In fact, hardly any work into the calculation or prediction of Bitcoin costs has been guided to date. Reference (Velankar et al.,2018) assessed Bitcoin's model-dependent value arrangements, taking into account data sorted in a few market power variables, engaging speculators in quality, and the global financial elements of large scale. They predict that Bitcoin will, however, cost with variation after some period the remaining and second factors listed above are fundamentally innocent. Different scientists restrict the number of regressors in order to encourage direct model analysis. (Karasu et al.2018) make predictions about the Bitcoin valuing process using artificial intelligence techniques such as repetitive neural systems (RNNs) and long present moment memory(LSTM), then compare their predictions with those obtained using autoregressive coordinated moving normal (ARIMA) models.

Predictive execution is bad on a system that was prepared uniquely with the Bitcoin value file and altered expenses. For example, the reference (Radityo et al.,2018) examines the accuracy of foreseeing Bitcoin price using binomial strategic relapse, bolster vector machine, and irregular woodland models.

While investigating the Bitcoin time scheme, there are few relevant and purposeful observational examinations that may be conducted. As part of this research, the author conducts a feasible analysis of the Bitcoin protocol in order to explain and forecast it. The author does so by using a Bayesian Neural Network (BNN), which can typically handle a growing number of important evaluation highlights. In a BNN, a legislative idea is combined with the goal of eliminating the overarching question, which is essential to our program's success. It is possible for a machine to become complicated when it takes into account a large number of variables, and the negative consequences of an overfitting issue may be felt by the operator. The budgetary subsidiary protection study was aided by the BNN models, which showed their effect (McNally et al.,2018). When combined with Bitcoin's (Jang and Lee,2017) organic market, the arrangement of the Blockchain distinguishes it from other monetary standards. Although macroeconomic variables have been considered, it has not been attempted to portray the process of Bitcoin cost via direct use of Block-chain data such as the hash rate, challenges, and square age rate. Filling in this gap, the current research effectively evaluates and explains the process of Bitcoin cost by showing and predicting Bitcoin costs based on blockchain data as well as a variety of macroeconomic factors.

ISSUES AND CHALLENGES

There are many difficulties and concerns associated with Bitcoin(Amjad et al.,2017) Prediction. On the basis of neural network prediction, some of them might be summarised as follows:

- They don't have enough analytical evidence to back up their assertions.
- Non-Linear, Complicated Connections: Deep neural networks can simulate non-linear, complex relationships between predictors.
- Robust: Deep learning models have proved to be resilient to the crypto market's continuous changes via constant training.
- Large Research Body: Quantitative finance research in deep learning is expanding at a quicker rate than any other field, resulting in a plethora of research ideas that may be applied to the crypto sector.
- Interpretability: Deep neural networks are complicated and, as a result, difficult to comprehend.
- Costly to Develop: Developing and maintaining deep learning models(Jang & Lee,2017) is computationally expensive.

METHODOLOGY

The proposed methodology for Bit-Coin prediction using Multi-Layer Perceptron Regressor(Radityo et al.,2018) requires various intermediate steps. The initial step involves the reading or capturing of the dataset in a CSV file format. This dataset only reads the head and disintegrates the data columns. Once it has been done the data is divided into training data, validation data, and testing set. This split is fed into Neural Network Regression. Using the SVR classifier the 2-degree regression is applied further the relevant feature selection is done using PCA. the next step involves feature selection using F-Regression which leads to Time-Series Analysis. The predicted graph has experimented on Keras Model Prediction with RNN(LSTM).

Figure 4. Proposed methodology for bit-coin prediction using multi-layer perceptron regressor

IMPLEMENTATION

The Historical Bitcoin dataset, has been taken for testing which is the everyday information from 2017 – 2019. The dataset comprises 8 headers and 266775 examples. With the end goal of the trial, many iterations done with preparing and testing division as 250000 pushes in preparing and rest in testing. Presently there are 8 highlights, which may not be that imperative to our models for learning the examples. Previously it was tested with each of the 8 features on a Neural Network Multi-Layer Perceptron Regressor. The outcome is getting the scaled Root Mean Square Error (RMSE) to be 16.95% and the a similar model is applied to Support Vector Regression (SVR) to correlate.

The approach taken is that of Feature Selection for example choosing the ideal subset out of a lot of as given components. One methodology used is Principal Component Analysis (PCA) which is utilized for dimensionality reduction. The model is re-run on the methods accumulated already and sees the outcomes. Finally, Feature Selection utilizing is applied (F-Regression) to see the autonomy of the highlights and recognize the ideal subset utilizing that.

Stage 1: Normalize the information

The first step is to standardize our information so that PCA functions properly. Eventually, the different strategies are subtracted from the numbers in the particular segment. If the author have two X and Y measurements, all X will be x- and Y will be y-. This provides a dataset with a null mean.

Stage 2: Calculate the covariance framework

Since the dataset the author took is 2-dimensional, this will bring about a 2x2 Covariance framework.

Matrix (Covariance)=[var(x1) Cov(x1,x2) Cov(x2,x1) var(x2)] (1)

Please note that Var(X1) = Cov(X1,X1) and Var(X2) = Cov(X2,X2).

Stage 3: Determine the eigenvalues and eigenvectors of the function.

The eigenvalues and eigenvectors for the covariance framework are calculated in the next step. Due to the fact that it is a square framework, it is possible to create an equivalent. If it is a response to the trademark condition, then it is an eigenvalue for a framework with the property:

Det (I - A) = 0 if and only if

In this case, I represent the network of identities of a common dimension such as A, which is also essential for the subtraction of the frames, and that represents a determinant of the grid. It is possible to find a corresponding proper vector v for any personal value by stating the following: (I - A) v = 0 (I - A)

Stage 4: Choosing the various components

I am the personality network of comparable measurement to A, which is a required requirement for the framework subtraction in this case as well, and it denotes that the grid is determined by the determinant. It is possible to get a corresponding eigenvector v for each eigenvalue by explaining: in addition to the vector structure of an element: They inquire for their own ideas from the highest to the least, which brings us the essential parts. This is the aspect that reduces dimensionality. If the author has a data set with n factors, has the comparative identical values and self-vectors at that point. For unknown reasons, the own vector is the essential part of the dataset as opposed to its highest value and our decision is for what number of values, The author chooses to carry out our work with. For each the quantities, the key proper p values are chosen and the others are ignored and misses some data at the same time, yet the author doesn't lose a lot if our own values are small.

First, for our case, the author is structuring a vector part, which is a vector network. It's only the lines The author needs to start using, reality is being stated. Since in the running model simply has two measures, The author can either select one that relates to the most prominent value or basically takes both.

Feature Vector = (eigen**1**, eigen**2**)

Stage 5: Creating the Primary Components:

This is the last step in organizing the important sections, and it makes use of all of the computations that the article has been concentrating on thus far. The transposition of the product matrix as well as the transposition of the first tuple to the left account for the difference. New data is equal to the product of the feature vector T and the scaled data T.

In this case, new data is the matrix, which is made up of the major components, highlights. Vector is the network which is framed using the eigenvectors and chose to retain and scaled data represents the scaled rendition of the initial dataset (the 'T' in the superscript represents the transposition of a grid, which is framed by swapping the lines for sections and the other way around). The size of the transposition in the case of a **2x3** grid is **3x2**).

In particular, if the author puts our own vectors in a scattered information system in the running case of 2-D, it turns out that the head-in-vector is really well-fit for the information (in terms of the highest value of its own).

All of the grid's own dimensions are opposite to each other. In this line, the first dataset in PCA, using these symmetrical (opposite) vectors, is talked to or changed from the typical x and y tomahawks. Our information targets were now ordered as a mixture of x and y commitments. The distinction is when one or many vectors are simply declined, thereby that the dataset dimension.

RESULT AND ANALYSIS

In this section, the article shows the results of our BMM model. It was noted during training that the higher the batch size of 200 the worst the prediction on the test set. Since the more training, the more prone to overfitting the model becomes. But the unique suggested approach not only captures Bitcoin's representation but also aggregates the hidden representations of other cryptocurrencies. The experimental findings indicate that the specified features are appropriate for our issue, and our proposed model outperforms all baselines with state-of-the-art performance. In addition, the article assesses the effect of different factors on our issues. Figure 4 below shows the graphical representation between the time duration and the bit Coin Rate. With every passing year, Bitcoin rates are towards the increasing end. In figure 5 given below on every year Bitcoin prediction is calculated on the training dataset using Bayesian Neural Network and validated on the test set. It can be observed that there is a gradual increase in the rate of Bitcoin Prediction.

CONCLUSION

Bitcoin is effective cryptographic money, and it has been widely contemplated in fields of financial matters and software engineering. The objective of the proposed work is met with a continuous regression applied via Bayesian Neural Network and the best feature dimensionality selected by Principal Component Analysis on the separated training, test, and validation dataset in the form of a CSV file format. In this examination, the author breaks down the time arrangement of Bitcoin costs with a BNN utilizing Block-chain data notwithstanding macroeconomic factors and addresses the ongoing exceptionally unpredictable Bitcoin costs. Thanks to the details, exploratory results show that the BNN model with the highlights selected is efficient with Bitcoin log cost procedures and log instability. The evaluation of the method provisionally shows BNN's esteemed implementation is equivalent to other tests on the Bitcoin log expense and volatility procedures.

Figure 5. Prediction set of bitcoin with respect to time

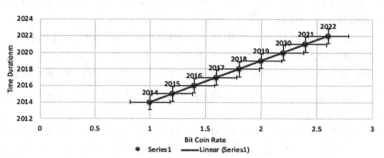

Through an experimental study, the BNN model represents the volatility in Bitcoin, usually later until August 2017. The BNN model does not usually prevail precisely as other benchmark models that anticipated a bomb direction. The BNN model is based on these test results so that subsequent knowledge can be tested comparably. With respect to the context of Bitcoin applications, it is common for the expansion and use of the BNN model to be feasible for the Bitcoin network inquiry and anticipation. Researching nonlinear connections between input capacities dependent on arranging investigation can clarify the examination of the Bitcoin value time arrangement. The fluctuation of Bitcoin must be demonstrated and anticipated all the more suitably. This objective can be accomplished by receiving other expanded AI techniques or considering new information capacities identified with the changeability of Bitcoin. Such an examination will add to rich bitcoin time arrangement investigation notwithstanding existing Bitcoin studies.

FUTURE RESEARCH DIRECTIONS AND APPLICATION

PCA is broadly used in spaces inclusive of facial recognition, PC perception, and visual pressure to reduce dimensionality. It is also used to explore designs for high-quality accounting, database processing, bioinformatics, brain research, etc. data measurement knowledge. Our research may pave the way for a real-world trading environment for investors in the future.

Figure 6. Training data set prediction

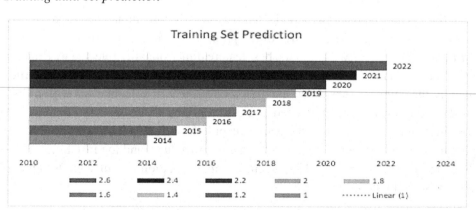

REFERENCES

Amjad, M., & Shah, D. (2017, February). Trading bitcoin and online time series prediction. In *NIPS 2016 Time Series Workshop* (pp. 1-15). PMLR.

Bariviera, A. F., Basgall, M. J., Hasperué, W., & Naiouf, M. (2017). Some stylized facts of the Bitcoin market. *Physica A*, *484*, 82–90. doi:10.1016/j.physa.2017.04.159

Bouri, E., Molnár, P., Azzi, G., Roubaud, D., & Hagfors, L. I. (2017). On the hedge and safe haven properties of Bitcoin: Is it really more than a diversifier? *Finance Research Letters*, *20*, 192–198. doi:10.1016/j.frl.2016.09.025

Cheah, E. T., & Fry, J. (2015). Speculative bubbles in Bitcoin markets? An empirical investigation into the fundamental value of Bitcoin. *Economics Letters*, *130*, 32–36. doi:10.1016/j.econlet.2015.02.029

Chen, Z., Li, C., & Sun, W. (2020). Bitcoin price prediction using machine learning: An approach to sample dimension engineering. *Journal of Computational and Applied Mathematics*, *365*, 112395.

Chu, J., Nadarajah, S., & Chan, S. (2015). Statistical analysis of the exchange rate of bitcoin. *PLoS One*, *10*(7), e0133678. doi:10.1371/journal.pone.0133678 PMID:26222702

Dyhrberg, A. H. (2016). Bitcoin, gold and the dollar–A GARCH volatility analysis. *Finance Research Letters*, *16*, 85–92. doi:10.1016/j.frl.2015.10.008

Dyhrberg, A. H. (2016). Hedging capabilities of bitcoin. Is it virtual gold? *Finance Research Letters*, *16*, 139–144. doi:10.1016/j.frl.2015.10.025

Jang, H., & Lee, J. (2017). An empirical study on modelling and prediction of bitcoin prices with bayesian neural networks based on blockchain information. *IEEE Access: Practical Innovations, Open Solutions*, *6*, 5427–5437. doi:10.1109/ACCESS.2017.2779181

Jiang, X. (2019). Bitcoin price prediction based on deep learning methods. *Journal of Mathematical Finance*, *10*(1), 132–139.

Jiang, Y., Nie, H., & Ruan, W. (2018). Time-varying long-term memory in the Bitcoin market. *Finance Research Letters*, *25*, 280–284. doi:10.1016/j.frl.2017.12.009

Karasu, S., Altan, A., Saraç, Z., & Hacioğlu, R. (2018, May). Prediction of Bitcoin prices with machine learning methods using time series data. In *2018 26th signal processing and communications applications conference (SIU)* (pp. 1-4). IEEE. 10.1109/SIU.2018.8404760

Katsiampa, P. (2017). *Volatility estimation for Bitcoin: A comparison of GA*. Academic Press.

Matta, M., Lunesu, I., & Marchesi, M. (2015, June). Bitcoin Spread Prediction Using Social and The author Search Media. In UMAP workshops (pp. 1-10). Academic Press.

McNally, S., Roche, J., & Caton, S. (2018, March). Predicting the price of bitcoin using machine learning. In *2018 26th euro micro international conference on parallel, distributed and network-based processing (PDP)* (pp. 339-343). IEEE. 10.1109/PDP2018.2018.00060

McNally, S., Roche, J., & Caton, S. (2018, March). Predicting the price of bitcoin using machine learning. In *2018 26th euro micro international conference on parallel, distributed and network-based processing (PDP)* (pp. 339-343). IEEE.

Nakamoto, S. (2008). Bitcoin: A peer-to-peer electronic cash system. *Decentralized Business Review*, 21260.

Radityo, A., Munajat, Q., & Budi, I. (2017, October). Prediction of Bitcoin exchange rate to American dollar using artificial neural network methods. In *2017 International Conference on Advanced Computer Science and Information Systems (ICACSIS)* (pp. 433-438). IEEE. 10.1109/ICACSIS.2017.8355070

Raju, S. M., & Tarif, A. M. (2020). *Real-Time Prediction of BITCOIN Price using Machine Learning Techniques and Public Sentiment Analysis*. arXiv preprint arXiv:2006.14473.

Urquhart, A. (2016). The inefficiency of Bitcoin. *Economics Letters*, *148*, 80–82. doi:10.1016/j.econlet.2016.09.019

Velankar, S., Valecha, S., & Maji, S. (2018, February). Bitcoin price prediction using machine learning. In *2018 20th International Conference on Advanced Communication Technology (ICACT)* (pp. 144-147). IEEE.

Compilation of References

ILCS 730 Blockchain Technology Act, (2020).

NY Comp Codes Rules and Regs §, (2015). https://govt.westlaw.com/nycrr/Browse/Home/NewYork/NewYorkCodesRulesandRegulations?guid=I7444ce80169611e594630000845b8d3e&originationContext=documenttoc&transitionType=Default&contextData=(sc.Default)&bhcp=1

A Big Lesson from the Delaware Blockchain Amendments. (2018). https://koreprotocol.medium.com/a-big-lesson-from-the-delaware-blockchain-amendments-9789e34f6c9f

ACT No. XXXI of 2018, (2018).

ACT No. XXXIII of 2018, (2018).

Admin, A. W. S. (2019). Ondiflo is using Blockchain to Revolutionize Oil and Gas Industry. *AWS Startups Blog*. https://aws.amazon.com/blogs/startups/ondiflo-is-using-blockchain-to-revolutionize-the-oil-and-gas-industry/

Administrative Commission of Zhongguancun Science Park. (2018, November 9). *Notice on printing and distributing the Beijing Fintech Development Plan (2018-2022)*. Available at: http://zgcgw.beijing.gov.cn/zgc/zwgk/ghjh/179396/index.html

Ahluwalia, S., Mahto, R. V., & Guerrero, M. (2020). Blockchain technology and startup financing: A transaction cost economics perspective. *Technological Forecasting and Social Change, 151*, 119854. doi:10.1016/j.techfore.2019.119854

Akar, S., & Akar, E. (2020). Is it a New Tulip Mania Age? A Comprehensive Literature Review Beyond Cryptocurrencies, Bitcoin, and Blockchain Technology. *Journal of Information Technology Research, 13*(1), 44–67. doi:10.4018/JITR.2020010104

Akbar, A. (2011). *Exclusion Clauses and the Reasonableness Test*. https://www.lawdit.co.uk/news/473/10/Exclusion-Clauses-and-the-Reasonableness-Test

Akgiray, V. (2019). *The Potential for Blockchain Technology in Corporate Governance*. OECD Publishing. https://www.oecd-ilibrary.org/content/paper/ef4eba4c-en

Alam, T. (2019). IoT-Fog: A communication framework using blockchain in the internet of things. *International Journal of Recent Technology and Engineering, 7*(6).

Alasbali, N., Azzuhri, S., & Salleh, R. (2020). A Blockchain-Based Smart Network for IoT-Driven Smart Cities. *Proceedings of the 2020 2nd International Electronics Communication Conference*.

Alketbi, A., Nasir, Q., & Talib, M. A. (2018). Blockchain for government services—Use cases, security benefits and challenges. *2018 15th Learning and Technology Conference (L&T)*.

Allen & Overy LLP. (2016). *Decentralized Autonomous Organization*. Retrieved from Allen & Overy LLP website: https://www.allenovery.com/en-gb/global/news-and-insights/publications/decentralized-autonomous-organizations

Allen, J. G., Rauchs, M., Blandin, A., & Bear, K. (2020). *Legal and Regulatory Considerations for Digital Assets*. https://www.jbs.cam.ac.uk/wp-content/uploads/2020/10/2020-ccaf-legal-regulatory-considerations-report.pdf

Allessie, D., Sobolewski, M., & Vaccari, L. (2019). *Blockchain for digital government*. https://joinup.ec.europa.eu/sites/default/files/document/2019-04/JRC115049%20blockchain%20for%20digital%20government.pdf

Al-Megren, S., Alsalamah, S., Altoaimy, L., Alsalamah, H., Soltanisehat, L., & Almutairi, E. (2018). Blockchain use cases in digital sectors: A review of the literature. *2018 IEEE International Conference on Internet of Things (iThings) and IEEE Green Computing and Communications (GreenCom) and IEEE Cyber, Physical and Social Computing (CPSCom) and IEEE Smart Data (SmartData)*.

Altoros. (2017). A Close Look at Everledger - How Blockchain Secures Luxury Goods. *Medium*. https://medium.com/altoros-blog/a-close-look-at-everledger-how-blockchain-secures-luxury-goods-5c3447d07373

Amjad, M., & Shah, D. (2017, February). Trading bitcoin and online time series prediction. In *NIPS 2016 Time Series Workshop* (pp. 1-15). PMLR.

Andoni, M., Robu, V., Flynn, D., Abram, S., Geach, D., Jenkin, D. P., McCallum, P., & Peacock, A. (2019). Blockchain Technology in the Energy Sector: A Systematic Review of Challenges and Opportunities. *Renewable and Sustainable Energy Reviews*, *100*, 143-174. doi:10.1016/j.rser.2018.10.014

Anti-Money Laundering Act of 10 October 1997, (1997).

Anti-Money Laundering Council. (2014). *Warning Advisory on Virtual Currencies*. http://www.amlc.gov.ph/2015-12-09-07-34-10/2015-12-14-04-11-34/request-for-amla-training/2-uncategorised/60-warning-advisory-on-virtual-currencies

AP. (2020). *China, top global emitter, aims to go carbon-neutral by 2060*. Retrieved from https://apnews.com/article/climate-climate-change-paris-xi-jinping-emissions-reduction-7a4216ad4026090adb8d600fab210406

Artemov, N. M., Arzumanova, L. L., Sitnik, A. A., & Zenin, S. S. (2017). Regulation and Control of Virtual Currency: To be or not to be. *J. Advanced Res. L. Econ.*, *8*, 1428.

Article 19. (2018). *Privacy and Freedom of Expression In the Age of Artificial Intelligence*. https://www.article19.org/wp-content/uploads/2018/04/Privacy-and-Freedom-of-Expression-In-the-Age-of-Artificial-Intelligence-1.pdf

Atiyah, P. S. (1971). *Consideration in Contracts: A Fundamental Restatement*. Australian National University Press Canberra.

Attaran, M. (2020). Blockchain technology in healthcare: Challenges and opportunities. *International Journal of Healthcare Management*, 1-14. doi:10.1080/20479700.2020.1843887

Autoriti Monetari Brunei Darussalam. (2017). *Public to Exercise High Caution with Cryptocurrencies*. https://www.ambd.gov.bn/

Autoriti Monetari Brunei Darussalam. (2018). *Autoriti Monetari Brunei Darussalam Reiterates Position on Cryptocurrencies*. https://ambd.gov.bn/

Back, A. (2002). *Hashcash-a denial of service counter-measure*. Academic Press.

Baghery, K. (2019). On the efficiency of privacy-preserving smart contract systems. *International Conference on Cryptology in Africa*. Beijing AI. https://www.baai.ac.cn/news/beijing-ai-principles-en.html

Bag, S., Ruj, S., & Sakurai, K. (2016). Bitcoin block withholding attack: Analysis and mitigation. *IEEE Transactions on Information Forensics and Security*, 1967–1978.

Baker, J. (2021). Blockchain and Sustainability: Oxymoron or Panacea? *Forbes*. https://www.forbes.com/sites/jessibaker/2021/05/25/blockchain-and-sustainability-oxymoron-or-panacea/?sh=6bfcca239af9

Balzli, T. R. (2021). *New tech act in Switzerland secures legal environment, allows blockchain to flourish*. Retrieved June 30, 2021 from https://www.imd.org/news/updates/new-tech-act-Switzerland-secures-legal-environment-blockchain-flourish/

Banafa, A. (2019). *Blockchain and AI: A Perfect Match?* https://www.bbvaopenmind.com/en/technology/artificial-intelligence/blockchain-and-ai-a-perfect-match/

Bangko Sentral ng Pilipinas. (2017). *BSP Circular No. 944*. https://www.bsp.gov.ph/Regulations/Issuances/2017/c944.pdf

Bank for International Settlements. (2018). *Annual Economic Report*. https://www.bis.org/publ/arpdf/ar2018e.pdf

Bariviera, A. F., Basgall, M. J., Hasperué, W., & Naiouf, M. (2017). Some stylized facts of the Bitcoin market. *Physica A*, *484*, 82–90. doi:10.1016/j.physa.2017.04.159

Bartolini, C., & Siry, L. (2016). The right to be forgotten in the light of the consent of the data subject. *Computer Law & Security Review*, *32*(2), 218–237. doi:10.1016/j.clsr.2016.01.005

Bashir, I. (2018). *Mastering Blockchain: Distributed ledger technology, decentralization, and smart contracts explained* (2nd ed.). Packt Publishing. https://books.google.com.my/books?id=3ZlUDwAAQBAJ

Baum, A. (2021). Tokenization—The Future of Real Estate Investment? *Journal of Portfolio Management*, *47*(7).

Bayle, A., Koscina, M., Manset, D., & Perez-Kempner, O. (2018). When blockchain meets the right to be forgotten: technology versus law in the healthcare industry. *2018 IEEE/WIC/ACM International Conference on Web Intelligence (WI)*.

Bejleri, E., & Fishta, A. (2017). Toward Virtual Business. *Mediterranean Journal of Social Sciences*, *8*(3), 275–280. doi:10.5901/mjss.2017.v8n3p275

Belchior, R., Vasconcelos, A., Guerreiro, S., & Correia, M. (2021). *A Survey on Blockchain Interoperability: Past, Present, and Future Trends*. arXiv:2005.14282

Benčić, F. M., & Žarko, I. P. (2018, July). Distributed ledger technology: Blockchain compared to directed acyclic graph. In *2018 IEEE 38th International Conference on Distributed Computing Systems (ICDCS)* (pp. 1569-1570). IEEE. doi:10.2139srn.3638991

Benjamins, R., Barbado, A., & Sierra, D. (2019). Responsible AI by Design in Practice. *Proceedings of the Human-Centered AI: Trustworthiness of AI Models & Data (HAI) track at AAAI Fall Symposium*.

Bennear, L. S., & Wiener, J. B. (2019). *Adaptive Regulation: Instrument Choice for Policy Learning over Time*. https://www.hks.harvard.edu/sites/default/files/centers/mrcbg/files/Wiener_2.14.19.transcript.pdf

Bentov, I., Lee, C., & Mizrahi, A. (2014). Proof of activity: Extending bitcoin's proof of work via proof of stake [extended abstract]. *Performance Evaluation Review*, 34–37.

Bessemer, C. (2019). Cryptocurrency: Legality and Role within US Financial Institutions. *Syracuse J. Sci.Tech. L.*, *36*, 3.

Biden, J. (2020). *The Biden plan for a clean energy revolution and environmental justice*. Retrieved from https://joebiden.com/climate-plan

Black, J. (2007). *Principles based regulation: risks, challenges and opportunities*. http://eprints.lse.ac.uk/62814/

Black, J. (2008). Forms and paradoxes of principles-based regulation. *Capital Markets Law Journal, 3*(4), 425–457. doi:10.1093/cmlj/kmn026

Black, J., Hopper, M., & Band, C. (2007). Making a success of principles-based regulation. *Law Financial Markets Review, 1*(3), 191–206. doi:10.1080/17521440.2007.11427879

Blakstad, S., & Allen, R. (2018). *FinTech Revolution: Universal Inclusion in the New Financial Ecosystem.* Springer International Publishing. https://books.google.com.my/books?id=0_VeDwAAQBAJ

Blockchain Working Group. (2020). *Blockchain in California: A Roadmap.* https://www.govops.ca.gov/blockchain/

Bonneville Environmental Foundation. (2016). *What Are Renewable Energy Certificates (RECs)?* http://www.b-e-f.org/learn/what-are-renewable-energy-certificates/

Bouri, E., Molnár, P., Azzi, G., Roubaud, D., & Hagfors, L. I. (2017). On the hedge and safe haven properties of Bitcoin: Is it really more than a diversifier? *Finance Research Letters, 20*, 192–198. doi:10.1016/j.frl.2016.09.025

Bourque, S., & Tsui, S. F. L. (2014). A Lawyer's Introduction to Smart Contracts. *Scientia Nobilitat Reviewed Legal Studies*, 4–23.

Bradshaw, S., Millard, C., & Walden, I. (2010). Contracts for Clouds: Comparison and Analysis of the Terms and Conditions of Cloud Computing Services. *Queen Mary School of Law Legal Studies.* https://ssrn.com/abstract=1662374 doi:10.2139/ssrn.1662374

Braithwaite, C. (2020). *Blockchain in Energy Markets.* lisk.com/blog/research/blockchain-energy-markets.

Brank, L., Dunaev, P., & Korotkova, E. (2021). *Russian Laws Advance Framework for the Use and Regulation of Digital Financial Assets and Currency.* https://www.jdsupra.com/legalnews/russian-laws-advance-framework-for-the-9925457/

Braun-Dubler, N., Gier, H. P., Bulatnikova, T., Langhart, M., Merki, M., Roth, F., ... der ETH Zürich, H. A. G. (2020). *Blockchain: Capabilities, Economic Viability, and the Socio-Technical Environment.* vdf Hochschulverlag ETH Zurich. https://books.google.com.my/books?id=QLbrDwAAQBAJ

Brilliantovaa, V., & Thurne, T. W. (2019). Blockchain and the future of energy. *Technology in Society, 57*, 38–54. doi:10.1016/j.techsoc.2018.11.001

Brownsword, R., & Goodwin, M. (2012). *Law and the Technologies of the Twenty-First Century: Text and Materials.* Cambridge University Press. doi:10.1017/CBO9781139047609

Brukhanskyi, R., & Spilnyk, I. (2019). Cryptographic objects in the accounting system. *2019 9th International Conference on Advanced Computer Information Technologies (ACIT).*

Bruyn, A. S. (2017). *Blockchain, an Introduction.* University Amsterdam.

Buccafurri, F., Lax, G., Nicolazzo, S., & Nocera, A. (2017). Overcoming limits of blockchain for IoT applications. *Proceedings of the 12th International Conference on Availability, Reliability and Security*, 1-6.

Buchanan, K. (2019). *Regulatory Approaches to Cryptoassets in Selected Jurisdictions-Indonesia.* https://www.lawscopelibrary.com/admin/articles/regulatory-approaches-to-cryptoassets-in-selected-jurisdictions/cryptoasset-regulation.pdf

Buck, K., Hanf, D., & Harper, D. (2015). *Cloud SLA Considerations for the Government Consumer Case Number 15-2504 J.* https://www.mitre.org/sites/default/files/publications/pr_15-2504.pdf

Bu, G. G.-B. (2019). G-iota: Fair and confidence aware tangle. In *IEEE Conference on Computer Communica- tions Workshops (INFOCOM WKSHPS)* (pp. pp. 644–649.). IEEE.

Burger, C., Kuhlmann, A., Richard, P., & Weinmann, J. (2016). *Blockchain in the energy transition a survey among decision-makers in the German energy industry.* https://shop.dena.de/fileadmin/denashop/media/Downloads_Dateien/esd/9165_Blockchain_in_der_Energiewende_englisch.pdf

Buterin, V. (2016). *A Next Generation Smart Contract and Decentralized Application Platform.* Ethereum White Paper.

Buttigieg, C. P., & Efthymiopoulos, C. (2019). The regulation of crypto assets in Malta: The virtual financial assets act and beyond. *Law Financial Markets Review, 13*(1), 30–40.

Buttigieg, C. P., Efthymiopoulos, C., Attard, A., & Cuyle, S. (2019). Anti-money laundering regulation of crypto assets in Europe's smallest member state. *Law Financial Markets Review, 13*(4), 211–227.

Cahill, D. G., Baur, D. G., Liu, Z. F., & Yang, J. W. (2020). I am a Blockchain too: How does the market respond to companies' interest in Blockchain? *Journal of Banking & Finance*, 105740. doi:10.1016/j.jbankfin.2020.105740

Carley, S., & Konisky, D. M. (2020). The justice and equity implications of the clean energy transition. *Nature Energy, 5*(8), 569–577. doi:10.103841560-020-0641-6

Castro, D., & McQuinn, A. (2019). *A Policymaker's Guide to Blockchain.* https://itif.org/publications/2019/04/30/policymakers-guide-blockchain

Castro, M. (1999). Practical Byzantine fault tolerance. OSDI, 99, 173-186.

Cath, C., Wachter, S., Mittelstadt, B., Taddeo, M., & Floridi, L. (2018). Artificial intelligence and the 'good society': The US, EU, and UK approach. *Science and Engineering Ethics, 24*(2), 505–528. doi:10.100711948-017-9901-7 PMID:28353045

Caytas, J. (2017). Blockchain in the US regulatory setting: Evidentiary use in Vermont, Delaware, and elsewhere. *The Columbia Science and Technology Law Review.*

CBIRC. (2020a, Mar.31). *Notice on Promoting the Incremental Expansion, Quality Improvement and Cost Reduction of Financial Services for Small and Micro Enterprises in 2020.* Available at: http://www.cbirc.gov.cn/cn/view/pages/govermentDetail.html?docId=896876&itemId=878&generaltype=1

CBIRC. (2020b, Jul.17). *The Interim Measures for the Management of Internet loans of commercial banks.* Available at: http://www.gov.cn/xinwen/2020-07/17/content_5527714.htm

Chang, S. E., Luo, H. L., & Chen, Y. (2020). Blockchain-Enabled Trade Finance Innovation: A Potential Paradigm Shift on Using Letter of Credit. *Sustainability, 12*(1), 188. doi:10.3390u12010188

Cheah, E. T., & Fry, J. (2015). Speculative bubbles in Bitcoin markets? An empirical investigation into the fundamental value of Bitcoin. *Economics Letters, 130*, 32–36. doi:10.1016/j.econlet.2015.02.029

Chen, G., Xu, B., Lu, M., & Chen, N.-S. (2018). Exploring blockchain technology and its potential applications for education. *Smart Learning Environments, 5*(1), 1–10.

Chen, L., Xu, L., Shah, N., Gao, Z., Lu, Y., & Shi, W. (2017, November). On security analysis of proof-of-elapsed-time (poet). In *International Symposium on Stabilization, Safety, and Security of Distributed Systems* (pp. 282-297). Springer. 10.1007/978-3-319-69084-1_19

Chen, R. Y. (2018). A traceability chain algorithm for artificial neural networks using T–S fuzzy cognitive maps in blockchain. *Future Generation Computer Systems*, 198–210.

Chen, Z., Li, C., & Sun, W. (2020). Bitcoin price prediction using machine learning: An approach to sample dimension engineering. *Journal of Computational and Applied Mathematics, 365*, 112395.

China News. (2020, December 9). *The Digital Currency Research Institute of the People's Bank of China signed a strategic cooperation agreement with UnionPay.* Available at: http://www.szzg.gov.cn/2020/szzg/gzdt/202012/ t20201209_5478980.htm

China Securities News. (2019, December 3). *CBIRC: Encourage insurance companies to conduct data docking with third-party credit reference institutions and various big data institutions.* Available at: http://ddcredit.dandong.gov.cn/ zh/News_18951.html

Chohan, U. W. (2017). The Decentralized Autonomous Organization and Governance Issues. SSRN *Electronic Journal,* (April). doi:10.2139/ssrn.3082055

Chokor, A., & Alfieri, E. (2021). Long and short-term Impacts of Regulation in the Cryptocurrency Market. *The Quarterly Review of Economics and Finance.*

Chou, I., Su, H., Hsueh, Y., & Hsueh, C. (2020). BC-Store: A Scalable Design for Blockchain Storage. *Proceedings of the 2020 2nd International Electronics Communication Conference,* 33-38.

Chu, J., Nadarajah, S., & Chan, S. (2015). Statistical analysis of the exchange rate of bitcoin. *PLoS One, 10*(7), e0133678. doi:10.1371/journal.pone.0133678 PMID:26222702

Cioara, T., Pop, C., Zanc, R., Anghel, I., Antal, M., & Salomie, I. (2020). Smart Grid Management Using Blockchain: Future Scenarios and Challenges. *19th RoEduNet Conference: Networking in Education and Research (RoEduNet).* 10.1109/RoEduNet51892.2020.9324874

Clarke, R. (2019). Regulatory alternatives for AI. *Computer Law & Security Review, 35*(4), 398–409. doi:10.1016/j. clsr.2019.04.008

Clayton, J. (2017). *Statement on Cryptocurrencies and Initial Coin Offerings.* https://www.sec.gov/news/public-statement/ statement-clayton-2017-12-11

CO Rev Stat § 11-110, (2018).

CodeC. (2015). https://www.economica.vn/Content/files/LAW%20%26%20REG/91_2015_QH13%20Civil%20Code.pdf

Código Orgánico Monetario, Y. Financiero. (2014). http://www.pge.gob.ec/documents/Transparencia/antilavado/REG-ISTROOFICIAL332.pdf

Coeckelbergh, M., Loh, J., Funk, M., Seibt, J., & Nørskov, M. (2018). *Envisioning Robots in Society – Power, Politics, and Public Space: Proceedings of Robophilosophy.* IOS Press. https://books.google.com.my/books?id=jLh9DwAAQBAJ

Cohen, J. (2019). *Cryptocurrency Regulations in Mainland Southeast Asia.* https://www.tilleke.com/wp-content/up-loads/2019/09/Cryptocurrency-Regulations-in-Mainland-Southeast-Asia_0.pdf

Colorado Department of Regulatory Agencies. (2018). *Interim Regulatory Guidance Cryptocurrency and the Colorado Money Transmitters Act.* Author.

Commissioner for Revenue. (2018). *Guidelines on the Income Tax Treatment of transactions or arrangements involving DLT Assets.* https://cfr.gov.mt/en/inlandrevenue/legal-technical/Documents/Guidelines%20-DLTs%20Income%20tax.pdf

Commodity Exchange Act, (1936).

Commodity Futures Trading Comm'n v. McDonnell, F. Supp. 3d 287 (Dist. Court, ED New York 2018).

Condos, J., Sorrell, W. H., & Donegan, S. L. (2016). *Blockchain Technology: Opportunities and Risks.* https://sos.ver-mont.gov/media/253f2tpu/vermontstudycommittee_blockchaintechnology_opportunitiesandrisks_finalreport_2016.pdf

Corbin, A. L. (1916). Offer and Acceptance, and Some of the Resulting Legal Relations. *The Yale Law Journal, 26*(169), 169–206.

Coyne, A. (2017). Dropbox 'inadvertently' kept users' deleted files for up to 7 years. *IT News*. https://www.itnews.com.au/news/dropbox-inadvertently-kept-users-deleted-files-for-up-to-7-years-448676

CPC Central Committee and State Council. (2019, February 18). *Outline of Development Planning for Guangdong, Hong Kong and Macao Bay Area*. Available at: http://www.xinhuanet.com/politics/2019-02/18/c_1124131474.htm

Crasswell, R. (2005). Contract Law: General Theories. Encyclopedia of Law and Economics, (3), 1–24.

Cumming, D. J., Johan, S., & Pant, A. (2019). Regulation of the crypto-economy: Managing risks, challenges, and regulatory uncertainty. *Journal of Risk Financial Management, 12*(3), 126.

Dalmia, V. P. (2020). *India: RBI ban on banks' crypto deals quashed*. https://globalbankingregulationreview.com/pro/content/cryptocurrency-verdict-imai-vs-rbi

Danaher, J. (2015). *Is effective regulation of AI possible? Eight potential regulatory problems*. https://philosophicaldisquisitions.blogspot.com/2015/07/is-effective-regulation-of-ai-possible.html

Das. (2002). *Comment, Forum-Selection Clauses in Consumer Clickwrap and Browsewrap Agreements and the "Reasonably Communicated"*. Academic Press.

Davydov, D., & Pitaikina, I. (2020). Blockchain Technology Is Changing the Innovation Aspect in the Digital Economy. In Avatar-Based Models, Tools, and Innovation in the Digital Economy (pp. 103-112). IGI Global. doi:10.4018/978-1-7998-1104-6.ch006

De Caria, R. (2019). The Legal Meaning of Smart Contracts. *European Review of Private Law, 6*, 731–752. www.bis.org/cpmi/publ/d137.pdf

de Haro-Olmo, F. J., Varela-Vaca, Á. J., & Álvarez-Bermejo, J. A. (2020). Blockchain from the Perspective of Privacy and Anonymisation: A Systematic Literature Review. *Sensors (Basel), 20*(24), 7171. doi:10.339020247171 PMID:33327652

de Jong, J., Meyer, A., & Owens, J. (2017). Using blockchain for transparent beneficial ownership registers. *Int'l Tax Rev., 28*, 47.

Deatherage, S. (2019). Mutually Evolving Technologies: Blockchain, Renewable Energy, and Energy Storage. *American Bar Association*. www.americanbar.org/groups/business_law/publications/blt/2019/12/evolving-tech/

Decker, C., & Wattenhofer, R. (2013). Information propagation in the bitcoin network. In IEEE P2P 2013 Proceedings (pp. 1-10). IEEE.

Deirmentzoglou, E. P. (2019). A survey on long-range attacks for proof of stake protocols. *IEEE Access: Practical Innovations, Open Solutions*, 28712–28725.

Deloitte. (2019). *Transparency and Responsibility in Artificial Intelligence*. Retrieved May 29, 2021 from https://www2.deloitte.com/content/dam/Deloitte/nl/Documents/innovatie/deloitte-nl-innovation-bringing-transparency-and-ethics-into-ai.pdf

Deng, Y. (2019, November 5). *Overview of current laws and compliance of blockchain: Young but not undependable*. Available at: https://lvdao.sina.com.cn/news/2019-11-05/doc-iicezuev7236612.shtml

Department of Finance. (2016). *Guidance for regulators to implement outcomes and risk-based regulation*. http://productivity.nsw.gov.au/sites/default/files/2018-05/Guidance_for_regulators_to_implement_outcomes_and_risk-based_regulation-October_2016.pdf

Department of Financial Service. (n.d.). *Virtual Currency Businesses: Request for Comments on a Proposed Framework for a Conditional BitLicense.* https://www.dfs.ny.gov/apps_and_licensing/virtual_currency_businesses/gn/req_comments_prop_framework#_edn1

Department of the Treasury Financial Crimes Enforcement Network. (2013). *Application of FinCEN's Regulations to Persons Administering, Exchanging, or Using Virtual Currencies.* https://www.fincen.gov/sites/default/files/shared/FIN-2013-G001.pdf

Dewey, J. (2021). *Blockchain & Cryptocurrency Regulation – USA.* https://www.globallegalinsights.com/practice-areas/blockchain-laws-and-regulations/usa

Dhanda, N., & Garg, A. (2021). Revolutionizing the Stock Market With Blockchain. In Revolutionary Applications of Blockchain-Enabled Privacy and Access Control (pp. 119-133). IGI Global.

Dignum, V. (2019). *Responsible Artificial Intelligence: How to Develop and Use AI in a Responsible Way.* Springer International Publishing. https://books.google.com.my/books?id=EEO8DwAAQBAJ

Dillenberger, D., Novotny, P., Zhang, Q., Jayachandran, P., Gupta, H., Hans, S., & Vaculin, R. (2019). Blockchain analytics and artificial intelligence. *IBM Journal of Research and Development, 63*(2/3), 5–1.

Dinh & Thai. (2018). AI and Blockchain a disruptive integration. *Computer, 51,* 48-53. http://www.people.vcu.edu/~tndinh/papers/IEEEComp18_Blockchain+AI.pdf

Directive, No. 10 /CT-TTg, (2018). http://ssc.gov.vn/ssc/faces/en/enlinks/endetail/investor/investoralert/enchitiet167?dDocName=APPSSCGOVVN162121076&_afrLoop=66504322089922874&_afrWindowMode=0&_afrWindowId=gflldph6f_51#%40%3F_afrWindowId%3Dgflldph6f_51%26_afrLoop%3D66504322089922874%26dDocName%3DAPPSSCGOVVN162121076%26_afrWindowMode%3D0%26_adf.ctrl-state%3Dgflldph6f_79

Disparte, D. A. (2018, July 21). Beware Of Crypto Risks - 10 Risks To Watch. *Forbes.* Available at: https://www.forbes.com/sites/dantedisparte/2018/07/21/beware-of-crypto-risks-10-risks-to-watch/?sh=f8cef5c5f17f

Disparte, D. A. (2019). Why Enterprise Blockchain Projects Fail. *Forbes Magazine.* www.forbes.com/sites/dantedisparte/2019/05/20/why-enterprise-blockchain-projects-fail/?sh=4f649a7d4b96

Dong, J., & Jing, X. (2020, Feb. 5). 2020 CPC Document No. 1 Announced Two Key Tasks. *The Xinhua News Agency.* Available at: http://www.gov.cn/xinwen/2020-02/05/content_5474860.htm

Doshi-Velez, F., Kortz, M., Budish, R., Bavitz, C., Gershman, S., O'Brien, D., . . . Wood, A. (2017). *Accountability of AI under the law: The role of explanation.* arXiv:1711.01134 [cs.AI].

Drake, E. (2021). *2 new blockchain bills head for US Senate.* Retrieved June 30, 2021 from https://coingeek.com/2-new-blockchain-bills-head-for-us-senate/

Drescher, D. (2017). Blockchain Basics: A Non-Technical Introduction in 25 Steps. APRESS. doi:10.1007/978-1-4842-2604-9

Dropbox Acceptable Use Policy. (n.d.). https://www.dropbox.com/privacy#acceptable_use>

Dubai Future Councils. (n.d.a). *Dubai Blockchain Policy.* https://www.smartdubai.ae/docs/default-source/policies-standards/dubai-blockchain-policy.pdf?sfvrsn=ddfaec24_4

Dubai Future Councils. (n.d.b). *Dubai Blockchain Policy Brief.* https://www.smartdubai.ae/docs/default-source/publications/brief---dubai-blockchain-policyd78f44970b3a47269cc95fd6a742df06.pdf?sfvrsn=2ff3e093_2

Duenser, T. G. (2020). *Legalize Blockchain: How States Should Deal with Today's Most Promising Technology to foster prosperity*. https://books.google.com.my/books?id=EcLoDwAAQBAJ

Dunjic, M. (2018). Blockchain Immutability ... Blessing or Curse? *Finextra*. https://www.finextra.com/blogposting/15419/blockchain-immutability--blessing-or-curse

Durovic, M., & Lech, F. (2019). The Enforceability of Smart Contracts. *Italian Law Journal*, 5(2), 493–512.

Dyhrberg, A. H. (2016). Bitcoin, gold and the dollar–A GARCH volatility analysis. *Finance Research Letters*, 16, 85–92. doi:10.1016/j.frl.2015.10.008

Dyhrberg, A. H. (2016). Hedging capabilities of bitcoin. Is it virtual gold? *Finance Research Letters*, 16, 139–144. doi:10.1016/j.frl.2015.10.025

Edelman, K., Hurley, B., Devan, P., Khan, A., & Bhat, R. (2018). *The future of regulation: The principles for regulating emerging technologies*. https://www2.deloitte.com/content/dam/insights/us/articles/4538_Future-of-regulation/DI_Future-of-regulation.pdf

Ekparinya, P. G. (2018). Impact of man-in-the-middle attacks on ethereum. In *2018 IEEE 37th Symposium on Reliable Distributed Systems (SRDS)* (pp. 11-20). IEEE.

El Faqir, Y., Arroyo, J., & Hassan, S. (2020). An overview of Decentralized Autonomous Organizations on the Blockchain. *Proceedings of the 16th International Symposium on Open Collaboration*, 1–8. 10.1145/3412569.3412579

El Kafhali, S., Chahir, C., Hanini, M., & Salah, K. (2019). Architecture to manage Internet of Things data using blockchain and fog computing. *Proceedings of the 4th International Conference on Big Data and Internet of Things*, 1-8.

Elfstrom, A. L. (2018). *Blockchain organizations: Decentralized Autonomous Organizations and the Law*. University of Gothenburg.

Ellul, J., Galea, J., Ganado, M., McCarthy, S., & Pace, G. J. (2020). Regulating Blockchain, DLT and Smart Contracts: a technology regulator's perspective. *ERA Forum, 21*(2), 209-220. doi:10.1007/s12027-020-00617-7

Energy Web. (2021a). Bebat Launches EasyBat, an Open-Source, Decentralized Solution for Battery Lifecycle Management. *Medium*. https://medium.com/energy-web-insights/bebat-launches-easybat-an-open-source-decentralized-solution-for-battery-lifecycle-management-281f2ace61e9

Energy Web. (2021b). Energy Web and Energy Peacg Partners Annouces Peace Reneable Energy Credit (P-REC) Digital Marketplace Platform. *Medium*. https://medium.com/energy-web-insights/energy-web-and-energy-peace-partners-announce-peace-renewable-energy-credit-p-rec-digital-6295ea233218

Energy Web. (2021c). ENGIE Energy Access and Energy Web Announce DeFi Crowdfunding Platform to Help Scale Solar, Mini Grids in Sub-Saharan Africa. *Medium*. https://medium.com/energy-web-insights/engie-energy-access-and-energy-web-announce-defi-crowdfunding-platform-to-help-scale-solar-mini-2142029ad84f

ENISA. (2009). *Benefits, risks and recommendations for information security*. https://resilience.enisa.europa.eu/cloud-security-and-resilience/publications/cloud-computing-benefits-risks-and-recommendations-for-information-security

Ernst & Young. (2020). *Tokenization of Assets*. Retrieved June 30, 2021 from https://assets.ey.com/content/dam/ey-sites/ey-com/en_ch/topics/blockchain/ey-tokenization-of-assets-broschure-final.pdf

Esmaeilian, B., Sarkis, J., Lewis, K., & Behdad, S. (2020). Blockchain for the Future of Sustainable Supply Chain Management in Industry 4.0. *Resources Conversation & Recycling, 163*, 105060. doi:10.1016/j.resconrec.2020.105064

European Banking Federation. (2019). *EBF position paper on AI in the banking industry.* https://www.ebf.eu/wp-content/uploads/2020/03/EBF-AI-paper-_final-.pdf

European Commission Joint Research Centre (EC-JRC)/Netherlands Environmental Assessment Agency (PBL) (2019). Emissions Database for Global Atmospheric Research (EDGAR), release EDGAR v5.0 (1970 - 2015) of November 2019. Author.

European Commission. (2020). *White Paper on Artificial Intelligence - A European approach to excellence and trust.* https://ec.europa.eu/info/sites/info/files/commission-white-paper-artificial-intelligence-feb2020_en.pdf

European Parliament. (2019). *Regulating disinformation with artificial intelligence: Effects of disinformation initiatives on freedom of expression and media pluralism.* https://www.europarl.europa.eu/RegData/etudes/STUD/2019/624279/EPRS_STU(2019)624279(ANN1)_EN.pdf

European Parliamentary Research Service. (2019). *Blockchain and the General Data Protection Regulation: Can distributed ledgers be squared with European data protection law?* https://www.europarl.europa.eu/RegData/etudes/STUD/2019/634445/EPRS_STU(2019)634445_EN.pdf

European Securities and Markets Authority. (2017). *ESMA alerts firms involved in Initial Coin Offerings (ICOs) to the need to meet relevant regulatory requirements.* https://www.esma.europa.eu/sites/default/files/library/esma50-157-828_ico_statement_firms.pdf

Eyal, I., & Sirer, E. G. (2014). Majority is not enough: Bitcoin mining is vulnerable. In *International conference on financial cryptography and data security* (pp. 436-454). Springer.

Eyers, J. (2019). *We need laws about AI, not self-regulation.* Retrieved May 29, 2021 from https://www.afr.com/technology/we-need-laws-about-ai-not-self-regulation-20191216-p53k8r

Fakhri, D., & Mutijarsa, K. (2018). Secure IoT communication using blockchain technology. In *2018 International Symposium on Electronics and Smart Devices (ISESD)* (pp. 1-6). IEEE.

Fan, X., & Chai, Q. (2018, November). Roll-DPoS: a randomized delegated proof of stake scheme for scalable Blockchain-based internet of things systems. In *Proceedings of the 15th EAI International Conference on Mobile and Ubiquitous Systems: Computing, Networking and Services* (pp. 482-484). 10.1145/3286978.3287023

Federal Act on the Adaptation of Federal Law to Developments in Distributed Ledger Technology, (2020).

Federal Council of Switzerland. (2018). *Legal framework for distributed ledger technology and blockchain in Switzerland: An overview with a focus on the financial sector.* https://www.newsd.admin.ch/newsd/message/attachments/55153.pdf

Federal Department of Finance. (2012). *Circular No. 36: Commercial securities trading.* Author.

Federal Law No. 259-FZ on Digital Financial Assets and Digital Currencies, (2020).

Fenwick, M., Kaal, W. A., & Vermeulen, E. P. (2016). Regulation tomorrow: What happens when technology is faster than the law. *American University Business Law Review, 6,* 561–594. doi:10.2139srn.2834531

Financial Conduct Authority. (2015, November). *Regulatory Sandbox.* Available at: https://www.fca.org.uk/publications/documents/regulatory-sandbox

Financial Conduct Authority. (2019). *Guidance on Cryptoassets.* Accessed at https://www.fca.org.uk/publication/consultation/cp19-03.pd

Financial Market Infrastructure Act of 19 June 2015, (2015).

Financial Services (Distributed Ledger Technology Providers) Regulations, (2020).

Finck, M. (2018). Blockchains: Regulating the Unknown. *German Law Journal*, *19*(4), 665–692. doi:10.1017/S2071832200022847

Finck, M. (2018a). *Blockchain Regulation and Governance in Europe*. Cambridge University Press. https://books.google.com.my/books?id=pMd6DwAAQBAJ

Fjeld, J., Achten, N., Hilligoss, H., Nagy, A., & Srikumar, M. (2020). *Principled artificial intelligence: Mapping consensus in ethical and rights-based approaches to principles for AI*. Berkman Klein Center Research Publication.

Flicker Guidelines. (n.d.). https://www.flickr.com/help/guidelines

Florea, B. C. (2018). Blockchain and Internet of Things data provider for smart applications. In *2018 7th Mediterranean Conference on Embedded Computing (MECO)* (pp. 1-4). IEEE.

Floridi, L. (2016). On human dignity as a foundation for the right to privacy. *Philosophy & Technology*, *29*(4), 307–312. doi:10.100713347-016-0220-8

Fosso Wamba, S., Kala Kamdjoug, J. R., Epie Bawack, R., & Keogh, J. G. (2020). Bitcoin, Blockchain and Fintech: A systematic review and case studies in the supply chain. *Production Planning and Control*, *31*(2-3), 115–142. doi:10.1080/09537287.2019.1631460

Fraenkel, M. (2018). Blockchain for Commodities: Trading Opportunities in a Digital Age. *Trading Opportunities in a Digital Age | S&P Global*. www.spglobal.com/en/research-insights/featured/blockchain-for-commodities-trading-opportunities-in-a-digital-age

Fulmer, N. (2019). Exploring the Legal Issues of Blockchain Applications. *Akron Law Review*, *52*(1), 5. https://ideaexchange.uakron.edu/akronlawreview/vol52/iss1/5

Furlonger, D., & Uzureau, C. (2019). *The Real Business of Blockchain: How Leaders Can Create Value in a New Digital Age*. Harvard Business Review Press. https://books.google.com.my/books?id=B5U4wQEACAAJ

Future of Life Institute. (2017). *Asilomar AI Principles*. Retrieved May 29, 2021 from https://futureofife.org/ai-principles/

Garcia, H. (2018). TheCrypto Emobility Company. *Medium*. https://medium.com/motion-werk/the-crypto-emobility-company-5223bfd81e29

Garcia, J., & Garcia, J. (2021). Blockchain & Cryptocurrency Regulation 2021 - Gibraltar. *Global Legal Insights*. https://www.globallegalinsights.com/practice-areas/blockchain-laws-and-regulations/gibraltar

Garcia-Teruel, R. M., & Simón-Moreno, H. (2021). The digital tokenization of property rights. A comparative perspective. *Computer Law & Security Review*, *41*, 105543.

Gat, A. (2002). *Electronic Commerce — Click-Wrap Contracts The Enforceability Of Click-Wrap Agreements*. https://edisciplinas.usp.br/pluginfile.php/2056275/mod_resource/content/1/enforceability%20of%20clickwrap%20%28Adam%20Gatt%29.pdf

Gaži, P., Kiayias, A., & Russell, A. (2018). Stake-bleeding attacks on proof-of-stake blockchains. In *2018 Crypto Valley Conference on Blockchain Technology (CVCBT)* (pp. 85-92). IEEE.

GBA Cities. (n.d.). *Guangdong-Hong Kong-Macao greater Bay area - Gba cities*. https://www.bayarea.gov.hk/en/about/the-cities.html

General Data Protection Regulation (GDPR), (2016).

Geng, J. (2020, Mar). Recognition of B-end Business of Digital Bank Under the Epidemic. *Fudan Financial Review*. Available at: https://fisf.fudan.edu.cn/ffr/content/292

Gesley, J. (2021). *Switzerland: New Amending Law Adapts Several Acts to Developments in Distributed Ledger Technology*. Retrieved June 30, 2021 from https://www.loc.gov/law/foreign-news/article/switzerland-new-amending-law-adapts-several-acts-to-developments-in-distributed-ledger-technology/

Gibraltar Financial Services Commission. (n.d.). *Distributed Ledger Technology Regulatory Framework (DLT framework)*. https://www.fsc.gi/dlt

Gilcrest, J., & Carvalho, A. (2018). Smart Contracts: Legal Considerations. *2018 IEEE International Conference on Big Data (Big Data)*, 3277–3281. 10.1109/BigData.2018.8622584

Ginart, A., Guan, M., Valiant, G., & Zou, J. Y. (2019). Making AI forget you: Data deletion in machine learning. *Advances in Neural Information Processing Systems*.

Google Privacy Policy. (n.d.). https://policies.google.com/privacy

Google. (2018). Artificial Intelligence at Google: Our Principles. *Google AI*. https://ai.google/principles

Gourisetti, S. N. G., Mylrea, M., & Patangia, H. (2019). Evaluation and demonstration of Blockchain applicability framework. *IEEE Transactions on Engineering Management*, 67(4), 1142–1156. doi:10.1109/TEM.2019.2928280

Government of Liechtenstein. (2019). *Report and application of the government to the parliament of the Principality of Liechtenstein concerning the creation of a law on tokens and TT service providers (Tokens and TT Service Providers Act, TVTG) and the amendment of other laws (No. 54/2019)*. https://www.naegele.law/files/Downloads/2019-07-12_BuA_TVTG_en_full_report.pdf

Government Office for Science. (2016). *Distributed ledger technology: beyond block chain*. https://www.gov.uk/government/news/distributed-ledger-technology-beyond-block-chain

Governor Gordon. (2021). *State of the State address, March, 2*. https://governor.wyo.gov/media/news-releases/2021-news-releases/governor-gordon-celebrates-states-resilience-lays-out-vision-to-address-w

Governor of Bank Indonesia. (2016). *Bank Indonesia Regulation Number 18/40/PBI/2016 Concerning Operation of Payment Transaction Processing*. http://intr.insw.go.id/files/ecommerce/7.%20Regulation%20of%20BI%20No%2018.40.PBI.2016%20on%20Concerning%20the%20implementation%20of%20payment%20transaction.pdf

Grewal, D. S. (2014). A Critical Conceptual Analysis of Definitions of Artificial Intelligence as Applicable to Computer Engineering. *IOSR Journal of Computer Engineering*, 16(2), 9–13. doi:10.9790/0661-16210913

Grigg, I. (2004). The Ricardian contract. *Proceedings - First IEEE International Workshop on Electronic Contracting, WEC 2004*, (September), 25–31. 10.1109/WEC.2004.1319505

Gudkov, A. (2017). Control on Blockchain Network. *Nova Law Review*, 42, 353.

Güntert, M., & Schnyder, F. (2021). *Ledger-based securities: introduction of DLT shares in Switzerland*. https://pestalozzilaw.com/en/news/legal-insights/ledger-based-securities-introduction-dlt-shares-switzerland/

Guo, F., Wang, J., Wang, F., Kong, T., Zhang, X., & Cheng, Z. (2020). Measuring China's digital financial inclusion: Index compilation and spatial characteristics [in Chinese]. *China Economic Quarterly*, 19(4), 1401–1418.

Gupta, N. (2020). Security and privacy issues of blockchain technology. In *Advanced Applications of Blockchain Technology* (pp. 207–226). Springer. doi:10.1007/978-981-13-8775-3_10

Gürcan, B. (2019). Various Dimensions and Aspects of the Legal Problems of the Blockchain Technology. *Comparative Law Working Papers, 3*(1).

Gurrea-Martínez, A., & Remolina, N. (2020). Corporate Governance Challenges in Initial Coin Offerings. *Singapore Management University School of Law Research Paper, 19.*

H.B. 0019, 64th Leg., Budget Sess (Wyo), (2018).

H.B. 0070, 65th Leg., Gen. Sess. (Wyo), (2018).

H.B. 0101, 64th Leg., Budget Sess (Wyo.), (2018). https://www.wyoleg.gov/Legislation/2018/HB0101

H.B. 0185, 65th Leg., Gen. Sess. (Wyo.), (2019). https://www.wyoleg.gov/Legislation/2019/HB0185

H.B. 1, 65th Leg., Gen. Sess. (Wyo.), (2019).

H.B. 1418, 29th Leg., Reg. Sess. (Haw.), (2017).

H.B. 182, Gen. Assemb., Reg. Sess. (Vt.), (2017).

H.B. 27, 65th Leg., Gen. Sess. (Wyo), (2020).

H.B. 868, Gen. Assemb., Reg. Sess. (Vt), (2016).

H.R. 2417, 53d Leg., 1st Reg. Sess. (Ariz.), (2017). https://www.azleg.gov/legtext/53leg/1r/bills/hb2417p.pdf

H.R. 3723, 117th Congress, (2021).

Haeberli, D., Oesterhelt, S., & Wherlock, A. (2021). *Blockchain & Cryptocurrency Regulation 2021 – Switzerland.* https://www.globallegalinsights.com/practice-areas/blockchain-laws-and-regulations/switzerland

Haggerty, J. H., Haggerty, M. N., Roemer, K., & Rose, J. (2018). Planning for the local impacts of coal facility closure: Emerging strategies in the US West. *Resources Policy, 57,* 69–80. doi:10.1016/j.resourpol.2018.01.010

Hamil, J. (2018). *Bitcoin is a 'bubble' and cryptocurrency trading relies on 'finding the greater fool', Bank of England governor Mark Carney warns.* https://metro.co.uk/2018/03/02/bitcoin-bubble-cryptocurrency-trading-fools-says-bank-england-governor-mark-carney-7356044/

Hangzhou Municipal Government. (2019, Oct. 31). *Implementation opinions of Hangzhou Municipal Government on accelerating the development of cross border E-commerce.* Available at: https://z.hangzhou.com.cn/2019/hzsrmzfgb/content/content_7645608.html

Hao, X., Yu, L., Zhiqiang, L., Zhen, L., & Dawu, G. (2018, May). Dynamic practical byzantine fault tolerance. In *2018 IEEE Conference on Communications and Network Security (CNS)* (pp. 1-8). IEEE.

Hassani, H., Huang, X., & Silva, E. (2018). Banking with Blockchain-ed big data. *Journal of Management Analytics, 5*(4), 256–275. doi:10.1080/23270012.2018.1528900

Ha, T. L. D., Lee, C., & Cho, S. (2021). VCG Auction Mechanism based on Block Chain in Smart Grid. *International Conference on Information Networking.*

Haufler, V. (2013). *A Public Role for the Private Sector: Industry Self-Regulation in a Global Economy.* Brookings Institution Press. https://books.google.com.my/books?id=TxKNYxTRA-cC

Hayes, A. (2018). Is Ethereum More Important than Bitcoin? *Investopedia.* https://www.investopedia.com/articles/investing/032216/ethereum-more-important-bitcoin.asp

Higgins, S. (2018). *SEC Chief Clayton: 'Every ICO I've Seen Is a Security'*. Retrieved June 30, 2021 from https://www.coindesk.com/sec-chief-clayton-every-ico-ive-seen-security

High-Level Expert Group on Artificial Intelligence. (2019). *Ethics Guidelines for Trustworthy AI*. https://digital-strategy.ec.europa.eu/en/library/ethics-guidelines-trustworthy-ai

Hirsch, D. D. (2010). The law and policy of online privacy: Regulation, self-regulation, or co-regulation. *Seattle UL Rev.*, *34*, 439.

HM Government of Gibraltar. (2020). *Gibraltar Regulator Refreshes Jurisdiction's Distributed Ledger Technology Regulation - 631/2020*. https://www.gibraltar.gov.gi/press-releases/gibraltar-regulator-refreshes-jurisdictions-distributed-ledger-technology-regulation-6312020-6206

Hofverberg, E. (2019). *Regulatory Approaches to Cryptoassets in Selected Jurisdictions-Denmark*. https://www.lawsco-pelibrary.com/admin/articles/regulatory-approaches-to-cryptoassets-in-selected-jurisdictions/cryptoasset-regulation.pdf

Homoliak, I. V. (2019). A security reference architecture for blockchains. In *2019 IEEE International Conference on Blockchain (Blockchain)* (pp. 390-397). IEEE.

Hon, Millard, & Walden. (2012). Negotiating cloud contracts: Looking at clouds from both sides. *Stan. Tech. L. Rev., 79*.

Houy, N. (2014). *It will cost you nothing to 'kill' a proof-of-stake crypto-currency*. Available at SSRN 2393940.

Hsiao, J. I.-H. (2017). "Smart" Contract on the Blockchain-Paradigm Shift for Contract Law? *US-China Law Review*, *14*(10), 685–694. doi:10.17265/1548-6605/2017.10.002

Hsieh, Y.-Y. (2018). *The Rise of Decentralized Autonomous Organizations: Coordination and Growth within Cryptocurrencies*. The University of Western Ontario.

HSV. (2020). Reneum Collaborate with Energy Web & Will Host the Companies Blockchain Enabling Aggregation with Other Brokers. *Medium*. https://hsvgts.medium.com/reneum-becomes-an-energy-web-affiliate-will-host-the-companies-blockchain-enabling-aggregation-a216fc16c6b9

Huang, Z., Li, Z., Lai, C. S., Zhao, Z., Wu, X., Li, X., Tong, N., & Lai, L. L. (2021). A Novel Power Market Mechanism Based on Blockchain for Electric Vehicle Charging Stations. *Electronics (Basel)*, *10*(3), 307. doi:10.3390/electronics10030307

Hughes, S. D. (2017). *Cryptocurrency Regulations and Enforcement in the US*. Academic Press.

Hughes, L., Dwivedi, Y. K., Misra, S. K., Rana, N. P., Raghavan, V., & Akella, V. (2019). Blockchain research, practice and policy: Applications, benefits, limitations, emerging research themes and research agenda. *International Journal of Information Management*, *49*, 114–129. doi:10.1016/j.ijinfomgt.2019.02.005

Hüllmann, T. A. (2018). *Are Decentralized Autonomous Organizations the Future of Corporate Governance*. Otto Beisheim School of Management., doi:10.13140/RG.2.2.34344.88327

Humayun, M., Jhanjhi, N., Hamid, B., & Ahmed, G. (2020). Emerging Smart Logistics and Transportation Using IoT and Blockchain. *IEEE Internet of Things Magazine, 3*(2), 58-62. doi:10.1109/IOTM.0001.1900097

IEEE Global Initiative on Ethics of Autonomous Intelligent Systems. (2017). *Ethically Aligned Design: A Vision for Prioritizing Human Well-being with Autonomous and Intelligent Systems, Version 2*. IEEE.

IL Public Act 101-0504, (2019).

In re Appraisal of Dell Inc, 143 A. 3d 20 (Del: Court of Chancery 2015).

In the Matter of: Coinflip, Inc., d/b/a Derivabit, and Francisco Riordan, WL 5535736 (2015).

Income Tax Act (1949).

Indigo Advisory Group. (2017). *Blockchain in energy and utilities use cases, vendor activity, market analysis.* https://www.indigoadvisorygroup.com/blockchain

Indonesia, K. P. R. (2019). *Bappebti Terbitkan Empat Peraturan Aset Kripto dan Emas Digital.* http://bappebti.go.id/resources/docs/siaran_pers_2019_02_18_gpfdzt8b_id.pdf

Inland Revenue Authority of Singapore. (2020). *IRAS e-Tax Guide: Income Tax Treatment of Digital Tokens.* https://www.iras.gov.sg/irashome/uploadedFiles/IRASHome/e-Tax_Guides/etaxguide_CIT_Income%20Tax%20Treatment%20of%20Digital%20Tokens.pdf

Intel. (2017). *Artificial Intelligence: The Public Policy Opportunity.* Retrieved May 29, 2021 from https://blogs.intel.com/policy/files/2017/10/Intel-Artificial-Intelligence-Public-Policy-White-Paper-2017.pdf

Internal Revenue Service. (2014). *IRS Notice 2014-21.* https://www.irs.gov/pub/irs-drop/n-14-21.pdf

International Monetary Fund, & Monetary and Capital Markets (MCM) Department. (2018). *Global Financial Stability Report, April 2018: A Bumpy Road Ahead.* International Monetary Fund. https://books.google.com.my/books?id=_K4ZEAAAQBAJ

Internet and Mobile Association of India v. Reserve Bank of India CPSC58 (SC 2020).

IRENA. (2018). *Global Energy Transformation: A roadmap to 2050.* International Renewable Energy Agency.

Ismail, L., Materwala, H., & Khan, M. (2020). Performance Evaluation of a Patient-Centric Blockchain-based Healthcare Records Management Framework. *Proceedings of the 2020 2nd International Electronics Communication Conference,* 39-50.

iWork.com Public Beta Terms of Service. (n.d.). https://www.apple.com/legal/iworkcom/en/terms.html

Izquierdo, L. C. J. (2017). *Aragon Network; a Decentralized Infrastructure for Value Exchange.* Retrieved from https://www.chainwhy.com/upload/default/20180705/49f3850f2702ec6be0f57780b22feab2.pdf

J, A.-J., & N, M. (2019). Blockchain in industries: A survey. *IEEE Access, 7,* 36500-36515.

Jang, H., & Lee, J. (2017). An empirical study on modelling and prediction of bitcoin prices with bayesian neural networks based on blockchain information. *IEEE Access: Practical Innovations, Open Solutions, 6,* 5427–5437. doi:10.1109/ACCESS.2017.2779181

Janssen, M., Weerakkody, V., Ismagilova, E., Sivarajah, U., & Irani, Z. (2020). A framework for analysing Blockchain technology adoption: Integrating institutional, market and technical factors. *International Journal of Information Management, 50,* 302–309. doi:10.1016/j.ijinfomgt.2019.08.012

Jentzsch, C. (2017). *Decentralized Autonomous Organization to Automate Governance.* Retrieved from Slock.it website: https://lawofthelevel.lexblogplatformthree.com/wp-content/uploads/sites/187/2017/07/WhitePaper-1.pdf

Jesse McWaters, R. (2016). The Future of Financial Infrastructure: An Ambitious Look at How Blockchain Can Reshape Financial Services. *World Economic Forum.* http://www3.weforum.org/docs/WEF_The_future_of_financial_infrastructure.pdf

Ji, J. Z. K., Wang, R., Chen, B., & Dai, C. (2018). Energy Efficient Caching in Backhaul-Aware Ultra-Dense Cellular Networks. *Proceedings - IEEE 2018 International Congress on Cybermatics: 2018 IEEE Conferences on Internet of Things, Green Computing and Communications, Cyber, Physical and Social Computing, Smart Data, Blockchain, Computer and Information Technology, iThings/GreenCom/CPSCom/SmartData/Blockchain/CIT 2018.*

Jiang, Y. W. (2018). A cross-chain solution to integration of iot tangle for data access management. In *2018 IEEE Interna- tional Conference on Internet of Things (iThings) and IEEE Green Computing and Communications.* IEEE.

Jiang, S., Jakobsen, K., Jaccheri, L., & Li, J. (2021). *Blockchain and Sustainability: A Tertiary Study.* IEEE.

Jiang, X. (2019). Bitcoin price prediction based on deep learning methods. *Journal of Mathematical Finance*, *10*(1), 132–139.

Jiang, Y. &. (2019). High performance and scalable byzantine fault tolerance. In *IEEE 3rd Information Technology, Networking, Electronic and Automation Control Conference (ITNEC)* (pp. 1195–1202). IEEE.

Jiang, Y., Nie, H., & Ruan, W. (2018). Time-varying long-term memory in the Bitcoin market. *Finance Research Letters*, *25*, 280–284. doi:10.1016/j.frl.2017.12.009

Johann, L. (2018). *Liechtenstein implements Distributed Ledger Technology (DLT).* Retrieved June 30, 2021 from https://bwb.li/blog/liechtenstein-implements-distributed-ledger-technology-dlt/

Joint Economic Committee. (2018). *H. Rept. 115-596 - Report of the Joint Economic Committee Congress of the United States on the 2018 Economic Report of the President Together with Minority Views.* https://www.congress.gov/congressional-report/115th-congress/house-report/596/1

Jolley, G. J., Khalaf, C., Michaud, G., & Sandler, A. M. (2019). The economic, fiscal, and workforce impacts of coal-fired power plant closures in Appalachian Ohio. *Regional Science Policy & Practice*, *11*(2), 403–422. doi:10.1111/rsp3.12191

Jonker, W., & Petkovic, M. (2008). *Secure Data Management: 5th VLDB Workshop, SDM 2008, Auckland, New Zealand, August 24, 2008, Proceedings.* Springer. https://books.google.com.my/books?id=8Bd_6cxbkDgC

Joy, J. G., & Sebastian, K. (2020). Blockchain in Real Estate. *International Journal of Applied Engineering Research*, *15*(9), 930–932.

Jurdak, R., Dorri, A., & Vilathgamuwa, M. (2021). A Trusted and Privacy Preserving Internet of Mobility Energy. *IEEE Communications Letters*, *59*(6), 89–95. doi:10.1109/MCOM.001.2000754

Kaal, W. A., & Evans, S. (2019). Blockchain-based securities offerings. *UC Davis Bus. LJ*, *20*, 89.

Kabra, N., Bhattacharya, P., Tanwar, S., & Tyagi, S. (2020). Mudrachain: Blockchain-based framework for automated cheque clearance in financial institutions. *Future Generation Computer Systems*, *102*, 574–587. doi:10.1016/j.future.2019.08.035

Karasu, S., Altan, A., Saraç, Z., & Hacioğlu, R. (2018, May). Prediction of Bitcoin prices with machine learning methods using time series data. In *2018 26th signal processing and communications applications conference (SIU)* (pp. 1-4). IEEE. 10.1109/SIU.2018.8404760

Kasprzyk, M. (2018). Comparative Review of Regulatory Framework of Virtual Currency (Cryptocurrency) In Selected Countries. *Review of European Comparative Law Working Papers*, *35*(4), 7–26.

Katsiampa, P. (2017). *Volatility estimation for Bitcoin: A comparison of GA.* Academic Press.

Kelly, L. (2019). What Is Enabled: How Blockchain Enabling Legislation Fails Commercial Contracts. *Rutgers JL Pub. Pol'y*, *16*, 1.

Kharitonova, A. (2021). Capabilities of Blockchain Technology in Tokenization of Economy. *1st International Scientific Conference "Legal Regulation of the Digital Economy and Digital Relations: Problems and Prospects of Development" (LARDER 2020).*

Kiayias, A. R. (2017). Ouroboros: A provably secure proof-of-stake blockchain protocol. *In Annual International Cryptology Conference* (pp. 357-388). Springer.

Kiayias, A., & Zindros, D. (2019, February). Proof-of-work sidechains. In *International Conference on Financial Cryptography and Data Security* (pp. 21-34). Springer.

Kieckhefer, B. (n.d.). *How Nevada Is Preparing For Blockchain Technology.* https://www.mcdonaldcarano.com/news/how-nevada-is-preparing-for-blockchain-technology/

Kiviat, T. I. (2015). Beyond bitcoin: Issues in regulating blockchain tranactions. *Duke Law Journal, 65,* 569.

Kondova, G., & Barba, R. (2019). Governance of Decentralized Autonomous Organizations. *Journal of Modern Accounting and Auditing, 15*(8), 406–411. doi:10.17265/1548-6583/2019.08.003

Kosnik, L.-R. (2014). Determinants of Contract Completeness: An Environmental Regulatory Application. *International Review of Law and Economics, 37,* 198–208. doi:10.1016/j.irle.2013.11.001

Kozakiewicz, A., & Fettes, K. (2021). *Impact of new Luxembourg law on the issuance and settlement of securities using blockchain.* Retrieved June 30, 2021 from https://www.ashurst.com/en/news-and-insights/legal-updates/impact-of-new-luxembourg-law-on-the-issuance-and-settlement-of-securities-using-blockchain/

Kriskó, A. (2013). Crypto currencies–currencies governed by belief Bitcoin, Piggycoin, Monero, Peercoin, Ethereum and the rest. Conference book Konferenciakötet.

Kroll, J. A. (2013). The economics of bitcoin mining, or bitcoin in the presence of adversaries. *Proceedings of WEIS, 11.*

Kulms, R. (2020). Blockchains: Private Law Matters Special Feature. *Sing. J. Legal Stud., 2020,* 63.

Kumar, N., Gayathri, N., Rahman, M. A., & Balamurugan, B. (2020). *Blockchain, Big Data and Machine Learning: Trends and Applications.* CRC Press. https://books.google.com.my/books?id=yzX7DwAAQBAJ

Kwon, J. (2014). *Tendermint: Consensus without mining.* Draft v. 0.6, fall, 1(11).

L'oreal Sa And Others V Ebay International Ag And Others [2009] EWHC 1094 (Ch), [2009] RPC 21

LabCFTC. (2017). *A CFTC Primer on Virtual Currencies.* https://www.cftc.gov/sites/default/files/idc/groups/public/documents/file/labcftc_primercurrencies100417.pdf

Lacity, M. (2020). Crypto and Blockchain Fundamentals. *Arkansas Law Review, 73,* 363.

Lamport, L. S. (1982). *The byzantine generals problem acm transactions on progamming languages and syetems.* Academic Press.

Lamport, L., Shostak, R., & Pease, M. (1982). The Byzantine Generals Problem. *ACM Transactions on Programming Languages and Systems, 4*(3), 387–389. doi:10.1145/357172.357176

Landen, X. (2018). Vt. Banks on Appeal, Lure Of Blockchain. *Valley News.* https://www.vnews.com/Vermont-bullish-on-blockchain-as-new-law-takes-effect-19810798

Lanzing, M. (2019). "Strongly recommended" revisiting decisional privacy to judge hypernudging in self-tracking technologies. *Philosophy & Technology, 32*(3), 549–568. doi:10.100713347-018-0316-4

Laster, J. T., & Rosner, M. T. (2017). Distributed Stock Ledgers and Delaware Law. *Business Lawyer, 73*, 319.

Law of 1 March 2019, (2019). https://legilux.public.lu/eli/etat/leg/loi/2019/03/01/a111/jo

Law of 22 January 2021, (2021).

Law on the State Bank of Vietnam. (2010). https://sites.google.com/a/ecolaw.vn/luat-tieng-anh/1-bo-luat-luat/-law-on-the-state-bank-of-vietnam

Law, A. (2017). *Smart Contracts and their applications in supply chain management*. MIT Thesis. Accessed at https://dspace.mit.edu/handle/1721.1/114082

Lee, J., & L'heureux, F. (2019). A regulatory framework for cryptocurrency. *European Business Law Review*. https://ore.exeter.ac.uk/repository/handle/10871/120627

Li, Jiang, Chen, Luo, & Wen. (2017). A survey on the security of blockchain systems. *Future Gener. Comput. Syst., 107*, 841-853. . doi:10.1016/j.future.2017.08.020

Li, R. (2020, December 28). Two blockchain scenario application platforms have been built in the Xiong'an area of Hebei free trade zone. *Beijing Daily*. Available at: http://ie.bjd.com.cn/5b5fb98da0109f010fce6047/contentApp/5b5fb9d0e4b08630d8aef954/AP5fe9de40e4b02f6bb4131f12.html

Liao, K. (2017). Incentivizing blockchain forks via whale transactions. In *International Conference on Financial Cryptography and Data Security* (pp. 264–279.). Springer.

Liechtenstein is the New Powerhouse for Digital Securities. (2021). Retrieved June 30, 2021 from https://www.lcx.com/liechtenstein-is-the-new-powerhouse-for-digital-securities/

Linoy, S., Stakhanova, N., & Matyukhina, A. (2019). Exploring Ethereum's Blockchain Anonymity Using Smart Contract Code Attribution. *15th International Conference on Network and Service Management, CNSM 2019*. 10.23919/CNSM46954.2019.9012681

Liu, Z., Luong, N. C., Wang, W., Niyato, D., Wang, P., Liang, Y.-C., & Kim, D. I. (2019). *A survey on applications of game theory in blockchain*. arXiv preprint arXiv:1902.10865.

Liu, Z., Tang, S., Chow, S. S., Liu, Z., & Long, Y. (2019). Fork-free hybrid consensus with flexible proof-of-activity. *Future Generation Computer Systems, 96*, 515–524. doi:10.1016/j.future.2019.02.059

Li, W., Andreina, S., Bohli, J. M., & Karame, G. (2017). Securing proof-of-stake Blockchain protocols. In *Data Privacy Management, Cryptocurrencies and Blockchain Technology* (pp. 297–315). Springer. doi:10.1007/978-3-319-67816-0_17

Lofstedt, R. (2003). The precautionary principle: Risk, regulation and politics. *Process Safety and Environmental Protection, 81*(1), 36–43. doi:10.1205/095758203762851976

MacCarthy, M. (2020). *AI needs more regulation, not less*. https://www.brookings.edu/research/ai-needs-more-regulation-not-less/

MacMillen, C., & Stone, R. (2004). Elements of The Law of Contract. University of London. doi:10.1201/9781003029250-6

Malkhi, D. N. (2019). Flexible byzantine fault tolerance. *Proceedings of the 2019 ACM SIGSAC Conference on Computer and Communica- tions Security*, 1041–1053.

Malta Financial Services Authority. (2018a). *Virtual Financial Assets Framework - Frequently Asked Questions*. https://www.legal500.com/developments/wp-content/uploads/sites/19/2019/03/MFSA-VFARFAQs-24.10.18.pdf

Malta Financial Services Authority. (2018b). *Virtual Financial Assets Rulebook - Chapter 1.* https://www.mfsa.mt/wp-content/uploads/2019/02/VFAR_Chapter1_FINAL.pdf

Marchant, G. (2019). "Soft Law" Governance of Artificial Intelligence. *UCLA: The Program on Understanding Law, Science, and Evidence (PULSE).* https://escholarship.org/uc/item/0jq252ks

Marchant, G. E., Allenby, B. R., & Herkert, J. R. (2011). *The growing gap between emerging technologies and legal-ethical oversight: The pacing problem* (Vol. 7). Springer Science & Business Media. doi:10.1007/978-94-007-1356-7

Marsden, C. T. (2004). Co-Regulation in European Media and Internet Sectors. *Communications and the Law, 9*(5), 187–195.

Marwala, T., & Xing, B. (2018). *Blockchain and Artificial Intelligence.* https://arxiv.org/abs/1802.04451

Massad, T. G. (2019). It's Time to Strengthen the Regulation of Crypto-Assets. *Economic Studies at Brookings*, 34-36.

Massinon, L., & Nickel, C. (2021). *Law of 22 January 2021 amending Luxembourg dematerialised securities law and financial sector law.* https://www.dlapiper.com/en/us/insights/publications/2021/01/law-amending-luxembourg-dematerialised-securities-law-and-financial-sector-law/

Matta, M., Lunesu, I., & Marchesi, M. (2015, June). Bitcoin Spread Prediction Using Social and The author Search Media. In UMAP workshops (pp. 1-10). Academic Press.

Maughan, A., Ford, C. D., & Stevenson, S. W. (2014). *Negotiating Cloud Contract.* https://media2.mofo.com/documents/141217negotiatingcloudcontracts.pdf

McFarlane, S. (2020). BP Bets Future on Green Energy, but Investors Remain Wary. *The Wall Street Journal.* Retrieved from https://www.wsj.com/articles/bp-bets-future-on-green-energy-but-investors-remain-wary-11601402304#:~:text=The%20deal%20is%20part%20of,investment%20in%20solar%20business%20Lightsource

McGill, D. H., Sauter, B. J., & Barnes, B. D. (2018). Cryptocurrency Is Borderless—but Still Within the Grip of US Regulators. *International Law Practicum, 31*(1), 11. https://www.huntonak.com/images/content/5/3/v2/53787/international-law-practicum-nysba.pdf#page=11

McKinney, R. E. Jr, Baker, C. W., Shao, L. P., & Forrest, J. Y. (2020). Cryptocurrency: Utility Determines Conceptual Classification despite Regulatory Uncertainty. *Intell. Prop. Tech. LJ, 25*, 1.

McLelland, R., Hackett, Y., Hurley, G., & Collins, D. (2014). *Agreements between Cloud Service Providers and their Clients: A Review of Contract Terms.* <https://www.girona.cat/web/ica2014/ponents/textos/id210.pdf>

McNally, S., Roche, J., & Caton, S. (2018, March). Predicting the price of bitcoin using machine learning. In *2018 26th euro micro international conference on parallel, distributed and network-based processing (PDP)* (pp. 339-343). IEEE.

McNally, S., Roche, J., & Caton, S. (2018, March). Predicting the price of bitcoin using machine learning. In *2018 26th euro micro international conference on parallel, distributed and network-based processing (PDP)* (pp. 339-343). IEEE. 10.1109/PDP2018.2018.00060

Medina, A. F. (2020). *Cambodia Launches Digital Currency: Key Features.* https://www.aseanbriefing.com/news/cambodia-launches-digital-currency-key-features/

Megha, S., Lamptey, J., Salem, H., & Mazzara, M. (2019). *A survey of blockchain-based solutions for Energy Industry.* arXiv:1911.10509.

Meiklejohn, A. M. (1994). Castles in the Air: Blanket Assent and the Revision of Article 2. *Washington and Lee Law Review.* https://scholarlycommons.law.wlu.edu/cgi/viewcontent.cgi?article=1602&context=wlulr

Mendki, P. (2019). Blockchain enabled IoT edge computing. *Proceedings of the 2019 International Conference on Blockchain Technology*, 66-69.

Merz, M. (2019, May 20). *Enerchain 1.0 is live!* https://enerchain.ponton.de/index.php/articles/2-uncategorised/37-enerchain10live

Metjahic, L. (2018). Deconstructing the DAO: The Need for Legal Recognition and the Application of Securities Laws to Decentralized Organizations. *Cardozo Law Review, 39*, 1541.

Microsoft. (2018). *Microsoft AI Principles*. https://www.microsoft.com/en-us/ai/responsible-ai?activetab=pivot1%3aprimaryr6

Mik, E. (2017). Smart Contracts: Terrminology, Technical Limitations and Real-World Complexity. *Law, Innovation and Technology, 9*(2), 269–300. doi:10.1080/17579961.2017.1378468

Milewski, K. P. (2020). *Illinois Embraces Smart Contracts with New Blockchain Legislation.* https://www.natlawreview.com/article/illinois-embraces-smart-contracts-new-blockchain-legislation

Miller, B. (2016). *Smart contract and the role of lawyers (Part 1) - About smart contracts.* http://biglawkm.com/2016/10/20/smart-contracts-and-the-role-of-lawyers-part-1-about-smart-contracts/

Miller, L. K., Comfort, P. G., & Stoldt, G. C. (2001). Contracts 101: Basics and Applications. *Journal of Legal Aspects of Sport, 11*(1), 79–89. doi:10.1123/jlas.11.1.79

Mills, A. (2017). *An Introduction To Blockchain Technology And Its Legal Implications.* https://www.mmmlaw.com/media/an-introduction-to-blockchain-technology-and-its-legal-implications/

Mingxiao, D., Xiaofeng, M., Zhe, Z., Xiangwei, W., & Qijun, C. (2017). *A review on consensus algorithm of blockchain. 2017 IEEE international conference on systems, man, and cybernetics.* SMC.

Ministry of Finance. (n.d.). *Draft Banning of Cryptocurrency & Regulation of Official Digital Currency Bill, 2019.* https://prsindia.org/billtrack/draft-banning-of-cryptocurrency-regulation-of-official-digital-currency-bill-2019

Ministry of Industry and Information Technology. the People's Bank of China, Ministry of Justice, Ministry of Commerce, State Owned Assets Supervision and Administration Commission, State Administration of market supervision and administration, CBIRC, State Administration of Foreign Exchange. (2020, September 18). *Opinions on standardizing the development of supply chain finance to support the stable circulation, optimization and upgrading of the supply chain and industry chain.* Available at: http://www.gov.cn/zhengce/zhengceku/2020-09/22/content_5546142.htm

Moalem, D., & Probst Larsen, K. (2020). *The Virtual Currency Regulation Review: Denmark.* https://thelawreviews.co.uk/title/the-virtual-currency-regulation-review/denmark#footnote-016

Mohanta, B. K., Panda, S. S., & Jena, D. (2018). An Overview of Smart Contract and Use Cases in Blockchain Technology. *International Conference on Computing, Communication and Networking Technologies 2018.* 10.1109/ICCCNT.2018.8494045

MoneroJ. (2016). *Fat Protocols.* https://www.usv.com/writing/2016/08/fat-protocols/

Monetary Authority of Singapore. (2019). *"Payment Services Bill" - Second Reading Speech by Mr Ong Ye Kung, Minister For Education, On Behalf of Mr Tharman Shanmugaratnam, Deputy Prime Minister and Minister-In-Charge of The Monetary Authority of Singapore on 14 Jan 2019.* https://www.mas.gov.sg/news/speeches/2019/payment-services-bill

Monetary Authority of Singapore. (2020). *A Guide to Digital Token Offerings.* https://www.mas.gov.sg/-/media/MAS/Sectors/Guidance/Guide-to-Digital-Token-Offerings-26-May-2020.pdf

Money Laundering and Terrorist Financing Prevention Act (2017).

Montreal Declaration. (2017). *Montreal Declaration for a Responsible Development of Artificial Intelligence.* https://recherche.umontreal.ca/english/strategic-initiatives/montreal-declaration-for-a-responsible-ai/

Moolman, J. (2017). *Are you ready for outcomes-based regulation?* https://www.linkedin.com/pulse/you-ready-outcomes-based-regulation-juanita-moolman

Moses, L. B. (2013). How to think about law, regulation and technology: Problems with 'technology' as a regulatory target. *Law, Innovation and Technology, 5*(1), 1–20. doi:10.5235/17579961.5.1.1

Muhanji, S. O., Flint, A. E., & Farid, A. M. (2019). eIoT: The Development of the Energy Internet of Things in Energy Infrastructure. Springer.

Nabilou, H. (2019). How to regulate bitcoin? Decentralized regulation for a decentralized cryptocurrency. *International Journal of Law and Information Technology, 27*(3), 266–291.

Nacer, M., Prakoonwit, S., & Alarab, I. (2020). TheChain: A Fast, Secure and Parallel Treatment of Transactions. In *Proceedings of the 2020 2nd International Electronics Communication Conference* (pp. 81-89). ACM.

Naim, B., Hronsky, M., & Klas, W. (2020). From Blockchain to Web: Paving the Last Mile for Releasing Chained Data from the Blocks. *Proceedings of the 2020 2nd International Electronics Communication Conference*, 24-32.

Nakamoto, S. (2008). *Bitcoin: A Peer-to-Peer Electronic Cash System.* Bitcoin White Paper.

Nakamoto, S. (2008). Bitcoin: A peer-to-peer electronic cash system. *Decentralized Business Review*, 21260.

Nakamoto, S. (2019). *Bitcoin: A peer-to-peer electronic cash system.* Manubot.

Nami, M. R. (2008). Virtual Organizations: An Overview. *International Conference on Intelligent Information Processing*, 211–219.

Nassar, M., Salah, K., & Rehman, M. H. (2020). Blockchain for explainable and trustworthy artificial intelligence. *Wiley Interdisciplinary Reviews. Data Mining and Knowledge Discovery, 10*(1), 1340. doi:10.1002/widm.1340

National Bank of Cambodia. (2018). *Joint Statement between The national Bank of Cambodia, the Securities and Exchange Commission of Cambodia and the General-Commissariat of National Police.* Author.

National Development and Reform Commission. (2019, Nov). *Regional Integration Development Strategy of Yangtze River Delta.* Available at: https://www.ndrc.gov.cn/gjzl/csjyth/201911/t20191127_1213169.html

Nayak, Narendra, & Shukla. (2018). *Saranyu: Using Smart Contracts and Blockchain for Cloud Tenant Management Salesforce Master Subscription Agreement.* https://www.salesforce.com/content/dam/web/en_us/www/documents/legal/salesforce_MSA.pdf

Neitz, M. B. (2020). How to Regulate Blockchain's Real-Life Applications: Lessons from the California Blockchain Working Group. *Jurimetrics: The Journal of Law, Science Technology, 61*(2).

Nev. Code. Title 32. Chp 361, NRS 361.228 (2010).

Nev. Const. Art. 10, §1.

Nevada Senate Bill 398 at https://www.leg.state.nv.us/Session/79th2017/BDR/BDR79_59-0158.pdf

NITI Aayog. (2018). *Discussion Paper National Strategy for Artificial Intelligence.* https://niti.gov.in/writereaddata/files/document_publication/NationalStrategy-for-AI-Discussion-Paper.pdf

No. 80/2016/ND-CP Decree, (2016). https://vanbanphapluat.co/decree-no-80-2016-nd-cp-amend-governments-decree-101-2012-nd-cp-on-non-cash-payments

Nuzzi, L. (2019). *Interoperability in the Age of Siloed Blockchains Pt.1.* https://medium.com/digitalassetresearch/interoperability-in-the-age-of-siloed-blockchains-pt-1-4d7393fbf420

NV Rev Stat § 719, (2013).

O'Brien, C. (2019). Startup of the Week: Share&Charge Foundation. *Medium.* https://innovator.news/startup-of-the-week-share-charge-foundation-359425b226c6

O'Shields, R. (2017). *Smart Contracts: Legal Agreements for the Blockchain.* https://scholarship.law.unc.edu/cgi/viewcontent.cgi?referer=&httpsredir=1&article=1435&context=ncbi

OECD. (2008). *APEC-OECD Co-operative Initiative on Regulatory Reform Proceedings of the Fourth APEC-OECD Workshop on Regulatory Reform.* OECD Publishing. https://books.google.com.my/books?id=gbBFF4_XXBUC

OECD. (2014). *Cloud Computing: The Concept, Impacts and the Role of Government Policy.* OECD Digital Economy Papers, No. 240, OECD Publishing. doi:10.1787/5jxzf4lcc7f5-en

Office of Assistant to Deputy Cabinet Secretary for State Documents & Translation. (2018). *Bank Indonesia Warns All Parties Not to Sell, Buy, or Trade Virtual Currency.* https://setkab.go.id/en/bank-indonesia-warns-all-parties-not-to-sell-buy-or-trade-virtual-currency/

Omezzine, F., & Schleich, J. (2019). The Future of Blockchain According to Experts in the Energy Sector. *The Conversation, 5*(Mar). theconversation.com/the-future-of-blockchain-according-to-experts-in-the-energy-sector-111780

Opinion of the Data Ethics Commission. (2019). *Data Ethics Commission of the Federal Government.* https://www.bmjv.de/SharedDocs/Downloads/DE/Themen/Fokusthemen/Gutachten

Oracle. (2019). *Data Processing Agreement for Oracle Cloud Services.* https://www.oracle.com/us/corporate/contracts/data-processing-agreement-011218-4261005.pdf

Ordano, E., Meilich, A., Jardi, Y., & Araoz, M. (2017). *Decentraland: White Paper.* Academic Press.

Oren, O. (2017). ICO's, DAO'S, and the SEC: A Partnership Solution. *Columbia Business Law Review, hs*(2), 617–657.

Osmani, M., El-Haddadeh, R., Hindi, N., Janssen, M., & Weerakkody, V. (2020). Blockchain for next generation services in banking and finance: Cost, benefit, risk and opportunity analysis. *Journal of Enterprise Information Management.*

Pagallo, U., Aurucci, P., Casanovas, P., Chatila, R., Chazerand, P., Dignum, V., . . . Valcke, P. (2019). *AI4People - On Good AI Governance: 14 Priority Actions, a S.M.A.R.T. Model of Governance, and a Regulatory Toolbox.* https://www.eismd.eu/wp-content/uploads/2019/11/AI4Peoples-Report-on-Good-AI-Governance_compressed.pdf

Pal, S., Dorri, A., & Jurdak, R. (2021). *Blockchain for IoT Access Control: Recent Trends and Future Research Directions*, arXiv:2106.04808

Pankratov, E., Grigoryev, V., & Pankratov, O. (2020). The blockchain technology in real estate sector: Experience and prospects. *IOP Conference Series. Materials Science and Engineering.*

Papajak, U. (2017). Can the Brooklyn Microgrid project revolutionize the energy market? *Medium.* https://medium.com/thebeammagazine/can-the-brooklyn-microgrid-project-revolutionise-the-energy-market-ae2c13ec0341

Paris Agreement. (2015). *Paris agreement.* Report of the Conference of the Parties to the United Nations Framework Convention on Climate Change (21st Session, 2015: Paris). https://unfccc.int/files/meetings/paris_nov_2015/application/pdf/paris_agreement_english_.pdf

Parker, L. (2017). *European Commission 'actively monitoring' Blockchain developments.* https://bravenewcoin.com/insights/european-commission-actively-monitoring-blockchain-developments

Partnership on AI. (2016). *Tenets.* https://www.partnershiponai.org/tenets/

Patel, Ranabahu, & Sheth. (n.d.). *Service Level Agreement in Cloud Computing.* Knoesis Center, Wright State University.

Paxos made simple. (2001). *ACM Sigact News, 32*(4), 18–25.

Payment Services (Amendment) Act 2021, (No. 1 of 2021).

Payment Services Act 2019, (No. 2 of 2019).

PBC (People's Bank of China). (2020, Jun.1). *Guidance on Further Strengthening the Financial Services for Small and Micro Enterprises.* Available at: http://www.gov.cn/zhengce/zhengceku/2020-06/02/content_5516693.htm

People's Daily. (2015, February 8). *CSRC: Using big data analysis to crack down on "rat trading" cases.* Available at: http://www.ce.cn/xwzx/xinwen/yw/201502/08/t20150208_4541771.shtml

Peraturan, B. P. P. B. K. N. (2019). *5 Tahun 2019 Tentang Ketentuan Teknis Penyelenggaraan Pasar Fisik Aset Kripto (Crypto Asset).* Di Bursa Berjangka.

Personal Data Protection Commission Singapore. (2019). *Model Artificial Intelligence Governance Framework.* https://ai.bsa.org/wp-content/uploads/2019/09/Model-AI-Framework-First-Edition.pdf

Philippines: Where, How, and What you can buy for bitcoins. (2018). https://medium.com/kriptapp/philippines-where-how-and-what-you-can-buy-for-bitcoins-4e6e28fb71d4

Phillips, J. P., Hahn, C. A., Fontana, P. C., Broniatowski, D. A., & Przybocki, M. A. (2020). *Four Principles of Explainable Artificial Intelligence* [Unpublished Paper]. https://www.nist.gov/system/files/documents/2020/08/17/NIST%20Explainable%20AI%20Draft%20NISTIR8312%20%281%29.pdf

Phillips, K. (2018). *Ohio Becomes The First State To Allow Taxpayers To Pay Tax Bills Using Cryptocurrency.* https://www.forbes.com/sites/kellyphillipserb/2018/11/26/ohio-becomes-the-first-state-to-allow-taxpayers-to-pay-tax-bills-using-cryptocurrency/?sh=77791f056b04

Politou, E., Casino, F., Alepis, E., & Patsakis, C. (2019). Blockchain mutability: Challenges and proposed solutions. *IEEE Transactions on Emerging Topics in Computing.* doi:10.1109/TETC.2019.2949510

Popov, S. (2016). A probabilistic analysis of the nxt forging algorithm. *Ledger*, 69-83.

Popov, S. (2016). *The tangle.* Academic Press.

Porru, S., Pinna, A., Marchesi, M., & Tonelli, R. (2017). Blockchain-oriented software engineering: challenges and new directions. In *IEEE/ACM 39th International Conference on Software Engineering Companion* (pp. 169-171). IEEE.

Prevention of Money Laundering and Funding of Terrorism Regulations (2018).

Prodent, L. (2021). *Vietnam to Start Regulating Cryptocurrencies.* https://www.aseanbriefing.com/news/vietnam-to-start-regulating-cryptocurrencies/

Prussen, E. H. (2021). *Luxembourg: Luxembourg Law Recognises Issuance of Dematerialised Securities In Blockchains*. Retrieved June 30, 2021 from https://www.mondaq.com/fin-tech/1034224/luxembourg-law-recognises-issuance-of-dematerialised-securities-in-blockchains-

Qi, Y., & Xiao, J. (2018). Fintech: Ai powers financial services to improve people's lives. *Communications of the ACM*, *61*(11), 65–69. doi:10.1145/3239550

Quasim, M. T. (2020). *Decentralised Internet of Things: A Blockchain Perspective* (Vol. 71). Springer Nature.

Quintais, J., Bodó, B., Giannopoulou, A., & Ferrari, V. (2019). Blockchain and the law: A critical evaluation. *Stanford Journal of Blockchain Law Policy, 1*.

Rackspace Terms of Use. (n.d.). https://www.rackspace.com/information/legal/websiteterms

Radityo, A., Munajat, Q., & Budi, I. (2017, October). Prediction of Bitcoin exchange rate to American dollar using artificial neural network methods. In *2017 International Conference on Advanced Computer Science and Information Systems (ICACSIS)* (pp. 433-438). IEEE. 10.1109/ICACSIS.2017.8355070

Raijmakers, J. (2020). *Entry into force of Swiss DLT bill*. Retrieved June 30, 2021 from https://www.loyensloeff.com/ch/en/news/swiss-dlt-bill-enters-into-force-n21037/

Raj, P., Saini, K., & Surianarayanan, C. (2020). *Blockchain Technology and Applications*. CRC Press.

Raju, S. M., & Tarif, A. M. (2020). *Real-Time Prediction of BITCOIN Price using Machine Learning Techniques and Public Sentiment Analysis*. arXiv preprint arXiv:2006.14473.

Rashid, F. Y. (2017). *Don't get bit by zombie cloud data*. https://www.infoworld.com/article/3190131/security/dont-get-bit-by-zombie-cloud-data.html

Rautenstrauch, T. (2002). *The Virtual Corporation: A strategic option for Small and Medium sized Enterprises (SMEs)*. Association for Small Business and Entrepreneurship.

Republic of Estonia Financial Intelligence Unit. (2020). *Estonia fully transposes the European Union money laundering directives*. https://fiu.ee/en/news/estonia-fully-transposes-european-union-money-laundering-directives

Republic of Estonia Tax and Customs Board. (2021). *Taxation of private person's virtual currency/cryptocurrency earnings*. https://www.emta.ee/eng/private-client/declaration-income/other-income/taxation-private-persons-virtual

Reserve Bank of India. (2013). *Press Release: RBI cautions users of Virtual Currencies against Risks*. https://www.rbi.org.in/scripts/BS_PressReleaseDisplay.aspx?prid=30247

Reserve Bank of India. (2017a). *Press Release: Reserve Bank cautions regarding risk of virtual currencies including Bitcoins*. https://www.rbi.org.in/scripts/BS_PressReleaseDisplay.aspx?prid=42462

Reserve Bank of India. (2017b). *Press Release:RBI cautions users of Virtual Currencies*. https://www.rbi.org.in/scripts/BS_PressReleaseDisplay.aspx?prid=39435

Reserve Bank of India. (2018). *Prohibition on dealing in Virtual Currencies (VCs)*. https://rbidocs.rbi.org.in/rdocs/Notification/PDFs/NOTI15465B741A10B0E45E896C62A9C83AB938F.PDF

Reyes, C. L. (2017). Conceptualizing Cryptolaw. *Nebraska Law Review*, *96*(2).

Ritz, N. (2018). Bitlumens: A New Energy Powered by IoT and Blockchain Technology. *Medium*. https://medium.com/@nina.d.ritz/bitlumens-a-new-energy-powered-by-iot-and-blockchain-technology-483cd212a6

Rizzo, P. (2014). *Bolivia's Central Bank Bans Bitcoin.* https://www.coindesk.com/bolivias-central-bank-bans-bitcoin-digital-currencies

Robert a. Hillman & Jeffrey j. Rach.insri, N.Y.U. Law (2002) Standard-Form Contracting In The Electronic Age. NYU Law Review. http://www.nyulawreview.org/sites/default/files/pdf/NYULawReview-77-2-Hillman-Rachlinski.pdf

Rohrer, E., & Tschorsch, F. (2019). Kadcast: A structured approach to broadcast in blockchain networks. In *Proceedings of the 1st ACM Conference on Advances in Financial Technologies*, (pp. 199-213). ACM.

Rohrmann & Cunha. (2015). Some legal aspects of cloud computing contracts. *Journal of International Commercial Law and Technology.*

Rong, Y., Zhang, J., & Bian, J. (2019). Erbft: efficient and robust byzan- tine fault tolerance. In *2019 IEEE 21st International Conference on High Per- formance Computing and Communications.* IEEE.

Roode, D., & G., U. I. (2018). How to break iota heart by replay- ing. In *2018 IEEE Globecom Workshops (GC Wkshps)* (pp. 1–7.). IEEE.

Rosenfeld, M. (2011). *Analysis of bitcoin pooled mining reward systems.* arXiv, preprint arXiv:1112.4980.

Rossi, F., Sekaran, A., Spohrer, J., & Caruthers, R. (2019). Everyday Ethics for Artificial Intelligence. *IBM Design Program Office.* https://www.ibm.com/watson/assets/duo/pdf/everydayethics.pdf

Roy, N., Shen, S., Hassanieh, H., & Choudhury, R. R. (2018). Inaudible voice commands: The long-range attack and defense. In *15th USENIX Symposium on Networked Systems Design and Implementation (NSDI 18)*, (pp. pp. 547-560). USENIX.

Rubinstein, I. (2016). The Future of Self-Regulation is Co-Regulation. In *The Cambridge Handbook of Consumer Privacy.* Cambridge University Press.

Rubio, M. (2020). *Cryptocurrency: The Complete Blockchain Guide for Beginners to Make Money and Passive Income (Understand Ethereum, Blockchain, Smart Contracts, Icos).* Martzel Rubio. https://books.google.com.my/books?id=53LgDwAAQBAJ

S.B. (2019). *19-023, 73rd Leg. Sess.*

S.B. 161, 80th Leg. Sess. (Nev.), (2019).

S.B. 162, 80st Leg. Sess. (Nev.), (2019).

S.B. 163, 80th Leg. Sess. (Nev.), (2019).

S.B. 164, 80th Leg. Sess. (Nev.), (2019). https://www.leg.state.nv.us/Session/80th2019/Bills/SB/SB164_EN.pdf

S.B. 269, Leg., Reg. Sess. (Vt.), (2017).

S.B. 398, 79th Leg. Sess. (Nev.), (2017).

S.B. 69, 149th Gen. Assemb., Reg. Sess, (Del), (2017). https://delcode.delaware.gov/title8/c001/sc07/index.html

S.F. 125, 65th Leg., Gen. Sess. (Wyo), (2019).

S.F. 38, 66th Leg, Gen. Sess. (Wyo), (2021).

Saad, M. S. (2019). *Exploring the attack surface of blockchain: A systematic overview.* preprint arXiv:1904.03487.

Saad, M., Spaulding, J., Njilla, L., Kamhoua, C., Shetty, S., & Nyang, D. (2019). *Exploring the attack surface of blockchain: A systematic overview.* preprint arXiv:1904.03487.

Sadiku, M. N. O., Eze, K. G., & Musa, S. M. (2018). Smart Contracts: A Primer. *Journal of Scientific and Engineering Research, 5*(5), 538–541.

Sahoo, P. K. (2017). Bitcoin as digital money: Its growth and future sustainability. *Theoretical Applied Economics, 24*(4).

Saif, I., & Ammanath, B. (2020). Trustworthy AI' is a framework to help manage unique risk. *MIT Technology Review.* https://www.technologyreview.com/2020/03/25/950291/trustworthy-ai-is-a-framework-to-help-manage-unique-risk/

Salah, K., Rehman, M. H. U., Nizamuddin, N., & Al-Fuqaha, A. (2019). Blockchain for AI: Review and open research challenges. *IEEE Access: Practical Innovations, Open Solutions, 7*, 10127–10149. doi:10.1109/ACCESS.2018.2890507

Salmon, J., & Myers, G. (2019). *Blockchain and Associated Legal Issues for Emerging Markets.* https://openknowledge.worldbank.org/bitstream/handle/10986/31202/133877-EMCompass-Note-63-Blockchain-and-Legal-Issues-in-Emerging-Markets.pdf?sequence=1&isAllowed=y

Salzman, N. H., Hung, K., Haribhai, D., Chu, H., & Karlsson-Sjöberg, J., & A., E. (2010). Enteric defensins are essential regulators of intestinal microbial ecology. *Nature Immunology.*

Samp, T., & Phillips, S. R. (2020). *White House issues guidelines for regulatory and non-regulatory approaches to artificial intelligence.* https://www.dlapiper.com/en/us/insights/publications/2020/01/white-house-issues-guidelines-for-regulatory-and-nonregulatory-approaches-to-artificial-intelligence/

Saraji, S., & Borowczak, M. (2021). *A Blockchain-Based Carbon Credit Ecosystem.* University of Wyoming, Whitepaper. www.uwyo.edu/research/advancing-research-and-scholarship/a-blockchain-based-carbon-credit-ecosystem.pdf

Sasson, A., C., C., G., M., G., I., M., E., T., & Virza. (2014). Zerocash: Decentralized anonymous payments from bitcoin. In *IEEE Symposium on Security and Privacy*, (pp. 459-474). IEEE.

Scherer, M. U. (2016). Regulating artificial intelligence systems: Risks, challenges, competencies, and strategies. *Harvard Journal of Law & Technology, 29*, 353–400.

Schwinger, R. A. (2018). *Cryptocurrencies held subject to US federal securities laws.* https://www.nortonrosefulbright.com/en-ug/knowledge/publications/b9789fd9/cryptocurrencies-held-subject-to-us-federal-securities-laws

Scoca, Uriarte, & De Nicola. (2018). *Smart Contract Negotiation in Cloud Computing.* Academic Press.

SEC v. WJ Howey Co, 328 US 293 (Supreme Court 1946).

Securities and Exchange Commission. (2017). *Report of Investigation Pursuant to Section 21(a) of the Securities Exchange Act of 1934: The DAO.* Author.

SF0111. 64th Leg., Budget Sess (Wyo), (2018). https://legiscan.com/WY/text/SF0111/id/1753980

Shabandri, B. (2019). Enhancing IoT Security and Privacy Using Distributed Ledgers with IOTA and the Tangle. In *2019 6th International Conference on Signal Processing and Integrated Networks (SPIN)* (pp. 1069-1075). IEEE.

Shanaev, S., Sharma, S., Ghimire, B., & Shuraeva, A. (2020). Taming the blockchain beast? Regulatory implications for the cryptocurrency Market. *Research in International Business and Finance, 51*, 101080.

Shanghai Pudong Government. (2018, Aug. 21). Shanghai Financial Court Officially Established. *Pudong News.* Available at: http://www.pudong.gov.cn/shpd/news/20180821/006001_7f36d025-0463-4204-8f63-11f86864e35f.htm. Official website: http://www.shjrfy.gov.cn/jrfy/gweb/index.jsp

Sharma, V. (2018). An Energy-efficient Transaction Model for the Blockchain-Enabled Internet of Vehicles (IoV). *IEEE Communications Letters.*

Shen, C., & Pena-Mora, F. (2018). Blockchain for cities—A systematic literature review. *IEEE Access: Practical Innovations, Open Solutions, 6*, 76787–76819.

Sichuan Provincial Bureau of Statistics. (2021, Mar.14). *Statistical bulletin of national economic and social development of Sichuan Province in 2020.* Available at: http://tjj.sc.gov.cn/scstjj/tjgb/2021/3/14/c64ac94ca86c4714adaf117789e47073.shtml

Singh, H., Jain, G., Munjal, A., & Rakesh, S. (2019). Blockchain technology in corporate governance: disrupting chain reaction or not? *Corporate Governance: The International Journal of Business in Society.*

Singh, M., Singh, A., & Kim, S. (2018). Blockchain: A game changer for securing iot data. In *2018 IEEE 4th World Forum on Internet of Things (WF-IoT)* (pp. 51–55.). IEEE.

Singh, U. P. (2021). *Indian Cryptocurrency Saga: Regulation And IP Protection.* https://www.mondaq.com/india/fintech/1084772/indian-cryptocurrency-saga-regulation-and-ip-protection

Singh, P. K., Singh, R., Nandi, S. K., Ghafoor, K. Z., Rawat, D. B., & Nandi, S. (2020). An efficient blockchain-based approach for cooperative decision making in swarm robotics. *Internet Technology Letters, 3*(1), 140. doi:10.1002/itl2.140

Six, N., Ribalta, C. N., Herbaut, N., & Salinesi, C. (2020). A Blockchain-Based Pattern for Confidential Pseudo-anonymous Contract Enforcement. *3rd International Workshop on Blockchain Systems and Applications.*

Skali Cloud. (n.d.). http://skalicloud.com/v4/wp-content/uploads/2013/10/SKALICloud-Leaflet.pdf

Smart Contracts Alliance. (2018). Smart Contracts: 12 Use Cases for Business & Beyond. In *Chamber of Digital Commerce* (Vol. 56). Retrieved from http://digitalchamber.org/assets/smart-contracts-12-use-cases-for-business-and-beyond.pdf

Smart Contracts. (2017). *Oxford faculty of law.* https://www.law.ox.ac.uk/business-law-blog/blog/2017/03/smart-contracts?cv=1

Song, L., Ju, X., Zhu, Z., & Li, M. (2021). An access control model for the Internet of Things based on zero-knowledge token and blockchain. *Journal of Wireless Communication Network, 105*(1), 105. Advance online publication. doi:10.118613638-021-01986-4

Sonksen, C. (2021). Cryptocurrency Regulations in ASEAN, East Asia, & America: To Regulate or Not to Regulate Notes. *Wash. U. Global Stud. L. Rev., 20*, 171.

Soto, E. A., Bosman, L. B., Wollega, E., & Leon-Salas, W. D. (2021). Peer-to-Peer Energy Trading: A Review of the Literature. *Applied Energy, 283*, 116268. Advance online publication. doi:10.1016/j.apenergy.2020.116268

Spinnell, J. J., & Zimberg, D. M. (2018). *Renewable energy certificate markets: blockchain applied.* Energy System Engineering Institute, Lehigh University.

Spiro, M. (2020). The FTC and AI Governance: A Regulatory Proposal. *Seattle Journal of Technology. Environmental Innovation Law, 10*(1), 2.

State Bank of Vietnam. (2017). *Dispatch No.5747/NHNN-PC.* Author.

Stifter, N. J. (2019). Revisiting Practical Byzantine Fault Tolerance Through Blockchain Technologies. In Security and Quality in Cyber-Physical Systems Engineering (pp. 471-495). Springer.

Stifter, N. S. (2019). Echoes of the past: Recovering blockchain metrics from merged mining. *International Conference on Financial Cryptography and Data Security*, 527-549.

Stifter, N., Judmayer, A., & Weippl, E. (2019). Revisiting practical byzantine fault tolerance through Blockchain technologies. In *Security and Quality in Cyber-Physical Systems Engineering* (pp. 471–495). Springer. doi:10.1007/978-3-030-25312-7_17

Strassman, R. (n.d.). Delaware Explicitly Legalizes Corporate Documentation via Blockchain. *Review of Banking & Financial Law, 37*. https://www.bu.edu/rbfl/files/2018/03/166-176.pdf

Su, S. (2020, May 19). The PBC has proposed "digital central bank" construction for four consecutive years, and financial digital transformation is urgent. *Securities Daily*. Available at: http://epaper.zqrb.cn/images/2019-04/19/A2/A2.pdf

Suda, M., Tejblum, B., & Francisco, A. (2017). Chain reactions: Legislative and regulatory initiatives related to blockchain in the United States. *Computer Law Review International, 18*(4), 97–103.

Sudhakaran, S., Kumar, S., Ranjan, P., & Tripathy, M. R. (2020). Blockchain-Based Transparent and Secure Decentralized Algorithm. In *International Conference on Intelligent Computing and Smart Communication 2019* (pp. 327-336). Springer. 10.1007/978-981-15-0633-8_32

Suzhou Daily. (2021, Jan.5). *Suzhou digital economy and digital development promotion conference are held*. Available at: http://www.suzhou.gov.cn/szsrmzf/szyw/202101/f6c44ccfc91740c0be40d3e384faa8c0.shtml

Swiss Federal Code of Obligations, (1911).

Syllaba, O. (2020). Internet Smart Contracts: Are They Really Smart? *Common Law Review, 16*, 19–22. Retrieved from https://heinonline.org/hol-cgi-bin/get_pdf.cgi?handle=hein.journals/comnlrevi16&section=9

Szabo, N. (1997). Formalizing and Securing Relationships on Public Networks. *First Monday, 2*(9). Advance online publication. doi:10.5210/fm.v2i9.548

Team, N. A. (2018). *Nebula AI (NBAI) decentralized ai blockchain whitepaper*. https://nebulaai.org/_include/whitepaper/NBAI_whitepaper_EN.pdf

Tehrani, bin Sabaruddin, & Ramanathan. (2017). *The problem of binary distinction in cloud computing and the necessity for a different approach: Positions of the European Union and Canada*. Academic Press.

Tehrani, P. M., Sabaruddin, J. S., & Ramanathan, D. (2018). Cross border data transfer: Complexity of adequate protection and its exceptions. *Computer Law & Security Review, 34*(3), 582-594. http://support.ptc.com/WCMS/files/164830/en/Acceptable_Use_Policy_Cloud_Services_Eng_Jan_2015_2.pdf

Telefonica. (2018). *Telefonica: Our Artificial Intelligence Principles*. Retrieved May 29, 2021 from https://www.telefonica.com/documents/

Teufel, B., Sentic, A., & Barmet, M. (2019). Blockchain Energy: Blockchain in Future Energy Systems. *Journal of Electronic Science and Technology, 17*(4), 100011. doi:10.1016/j.jnlest.2020.100011

The DAO: Theft is property. (2016). *The Economist, 419*(8995), 66.

The People's Bank of China. (2019, August 23). *The People's Bank of China issued the development plan of FinTech (2019-2021)*. Available at: http://www.gov.cn/xinwen/2019-08/23/content_5423691.htm

The People's Bank of China. (2019, December 5). *The People's Bank of China Launched the FinTech Innovative Regulation Pilot*. Available at: http://www.pbc.gov.cn/goutongjiaoliu/113456/113469/3933971/index.html

The People's Bank of China. (2020, April 27). *The People's Bank of China Expands the FinTech Innovative Regulation Pilot in cities (districts) including Shanghai.* Available at: http://www.pbc.gov.cn/goutongjiaoliu/113456/113469/4014870/index.html

The People's Bank of China. (2020, November 7). *The People's Bank of China issues China's financial stability report (2020).* Available at: http://www.gov.cn/xinwen/2020-11/07/content_5558567.htm

The State Council. (2021, March 5). *Government Work Report.* Available at: http://www.gov.cn/guowuyuan/zfgzbg.htm

Thematic Report. (2019). Legal and regulatory framework of blockchains and smart contracts. *EU Blockchain.* Accessed at https://www.eublockchainforum.eu/sites/default/files/reports/report_legal_v1.0.pdf

Thierer, A. (2014). *Problems with Precautionary Principle-Minded Tech Regulation & A Federal Robotics Commission.* https://medium.com/tech-liberation/problems-with-precautionary-principle-minded-tech-regulation-a-federal-robotics-commission-c71f6f20d8bd

Thukral, M. K. (2021). Emergence of blockchain-technology application in peer-to-peer electrical-energy trading: A review. *Clean Energy, 5*(1), 104–123.

Tian, A. (2016, March 25). National Internet Finance Association is officially established. *China Daily.* Available at: http://www.cac.gov.cn/2016-03/25/c_1118478823.htm

Tinianow, A., & Klayman, J. A. (2017). *Enabling or Crippling? The Risks of State-by-State Blockchain Laws.* https://www.coindesk.com/enabling-crippling-risks-state-state-blockchain-laws

Tinianow, A., & Long, C. (2017). *Delaware blockchain initiative: transforming the Foundational Infrastructure of Corporate Finance.* Harv. L. Sch. F. on Corp. Governance Fin. Reg.

Token- und VT-Dienstleister-Gesetz, (2019).

Tu, K. (2020). Blockchain Stock Ledgers. *Industrial Law Journal, 96,* 223.

Turesson, H. R. (2019). *Privacy-preserving blockchain mining: Sybil-resistance by proof-of-useful-work.* arXiv preprint:1907.08744.

Twentieth Century Fox Film Corporation And Another V Newzbin Ltd [2010] [2010] EWHC 608 (Ch) *Unfair Contract Terms Act 1977* S(3)

United States v. Zaslavskiy, 2018 WL 4346339 (2018).

Urquhart, A. (2016). The inefficiency of Bitcoin. *Economics Letters, 148,* 80–82. doi:10.1016/j.econlet.2016.09.019

Uzsoki, D. (2019). *Tokenization of Infrastructure- A blockchain-based solution to financing sustainable infrastructure.* https://www.iisd.org/system/files/publications/tokenization-infrastructure-blockchain-solution.pdf

van Asselt, M., Vos, E., & Fox, T. (2010). *Regulating technologies and the Uncertainty paradox.* Wolf Legal Publishers.

Vasey, G. M. (2019). *VAKT, Blockchain, Consortia and Solving Industry Problems.* https://www.ctrmcenter.com/blog/opinion/vakt-blockchains-consortia-and-solving-industry-problems/

Vasin, P. (2014). *Blackcoin's proof-of-stake protocol v2.* https://blackcoin.co/blackcoin-pos-protocol-v2-whitepaper

Vaughn & Outzen. (2017). *Understanding how blockchain could impact legal industry.* https://www.law360.com/articles/879810/understanding-how-blockchain-could-impact-legal-industry

Velankar, S., Valecha, S., & Maji, S. (2018, February). Bitcoin price prediction using machine learning. In *2018 20th International Conference on Advanced Communication Technology (ICACT)* (pp. 144-147). IEEE.

Verberne, J. (2018). *How can blockchain serve society?* Retrieved June 30, 2021 from https://www.weforum.org/agenda/2018/02/blockchain-ocean-fishing-sustainable-risk-environment/

Villaronga, E. F., Kieseberg, P., & Li, T. (2018). Humans forget, machines remember: Artificial intelligence and the right to be forgotten. *Computer Law & Security Review, 34*(2), 304–313. doi:10.1016/j.clsr.2017.08.007

Virtual Financial Assets Act (2018).

Vitale, J., Tonkin, M., Ojha, S., Williams, M.-A., Wang, X., & Judge, W. (2017). Privacy by design in machine learning data collection: A user experience experimentation. *The AAAI 2017 Spring Symposium on Designing the User Experience of Machine Learning Systems Technical Report.*

Wachter, S., & Mittelstadt, B. (2019). A right to reasonable inferences: Re-thinking data protection law in the age of big data and AI. *Colum. Bus. L. Rev.*, 494.

Walch, A. (2017). The Path of the Blockchain Lexicon (and the Law). *Boston University Review of Banking & Financial Law*, (36).

Walch, A. (2016). The path of the blockchain lexicon (and the law). *Rev. Banking Fin. L., 36*, 713.

Walch, A. (2017). Blockchain's treacherous vocabulary: One more challenge for regulators. *Journal of Internet Law, 21*(2).

Waldman, A. E. (2019). Privacy's Law of Design. *U.C Irvine Law Review, 9.* https://scholarship.law.uci.edu/ucilr/vol9/iss5/8

Walker, C. (2019). *Immutability, Friend or Foe: An Analysis of Smart Contracts Against the Fundamentals of Contract Law.* Academic Press.

Wallace, N., & Castro, D. (2018). *The impact of the EU's new data protection regulation on AI.* Centre for Data Innovation.

Wamba, S. F., & Queiroz, M. M. (2020). *Blockchain in the operations and supply chain management: Benefits, challenges and future research opportunities.* Academic Press.

Weaver, J. F. (2014). *We Need to Pass Legislation on Artificial Intelligence Early and Often.* https://slate.com/technology/2014/09/we-need-to-pass-artificial-intelligence-laws-early-and-often.html

Weber, Lenne, & Poirier. (2020). AI, Machine Learning & Big Data: France. Academic Press.

Weinstein, J., Cohn, A., & Parker, C. (2019). *Promoting innovation through education: The blockchain industry, law enforcement and regulators work towards a common goal.* https://www.acc.com/sites/default/files/resources/vl/membersonly/Article/1489775_1.pdf

Weitzenböck, E. M. (2012). *English Law of Contract: Consideration.* Norwegian Research Center for Computers and Law.

Wischmeyer, T., & Rademacher, T. (2019). *Regulating Artificial Intelligence.* Springer International Publishing. https://books.google.com.my/books?id=FQ3BDwAAQBAJ

Wolfson, R. (2019). *Majority Leader of California State Assembly Pushes for Legal Certainty for Blockchain.* Retrieved June 30, 2021 from https://cointelegraphs.com/news/majority-leader-of-california-state-assembly-pushes-for-legal-certainty-for-blockchain

Wood Mackenzie. (2018). *Thinking Global Energy Transitions: the what, if, how, and when.* https://www.woodmac.com/news/feature/global-energy-transition/

Wood, G. (2014). *Ethereum: A secure decentralised generalised transaction ledger.* Ethereum project yellow paper.

Wood, G. (2016). *Polkadot: Vision for a Heterogeneous Multi-chain Framework.* Polkadot Whitepaper.

World Economic Forum. (2020). *Fostering Effective Energy Transition.* Retrieved from http://www3.weforum.org/docs/WEF_Fostering_Effective_Energy_Transition_2020_Edition.pdf

Wright, D., Gutwirth, S., Friedewald, M., Vildjiounaite, E., & Punie, Y. (2008). *Safeguards in a World of Ambient Intelligence.* Springer Netherlands. doi:10.1007/978-1-4020-6662-7

WrightA.De FilippiP. (2015). Decentralized Blockchain Technology and the Rise of Lex Cryptographia. doi:10.2139/ssrn.2580664

Wrigley, S. (2018). Taming Artificial Intelligence: "Bots," the GDPR and Regulatory Approaches. In Robotics, AI and the Future of Law (pp. 183-208). Springer.

Wu, Y. (2019, August 22). The People's Bank of China proposed the Fintech Three-year Development Plan. *The Xinhua News Agency.* Available at: http://www.gov.cn/xinwen/2019-08/22/content_5423531.htm

XELS. (2021). *Award-Winning Carbon Broker to Assist XELS With Offset Procurement and Strategy.* https://www.prnewswire.com/news-releases/award-winning-carbon-broker-to-assist-xels-with-offset-procurement-and-strategy-301281322.html

Xi, J. (2016, Sep.3). A new starting point for China's development and a new blueprint for global growth——Keynote speech at the opening ceremony of G20 Business Summit. *Xinhua News Agency.* Available at: http://www.gov.cn/xinwen/2016-09/03/content_5105135.htm

Xiao, X. (2017, December 6). Ten characteristics of FinTech in China. *China Times.* Available at: https://www.chinatimes.net.cn/article/72955

Xiao, Y., Zhang, N. J. L., & Lou, A. Y. (2019.). Distributed consensusprotocols and algorithms. Blockchain for Distributed Systems Security, 25.

Xinhua News Agency. (2014, September 1). *The Decision of the Standing Committee of the National People's Congress on the establishment of intellectual property courts in Beijing, Shanghai and Guangzhou.* Available at: http://www.npc.gov.cn/npc/c12489/201409/9d38b14721f44b35817082f371afb76a.shtml

Xinhua News Agency. (2021, March 29). *Green, innovation and intelligence: decoding the high standard and high-quality development of Xiong'an New District.* Available at: http://ie.bjd.com.cn/5b165687a010550e5ddc0e6a/contentApp/5b16573ae4b02a9fe2d558fa/AP6061ce2fe4b0b87b6752b7e3.html

Yanisky-Ravid, S., & Hallisey, S. (2018). 'Equality and Privacy by Design': Ensuring Artificial Intelligence (AI) Is Properly Trained & Fed: A New Model of AI Data Transparency & Certification As Safe Harbor Procedures. *Fordham Urb. L.J., 46*(2).

Ye, Y. (2021, Jan. 29). "Yangtze River Delta credit chain application platform" realizes the interconnection of enterprises' credit information, with 7.89 million enterprises on the chain. *Suzhou Daily.* Available at: http://www.subaonet.com/2021/szyw/0129/157360.shtml

Yeah Host Terms. (n.d.). https://www.yeahhost.com.my/terms

Yu, P., Hu, Y., Waseem, M., & Rafay, A. (2021). Regulatory Developments in Peer-to-Peer (P2P) Lending to Combat Frauds: The Case of China. In A. Rafay (Ed.), Handbook of Research on Theory and Practice of Financial Crimes (pp. 172-194). IGI Global. doi:10.4018/978-1-7998-5567-5.ch010

Zainelabden, Kliazovich, & Bouvry. (2016). *16th IEEE/ACM International Symposium on Cluster, Cloud, and Grid Computing*. https://ieeexplore-ieeeorg.ezproxy.um.edu.my/stamp/stamp.jsp?tp=&arnumber=7515740

Zhang, C., Wu, J., Zhuo, Y., Cheng, M., & Long, C. (2018). Peer-to-Peer Energy Trading in a Microgrid. *Applied Energy, 220*, 1–12. doi:10.1016/j.apenergy.2018.03.010

Zhang, H., Uwasu, M., Hara, K., & Yabar, H. (2011). Sustainable Urban Development and Land Use Change—A Case Study of the Yangtze River Delta in China. *Sustainability, 3*(7), 1074–1089. doi:10.3390u2071074

Zharova, A., & Lloyd, I. (2018). An examination of the experience of cryptocurrency use in Russia. In search of better practice. *Computer Law & Security Review, 34*(6), 1300–1313.

Zheng, W., Zheng, Z., Chen, X., Dai, K., Li, P., & Chen, R. (2019). Nutbaas: A Blockchain-as-a-service platform. *IEEE Access: Practical Innovations, Open Solutions, 7*, 134422–134433. doi:10.1109/ACCESS.2019.2941905

Zheng, Z. X. (2018). Blockchain challenges and opportunities: A survey. *International Journal of Web and Grid Services*, 352–375.

Zhou, J., Conti, M., Ahmed, C. M., Au, M. H., Batina, L., Li, Z., . . . Majumdar, S. (2020). *Applied Cryptography and Network Security Workshops: ACNS 2020 Satellite Workshops, AIBlock, AIHWS, AIoTS, Cloud S&P, SCI, SecMT, and SiMLA, Rome, Italy, October 19–22, 2020, Proceedings*. Springer International Publishing.

Zhou, Y., & Pang, D. (2016, July 15). NIFA: Accelerate the construction of Internet financial statistical monitoring and risk early warning system. *Financial Times*. Available at: https://finance.sina.com.cn/roll/2016-07-15/doc-ifxua-pvw2010011.shtml

Zhou, Y., Wu, J., Long, C., & Ming, W. (2020). State-of-the-art analysis and perspectives for peer-to-peer energy trading. *Engineering, 6*(7), 739–753. https://doi.org/doi.org/10.1016/j.eng.2020.06.002

About the Contributors

Muhammad Abdullah Fazi is serving as lecturer at the faculty of law, Multimedia University Melaka. He has received his doctoral degree in international law from the University of Malaya, Malaysia. He has a special interest in International law, global human rights regime with respect to the law of armed conflict, Law and technology, Refugee law and strategic Implications of international law.

Ruixin Gong is an independent researcher. Her research interests include RegTech, FinTech and Cryptocurrencies.

Aatif Jamshed is currently working with ABES Engineering College, Ghaziabad. Since 20th June 2019 Pursuing Ph.D. from Uttarakhand Technical University Dehradun, A State Govt. University. Master in Technology in Computer Science and Engineering from JamiaHamdard University (New Delhi). Experience in real world projects in leading IT company in India with proficiency in Java, J2EE.

Karisma is a PhD student at the Faculty of Law, University of Malaya. Her research interests centre around law and technology from an interdisciplinary and comparative perspective. The project that she is currently involved in relates to the commercial viability of blockchain technology in the energy sector, particularly on the legal and regulatory aspects. She has developed a keen interest in the integration of law with emerging technologies, such as Blockchain Technology and Artificial Intelligence. Before pursuing her PhD, she was a law lecturer in a private higher educational institution in Malaysia.

Christelle Khalaf is the Associate Director for the Center for Business and Economic Analysis at the University of Wyoming. In this role, she conducts research on business and economic conditions across the state for government, industry, and other stakeholder groups. Previously, she worked as an Economist at Ohio University's Voinovich School of Leadership and Public Affairs, where she served as task lead on multiple U.S. Economic Development Administration projects, among other undertakings. She has also served as a member of the Ohio Economic Roundtable convened by Governor DeWine to discuss the state's economic outlook given the COVID-19 health pandemic. Dr. Khalaf has published peer-reviewed papers in journals such as Economic Development Quarterly, Economic Inquiry, and Journal of Labor Research, among other academic publications. She holds a Ph.D. in Economics from North Carolina State University (NCSU), where she received the Jenkins Dissertation Fellowship in recognition of the quality of her research.

Mohamed Ikbal Nacer holds a master's and a bachelor's degree in mathematics and computer science from the University of Abdel Hamid Maheri, Constantine 2 with an A grade and is currently a doctoral candidate at the University of Bournemouth. His doctorate focuses on distributed systems and more specifically on blockchain technology. He received a doctoral scholarship for the project: A New Method of Artificial Intelligence for the Decision Chain in Blockchain Technology. He enjoyed working in many fields related to IoT, Android, and web development, besides working in the automotive industry for the packet loss investigation within the MDA8 engine calibration system.

Simant Prakoonwit, after graduating with a BEng in Electronic Engineering, Chulalongkorn University, Bangkok, won the British Government's Colombo Plan Scholarship to study in Britain. He began research in artificial intelligence (AI)/3D computer vision when studying for an MSc in the Dept of Electrical and Electronic Engineering, Imperial College London. He then did a PhD research on AI/3D computer vision, reconstructing 3D objects from X-ray, also at Imperial. Subsequently, he worked as a Postdoctoral Research Assistant in Imperial College's Dept of Bioengineering, on 3D computer vision (grant from Home Office, UK). His work can be applied to both security, e.g. airport weapon and bomb scanning, and medical applications. His doctoral and postdoctoral research is patented by Imperial. He joined the Dept of Systems Engineering, Brunel University, UK, as a lecturer in 2000. A year later, he received the Brunel Research Initiative Enterprise Fund Award for his work on AI and assistive technology. In 2004, he took up a lectureship in biomedical engineering/cybernetics in the School of Systems Engineering, University of Reading. He also worked as a consultant to the UK Ministry of Defence (DSTL), supervising projects on security X-ray imaging. He joined University of Bedfordshire, in 2011, as a Principal Lecturer in Computer Science and the Postgraduate Academic Director. Dr Prakoonwit moved to Bournemouth as an Associate Professor in 2015 (also as Head of Education, until 2017). Currently, he teaches artificial intelligence (AI) and works on many funded AI-related research projects. Dr Prakoonwit has won research awards and recognitions, e.g. IEEE Innovation and Creativity Award, Brunel Research Initiative Enterprise Fund Award, Bedfordshire's Rising Star/Research Investment Programme Award, best papers at conferences and journal special issues.

Andasmara Rizky Pranata is a PhD student in Faculty of law, University of Malaya. His researches focuses on technology law and corporate law.

Dhiviya Ram is a Master's Student from University Malaya. She was formerly working as a Research Assistant. She subsequently joined an Intellectual Property company in which she served as an in-house Legal Advisor. She is currently working for a Fortune 500 company in their in-house legal department. She has a great interest in research and plans to pursue her Ph.D. in the near future.

Michael Sampat is an independent researcher working in a number of different disciplines including sociology, political science, and biblical studies.

Soheil Saraji is an assistant professor of Petroleum Engineering and co-director of the Hydrocarbons Lab at the University of Wyoming. Prior to joining the Petroleum Engineering Faculty, he was Postdoctoral Research Scientist at the Centre of Innovation for Flow Through Porous Media at the University of Wyoming. Dr. Saraji has more than fifteen years of experience in energy and engineering research and has published more than twenty-five papers in this field. His research interests lie in enhanced oil recovery techniques, carbon Geo-Sequestration, carbon economy, energy transition, and blockchain technology in energy.

Poshan (Sam) Yu is a Lecturer in Accounting and Finance in the International Cooperative Education Program of Soochow University (China). He is also an External Professor of FinTech and Finance at SKEMA Business School (China), a Visiting Professor at Krirk University (Thailand) and a Visiting Researcher at the Australian Studies Center of Shanghai University (China). Sam leads FasterCapital (Dubai, UAE) as a Regional Partner (China) and serves as a Startup Mentor for AIC RAISE (Coimbatore, India). His research interests include financial technology, regulatory technology, public-private partnerships, mergers and acquisitions, private equity, venture capital, start-ups, intellectual property, art finance, and China's "One Belt One Road" policy.

Index

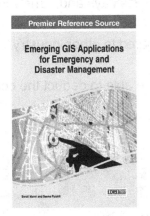
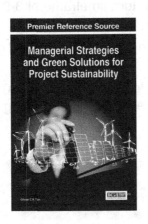

IGI Global Author Services

Providing a high-quality, affordable, and expeditious service, IGI Global's Author Services enable authors to streamline their publishing process, increase chance of acceptance, and adhere to IGI Global's publication standards.

Benefits of Author Services:

- **Professional Service:** All our editors, designers, and translators are experts in their field with years of experience and professional certifications.

- **Quality Guarantee & Certificate:** Each order is returned with a quality guarantee and certificate of professional completion.

- **Timeliness:** All editorial orders have a guaranteed return timeframe of 3-5 business days and translation orders are guaranteed in 7-10 business days.

- **Affordable Pricing:** IGI Global Author Services are competitively priced compared to other industry service providers.

- **APC Reimbursement:** IGI Global authors publishing Open Access (OA) will be able to deduct the cost of editing and other IGI Global author services from their OA APC publishing fee.

Author Services Offered:

English Language Copy Editing
Professional, native English language copy editors improve your manuscript's grammar, spelling, punctuation, terminology, semantics, consistency, flow, formatting, and more.

Scientific & Scholarly Editing
A Ph.D. level review for qualities such as originality and significance, interest to researchers, level of methodology and analysis, coverage of literature, organization, quality of writing, and strengths and weaknesses.

Figure, Table, Chart & Equation Conversions
Work with IGI Global's graphic designers before submission to enhance and design all figures and charts to IGI Global's specific standards for clarity.

Translation
Providing 70 language options, including Simplified and Traditional Chinese, Spanish, Arabic, German, French, and more.

Hear What the Experts Are Saying About IGI Global's Author Services

"Publishing with IGI Global has been an amazing experience for me for sharing my research. The strong academic production support ensures quality and timely completion." – **Prof. Margaret Niess, Oregon State University, USA**

"The service was very fast, very thorough, and very helpful in ensuring our chapter meets the criteria and requirements of the book's editors. I was quite impressed and happy with your service." – **Prof. Tom Brinthaupt, Middle Tennessee State University, USA**

Learn More or Get Started Here:

For Questions, Contact IGI Global's Customer Service Team at cust@igi-global.com or 717-533-8845

IGI Global
PUBLISHER of TIMELY KNOWLEDGE
www.igi-global.com

Printed in the United States
by Baker & Taylor Publisher Services